Making it HUGE in Video Games

Making it HUGE in Video Games recounts the astonishing journey of an unassuming, middle-of-the-bell-curve young man, rising from mundane beginnings to scale the dizzying heights of artistic distinction and financial success in the worldwide video game industry.

This is the story of Chance Thomas, a moderately talented musician who struggled and grew to compose original scores for some of the most well-known entertainment properties in the world. Detailed personal accounts and instructive side bars carry readers across the jagged peaks and valleys of an absolutely achievable career in video games. World-famous IPs get personal treatment here – *The Lord of the Rings, Marvel, Avatar, Dungeons & Dragons, Warhammer, DOTA 2, King Kong, The Settlers*, and many more.

Readers will discover unvarnished true stories about starting out, pitching and pursuing gigs, negotiating contracts, composing and producing scores, multinational corporations and personalities, funny anecdotes, daunting challenges, glorious successes, and instructive failures. Autobiographical details throughout provide intimate perspective, vibrant color, and inspiration. This book is written in a comfortable, conversational style.

Think of this as a career guidebook wrapped around a personal retrospective; a professional how-to manual woven into a memoir.

Making it HUGE in Video Games

Video Games
Memoirs of Composer Chance Thomas

Chance Thomas

CRC Press
Taylor & Francis Group
Boca Raton London New York

CRC Press is an imprint of the
Taylor & Francis Group, an **informa** business

First edition published 2024
by CRC Press
2385 Executive Center Drive, Suite 320, Boca Raton FL 33431

and by CRC Press
4 Park Square, Milton Park, Abingdon, Oxon, OX14 4RN

CRC Press is an imprint of Taylor & Francis Group, LLC

© 2024 Chance Thomas

Library of Congress Cataloging-in-Publication Data
Names: Thomas, Chance, 1961- author.
Title: Making it huge in video games : memoirs of composer Chance Thomas / Chance Thomas.
Description: [1.] | Boca Raton, FL : CRC Press, 2024. | Includes bibliographical references and index.
Identifiers: LCCN 2023017677 (print) | LCCN 2023017678 (ebook) | ISBN 9781032022604 (paperback) | ISBN 9781032058146 (hardback) | ISBN 9781003199311 (ebook)
Subjects: LCSH: Thomas, Chance, 1961- | Video game composers—United States—Biography. | LCGFT: Autobiographies.
Classification: LCC ML410.T442 A3 2024 (print) | LCC ML410.T442 (ebook) | DDC 781.5/4092 [B]—dc23/eng/20230519
LC record available at https://lccn.loc.gov/2023017677
LC ebook record available at https://lccn.loc.gov/2023017678

ISBN: 9781032058146 (hbk)
ISBN: 9781032022604 (pbk)
ISBN: 9781003199311 (ebk)

DOI: 10.1201/9781003199311

Typeset in Minion
by codeMantra

Access the Support Material: www.HUGEsoundRecords.com/Memoir

Contents

"Make no little plans. They have no magic to stir men's blood and probably will not themselves be realized. Make big plans, aim high in hope and work."

– Daniel Burnham

"We are all meant to shine. As we let our light shine, we unconsciously give other people permission to do the same. As we are liberated from our own fear, our presence actually liberates others."

– Marianne Williamson

Introduction

IMAGINE WE ARE SITTING down together for lunch or cold drinks. Relaxed and comfortable, let's take a few minutes and get acquainted.

My name is Chance Thomas. I have been composing music for video games, film, and television since the 1990s. I have had my share of failures, but also experienced many thrilling victories, including an Oscar win, an Emmy win, and billions of dollars in video game and film sales worldwide.

Though I was never blessed with generation-defining talent, I was given just enough talent coupled with an outrageous work ethic.

In terms of financial success, I am certainly no billionaire. But I did eventually become a millionaire. A multimillionaire, to be transparent.

You may be similar to me – good mind, decent health, raw talent, lofty ambitions, ready to work hard, willing to study and learn. Not necessarily an outlier of nature, you may find yourself somewhere in the wide central span of the Bell Curve.

That's okay. I am right there with you. Like millions of others on this planet, my life began in the most humble of circumstances. No extraordinary endowments of intelligence, looks, or means.

But along the way, something astonishing happened, something which empowered me to contribute to many of the world's most valuable entertainment properties: *Avatar, Marvel, The Lord of the Rings, Star Wars, Dungeons & Dragons, King Kong, DOTA 2, Might & Magic,* and more.

What happened? What code did I crack? What blueprint did I discover?

Not surprisingly, the answer comes into focus a few puzzle pieces at a time, little treasures buried in the daily fabric of life. Throughout this memoir, I will unearth many of those treasures and share them all with you.

I share these stories with the loving hope that some parts of my journey will resonate deeply with you. I believe that in reading, you will gather precious intel and inspiration for your own pursuits.

It is my core belief that human beings can achieve some, most, or even all that they dream. You may even surpass your dreams. The world has

DOI: 10.1201/9781003199311-1

space for a vast multitude of creative voices in the tapestry of modern culture. That means there's room enough for all of us.

ABOUT THIS BOOK

Making It HUGE in Video Games is a career guidebook wrapped around a personal retrospective. It is a professional how-to manual woven into a memoir.

Let's get to it!

CHAPTER 1

Music Degree...
What Now?

I T WAS AUGUST OF 1987. I held a newly minted music degree in my hands from Brigham Young University. Generous donors and hard work made it possible for me to attend college on academic scholarships. Someday I hoped to endow a scholarship of my own. But after posing for pictures in a rented black gown and tasseled cap, all I could afford for graduation celebration was a medium Domino's pizza. Money was scarce, and the future was uncertain.

The world does not beat a path to the door of most music school graduates. Rather, the opposite is true. Musicians have to beat their own paths to wherever they hope to go. For those who have never cleared a trail, plowed a garden, or harvested sod, trust me when I tell you – beating a path is the right metaphor. It is backbreaking work.

After my graduation, I beat many different paths in my efforts to alchemize a music education into a living wage. The amount of work involved in trying to *find* work could be overwhelming.

All I wanted was to create original music that would light people up inside, and make a good living at it.

My university degree program had focused on music recording and production, which provided useful knowledge and skills. For my senior project, I had composed, arranged, performed, and produced a solo pop album called *Take A Chance*. I hoped that album would jump start a promising career after graduation. I ordered 1,000 cassette copies of the

DOI: 10.1201/9781003199311-2

album, but had little success in selling them. The reaction to my singing was withering. Many people said I sang like a girl (Madonna and Minnie Pearl were both mentioned). The response to my songwriting was lukewarm. And peers thought my arrangements were too busy. I once resorted to going door to door in apartment complexes, introducing my album from a boombox. I did sell a few tapes, but only enough for pocket change.

I had no plan B for making different kinds of original music that might be marketable. But rent does not wait on epiphany. I needed to find another way to generate income right away.

What would you do in this situation? Would you explore other ways of making money with music? Would you get a day job and pursue music on the side?

PIANO MAN

I decided to try using music in another way. I noticed that many upscale gathering spots had piano players who performed elaborate arrangements of old standards and popular songs. I bought a Liberace record and studied the way he presented melodies, often in octaves; how he comped and arpeggiated a song's harmony to transform and progress the piece; and how he employed a variety of formulaic flourishes as embellishment. I started putting my own arrangements together until I had a few dozen songs memorized. Adding some George Winston-style improvisation between tunes, I could probably cover three or four hours.

Hotels, country clubs, malls, reception centers, restaurants, and even the state Governor's mansion were all possible venues for a piano player. I cold-called most of them. "Do you have a piano? May I stop by and play it for you? Could I audition to become part of your crew?"

When I auditioned, I would dress sharp, but not formal. I played the most recognizable parts of several songs, but never played any one song all the way through. My usual lineup was *Summertime*, by George Gershwin, *Send in the Clowns*, by Stephen Sondheim, *New York, New York*, as sung by Frank Sinatra, *Charade*, by Henri Mancini, and whatever new movie theme was popular on the radio at the time. I would smile and talk with the manager and employees while playing to keep them engaged.

It took months to fine tune my audition formula. But once I did, it was like money in the bank. To a potential employer, my audition demonstrated talent, versatility, flair, relevance, and charisma. I can't remember a time when I didn't get hired with that approach.

As a side note, some of the same principles that produced a successful piano audition resurfaced later in my composing career. For example, I would only feature short music excerpts in promotional materials and websites. I would dress sharp for meetings with clients, prospects, and business partners. For pitch meetings, I preferred an engaging conversation, rather than a one-way show and tell. I learned that many principles of success are portable, with relevance far beyond their original application.

Now back to the piano. Becoming successful at consistently landing piano jobs felt great. On the other hand, I was fired from most of those jobs within a few months. Why? Simply put, I became complacent about my repertoire. I got lazy. After building my core repertoire, I would only add two or three new songs a year. Not surprisingly, the same managers who loved my audition became exasperated hearing the same songs every night. Eventually they gave me the boot.

Was there a silver lining? Getting fired so many times eventually taught me to stop being complacent. As artists, we should always be growing, improving our craft, adding to our skillset, refining our style, and testing innovative ideas. Fortunately, in this case, failure became a teacher. I determined that in the future, no one was ever going to outwork me.

Let's consider another lesson I learned from piano gigs.

When I first started, I was charging $20 per hour. One evening, my wife and I were having dinner with a friend from Canada, Angelique DeGoulette. Angelique had been a successful recording artist for Mercury Records in the 1960s, and she was still a firecracker. I mentioned to her that I was playing piano at the Governor's mansion, and she asked, "How much are they paying you?" I told her, "$20 per hour." She scolded me, "Don't you ever sell yourself short like that! Don't you know? People will only value you as much as you value yourself." She insisted that I double my rate, and then double it again. I balked, not wanting to lose the jobs I had. "At least raise your fees to $50 per hour," she countered. "Start with the Governor's mansion gig, and see what happens."

She promised that future clients wouldn't even bat an eye. They might even brag about their expensive piano player.

I thought she was crazy. But I hoped she was right.

Next time the Governor's event planner called to book me, I gulped and told her my new price was $50 per hour. She didn't flinch. Wait, could it really be that easy? I was happy, but still skeptical. Could this work with my other gigs too?

One of my steady bookings was at the Stein Erickson Lodge in Deer Valley, a posh ski resort outside Park City, Utah. Two nights a week, I sat in a vast luxurious lobby, playing an exquisite black Kawaii grand piano. When I told the manager I was raising my rates, he demanded to know why. I tensed up. What now? I was nervous, but I told him, "My new career consultant insists that $20 per hour is way below market value. $50 per hour is more in line with what prestigious hotels should be paying their musicians." There was an awkward silence while I waited to see if he would buy it. He furrowed his brow, stroked his chin for a minute, and then said, "OK. Our clientele really like you. We don't want to be out of step with the competition."

Just like that, my hourly rate had more than doubled. On the spot!

Angelique was right. Sometimes we undervalue ourselves. We love making music so much! And maybe we fear rejection. So we offer to work for very little money, or even no money. I think that is usually a mistake. We should be aware of whatever the low, median, and premium rates are for our services in any market we enter, and position ourselves as assertively as we can.

Playing at the Stein Erickson Lodge was enriching in other ways too. As a celebrity hot spot in the 1980s, many superstars listened to me play there – Tom Cruise, Bruce Willis, John Travolta, Sidney Poitier, Abigail Van Buren, and others.

Playing at the Governor's mansion also expanded my horizons. Ambassadors from Europe and South America would gather around the piano while I played. The Lord Mayor and Lady of London listened graciously for an afternoon. Leaders of government, business, education, and religion would come and go. Playing the piano in these spaces helped me see powerful people in a more relaxed way.

During this time, a local television station christened me "Utah's Piano Man," and I began using that nickname in my promotional materials. Audiences were being entertained, money was coming in, I was working hard, and opportunities were growing. Chance Thomas was slowly becoming a slightly visible fish in a very tiny pond.

CRUISING

I wasn't the only pianist working at the Stein Erickson Lodge. One night the other piano player stopped by to see me. He said he was heading out of the country in a couple of weeks to work on a cruise ship for a short contract. Would I cover for him? Of course, I would cover for him. I was thrilled to have his extra nights. I had no idea that something much bigger was about to unfold.

When I got home, my wife Pamela asked about how things went at work. I mentioned the conversation with the piano player, and she said, "Oh, I like the sound of a cruise ship! Maybe you could perform on a cruise ship too. And I could work in the gift shop!"

That did sound like fun. I began researching the cruise industry. Twelve cruise lines floated to the top, offering the best ships and itineraries. I cold-called each one in order to learn who booked their entertainment, and obtained their contact information. Before long, 12 promotional packages were winging their way to Miami and Los Angeles.

Two weeks later, Joe McGrath from Regency Cruises was on the phone. I had sent him promos for *Utah's Piano Man* and *The Chance Thomas Digital Trio*. The digital trio was just me playing bass on one synth, while comping chords/melody on another synth, accompanied by a drum machine. "I like your stuff!" he said, "But we only hire real duos and trios. Can you add a guitar player or a bass player?" I thought about it, but was really hoping to talk with him about Pamela working in the gift shop. Instead, I blurted out, "My wife sings."

Actually, she didn't.

At least, she didn't sing any more than the next person. Sure, she would join a congregational hymn at church, or hum along with the radio. But Pamela did not "sing" in any kind of professional sense. She had never performed, never even done karaoke. Why had I said that?

"Great!" said Joe. "Send me a photo and a tape of her singing within a couple of weeks so we can evaluate, and I'll get back to you. Goodbye."

Wait... a tape? He wanted a *TAPE*???

I was nervous. When Pamela came home later, I told her, "Remember how you wanted to work on a cruise ship? Good news! I got a call from Regency Cruises today expressing interest. Just one catch. You have to become a professional singer in the next two weeks."

She was surprisingly open to the idea. In fact, she got excited about it. We chose four songs with limited vocal ranges, and selected a 30-second segment from each song to rehearse and record. Pamela worked hard and made good progress. At her vocal sessions, we recorded lots of takes of her singing each tune. Was there some studio magic involved in the final editing and mixing of that demo? What happens in the editing/mixing room stays in the editing/mixing room...

The final demo sounded good. Joe heard the tape, called us back, and offered us a job. All expenses would be paid. They would provide travel, meals, and a ship cabin for us. We would soon be on our way to Montego Bay, Jamaica, with a four-month contract aboard the luxury cruise ship, *Regent Star.*

We packed up everything we owned and put it in two cheap storage units. Rent for both units was about $75 per month. Everything else we earned on the ship could go into savings. It was a windfall. Who could have imagined this, back when it was a splurge to buy a pizza for my graduation celebration? Things were looking up; in fact, they were looking downright *irie*. Onward to Jamaica!

As months progressed, Pamela's singing outstripped my wildest hopes. She developed into a dazzling entertainer with a gorgeous voice. We started making business plans for a post-cruise pop act. We started writing songs together. Working together on cruise ships had been an incredible gift for our relationship. No surprise there – a young couple touring the most beautiful places in the world on luxury cruise ships with all expenses paid? Are you kidding me?

We signed on for six more cruise contracts with four different companies. These ships took us all over the Caribbean, South America, down the California coast to Mexico, through the Panama Canal, over to the West Indies, from Florida to the Bahamas. Ruins at Tulum, botanical gardens and Dunn's River Falls in Jamaica, parasailing at Paradise Island, jet-skiing in Barbados, swimming in Trunk Bay, snorkeling everywhere. It was fabulous.

As a side note, we discovered a disturbing caste system on the cruise ships where we worked. Many employees lived in very poor conditions. The higher up your official status, the more perks and benefits you received on the ship. I did not fully understand that until our fourth ship contract, with our treatment on the first three ships being wildly inconsistent. But by our fourth ship, *The Sun Viking*, I had learned to negotiate for "entertainer status," plus more money, limited and clearly defined hours, and Sundays off. With entertainer status, we ate in the dining room with the passengers (mm, shrimp scampi every Tuesday for six months). We accompanied passengers on shore excursions for free, and lived in a decent cabin above the water line. The cabin even had a porthole.

Lest you think I was permanently distracted by sunshine and sandy beaches from my dream of creating original music, let me assure you I was not. Between cruise ship contracts, Pamela and I recorded a killer demo of original pop songs we had written together. We went to Hollywood and pitched to A&R reps, publishers, radio program directors, managers, and publicists. The Hollywood professionals we talked with praised us and our work. They promised to open doors for us, introduce us to powerful partners, and give us a shot at the big time. We were so pumped! But soon after leaving their offices, it was like we had never been there. Whenever I tried following up with them, it was nothing but crickets.

Rock star Richard Marx had just released a song with these lyrics, "It don't mean nothing, The words that they say. It don't mean nothing, The games that people play. It don't mean nothing, No victim no crime. It don't mean nothing till they sign it on the bottom line..." I was just beginning to understand that myself.

It was dawning on me that people in Hollywood don't always mean everything they say. I felt like Balthazar in *Galaxy Quest*, when he realizes that Taggart is just an actor, not a real starship commander.

Movie producer Lynda Obst (*Interstellar, Contact*) pulled the curtain back further in her excellent expose and career survival guidebook: *Hello, He Lied & Other Truths from the Hollywood Trenches*. The rose-colored glasses of my naiveté were beginning to crack.

Back on cruise ships for one final contract, we boarded the *Azure Seas* based out of San Pedro, California. The *Azure* did three- and four-day cruises down to Catalina Island, San Diego, and Ensenada, Mexico. One night, we really had the crowd going with our 50s and 60s show. Next up on our set list was *Pretty Woman* by Roy Orbison. I had a naturally high-tenor singing voice, which was well-suited to imitating Orbison. But that night I knocked it out of the park.

When we finished our set, a distinguished–looking older gentleman approached me and handed me his business card, *Bill Young, Senior Vice President of Production, Warner Brothers Pictures*. He had my attention. "I'd like to talk with you about auditioning for the role of Roy Orbison in a film we're making about his life. It's still a ways off, but could you come and see me next time you're in Los Angeles?"

Me? Acting in a film about Roy Orbison? I never saw that one coming, but wasn't about to blink at the invitation. A few weeks later, Pamela and I were sitting in Bill's office at Warner Brothers Pictures, talking about me playing Roy Orbison in a Hollywood feature film. Bill was gracious and measured, a statesman among the many entertainment industry types I had met before. We pursued some preliminary steps, even produced new recordings of me singing *Crying* and *Pretty Woman*. Bill was encouraging and responsive, but nothing else materialized. The film was never made, just another black hole.

We completed our final cruise contract and said bon voyage to ship entertaining forever. We moved to Salt Lake City, Utah, to settle down and start a family. I kept writing new pop songs and working on arrangements. We made new recordings and kept pushing to gain traction in the record business. Every effort seemed to disappear into a new black hole. Vapid pleasantries continued to float back at us (*love your work, you've got potential, let's do lunch…*), but nothing real ever came from any of it. Absolutely nothing.

It was time to move on from pop music. This epiphany struck me while calculating how much money we had *spent* trying to advance our recording career – demos, photography, promo packages, travel, and the like. I compared that figure to what we had *earned* from original music and it was humiliating. Tons of money going out, almost nothing coming in. This was not a tenable position. I needed a better strategy and a new direction. I just didn't know what or where yet.

ASTRO-BURGER

Time passes slowly for the unemployed. Not long after returning to Utah, I found myself driving aimlessly around Salt Lake City, obsessing about how to possibly make a living with original music.

Heading north on State Street one afternoon, I noticed a restaurant called Astro-Burger. "That's a catchy name," I thought while driving past. Instinctively, my finger started tapping on the steering wheel. A riff formed in my mind, with a hooky melody not far behind. Lyrics began to emerge: *"Astro-Burger… Gimme an Astro-Burger… I want my Astro-Burger… Now!"*

Maybe this would be worth putting some energy into. I drove to Suite Sound, a friend's studio where my bare-bones music gear was set up. I started writing a jingle, and within a short time, an uptempo track emerged. I added a gutsy lead vocal with overdubbed harmony parts, and then mixed it down to DAT tape. I made a cassette copy, grabbed my boombox, and headed over to Astro-Burger to make the pitch.

I stepped inside the restaurant and asked to speak with a manager. Astro-Burger was a medium-sized fast food restaurant resembling McDonald's, but with extra layers of grease coating the floor and walls. The store manager came out from behind the counter and greeted me. He was a large, balding Greek man with gaps in his teeth. I told him I had written a commercial song for his business, and asked if he would like to hear it. He responded, "Yes, yes, let us hear it!" A bouncy groove erupted from the speakers, vocals dancing in the air. Several employees started tapping their feet. "Do you like it?" I asked the owner. "Yes, yes, very much! Play it again." I played it a couple more times. Everyone was smiling. I went in for the close, "I'm really happy that you like this commercial song. You can purchase it to use in your advertising. It will be exclusively yours with no limits, and with no date of termination. This will only cost $1,000."

The owner's demeanor changed abruptly, and a sudden silence fell over the room. His eyebrows bent forward, his lips twisted down. He growled at me with surprising volume and rising pitch, "1,000 dollars? No. No! Get out. Get out!"

I did not try to dissuade him, quickly gathering my things and fleeing from the restaurant. I jumped into the car and sped away.

Oof. That went well.

The owner's spin-on-a-dime rejection had startled me. Honestly, it flattened me too. All the employees who had been listening clearly liked the song. The owner himself even liked the song. But when it came time to value my work, it wasn't even worth $1,000.

Discouraging thoughts began to multiply, "I can't break into the record business. Can't even sell a lousy jingle. Maybe I should get an accounting degree." Many music artists, at some point in their careers, have been similarly discouraged. You may be facing some career discouragement yourself.

By now the car was hurtling down State Street, but my mind was a hundred miles away. What was I going to do? Rounding a corner, I noticed a grand opening sign at a new car detail shop – Supersonic Car Wash. Whatever. But a moment later, one of my fingers started tapping on the steering wheel. Then a riff emerged, and an old melody with a new, yet familiar lyric... *"Supersonic... Gimme a Supersonic... I want a Supersonic... Car wash!"* Jolted from my melancholy, I realized, "Hey! Supersonic is a perfect fit for the Astro-Burger jingle!"

With cautious enthusiasm, I went back to Suite Sound, re-sang the jingle with new words, did a quick mix and hurried over to Supersonic corporate headquarters. I arranged to meet with the owner and his marketing executive. We listened to the tune two or three times. Their feet were tapping and their lips were smiling. Once again, I went for the close. "...and it will only cost you $1,000." The two men looked at each other, nodded their heads, then turned to me and said, "We'll take it. And we'll throw in some car wash tickets too." Boom!

The lesson here may be self-evident, but let's review it anyway. If a falling tree crashes across your path, don't abandon the entire journey. You may just need to go around it, something like re-singing your jingle with different lyrics. As NBA superstar Michael Jordan once taught, "Obstacles don't have to stop you. If you run into a wall, don't turn around and give up. Figure out how to climb it, go through it, or work around it."

Human intelligence has a built-in homing beacon. It always leads us to the next step of our most ardent desire. Some call this the universe, while some call it God. Wherever the source, this much is clear. When we obsess about a desire, when a quandary dominates our thoughts, and when we seek earnestly for a solution, illumination always comes. It may arrive at unexpected times, in unexpected ways. But whenever we seek answers with real diligence, enlightenment always comes.

THE AD BUSINESS

With Supersonic, I had sold an original jingle. Now with one success under my belt, I began pursuing other businesses, mostly taking the same approach. I would create a commercial song for some company, make a cassette, visit with the management team, and offer to sell it to them. The success ratio was not great, but persistent work and sheer volume allowed me to make a meager living. Some of my commercial songs began showing up on television and radio stations – Supersonic Car Wash, Food 4 Less, RC Willey Home Furnishings, Super Ford Store, Scone Cutter, Utah Jazz, Las Vegas Stars, and others.

A track record was beginning to emerge. Armed with familiar credits, I now had front-end credibility with new prospects. Front-end credibility was great, because it eliminated the need to always create music on spec. What a relief. Credits alone were now starting to open doors for me.

Even so, the phone was not ringing off the wall. I still had to hustle all the time, make cold calls, ask for referrals, and give presentations. It was hard work, and sometimes I made dumb mistakes. For example, I once gave a presentation to a large group of media producers. I thought it would be memorable to close my presentation by singing an original song live. It was memorable all right, but only for the awkwardness. Another time, I tried to pitch a grocery store owner while he was busy checking inventory. So clueless! I had to learn a lot of lessons the hard way. But the point is, I did learn. And now finally, it was happening. Several years after graduation, I was finally beginning to make a modest living from original music.

I was getting smarter about business too. To secure an affordable production space, I build a small studio in my home. To create an easily recognizable handle, I coined the company name, byChance Productions. To memorably and deliciously thank my clients, I gifted boxes of homemade chocolate turtle cookies, baked fresh from scratch. One client said he only kept hiring me for the cookies!

By now, opportunities had expanded from jingles to custom commercial scoring and infomercials. Ad agencies would give me a long-form commercial or TV spot, and I would compose original music to underscore its content. The work was enjoyable, but deadlines were a beast. I once had to score 13 public service announcement for Salvation Army overnight. Nothing focuses creativity like an insanely tight deadline.

THE NATURE OF MUSIC

In the midst of all this ad work, an awakening dawned on me about the nature of music. I began realizing that certain musical constructs corollate directly with universally resonant ideas and specific human emotions. Musical harmonies and rhythms connect with human physiology and psychology in ways that evoke *predictable emotional responses*. Music can change our body chemistry, our pulse rate, skin conductivity, even body temperature. Comprehending this was like suddenly uncovering the secret to an impossible magic trick.

This understanding is vital for media composers. Manipulating human emotion in lockstep with narrative is really the fundamental skill of any score composer. It is the essence of what we do. This was a HUGE revelation. For a deeper dive into this subject, please refer to Chapter 3 of *Composing Music for Games: The Art, Technology and Business of Video Game Scoring*, where this phenomenon is explored in some detail.

Now I began reaching out to video production companies, independent directors and producers, even some film studios. A big break came when I met Quinn Orr, a producer from the audiovisual department at the Church of Jesus Christ of Latter-day Saints (see Chapter 20). Quinn asked if I would be interested in scoring a short video vignette to present at an upcoming conference.

Quinn and I hit it off, and I began working for him frequently. He was a clever writer, a straightforward director, and an astute producer. We did good work together. One of our projects, an animated instrumental music video called *Rise above the Blues*, won an Emmy Award for Outstanding Regional Film PSA.

Before long, Quinn's colleagues started calling too. They hired me to score short form videos, public service announcements, trailers, and commercials. Everything we did was wholesome and uplifting. One PSA campaign I especially enjoyed was called *Home Front*. These spots were tender, witty, beautifully shot, and focused on building strong family relationships. I eventually scored more than 80 media projects for the church, allowing me to send lots of good vibes out into the world.

Many of these directors wanted the sound of a live orchestra in their scores. Suddenly the opportunity to learn orchestral writing, arranging, and production was thrust upon me. I had studied the orchestra briefly in college, but had very little orchestral experience in the real world. Samuel Adler's book, *A Study of Orchestration*, became my new best friend. I devoured it, taking copious notes, creating a notebook filled with orchestration tips and techniques. Orchestral samples became the new hotness in my slowly expanding composing rig. To learn on the job like this was an opportunity of a lifetime.

What would you do if you were suddenly handed a vibrant canvas to practice skills of orchestral writing, arranging, and production? Would you hire expert collaborators to guide you through? Would you jump into the deep end of the pool yourself? Maybe you would turn it down and walk away?

I decided to jump into the deep end of the orchestration pool myself. Through experimentation, with lots of trial and error, I learned where to place melodies, how to double and couple effectively, how to build and vary harmonic support. I learned how to prepare sheet music, and how to work with classically trained musicians in the studio. I learned important differences between working with digital samples and working with live instruments. Inevitably over time, I did gain a measure of proficiency. Working with an orchestra became a bright and shiny new tool in my scoring belt. And it was about to open a new career door for me I had never imagined.

VIDEO GAMES

It was the summer of 1996. One of my neighbors rang me up and said, "Chance, my favorite video game company just posted a music job online. You should totally apply!"

I was offended.

After all, I was a *composer*. Video games? They did not use real music. They just spewed inane electronic noise.

Granted, my knowledge of video games was mostly informed by the Atari 1040-ST, a computer I brought onboard cruise ships for composing. It hosted a program called SMPTE Tracks Gold, ideal for writing and arranging. But it also came installed with *Pong, Space Invaders, Oids,* and *Yahtzee.* All of those games were fun to play, but the soundtracks were just silly. Apply for a job making music for games? No way, not me.

After all, I was a *composer.*

"Chance, you write jingles for car dealers," he retorted. "No offense. Come over to my house and let me show you how cool this stuff is."

Later that afternoon, I found myself watching a large CRT monitor in a small home office. My friend showed me two video games featuring live-action film interspersed with graphic animation. Pretty cool, I had to admit. I didn't know that live actors could interact with animation in games. These games even had music with real melody and harmony! But it was super cheesy. And the MIDI instruments sounded terrible. I wasn't impressed.

Then he pulled up a brand new game called, *Gabriel Knight.* This game featured a level built around an opera. Literally, an opera. A 20-minute opera inserted inside a video game! The music was still MIDI, but I was awakened to a vast potential in games that I had never imagined before. I thanked him and returned home to ponder the possibilities.

The wheels of obsession started turning toward California, toward Sierra Online, the video game company that had produced *Gabriel Knight.*

Maybe I would apply for that job after all.

CHAPTER 2

Quest for Glory and Grammy Awards

G RIPPING THE PHONE TIGHTLY, I swung my left arm out of the car window and pressed "record". Endless waves of shaggy evergreens whizzed past, stretching skyward, filling the car with a wonderfully spicy aroma. This was Oakhurst California, home of Sierra Online, the famed adventure game company. I was entering town for a job interview and wanted to capture the moment.

Sierra was seeking a full-time composer and I had applied for the job. After submitting my resume and several music samples, the team wanted to take a closer look.

The world of video games was new to me. I was intrigued and excited. But I was also astonishingly ignorant. Only a brief glimpse at *Gabriel Knight* had shown me the potential of this rapidly evolving medium.

I spent a quiet night at the Ramada Inn on Highway 41, and prepared to visit Sierra's game studio the next morning.

Job interviews can be stressful. But as a freelancer working in the advertising business, I had developed a knack for stepping into new situations with a smile. Confidence and flexibility were important, but making a good impression often hinges on simply liking the people you meet and being likeable in return. With this group, that was especially easy to do.

Jay Usher led the first meeting. He had been a composer at Sierra for several years, and was now branching out to take on a wider range of responsibilities. In fact, he had just been promoted to game producer. Jay was tall

DOI: 10.1201/9781003199311-3

and thick, with short cropped hair, glasses, and an easy smile. He wore a starched plaid shirt tucked into khaki pants, with a brown leather belt. My first impression was of a typical middle manager in the tech industry.

Jason Hayes and Victor Crews also joined us, both currently working as company composers. Jason was magnetic, with a youthful musician vibe that oozed from his long brown hair, energetic bearing, and trendy banter. But he was no lightweight. Behind the cool slang and quick laugh was a piercing intellect pulsing with curiosity. His mind cut with razer precision, always innocuously. No self-serving agendas or malicious intent. Jason and I became life-long friends. Incidentally, Jason would eventually leave Sierra to become a trail blazer at Blizzard Entertainment, helping to define and develop *World of Warcraft*'s musical style for a generation of gamers.

Victor was the most serious of the group. He was a recent graduate of Indiana University with a computer music degree. Older, with a tangled mop of black hair and piercing dark eyes, Victor was quiet and measured his words carefully. He carried himself with a trace of aloofness and hint of skepticism. Victor could write music that was consummately cool but also kind of bizarre. We came at music from very different places, but I had great respect for Victor and his work. Years later, while working as a Studio Audio Director for EA Games, I would hire Victor to work as an audio designer on our team. Funny how life can cycle around.

The interview was a breeze. We basically just talked music, and they geeked out a little bit over my demo. Who wouldn't love that? But after lunch, the hard questions came. How familiar was I with Sierra's adventure games? Could I be comfortable composing in Cakewalk? What sort of score would I envision for an action/adventure title set among ancient Greek islands?

I wrapped most of those questions into questions of my own. How much did they want the music to reflect the setting, and how much did they want the music to reflect the story? What ambitions were they imagining for the future of music scores in adventure games? What were the benefits they found composing in Cakewalk as opposed to using a Mac-based system? On a personal level, how did they like living in the small mountain community of Oakhurst? More importantly, how did their wives like living there? Round and round we went.

By the end of the day, everyone had a good sense of connection, camaraderie, and shared vision for the future. They offered me a job, and after discussing things with Pamela and praying about our decision, I accepted. We were moving to California.

I was being hired to compose the original music score for Lori and Corey Cole's newest action/adventure game, *Quest for Glory V: Dragon Fire*. As I got up to speed on the game design, my ambition for the score became crystal clear. This game needed a live orchestral score, peppered with ethnic acoustic instruments and layered vocals. In 1996, that ambition sounded crazy to most of the team. But Jay liked it. He said he would get behind it if we could figure out how to make it work within the constraints of current PC tech limitations (memory footprint, digital audio playback system, etc.). We had a couple of years of development ahead of us, and I was certain we would figure it out.

COLLABORATION

As the fifth game in a popular franchise, *Quest for Glory V: Dragon Fire* had a veteran development team in place and a built-in fan base with deeply ingrained expectations. I learned early in the process to share my formative music ideas with Jay and key members of the team. Terry Robinson, the game's gently brilliant art director, proved especially useful in offering early feedback and direction. Jason and Victor were also generous and insightful in giving comments on my work-in-progress cues.

I have to admit, I loved working as part of a team. After so many years of composing music alone in my basement, the communal vibe was invigorating. I loved bouncing ideas spontaneously off other creative minds, evolving music through various iterations, improving the custom fit for a particular game state, and enhancing the breadth of appeal to an ever-widening audience.

Soon I wanted even broader feedback than the team could provide. I wanted to connect directly with the fans. In 1996, this was just becoming practical.

Sierra had developed an electronic mailing list for fans of their games, and Paul Trowe, the game's associate producer, was curating a regular and widely read newsletter for the QFG fans. I proposed sending an early version of my main theme out through Paul's newsletter. He agreed, and I wrote a short introductory article, imbedding an mp3 link so they could hear the work-in-progress theme. Oh man! The fans hated it, and really gave it to me with both barrels. Thankfully amid the backlash were some excellent suggestions for improvement.

In the next newsletter I thanked everyone for their suggestions and promised I would go back to the drawing board to try again. Once they knew I had listened to them, and respected their feedback, the fans became invested in the outcome. I did not want to disappoint them.

Version two of the theme was much better. We called it the *Quest for Glory V Overture*, and it was an epic track. Nearly all of the general feedback from the fans had been woven into the rewrite, including a few specific suggestions. I pointed that out in a short article, and imbedded a new link in the newsletter's next issue.

The fans loved the reworked theme and their enthusiastic response energized me. I wrote like crazy over the following months, churning out track after track of battle music, exploration ambience, tavern songs, you name it. And the music was coming out in game-ready, adaptive segments – introductory pieces, variations, loopable bits, stingers, and outros. I was having such a blast.

TECHNICAL REVOLUTION

Only problem was, the team only had reliable tech in place to deploy MIDI files interactively, driving downloadable sample sets (DLS). I hated that option because the DLS sounds of the day sounded terrible. There was no solution yet for deploying digital audio files in an interactively adaptable way. I needed to find a brilliant ally on the programming team.

Enter Eric Lengyl. Eric was a new hire like me. He was young and energetic, with innovative ideas of his own. He had successfully persuaded the dev team to switch the game's art assets from sprites to voxels and seemed to have a knack for thinking outside the box.

I also noticed that he loved pizza and frequently stayed late at the office, as did I.

Oakhurst, California had one of the best pizza restaurants on the planet, The Pizza Factory. Their pepperoni special with extra cheese was legendary. One night while Eric and I were both working late, I knocked on his door with a box of steaming hot pepperoni pizza and some cold drinks. I asked if Eric would like to share it with me and cracked open the lid. One whiff of the aroma was all it took. He invited me right in.

We talked about all kinds of interesting things while getting acquainted. Eric was a math whiz and a runner, indicative of his smarts and competitive drive. He admitted he did not plan to stay long at Sierra, and hinted at lofty ambitions for the future. He really hoped to advance his career by pioneering technical innovations in this game. When I heard that, I pivoted our discussion to the archaic music system we were currently using, and explained how it was limiting our ability to innovate.

I suggested two new functions that would elevate the music experience for our players. We needed an exploratory music system that could call up variations of a theme from different asset buckets, playing them back randomly with increasing intervals of time. We also needed a combat music system that could adapt to six different game states, all required to match and underscore the shape of battle inside the game.

"Oh, and one more thing," I nibbled, "All of this functionality has to trigger digital audio files, rather than MIDI." In 1996, that was truly undiscovered country.

I had thrown down the gauntlet.

We brainstormed and scribbled lots of notes on the whiteboard. By the time I left hours later, we had worked out the hooks and rudimentary language necessary to make a custom music plug-in for the game engine, a plug-in that could deliver all of the interactive functions required for this ambitious music design.

When I returned the next morning, Eric had already started writing the code.

By 1997, we had the new tech working in the game. This kind of interactive functionality with digital audio was virtually unheard of across the industry. LucasArts had figured out something similar with their iMuse system. But by and large, no one else was doing interactive music with digital audio files yet. That was meaningful, because using digital audio freed us from the captivity of cheesy DLS sound banks. Instead, we could now record our score with a live orchestra, ethnic musicians, and great singers. I was over the moon.

PRODUCTION

With the game and its score coming to completion, it was time to think about recording. I knew the Salt Lake City, Utah studios and talent base from my years working on advertising music there, so it seemed the natural place to go. I pulled out all the stops. I hired a 65-piece orchestra, which we recorded at LA East Studios, with veteran engineer Glen Neibaur behind the console. Most of the musicians were puzzled to be told they were recording music for a video game, and I daresay the scope and sweep of the score surprised them. The performances were very good, and I was pleased to have composed and produced one of the very first live orchestral scores in video game history.

I overdubbed soloists at Lakeview Recording Studio, a small shop run by veteran recording engineer Steve Lerud. I hired Rich Dixon, a legend in guitar circles, to play all of the nylon string acoustic guitar parts in the score. While we had him in the studio, I also asked Rich to improvise additional variations for our ambient music system. Daron Bradford played the oboe d'amore, flute, and English horn, which we sprinkled throughout the score for exotic flavor. Jenny Jordan recorded the layered vocal parts, including the glorious harmonies in what would later become the most popular cue in the score, *The Dance of Mystery and Intrigue.*

The score was a grand slam. We picked up Music of the Year from IGN in 1998. Nearly every game review raved about the music. The fact that we had pulled off a live orchestral score, while also making the music interactive, was a huge win. We released a commercial soundtrack of the game music both independently and as a bundled product. More than 50,000 units sold, which was a high bar for a soundtrack, let alone a video game soundtrack. It remains one of the best-selling game soundtracks from the pre-digital music era.

THE GRAMMY CAMPAIGN

All of this positive response stirred up a crazy idea in my mind. What if we could get game music into the Grammy Awards?

We had a savvy PR executive on site named Monica Moulin. I ran the idea past her, and she loved it. She agreed to rally support in the press if I proceeded. We also had a visionary general manager named Craig Alexander, to whom I also pitched the idea (much more on Craig later). He liked it, and asked how I planned to pursue this goal. I told him I would meet with the leadership of the National Academy of Recording Arts and Sciences (NARAS) and float a proposal. But first I ought to get acquainted with some of their key people. I suggested visiting an upcoming NARAS chapter party in San Francisco, and he agreed that Sierra would foot the bill.

The night of the party arrived, and I pushed my way into the crowded nightclub. A mobile DJ booth was pulsing over in the corner. Red and blue lights flickered from the ceiling, tickling a small dance floor. Music industry insiders were everywhere. Suddenly, I spotted the man I had come to see.

Chatting with a group of record execs was C. Michael Greene, Chief Executive Officer of the Recording Academy, otherwise known as "the Grammy guy." I wasted no time getting next to him.

I introduced myself as a new member of the Recording Academy, and mentioned that I composed music for video games. He nodded, but seemed disinterested and distracted, his eyes darting around the room. I pressed on, posing the question I had driven to San Francisco to ask, "Is it possible to have a new Grammy Award category for video game music?"

His eye-wandering stopped, and he looked down at me – straight down his long, thin, slightly crinkled nose, "You mean like Pac Man and Donkey Kong?"

"No, not really," I answered. "More like live orchestra, layered voices, classical guitar, and ethnic soloists. Sort of like what you're hearing right now."

Prior to our conversation, I had arranged with the DJ to spin up a copy of my *Quest for Glory V: Dragon Fire* original soundtrack. The first song was already sweeping across the room when I mentioned the new category.

I continued, "This is my latest video game score." Greene cocked his head toward the ceiling and began listening intently. Cigarette smoke drifted upward, dancing hazy circles around the lights, but his eyes were fixed far away. I could see the concentration on his face, lips pursed, eyebrows furrowed, an outdated paradigm shifting in real time.

Finally, he turned to me and said, "You may be on to something here. Get in touch with our VP of Awards, Diane Theriot. Show her what you've got. I'll tell her you're calling. Let's see where this goes."

I made the appointment and prepared my pitch. The false impression held by the Recording Academy's president, namely that all video game music sounded like *Pac Man* and *Donkey Kong* (8-bit), was widely held in the late 90s. If I was going to make any headway with the VP of Awards, I needed to blow that perception out of the water. I packed a copy of the *Quest for Glory V: Dragon Fire* soundtrack, and also brought along the best examples of peer work I could find – *Jurassic World* by Michael Giacchino, *Quake* by Nine Inch Nails, *Grim Fandango* by Peter McConnell, and a few more. Thusly armed, I made my way to NARAS' worldwide headquarters in Los Angeles, California for an appointment with the VP of Awards.

Diane Theriot was the epitome of hard-earned, effortless class. Imagine the congenial charm of Oprah Winfrey with the seasoned wisdom of a diplomat. Not a perfect description, but that's pretty close.

As I entered Diane's dazzling corner office, she rose up quickly and stepped out from behind her desk, extending a warm greeting. Dressed in a well-tailored business suit, she carried herself with an ease few could manage, even in their favorite sweats.

We soon relaxed into unhurried small talk. I don't think I had ever felt such natural affinity from a top executive before. At length Diane addressed the purpose of my visit. "I understand you would like to discuss a new Grammy Award category to honor music from video games? Please tell me what I ought to know about this."

My presentation was locked and loaded. Game on.

I focused first on quality. Quality of composition and production. She had a superior sound system in her office, and we listened to several tracks from the CDs I had prepared. She admitted both surprise and respect at the work we had been doing.

Next, I talked about relevance. By 1998, the video game industry had grown into an entertainment industry juggernaut. For millions of youth around the world, video games were "the new rock and roll,"[1] and those of us composing game music were providing the soundtrack for their lives. The reach of games was enormous and growing rapidly, and I showed Diane the graphs and sources to prove it. The Academy would be flirting with future irrelevance by ignoring such a significant demographic shift.

She got it. But on behalf of the Academy, she raised some strategic concerns. First and foremost, was video game music really a different art form that needed separate recognition? Second, were there enough Academy members participating in game music to create a critical mass of Grammy voters? Finally, would there be a respectable pool of game soundtrack albums released each year, enough to nominate and judge from? She set those challenges before me and suggested we meet again when I could answer those questions satisfactorily.

Keep in mind, I had only been involved in game music for a couple of years. Getting video game music into the Grammy Awards would be a huge task, much bigger than me. I needed allies of additional breadth and depth, peers who were at least as invested in the idea as I was, but who also had more history in the business. What if I put together a Game Music Grammy Committee, gathering the who's who of video game music in 1998? It would take research, logistical support, and funding. Most of all, it would take time. My time. I met with Craig Alexander again to update him on my progress and share my new strategy. He approved the use of additional company time and funding to continue the pursuit.

Several names floated to the top in my research – George "the Fat Man" Sanger, Tommy Tallarico, Brian Schmidt, Michael Land, Alexander Brandon, Bobby Prince, Greg Rahn, Mark Miller, Ron Hubbard, and Tom White. I set the date for an introductory meeting in San Francisco, California and booked a Crowne Plaza hotel conference room for the conversation. Invitations were extended, and everyone showed up. It was incredible to see so much formidable talent gather in the same room. Some had been deeply adversarial in years prior, but everyone "checked their egos at the door" and came together in unity for this Grammy discussion.

The meeting was amiable and productive. In the end, we agreed on three resolutions: (1) Our committee would undertake a campaign to evangelize the regular production and release of game soundtrack albums, not a common practice at the time. (2) We would encourage our peers to join the Recording Academy and get involved. (3) Members would elect one of us to create and publicize a formal proposal to form a new category.

On this third point, the committee unanimously elected me.

When I returned to Oakhurst and to Sierra, I reported back to Craig and Monika about the results of our Grammy Committee meeting. They were encouraged and offered continued support. Monika was especially helpful as we brainstormed a publicity campaign about our grassroots efforts to create a new Grammy category for video game music. It was the right time, and she had the right connections. I began interviewing with mainstream media outlets and entertainment industry press regularly, giving my pitch, pointing them to *Quest for Glory V, Grim Fandango*, and other substantial soundtracks of the day. Articles started coming out in the *New York Times*, *USA Today, LA Times, Entertainment Weekly, Hollywood Reporter, IGN, GameSpot*, and most game industry magazines and websites.

I became active in NARAS' San Francisco chapter, and with Diane's introduction, connected with Leslie Ann Jones, an influential member of the Academy's Board of Governors. Leslie became a powerful ally in our quest. In the midst of Sierra's press campaign, several members of the Game Music Grammy Committee joined me for another summit in San Francisco. I presented Leslie with the proposal I had drafted for a new Grammy Awards category for video game music, and she agreed to bring it up at the next Academy Board meeting in LA.

At the meeting, many Academy Board members contended that game music was not substantively different from other forms of underscore, such as music for film and television. Of course, those of us working on games disagreed because of the interactive component, but there weren't enough games deploying quality interactive music to make a persuasive case. And besides, they argued, the Grammy Awards honor audio recordings as stand-alone products – singles and soundtrack albums, not music playing inside games. The game industry was sorely lacking soundtrack releases, but even the few releases we did have were just linear music.

As a compromise, I drafted a new document proposing the creation of three new Grammy categories, which would lump game music together with film and TV music – Best Soundtrack Album for Motion Picture, Television or Other Visual Media; Best Song for a Motion Picture, Television, or Other Visual Media; and Best Instrumental Composition for Motion Picture, Television, or Other Visual Media. Our committee approved it, and I sent it to Leslie and Diane, who also expressed their support. At the next meeting of NARAS' Awards and Nominations Committee, the proposal was approved.

In 2001 video game music became part of the Grammy Awards for the first time in history. It was a great victory, but not the final step.

Twenty-one years passed. In 2022, NARAS finally agreed to give video game music its own Grammy Awards category. That was always the objective. The three mixed media categories laid the ground work, but the job was never finished until we finally had our own category. On February 5, 2023, Stephanie Economou became the first composer in history to win a Grammy Award for Best Score Soundtrack for Video Games and Other Interactive Media. Her winning score was the music from *Assassin's Creed Valhalla: Dawn of Ragnarök*.

Victory! I was thrilled for the win, and happy to see the fulfillment of our original objective. Nevertheless, I was reminded that patience is an essential attribute for those on the vanguard of change. Some goals can take decades to fully blossom.

To watch video and listen to music from Quest for Glory V: Dragon Fire, *as described in this chapter, please visit: HUGEsoundRecords.com/Memoir-02*

NOTE

1 Dan Irish, *The Game Producer's Handbook,* Thomson Course Technology PTR, 2005.

CHAPTER 3

The Lord of the Rings, Part One

A LOUD KNOCK AT THE door startled me. I was reviewing a newly mastered soundtrack album, lost in a dance of sonic colors, oblivious to the world around me. Shaken from my reverie, I pushed the pause button and opened the door, welcoming Daniel James into my studio. Daniel was a new hire at Sierra Online, where I worked as senior music producer. He had been brought onboard to assist with the design of *J.R.R. Tolkien's Middle-earth Online* (MEO), the company's top secret new online game.

First impressions are unfiltered, and with a glance I liked Daniel already. He was a lanky Brit with mischievous eyes and a crooked smile, topped with a messy mop of brown ringlets, scraggled in every possible direction. Cradled in his left arm was a pile of books.

He plopped the books on my desk. "Your summer reading material," he announced.

Unevenly stacked from top to bottom were five thick paperbacks from Ballentine Publishing: *The Hobbit*, *The Fellowship of the Ring*, *The Two Towers*, *The Return of the King*, and *The Silmarillion*. It was a formidable stack.

Daniel announced his intention to make *MEO* into a truly spectacular game. He raved about the source material in the books, unrivaled in all the world of fantasy. "Besides," he explained, "Sierra's video game license is based exclusively on J.R.R. Tolkien's writings, so everyone on the game

DOI: 10.1201/9781003199311-4

team needs to be thoroughly versed in this literature." I had been appointed to tackle *MEO* as my next project. It was a dream come true, an appointment I had lobbied for vigorously.

Daniel and I spent the better part of an hour discussing his vision for the game, and as we concluded, I said I looked forward to receiving my marching orders. He pointed an eager finger toward the pile of books on my desk and said, "Orders received!"

DISCOVERING MIDDLE-EARTH

This was the summer of 1998 and I will admit, at almost 37 years old, I had never read *The Lord of the Rings*. Of course, *The Hobbit* was familiar from my seventh-grade English class. But most of its details had long faded from memory. This embarking would take me through mostly virgin territory, an unpredisposed journey to the final chapters. I fanned the five books across the desk and instinctively drew *The Fellowship of the Ring* toward my chest. "Yes," I thought. "This is where I will begin my exploration." I turned back the cover, and thumbed through the first few pages. They felt crisp with newness between my fingers. I settled on page seven, where the following words were printed in italics:

> *Three Rings for the Elven-kings under the sky,*
> *Seven for the Dwarf-lords in their halls of stone,*
> *Nine for Mortal Men, doomed to die,*
> *One for the Dark Lord on his dark throne*
> *In the Land of Mordor where the Shadows lie.*
> *One Ring to rule them all, One Ring to find them,*
> *One Ring to bring them all and in the darkness bind them.*
> *In the Land of Mordor where the Shadows lie.*[1]

My *LOTR* journey had begun.

For the next several months, I disappeared into Tolkien's web of fantasy – wizards and Hobbits, Orcs and Uruk-Hai, Elves and Dwarves, warriors and kings. Threading magically through it all was music. My mission was to understand with authority how J.R.R. Tolkien had envisioned music throughout the breadth and depth of Middle-earth, across all of its ages.

Each day I spent long hours researching and annotating Tolkien's books for everything they revealed about music. I found passages describing specific musical instruments used by various races. I found passages describing vocal tone qualities. I found more than 60 different songs in the books and studied them all, including song forms and styles. It was fascinating to read about the impact of music on characters, personality traits, and even the environment. I sought to capture the author's magnificent vision, interpret it in contemporary musical terms, and give it pure expression through the music in our game.

From my literary notes, I drafted a 26-page Tolkien Music Style Guide. This Guide provided guardrails to keep my creativity from drifting wildly or even mildly off course. It insured that my composing and producing efforts would remain aligned with the literature, always in harmony with Tolkien's vision.

Let us dig into the some of those details.

HOME KEYS

Each race's music was centered in its own distinct home key. For example, Elves were based in A minor, Hobbits in C major, Dwarves in D minor, Men in E major, and monsters in F# minor.

The home key idea was born from two branches of theoretical thinking. First, nodes and overtones vibrate at different frequencies in different keys. These frequencies interact with human physiology in ways that are consistent, predictable, and unique to each key. Thus, hearing music in a certain key tends to create a recognizable resonance with emotional characteristics most associated with that key. For example, A minor triggers sad and sweet emotions within us, descriptors given to the Elves. C major elicits feelings of happiness and safety, a perfect fit for our Hobbits. Dwarves are a stout race acquainted with mourning and gloom, impressions reinforced in D minor. And so on.

The second theoretical support comes from contrasting ideas of "familiar" and "foreign." The design for *MEO* required an unimaginably vast online world. As players ventured far from their point of origin, I wanted them to feel a sense of displacement from home in their journey. Each player would begin the game in the origin territory and home key of their character's race before venturing out. So, for instance, by the time a Hobbit left The Shire, the player would be subliminally steeped in C major music. C major created the "familiar" resonance for that player. Thus, when entering territory belonging to Dwarves or Elves, Orcs or Uruk-Hai, the change in key would feel unexpectedly "foreign" to their own internal home key. When the player returned to The Shire, the "familiar" resonance of C major would give the player an internally subliminal sense of safety and belonging. They had come home.

PALETTES

The Style Guide assigned stylistic, vocal, and instrumental palettes to each race. Each palette was based on references and inferences taken directly from Tolkien's writings. This is easier to understand if we look at a few specifics:

Elves (A minor)

Emphasis within the orchestra: *Violin section, reed family, and pedal harp (gut strung).*

Emphasis in small ensembles, accompaniment, or solo instruments:

Lute, gemshorn, and oboe di amor for High Elves of Rivendell; Theorbo, English horn, and Italian carnival whistle for Wood Elves of Mirkwood; Harp (gut strung), viola di gamba, oboe, and tin whistle for Elves of Lothlorien.

Vocal palette: *Counter-tenor and tenor males; soprano and mezzo-soprano females. All voices clear and pure.*

Stylistic palette: *Generally ethereal, magical, sad, and sweet. Includes regional variants, as needed:*

Worshipful, approaching classical for High Elves of Rivendell; Folksy, and mischievous for Wood Elves of Mirkwood; Dreamy and warm for Elves of Lothlorien.

Dwarves (D minor)

Emphasis within the orchestra: *Cello and double bass sections, trombone section, bass clarinet, timpani, and gran casa.*

Emphasis in small ensembles, accompaniment, or solo instruments: *wire-strung harp, crumhorn, clarinets, and large bodhran played heavily in the center.*

Vocal palette: *Bass and baritone males with contralto females. All voices deep-throated and rugged.*

Stylistic palette: *Stately, plodding, stout, and mythical.*

On it went through each race and palette. The underscore for each race was also given harmonic, melodic, and rhythmic guidelines inferred from references in the text. Other sections in the Style Guide outlined production quality standards, music design matrices, implementation alternatives, music delivery specifications, and much more. It was wonderfully comprehensive.[2]

How could it be anything less than comprehensive and authoritative? The Tolkien works are highly esteemed by millions of readers across the globe. For the fantasy genre faithful, *Lord of the Rings* nearly approaches the status of canon. Daring to mingle my own efforts with those of Tolkien was a risky venture – not a quest for the superficially inclined. I needed to draw this music from the very pen of Tolkien's writings, ringing of truth to anyone familiar with its pages.[3] That's why I undertook the research with such meticulous and exhaustive standards.

Only after completing an authoritative Style Guide did I finally start composing.

CRAWL, WALK, RUN

Creating guidelines was one thing. Crafting glorious music to reflect those guidelines was something else entirely. My first attempts, I'm sorry to say, turned out abysmally.

My first setting of *A Elbereth Gilthoniel*, a sacred song of Elven worship, was a disaster. The melody I wrote meandered aimlessly to nowhere. The child soprano I hired to sing the song brought an odd flavor to the recording I hadn't anticipated. The string section accompaniment was bland and anemic. I cannot even listen to the song now, it just sets my teeth on edge.

That wasn't the only dud I penned during the early days of writing. It was much harder than I imagined to reconcile my raw composing style with the sophistication outlined in the Tolkien Music Style Guide. But one good character trait I have always possessed was an appetite for work. The more I worked at it, the closer I got to creating something good.

Eventually I started to find my footing. One particular set of stanzas from Tolkien's poetry truly inspired me:

> *I sang of leaves,*
> *Leaves of gold,*
> *And leaves of gold there grew...*[4]

In this part of *The Fellowship of the Ring*, Tolkien introduces his readers to the Elven Lord of Lothlorien, Celeborn. Following his introduction, he adds these beautiful words,

"Behind him stood Galadriel, tall and white; a circlet of golden flowers was in her hair, and in her hand she held a harp, and she sang. Sad and sweet was the sound of her voice in the cool, clear air..."[5]

Reading that section, I could see it, hear it, almost taste it. Music began to pour out of me more naturally than ever before. Yes! This felt much better than my earlier attempts. The melody was sweet and memorable. The harmony brought a feeling of reflection on better days. Rich textures from the Style Guide conjured an ethereal feeling – intricate harps (six tracks), flutes, theorbo, viola di gamba, and an occasional touch of piano. The vocalist, Jenny Jordan, was practically plucked from Lothlorien itself. I titled the song, *Leaves of Gold*. Now we were finally getting somewhere.

Many talented people were featured in the recording. Sterling Price played the theorbo. Patricia Zwick played viola di gamba. Rich Dixon laid down the nylon string acoustic guitar parts. All the harp tracks were performed by Janet Peterson. I played the piano and rounded out the rest of the arrangement with virtual instruments. We recorded the song at Lakeview Recording in Orem, Utah, with Steve Lerud engineering. I did the mix at Sierra. It turned out nicely, the first piece of music I had written for *MEO* that did not make me cringe.

THE DARK LORD OF CORPORATE FRAUD

Just as things were starting to gel with the music, a bombshell dropped.

February 22, 1999, was a chilly, overcast morning in central California. At 10:30 am, all Sierra employees were summoned and herded into two large meeting rooms to receive shocking news. There had been massive fraud allegations leveled against the parent company of Sierra's parent company. Our studio was being closed. 250 people lost their jobs that morning, including me. We were told to save and archive our work, gather our things, and exit the premises by the end of the day.

I was stunned. And desperate. A handful of employees had been offered relocation packages to move to Sierra's new corporate headquarters in Bellevue, Washington, but I was not among them. How could that happen? There was no way I was returning to the scratch-and-claw life of freelancing full-time without a fight. The visiting rep from corporate would be around all day. I hatched a plan to save my job.

The music from *Quest for Glory V: Dragon Fire* had generated rave reviews all over the world of gaming. I printed copies of as many as I could find and placed them in a binder.

The game music Grammy campaign had brought publicity to Sierra from mainstream media giants such as the *New York Times, Los Angeles Times, Entertainment Weekly,* and *USA TODAY.* I printed copies of those articles too, underlining the mentions of Sierra with yellow highlighter, and placed them in the binder.

My employee evaluations, a regular part of corporate administration, were stellar. They outlined initiatives I had undertaken to help raise our audio team to higher levels of innovation and excellence, including pushing new technologies, inventing new methods of interactive deployment, and skill training in orchestration, recording, and mixing. Those all went in the binder too.

I gathered all of this evidence to support my pitch that I was indispensable to the company, and set an appointment with the company rep. My buddy Tim Larkin, a sound designer hired for *MEO,* teased me, "Don't you know who I am?" he playfully mocked, as I showed him my arsenal. I just laughed. I had my binder, I was ready to roll.

Our appointment arrived and I walked with brisk confidence into the room. The rep from headquarters was distracted, on his phone, then on his laptop, then back on his phone again. The smell of old coffee filled the air. He briefly looked up at me, "Yes, what do you want?" I took a beat, pondering the good work I had been doing at Sierra and remembering how difficult freelance life had been in Salt Lake City, Utah. There was no going back. I had to get this man's attention.

I launched my opening salvo. "Did you know that the *Quest for Glory V* soundtrack album, which I produced, was more profitable than the game?" He sat up a little straighter and looked at me, as if for the first time.

"I'd heard some good things," he said, "But I didn't know all that." I showed him the Excel spreadsheet with numbers I had gotten from accounting and continued, "Yes, and did you know that I launched a nationwide campaign to bring video game music into the Grammy Awards?" "No, I wasn't aware," he said. I continued, "Yes, that campaign got Sierra highlighted in the *New York Times, Los Angeles Times, Entertainment Weekly,* and *USA TODAY.*" I opened the binder and thumbed through each article for him.

"OK, that's cool, but why are you telling me this?" he asked. I looked as incredulous as possible and replied, "Well, because I'm not on the list of employees getting relocation offers. Someone didn't do their homework."

I continued to visit with him, sharing some of the other evidences I had gathered. Things went well. He offered to keep me on the local payroll until they could make a decision about potentially moving me to Bellevue.

A few days later, a member of Sierra's corporate HR team whisked in from the airport in high heels and heavy hair spray to negotiate salary packages with those employees who were headed north. I gave her the same binder presentation I had given her colleague. It must have impressed her. She renewed my employment, offered to relocate me to Washington, and gave me a 40% pay raise on the spot.

SEATTLE

A few weeks later, I was flying to Seattle, Washington, to visit the company's headquarters in Bellevue. The core *MEO* team had relocated there already, and everyone was hard at work on the game. I had been working on the game in California, communicating with the team remotely, but it was bonding to see everyone and reconnect in person.

Bellevue and Seattle were lovely cities, with incredibly beautiful surroundings. Pamela came with me, and we looked at several neighborhoods and homes, eventually focusing on a property we liked near Lake Sammamish. Somewhere in the process, I picked up a *Welcome to Seattle* pamphlet and thumbed through the pages. Turning over the back cover I read: "Sixty-three days of sunshine annually!" I wondered why anyone would add something like that to a welcome brochure, as if it were a selling point? I was unsure if this California kid could survive on such a sunshine-starved diet. We hopped on the plane and headed back home.

Pamela and I have always made our big decisions together. We talk about the pros and cons. We share our points of view and feelings. We compare and contrast potential opportunities against costs and probable side effects. We even involve a spiritual dimension, praying for guidance in making choices that would be best for our family's overall health and well-being. For whatever reason, we did not feel settled about making the move to Bellevue.

Instead, Sierra agreed to let me stay in California, fully employed, working remotely from my music studio in the old Oakhurst office building. The building was up for sale, but there were not many prospects for such a large office space in a small town. Sierra had once been the largest employer in the area, at one point engaging hundreds of employees and supporting a large warehouse.

Now I was the only person working in the entire building. I composed new music for *MEO* each day and turned the lights off each night when I left. Sound designer Tim Larkin later took the same deal, and soon joined me in working there. Now there were two of us in that huge ghost building. Having Tim around was pretty cool. Two friends, all alone in that enormous building, crafting music and sound for Middle-earth in our old studios. Sometimes we played pranks on each other to keep things loose. It was a good season.

HUGESOUND

A few months into this arrangement, Sierra made the decision to change my status from employee to contractor. At that point, I decided to launch my own game audio services company. I would retain Sierra as my fist client. I called my new company HUGEsound (see Chapter 15).

Sierra still had not sold the building, so they allowed me to remain there while I was under contract for *MEO*. But I sensed a change in the air beyond my employment status. I wondered if Sierra had tipped their hand. Could the writing be on the wall for *MEO*?

Sure enough, a short time later, Sierra announced the complete cancellation of *MEO* and entered into litigation with the licensing agent for the Tolkien estate. All the Sierra team members who had moved to Bellevue were laid off. When my contract ran its course, it was not renewed. At least during that time I had been able to continue refining my approach to music in Middle-earth, and to think about what I could do next.

The Two Towers

While Sierra's license based on Tolkien's books became embroiled in legal battles, EA Games managed to secure a separate license to build games based on the new Peter Jackson films. Jackson's films were every nerd's dream. As a student of the books, I was especially impressed with the authenticity which this unlikely Kiwi and his formidable team brought to the silver screen.

EA's first *LOTR* game would match the events in the first two films. The game would come out on the same day that *The Two Towers* film was released. Don Veca was audio director over the project. Don is a tough dude. He looks like a Hell's Angel and he knows great audio. He had access to all of Howard Shore's music cues from the films, so there was no need for anyone to write new music for the game. But Don did need a music editor, someone who could slice Shore's music up and edit new underscore into the cinematics scattered throughout the game. I pitched my services, won the contract, and went to work.

Fascinating experience! I was so curious to compare Howard Shore's choices for the film score with my own choices for *MEO* and the Tolkien Style Guide. We were both drawing from the same source material, so it is not surprising that Shore and I made surprisingly similar choices in many areas. We also diverged in other ways, though not in the extreme. I was reminded that, "Music scoring is a language. It is comprised of known components, predictable structure and creative variation. It is a codified means of communicating ideas to the human mind. It is knowable, learnable and repeatable."[6]

The Fellowship of the Ring and The Hobbit

Working on *The Two Towers* for EA only whet my appetite for more.

Sierra managed to reacquire the book-based games license, and I began searching for opportunities within that franchise. Sierra had been reorganized under Universal Studios' game division, and I hoped that might provide the company with greater stability and longevity, yielding even more opportunities.

One of Universal's development teams was working on a *Fellowship of the Ring* adventure game, and I learned that they planned to produce a trailer for E3. I approached Mark Hood, Sierra's GM and asked, "Have you contracted with anyone for music and sound yet?" He replied that they had not even thought about audio yet, so I pitched HUGEsound as a total audio solution. Because of my work with the MEO team, Hood gave me the green light. I composed an original score and hired Tim Larkin to do the SFX. It was a tiny little project, but we did a great job. I hoped that would leave a good taste with the teams.

When the trailer launched at E3, I attended the expo and heard a rumor that Sierra was going to develop a platformer based on *The Hobbit*. Poking around on the Internet, I learned that Inevitable Entertainment in Austin, Texas, was developing the game. I discovered on LinkedIn that Marc Schaefgen was the audio director at Inevitable Entertainment. I copied his contact information and cold-called him. Marc was a sweet man with an easy wit and serious technical chops. I told him about the Tolkien Music Style Guide and my work on *MEO*, *The Two Towers*, and *The Fellowship of the Ring*. He was impressed and invited me to stay in touch, which I did.

Within a few short months, Marc said he would like for me to score *The Hobbit.* I was thrilled. This would be a huge win for my composing career. I felt grateful to Marc for opening this door for me. I began looking forward to learning more about the game and getting started on the music. In fact, I was counting on it.

But things can change in a hurry. The GM at Inevitable Entertainment stepped in and insisted that Marc hold an open audition for composers. Instead of handing me the score, Marc had to conduct a blind music test with the dev team. Whichever music demo received the most votes, its composer would receive the contract to score the game. With management now demanding a bake-off, I pulled some of my *MEO* Shire music together and submitted.

I will never forget Marc calling me a few weeks later, telling me the team had selected a different composer. I was so upset. I diplomatically expressed my disappointment to Marc, and asked if he would mind sending me a copy of the winning demo. Graciously, he agreed. I spun it up and listened to one of the best demos I had ever heard. The orchestration was perfect, the memorable melody faithfully captured the essence of Hobbits, and the production values were excellent. I called Marc back and told him, "I understand now. Whoever created that demo nailed it. They deserved to win, absolutely. Would you mind if I asked who submitted it?" Marc told me, "It was Rob Abernethy and Dave Adams."

I saw Rod and Dave a month later at the Game Developers Conference in San Francisco. I went right up and congratulated them. They knew I had pitched against them and lost, but did not gloat about it. We were professional and gracious to each another. Marc had already told them about me, and how positively I reacted to their demo. They were touched by sincere praise coming from a competitor.

I think that is how it should always be among peers, even competitors. Respect for merit. Respect for talent. Respect for honor among fellow travelers on the road.

Here's something I should point out. When you behave well in the face of disappointing news and unexpected circumstances, you can win the trust and respect of those who were watching you. Marc had been watching me, and respected the way I had handled myself with *The Hobbit* pitch, and afterwards with Rod and Dave. Later, when Marc picked up some intel that Universal Studios' game division was planning an entire franchise of new video games based on Sierra's Tolkien book license, he called me up and told me. In fact, Universal was launching a whole new corporate division to manage their Tolkien franchise. The new division was called Black Label Games.

BLACK LABEL GAMES

Scouring the Internet, I found a few articles that mentioned the formation of Black Label Games. Featured in each article was the name of the label's new president, Torrie Dorrell. LinkedIn gave me Torrie's contact information, and a couple of cold calls later, I had secured an appointment to present my ideas for music in Tolkien-based games to Torrie in person.

I took that appointment very seriously. I built a PowerPoint presentation highlighting my research in the literature, the Tolkien Music Style Guide, and music samples from *MEO* and *The Fellowship of the Ring* trailer. I wanted to impress upon Torrie that I knew Tolkien from a music perspective, better than anyone else in the business, perhaps better than anyone else in the world.

The day came. I made the four-hour drive down from Oakhurst, California, to Los Angeles, arriving about 10 minutes early for my appointment. I took a seat and waited nervously in the lobby.

I was shown into a small office, where Torrie faced me from the opposite side of a long desk. She was typing furiously at her keyboard, but paused shortly after I entered the room, standing to greet me with a warm smile and firm handshake. We made small talk for a few minutes, then I turned to the business of my visit. I asked for her permission to come around to the other side of her desk and share my presentation. I gave her a thumb drive, and she opened up my presentation on her screen.

Torrie was gracious and engaged, curious and methodical as I went through slide after slide. One of the points I hammered home was the need for all Tolkien games to orbit around a common musical center. In that way there would be a cohesion between the games, a subconscious familiarity with Tolkien's world for the players. "The Tolkien Music Style Guide offers just enough gravity to achieve that," I told her. Torrie seemed completely sold on my vision, and agreed with the conclusions I shared from the Style Guide. She suggested that I meet next with her VP of Production, VJ Lakshman.

While Torrie had been open-minded, VJ came across as adversarial. Behind his furrowed brows and dark eyes, VJ's black hair and muscular frame added an exclamation point to each aggressive question he levied about my qualifications, ideas, and assertions. That was OK. I was ready to be fully vetted and I held my own. Nothing was bigger in my career right now than landing a role composing music for this new *LOTR* franchise. Turned out, the opportunity was even bigger than I imagined.

TOLKIEN FRANCHISE MUSIC DIRECTOR

Near the end of our interview, VJ informed me that the Tolkien estate and their licensing entity, Tolkien Enterprises, was requiring Universal to hire franchise-wide Directors over story, art, and (wait for it…) music.

These Directors would have the responsibility to insure that each game played, looked, and sounded like Tolkien. The Franchise Music Director's job was specifically to insure that music in all of Universal's Tolkien games reflected an aesthetic that was tied directly to Tolkien's literature. This was exactly what I had been preaching since *MEO!* That was precisely what my Style Guide had been designed to do! I was thrilled.

Shortly after my interviews at Black Label, Torrie and VJ called to offer me a contract to serve as the Tolkien Franchise Music Director, supervising music development for all of Universal's upcoming *LOTR* titles. My Tolkien Music Style Guide would be universally adopted into their pipeline. I would visit each development team, assess the musical needs for their game, assist in hiring composers to fill those needs, and oversee the composition, production, and implementation of all game music. This was a dream come true gig, and I negotiated a generous rate that would be billed by the quarter hour.

My first meeting as the new music director was at Surreal Software in Seattle, Washington. Kristofor Mellroth was the audio director at the time, and he welcomed me upon my arrival. A bit unkempt, and sporting a wrinkled black T-shirt with baggy jeans, Kristofor fit the perfect stereotype of a game developer. During our conversation, he quickly acknowledged the value of a shared musical solar system for the franchise. He was, of course, deeply concerned about any technical and creative ramifications affecting his particular game, already in development. He suggested we meet with other key members of the team after lunch, including the game's composer and sound designer Brad Spear.

As engaging and cordial as Kristofor had been, Brad was the opposite. From the moment I walked into the conference room after lunch, Brad glared at me with suspicious eyes, peering out from under a tweed paddy cap and accusing eyebrows. He spoke up defensively and combatively many times during the meeting, making his point that I was an unnecessary intrusion into his creative process. I validated some of his concerns. After all, what composer relishes the thought of another composer suddenly having input and some degree of control over your score? His bristle was understandable.

But at the end of the day, we had to abide by the golden rule – those with the gold make the rules. In this case, Universal Studios' game division had the gold through its funding, and Tolkien Enterprises held the gold through its franchise license. Both had assigned me the gatekeeper for music in their games. Surreal's team, including Brad Spear, would have to accept my role as music director. I am not sure if Brad ever made peace with my involvement, but he settled into a professional mode, and complied with my input throughout development.

Other meetings followed with other teams – Liquid Entertainment in Los Angeles, California; Turbine Entertainment in Boston, Massachusetts; and Saffire Studios in Provo, Utah. All meetings were productive, and I loved collaborating with so many smart and talented people. I promised each team that I would give my best efforts to insure that their game's music met with Tolkien Enterprises' approval, and deliver their players an aesthetically exceptional experience. Everyone was onboard.

I even met with Inevitable Entertainment in Austin, Texas. In an ironic twist of fate, I became music director over *The Hobbit*, working directly with Marc Schaefgen and overseeing Rod Abernethy and Dave Adams in developing the game's original music score. Who would have ever seen that coming?

TOLKIEN FRANCHISE THEMES

Coming away from that first tour of meetings with such a diverse group of developers, I arrived at the conclusion that something more than the Style Guide document might be required to create sufficient gravity to hold each score in orbit. By now Universal Studios games division had merged with a large French entertainment conglomerate to form Vivendi-Universal Games. This seemed like a good time to update the Style Guide.

I added a recommendation for the development of a collection of thematic suites to identify the musical essence of each key race in the story. Themes from these suites could be deployed in every *LOTR* game to create a cohesive musical underpinning for each game score. The themes would serve as musical landmarks in our games, tying all the scores together with a series of common musical motifs and palettes. As Franchise Music Director, I assigned myself the task of composing and producing these thematic suites.

I proposed to showcase each group of themes by composing five overtures to tell key parts of the *LOTR* story in music. Not only would this model the Style Guide in a broad range of potential gameplay situations, but it would also provide a plethora of multiple-utility music assets for developers to use directly in their games. These assets would include dozens of high-quality music cues and sectional stems (choir, strings, brass, and woodwinds) from the live recording sessions. Also included were

MIDI files of each composition to start each composer on the right track. Wrapping up the deliverables would be feature-length tracks appropriate for a music CD or digital download.

For example, the yield from the single five-minute overture for the Elves was truly a bumper crop of musical assets:

- Eight recorded examples of Style Guide-based thematic scoring for the race of Elves.
- Five fully orchestrated music cues to introduce key areas in the game, ready for implementation directly in a game score.
- Dozens of stems and lesser cues (harp, strings and voice, woodwinds and psaltry, etc.) from each movement for implementation directly in a game score.
- The source MIDI files to give supporting composers an accurate starting point for their own scoring efforts.
- An adventurous, soundtrack-style overture for music lovers, which tells much of the Elves' story.

To my knowledge, planning such a detailed musical framework, designed in advance for an entire series of games, had never been done before. VUG approved the Franchise Themes as outlined, and we were off to the races. This would deliver innovative and efficient music design at a global level. I was very proud of that.

I was also proud of the music I was writing, but was wary of becoming rootbound by the limitations of my own writing style. In order to ensure the broadest possible appeal and safeguard against biases, I composed the five thematic overtures in full cooperation with our development teams, VUG management, and the other Tolkien Directors (Story and Art). Let me describe some of the process we went through.

First, I sent everyone early MP3 drafts of each thematic suite, with an invitation to return feedback. Many good suggestions came in. Kristofor Mellroth suggested that we use some of the Black Speech in Sauron's theme. Chris Pierson, the lore master at Turbine Entertainment, suggested specific lines of Dwarvish for the battle movement in the Dwarves thematic suite. Daniel Greenberg, our Story Director, helped steer me toward a better feel for the music in Mirkwood. Even Vijay Lakshman got into the act, suggesting I beef up the drums in the Dwarves' theme. It was a total team effort, and the end result was a collection of compositions we could all feel very good about.

Speaking of the Dwarves theme, let me take a brief sidebar. When I was working on the Dwarves themes, I would often go outside to walk along a river, just down the hill from my studio. Or I would sit and watch the nearby waterfall, or climb up some large rocks along the river bank. In that setting, I would imagine different musical phrases and possible approaches for the Dwarves' main theme. Eventually a piece of music began to come together in my mind, complete with primary elements for the orchestration. Once I heard the theme clearly in my mind, I went back inside the studio and started hammering out parts on the keyboard, bringing craftsmanship, knowledge, experience, and technology to bear. The process was an organic combination of inspiration and craft, with both playing an essential role.[7]

PRODUCING THE THEMES

There was never any question that I would record the themes with as many live components as possible, striving for the highest quality standard I could achieve. Tolkien's conceptualization of music was far too idealized for anything less. He talks of musical instruments "of perfect make and enchanting tones." He describes singing as "clear jewels of blended word and melody." He refers to "power" in old songs, and even yields the ultimate power of creation to music sung by the gods.

That meant finding the best orchestra, choir, and ancient acoustic instrumentalists available and within the reach of VUG's budget.

I quickly narrowed my orchestra list down to four – Hollywood Symphony, Northwest Sinfonia, Utah Film Orchestra, and Prague Philharmonic. Prague was the least expensive, but I never cared for the sound quality of scores recorded there. Hollywood was the high bar for quality, but also the high bar for cost. Seattle was on the high side of affordable, and I heard great sounding scores coming from there. But recording in Seattle would burn all of my budget on the orchestra, leaving me nothing else for soloists and mixing.

The cost to record in Salt Lake City was lower than Seattle and I had recorded in Salt Lake City previously with good results. I knew the talent pool and engineering resources well. In the end I went with the cost savings and personal experience. I chose Salt Lake City.

The Orchestra

Speed and efficiency matter when recording an orchestra. On the other hand, nothing evokes such a sick feeling as leaving the studio with an out-of-tune phrase that could have been fixed with one more take. That is why producing a live recording is such a balancing act. On one side you have aesthetics – timing, tuning, dynamics, all of the elusive ingredients that make emotive magic. On the other side there is the budget – only so much money, and if you exceed the allotment in one area, you have to cut somewhere else. Under the incredible pressure of the moment, making those decisions judiciously is the key to producing effective orchestral recording sessions.

We started with the strings, but things did not exactly get off to a smooth start. Version incompatibility between my Windows XP drives and the studio's Windows ME drives made it impossible to transfer the guide tracks directly. While the studio engineers scrambled to find a workaround, the orchestra grew restless. An outburst by a prominent member of the orchestra only added to the building tension. As we waited on the tech team, I watched the dollars slip into the chasm, and felt my blood pressure rising.

The control room finally called down with an interim solution. I rose to the podium and took a moment to gauge the atmosphere of the room. The players were unfocused, uneasy, and some seemed antagonistic. I was outwardly calm but rattled on the inside. This was no way to start a session, especially for *Lord of the Rings* themes.

I decided to do something I had never done in a recording session before. I announced to the orchestra that I was going to pray, and before they could protest I bowed my head and started talking loud enough for everyone to hear. I gave thanks for everyone's talents and professionalism, and gave thanks for the rare privilege we had of making music for a living. I asked for help in capturing a performance that would live up to the lofty standard of the literature. I said, "Amen," picked up my baton, and with surprisingly invigorated focus, I led the orchestra through the rousing first cue.

The Choir

In contrast to the orchestra, the choir was a hit right from the start. Many of the contracted studio singers also sang with the world-renowned Tabernacle Choir. In many ways, the choir far surpassed my expectations.

For *Sauron's Theme*, I took the inscription from the Ring of Power – *Ash nazg durbatuluk, Ash nazg gimbatul, Ash nazg thrakatuluk agh burzum, Ishi krimpatul* – and set the words to music. The choir was almost too good at this. During the session I teased them, "What will your director say when you confess to singing the Black Speech of Mordor, and that you were really good at it?" One of the baritones quipped, "That's true, we can always repent later."

After recording *Sauron's Theme* we moved to the Dwarves overture. During the first few takes, the singing was exceptional, but the feel of the caverns and the monotonous labor of the Dwarves was not coming through. I asked the men's choir to march in place, swaying from side to side for the next take. In an instant, their singing was altered. It was uncanny. As videographer John Pratt later wrote of that moment in the session: "To my amazement, simply excellent singing was transformed into the grandeur of generations of tireless hammers echoing into songs of celebration in the finished halls of Khazad-dûm!"

I was reminded that music producers need a lot of tricks up their sleeve.

Ancient Instruments

Rare, antique acoustic instruments can bring an ancient flavor to a game that nothing else in the world can. In truth, the sounds of these instruments are the only game elements that actually do come from another place and time. Getting some of these instruments into our *Lord of the Rings* recordings was essential.

Some of the specialty instruments we booked to record the Franchise Themes included the hurdy-gurdy, viola di gamba, psaltry, penny whistle, recorder, mandolin, rebec, dulcimer, and even an arch lute, also known as a theorbo.

I cannot tell you how interesting and challenging it was to work with those old instruments. Tuning was the most difficult part of the experience. The hurdy-gurdy seemed to rattle itself out of tune every five or six rotations. The arch lute's sixteen strings needed retuning several times during our recording session. Another difficulty was blending the thin and scratchy sounds of these ancient instruments with the full and rich tonality of modern instruments. The rebec was especially unpleasant in its natural state, requiring clever mic placement from underneath and behind, combined with an aggressive EQ carving to make it listenable.

Still, it was worth the added effort. The unique textures gained by including these soloists in the score could have come in no other way.

Getting in the Game

Once the recordings were complete, I brought all the music tracks back to my Yosemite area studio in five massive Pro Tools sessions and started carving out music cues. Every thematic suite was cut into six or seven cues of the full orchestration, each lasting up to two minutes each. That yielded 35 usable cues from the five thematic suites to share with our developers.

Next, I went to work creating variations on these cues with different mixes. For example, from one section in the overture for the race of men, I generated a full orchestral mix, a brass-only mix, a harp and flute mix, a strings-only mix, a woodwinds-only mix, and a strings plus woodwinds mix. Each mix sounds different and conveys a unique atmosphere. Thus, each is useful for a different scoring purpose. Culling through all five overtures and making remixes like these raised the number of usable music cues to nearly 100.

I uploaded every music cue to the corporate FTP site and made them available to the developers. I also included the original MIDI files and sectional stems. Each developer received a full asset list with recommendations for using them within their game. I followed up with a personal visit, meeting with each composer, offering further instruction, encouragement, and clarification. Here are two examples.

WAR OF THE RING

Composer Lennie Moore and the team at Liquid Entertainment took full advantage of every aspect of this design. Lennie took the MIDI files and used them as a starting point for 75%–80% of his compositions. He generally began by quoting one of the themes, working into a variation of the theme, then ventured off with a completely original idea. In producing the score, he made generous use of the choir stems, especially the phrases sung in Sauron's *Black Speech*. Each of the sectional stems were utilized to add texture and definition to the score. One highlight was his use of a solo fiddle stem from *The Overture of Men*, mixed into one of his own compositions. In addition, extra brass, pipes, voices, and Irish whistle sessions were contracted to record fresh material and some wild variations on Sauron's theme. Finally, music cues from the main themes were utilized in scoring the game's cinematics and key game events and transitions. The result is an artfully complete score that is perfectly in harmony with the Tolkien Music Style Guide. Lennie's score sings the main themes with clarity and variety, and creates a unique identity for *War of the Ring* within the body of VUG's solar system of Tolkien franchise game music.

MIDDLE-EARTH ONLINE

Instead of relying on MIDI files like Lennie Moore did for *War of the Ring*, developer Turbine Entertainment and composer Geoff Scott preferred sprinkling the game world with the ready-made digital music files pulled from the overtures. These fully produced theme segments were a perfect fit for the MMO. There were at least 90 different cues that they identified for implementation in the game. This abundant thematic foundation allowed Geoff to concentrate on creating source music and specialty tunes for the game. In addition, he contracted additional recordings on lute, solo woodwinds, and guitars, quoting some of the main themes by ear and offering grassroots variations for the score.[8]

AN EPIC JOURNEY

Great literature is a wonderful catalyst for the imagination, and very few works of literature inspire better than *The Lord of the Rings*. With the authoritatively documented Tolkien Music Style Guide, meticulously produced thematic overtures for each race, and successful franchise music design, each game score was set up to orbit convincingly around an authentic Tolkien center, while offering its own unique adaptation and interpretation of the material. The result is a desirable union of individuality and continuity.

In deference to *LOTR* fans, I tried to be as thorough, scholarly, and authoritative as possible in adapting these works for music. So did the various composers who worked with me. It was my brightest hope that music fans, gamers, and even Tolkien afficionados would find the music in every VUG Tolkien game evocative, authentic, of award-winning quality, and ultimately irresistible.

To listen to music from Vivendi-Universal's Lord of the Rings *franchise, as described in this chapter, please visit: HUGEsoundRecords.com/Memoir-03*

NOTES

1 J.R.R. Tolkien, *The Fellowship of the Rings*, p. 7; New York: Ballantine Books, 1955, 1965, 1973, 1982
2 https://www.gamedeveloper.com/audio/interview-with-chance-thomas-game-composer
3 Ibid.
4 J.R.R. Tolkien, *The Fellowship of the Rings*, p. 439; New York: Ballantine Books, 1955, 1965, 1973, 1982.
5 Ibid.
6 Chance Thomas, *Composing Music for Games: The Art, Technology and Business of Video Game Scoring*, p. 11; Boca Raton: CRC Press, 2016.
7 https://www.gamedeveloper.com/audio/interview-with-chance-thomas-game-composer
8 Ibid.

CHAPTER 4

King Kong

B Y 2004, PETER JACKSON was a household name. His *Lord of the Rings* movie trilogy was a triumph by any standard. With worldwide commercial success and critical acclaim, Jackson had carte blanche for whatever he wanted to do next. And what he wanted to do more than anything was to remake a classic that had captivated his imagination as a child – *King Kong.*

I had been following this closely in the news. It was not difficult. Every entertainment website, trade magazine, and news outlet seemingly reported Jackson's every move. And while reading about his love for high frame rates and going barefoot was mildly entertaining, that was not the kind of news that interested me. I needed to know who was making the *King Kong* video game. And I wanted to find out as early in the process as possible.

By today's standards, my Internet sleuthing skills were shockingly primitive. But what I lacked in know-how I made up for in volume. Article after article, day after day, searching for news, tidbits of information, anything that might lead to a publisher or a game developer. So much to sort through.

Here is a profile on actor Andy Serkis, there is an interview with VFX supervisor Joe Letteri. Here is a description of WETA's sound stages, there is a story on Jack Black. Hundreds of articles and not one of them useful to my purpose.

Until one day, a useful article suddenly appeared.

DOI: 10.1201/9781003199311-5

In the second or third column of an obscure story about film financing, I spotted a photo of Peter Jackson with three Frenchmen. The photo caption listed their names – Jacques Exertier, Xavier Poix, and Michel Ancel. I immediately recognized Michel Ancel's name as the designer for Ubisoft's highly lauded game, *Beyond Good and Evil*. This was exactly the kind of information I needed!

Researching each name through LinkedIn, I discovered that designer Michel Ancel and producer Xavier Poix both worked at Ubisoft's Montpellier, France studio. If I had been flush with cash, I might have hopped on a plane right then and pitched them in person. But as a poor young freelance composer, I had to find another way.

Michel's LinkedIn profile did not list any contact info. But Xavier's profile did include an email address. Cold call emails are notoriously ineffective, but what did I have to lose? I wrote Xavier and told him I had seen the article. I suggested that if his studio was developing a *King Kong* video game, I would love to audition for the score. I complimented the great work they had done with *Beyond Good and Evil*, and briefly touched on some of my own relevant work. I closed with my contact info and a scoring reel link.

Click... send!

Weeks went by with no reply. Meanwhile, my eyes turned bloodshot searching out additional information about the game. There was nothing new to be found.

Waiting and wondering is a corked volcano for impatient young aspirants. So much to release, but no outlet!

And then, early one Spring morning, an Outlook notification alerted me to a reply from Xavier Poix. This was a high-level reply from a cold call email and I was elated. Xavier's note was brief and gracious. He thanked me for my interest, and said my inquiry had been forwarded to his audio team. If they decided to follow up with me, I would hear back from them directly.

That was just enough hope to hang a rope on. I wrote back and thanked him profusely. And by the way, if the audio team decided to follow up, which team member would be reaching out? Having that name could help me make another direct contact, very valuable. But Xavier did not take the bait. Without another name to tie onto, I was left hanging by a thread.

Has anything like that ever happened to you?

Do not fret too much. Young composers often experience seasons of rejection, failure, or radio silence during their careers. That does not mean the harvest is over. Plant enough seeds, and learn enough about gardening, and some of your seedlings are bound to take root and grow.

Three or four weeks after hearing from Xavier, I received another fortuitous email from Aurelien Baguerre, the music supervisor at Ubisoft Montpellier. He briefly introduced himself and announced that he was inviting several composers to audition for Ubisoft's upcoming video game, *Peter Jackson's King Kong.* Jack Wall, Inon Zur, Jason Hayes, Jeremy Soule, and many others were on his list. I had been added after reaching out to Xavier.

In his invitation to submit a demo, Aurelien offered a description of the desired music style for the game, and outlined details for uploading submissions. He closed with the instruction that all submissions were due by the end of the week

I would not wait another moment to get started.

Firing up my workstation, I composed a piece of music that told a plausible Skull Island story – mysterious intro, exploratory A section, combat B section, with a big flourish at the end. The arrangement featured massive drums, ethnic flute, and marcato strings. Nothing exceptionally imaginative, but safely within the genre. The overheated outboard gear was beginning to smell by the time I finished mixing. I bundled up the track and pushed send, hurtling the demo across the Atlantic, crossing my fingers for a favorable outcome.

I waited for two days, then sent a follow up note, asking if my submission had been received. Still early morning for me in California, I hoped to catch Aurelien before he left work for the evening in Montpellier. He wrote back immediately, with a maddeningly brief response, "Yes, I received the demo."

I was hoping for more information than that, so I wrote again, "Did my demo hit the target you were looking for." Aurelien responded again, but candidly told me it was not what he had in mind.

I felt claws of disappointment digging into my chest. It can't end like this, can it? I ventured one further inquiry. "Would you be open to an updated submission from me?"

A trickle of sweat dripped from my temple. I was crouched over my computer, staring at the screen, waiting for Aurelien's reply. Oh, the agony of anticipation! Some of you know exactly what I'm talking about.

When the notification alert brought Aurelien's reply back to my desktop, it was worth the wait. He wrote that if I really wanted to make another submission, he would try to find time to review it. Not exactly the red carpet, but just enough sliver of daylight to push forward.

If only I had a few screenshots to conjure up the right setting! Or at least a level description to really focus my target. Without such references, I could only sort out which flavors were likely – jungle, tension, awe, fight, flight. I had touched on all of those in my first demo, but not enough to impress. It was time to take it up a notch.

This time I created a single track for exploratory tension. It was intense, with tremolo strings, overblown Ney flute, growling brass clusters, harmonic swells in the woodwinds, and an occasional booming drum in the distance. Listening back, the music set my teeth on edge in a good way, and sent shivers straight through my heart.

I was not done yet.

There had to be a second piece of new music. Skull Island had to offer gamers more than just a dark pit of terror. There must be mountain tops with panoramic views, awe-inspiring canyons, fertile jungle flora, and a vast surrounding ocean. What music could I conjure that would welcome players to such inspiring vistas? Maybe an epic theme, with bold leaps in the harmony, and lush orchestration colors. I had to sweat it out for this one. But the final track was exhilarating, exotic, and HUGE.

I wanted to reward Aurelien for giving me a second chance. I needed to take this submission completely over the top.

So I composed a third track. A battle music track. Taking the combat segment from my original demo, I extended it, added a new section, and beefed up the orchestration. The result was hardly riveting, but it was a totally serviceable piece of combat music.

Certainly, I thought, sending *three* new audition tracks was bound to impress Aurelien. I zipped the files and sent them winging on their way.

Two more days passed and, true to form, I checked in again. Did he receive the files? Did I hit the target this time?

It was like the thrill of victory and agony of defeat in the same email. He loved the exploratory tension track and the epic panorama track. But the combat music still fell short. He added that there would be a lot of fighting in this game, so the combat music had to be exceptional. "And," he said, "There is an important flavor still missing from the fight music."

Sigh.

I summoned my last ounce of grit. I asked for one more shot. He agreed, if I could make it by the deadline.

The deadline was the following day.

This would be the fifth music track I would write as part of this pitch. Keep in mind, there were no demo fees. Everything was on spec, hoping the music would find resonance with the team and lead to a scoring contract. By now I was too invested to call it quits.

One final question came to my mind. Had Aurelien been listening to any temp music? "Actually yes," he said, so I asked if he would send me a sample track. Maybe this would help me understand what extra nuance he was looking for.

I listened carefully to the temp track. Nothing out of the ordinary, except... I zeroed in on the percussion track. There was a relentlessness to the rhythm that was infectious, hypnotic. It grabbed you with both hands and never let up for a second. Perhaps this was the puzzle piece I had been missing.

With only a day to write, I opened with a simple rising string vamp as an A section, answered by falling growls in the brass. The B section featured marcato strings in double time, with a desperate rise in the horns and tenor bones, accented with staccato trumpets. Nothing earth-shatteringly difficult, but highly effective for combat music. I spent the rest of the day working on the percussion track. Gran casa and timpani, of course. Some concert snare to rat-a-tat the tune along. Native American leather-skin drums of various sizes for the tribal flavor.

It was almost there, but something was still missing. What was it? I tried adding more drums. That just muddied the mix. I tried wooden shakers, but the music was already teetering on overly busy. What was I missing?

Frantically scrolling through every percussion sample in my vast library, I was desperate to find the missing spark. In the "Metals" folder my eye caught a list of anvil strike samples. Could something like that work? I tried adding an anvil strike to the score, initially playing it on the second beat of each measure. That sounded cool. It cut through the thick orchestration and brought some extra energy. I added another strike on beat four. Now the track was grooving. But it wasn't relentless yet. One more try. I played the anvil strike on every beat and suddenly the full hypnotic relentlessness materialized. I had found the missing ingredient.

I finished the arrangement, mixed the tracks, and bounced out a stereo mp3 for Aurelien and the team. They were already well into their work day when my final submission arrived.

Utter exhaustion set in. For a full week I had poured myself into making those five demos. Round the clock effort, with plenty of orange juice and adrenaline, had kept me revved. But now I was completely spent. Too weary to feel anxious about the outcome, I crawled into my bed and crashed. Whatever would be, would be.

I woke up a day and a half later to some thrilling news from Montpellier. I had won the pitch.

Chance Thomas was going to score *Peter Jackson's King Kong* for Ubisoft! That was a HUGE boost to my confidence. It would be my first console game. It would be my first project for Ubisoft, one of the titans of video gaming. Peter Jackson and WETA would be deeply involved with the design, look, and feel of the game. Certainly that kind of direct involvement would dramatically increase the odds of the project being successful. I thought I had been handed the golden ticket to success.

As a side note, that fifth demo track, the one that sealed the deal for me, made it all the way into the final game score, mostly unchanged.

E3 TRAILER

Right away the team needed a promotional trailer scored for E3. They also needed a contract for the game music. I was thrilled to get started on the music, but was stressing about negotiating the agreement. Normally I looked forward to contract negotiations, as I had developed some skills in that arena. But it took a lot of preparation. To handle contract negotiations while also composing the first notes the world would ever hear from my *King Kong* score? My shoulders sagged.

The thought occurred to me that I might try using an agent. I had always negotiated my own contracts, but music agent Bob Rice had recently been inquiring about representing me. Bob claimed he could get much more money from Ubisoft than I could. I remember his closing line, "If we get in a boxing ring, and go toe-to-toe composing music, you'll definitely beat me. But if we jump into the ring to negotiate a deal? I'll win every time."

Bob first came to my attention during a Game Developers Conference in San Jose, California. He impressed me with a wry sense of humor and great story-telling. Bob certainly stood out. He was probably the oldest man at GDC, bald as a lake-skipping rock, rail thin, and bent forward at the shoulders. A cartoonist might draw him like Montgomery Burns, Homer's boss from *The Simpsons*. You could not miss Bob's voice either – a resonant, distinctive, gravelly baritone – compliments of DJ training and a long-term smoking habit.

Bob persisted, and I thought, "Why not give him a try?" He could negotiate the game scoring agreement while I am writing music for the trailer. Could be a good thing, especially since his offer to represent me was non-exclusive. If I was not impressed with his work, there was no obligation. I took the plunge, removing a huge burden from my shoulders. It was time to write the best music of my life.

Opening the trailer video for the first time, I could not believe how incredible Skull Island looked. You could tell that the art team had pulled out all the stops, with a heavy infusion of WETA's influence. The jungle was elaborate, rich, and terrifying. The dinosaurs were enormous, shaking the screen with each step. Everything had a cinematic vibe I had never encountered in video games before.

That trailer inspired one of the most strangely beautiful motifs I had ever written. Bb-A-E-Ab-G-C. Nothing else from the E3 trailer music was honestly memorable. But that motif, the beginnings of *Kong's Theme*, would become the backbone of the entire game score.

LOREENA MCKENNITT

Come with me now on a colorful flashback, a time warp, if you will. We need to visit an important part of my backstory before digging into the brawny particulars of *Kong's Theme*.

In 1997, while I was working at Sierra Online, Canadian recording artist Loreena McKennitt released a stunning album called, *The Book of Secrets*. Her album completely captured the imagination of my boss at the time, Craig Alexander, and with good reason. Loreena's intricate harp, haunting voice, and Celtic/Medieval orchestrations reminded him of J.R.R. Tolkien. Craig had, after all, just concluded negotiating unprecedented rights for a massively multi-player online game based on Tolkien's writings. The game would be called, *J.R.R. Tolkien's Middle-earth Online*, or *MEO* for short.

A year later, Sierra was deep in development of *MEO*. One day, Craig abruptly opened the door to my studio and handed me the *Book of Secrets* CD. He said, "Here, I want you to listen to this. Can we get her to do a song for *MEO*?"

I was unfamiliar with Loreena and her work. But as I spun the disc up, *Book of Secrets* captivated me. I delved into Loreena's background, including listening to previous albums. I discovered an artist with deep Celtic roots, a mystical appreciation for old European literature, and an uncanny ability to synthesize disparate world music influences into a unified style all her own. It was very impressive.

If she could compose music to one of Tolkien's poems, and produce a recording to play in the game, that track would be an artistic and marketing triumph for us. This was 1998, and most games were still mired in the musical mediocrity of MIDI-triggered DLS sounds. {shudder}

But how would I open a dialog? Digging into Loreena's portfolio of music businesses, I eventually found a phone number for her Canadian record label. I called and spoke politely to an assistant, mentioning that I had a business opportunity related to the works of J.R.R. Tolkien. However, I would need to speak with Loreena directly in order to assess artistic fit. Not only was Loreena at the office when I called, but she miraculously agreed to take my call.

Loreena was pleasant, curious, and savvy. Though unfamiliar with video games in general, she quickly grasped the relevant artistic, logistical, and business issues involved in our proposal. We spoke for about 30 minutes, and she agreed to have her manager call me to explore next steps. I was stoked.

As negotiations proceeded, it became clear that Loreena's schedule was too busy to compose a song for our video game. Nor would she have the time to produce her own recording. But I was unwilling to give up. We explored a number of lesser options, eventually settling on having me write a song and build an arrangement. I would record the instrumental tracks, then fly out and record Loreena singing lead vocal at a studio of her choosing. Sierra would, of course, pay for it all, including probable royalties.

Everything was looking good until catastrophe intervened.

Shatteringly, in the midst of our negotiations that summer, unimaginable tragedy struck. A boating accident took the life of her fiancé, Ronald Rees. I spoke to Loreena shortly afterward, expressing profound sorrow and sympathy for her loss. She was soft-spoken, broken-hearted, and apologized that she would be withdrawing from any further discussions about this project (and many others) for the foreseeable future. Our discussions concluded graciously.

KONG'S THEME

Six more years passed. It was now 2004. I was just starting on my game score for *Peter Jackson's King Kong*. The score needed a theme, a main theme that would be epic enough to match the incredible source material. For some reason, my mind drifted back to Loreena McKennitt. I wondered how she was doing, if she was working again in music? Would she be interested in working with me on a main theme for *King Kong*? I still had her phone number and thought I might venture a call.

She was gracious and open-minded, pleasant, and smart like before. She referred me again to her manager, and we began talks. Similar to our MEO negotiations, I would write a song, create and record background orchestration, then record Loreena's vocal remotely. Money was still a question mark, but I had confidence we would plow through any obstacle.

I went to work on the theme.

Everyone at Ubisoft Montpellier liked my motif from the E3 trailer, but it was only a motif. To become a full-fledged theme, the music would need to be fleshed out and imaginatively developed. I imagined different ideas while mowing my lawn, walking around the neighborhood, hiking in the hills near my home. I would sing melodies, testing lots of options, searching for lines that felt most natural. Being outside seemed to spark the better parts of my imagination.

The melody was solidifying into a traditional verse/chorus structure. And it was good – singable, memorable, evocative, epic. Definitely one of my better songs. But I needed good lyrics for Loreena to sing, and that was where I bogged down. I wanted to frame *King Kong* as a tragic hero for Ann Darrow, something like a beloved spirit animal, giving its life to protect an owner on an enormous, *Kong*-sized scale. While the melody succeeded in capturing that spirit, every lyric I wrote just sounded silly.

It turned out to be a mute point. As financial discussions with Loreena's manager drug on, Ubisoft lost interest and asked me to pull the plug on the idea. I never figured out if the sticking point was upfront cost, royalty payments, licensing entanglements (between Ubisoft, Universal, and WETA), or what. But at some point, Ubisoft instructed me to drop Loreena and go forward with an instrumental theme. I was terribly disappointed, but wished Loreena all the very best as we again graciously concluded our discussions.

Sometimes things just don't work out. Twice I had pursued opportunities to add Loreena's formidable talents to my own. She was willing, I was willing. Each time I invested substantial time, energy, emotion, and imagination trying to pull it together. Different circumstances prevented the collaboration from happening both times. I acknowledged my disappointment, allowing myself to grieve for a brief moment, then went back to work. The game still needed a theme.

Fortunately, all of my melodic ideas were scribbled on scraps of paper. I had roughed out some basic chords on the piano too, but lacked any meaningful orchestration ideas yet. I opened a new sequence in my customized *King Kong* sequencer template, and set to work.

The melody went in first. With no singer, I decided to give the opening line to the celli. That sounded nice, though not quite exotic enough. I tried doubling the cello section with a solo bassoon, and that sounded interesting. As the melody developed, the celli were also joined by French horns, and finally by the rest of the strings, trumpets, and flutes in a tutti ensemble, rising up to the chorus.

By now my fingers were flying across the keyboard. Parts were flowing from my imagination freely, rapidly, with neither compulsion nor hesitation. Many composers have had such experiences, where the inspiration comes unbidden and floods the mind with ideas perfectly tailored for their purpose. Resembling a download rather than a construction project, *Kong's Theme* was forming organically before my ears, as daylight passed into nightfall, hours disappeared into the darkness, and daybreak found me still at the keyboard, putting the finishing touches on my theme.

This had been an epic all-nighter, fueled by imagination, feedback, and flow. With jugs of filtered water along the way. I had been in the zone for hours and hours, and it had felt magical. As my family finished their morning breakfast and turned their attention to school, I leaned back in my swivel chair and listened to *Kong's Theme* rise from the speakers and fill the air with longing, loyalty, love, triumph, and tragedy. Yes, this was a fitting theme for the King of Skull Island. A deep satisfaction filled my heart.

To this day *Kong's Theme* is the only instrumental piece of music I have ever written that won a top award – Best Original Instrumental from the 2005 Game Audio Network Guild Awards. Many other tracks have been selected as nominees or finalists (from *Avatar, Riders* of Rohan, DOTA 2, Left Behind, Mines of Moria, Quest for Glory V, Shadows of Angmar, etc.), but only Kong's Theme delivered the winning hardware.

COMPOSITION

Never before had so much music been required of me in such a short time. The contract called for 90 minutes of game score, with 90 days on the production schedule. I was still relatively new to score composing, and had never needed to generate so many fresh ideas in such a short window. It was both intimidating and excruciating for me.

Nevertheless, what else can you do but dig in and start cranking out ideas?

It was painfully slow at first, as I would sit for hours at the keyboard noodling around until I stumbled upon something intriguing. Such a grind! I remember thinking one day, "I used to enjoy writing music…" At this rate, there was no way I was going to hit my deadlines. What options did I have?

One day, while working on music to underscore a V-rex level where the dinosaur suddenly appears from the jungle and chases the player up a narrow ravine, I made a discovery that sent a seismic tremor through my craft. I was noodling around with the same old approach and nothing sounded good to me. In frustration, I finally got up and left the studio so I could clear my head.

At the time, my studio was situated in the forested foothills outside Yosemite National Park in central California. I had a second-floor deck adjacent to the studio overlooking the forest, so I stepped outside to cool off. A gentle breeze was blowing, which caused the tops of trees to sway slowly back and forth. As I became lost in thought, I looked off in the distance and noticed two trees swaying in opposite directions, the wind momentarily moving them apart. I thought, "That's exactly what it would look like if a V-rex was forcing its way through those trees." I followed that train of thought and imagined an entire path of trees being pushed apart, steadily moving in my direction. "Yes," I thought, "It would be just like that if a dinosaur was on the move, coming closer to me." Soon, I was imagining the growing thunder of dinosaur footfalls on the forest floor. My heartbeat actually ticked up a notch.

Now I had completely given myself to the scenario. I imagined the crashing of branches coming ever nearer, the shaking of the ground nearly toppling me from my feet, and then finally, the very branches in front of me bursting apart with the thrust of the predator's head, beady eyes drilling through me, with the hot breath of its nostrils in my face. I could almost see the serrated inner edges of the beast's off-color teeth. By this time, I was actually feeling panic.

And that is when it happened.

I started to hear music in my mind. Music that was a perfect fit for what I was feeling. I heard the pounding of tribal drums, the dynamic stabs of cimbasso and bass trombones, with tremolos in the double bass and cello. I heard the cacophony of trumpets desperately climbing over each other and violins racing to a crescendo. The French horns snarling down a half-step, with woodwinds caught in a dissonant duel. This music reflected exactly what I was feeling!

I rushed back inside and began playing parts into my sequencing program. It was almost like lifting an arrangement from a CD – I would listen as the music played back in my mind, then play in the parts as I heard them. It was such a rush. When I finished transcribing, it only totaled about 30 seconds of music. But honestly, that is all the inspiration I needed. Craft, instincts, and experience could take over from there. I just needed the right start.

As an editorial aside, I can tell you that from that day forward I have tried to approach each score much like a method actor. I imagine myself totally immersed in the scenario I am scoring, complete with all the sights, sounds, smells, excitement, adrenaline – whatever I can conjure up. The more vividly I can imagine the situation, the more likely the right emotions from my own heart will start to rise. And the more intimately and powerfully I can experience the emotions of the scene, the more likely it is that I will imagine music that is the right emotional fit for that scene.

My writing began to flow more quickly after that. I hit the deadline with time to spare.

PRODUCTION

We arranged to record the score in Seattle, Washington, at Studio X, the one-time home of world-famous rock band Heart. I selected that studio because I thought the long, narrow room would lend a vintage sound to the orchestra, giving a nod to Max Steiner's 1933 score for the original *King Kong*.

The studio did that and more for us. The recorded sound of the orchestra was raw and close, intense, and inescapable, like the island itself. The musicians played with a vigorous edge I had not heard in my Salt Lake City, Utah, recording sessions. At times, it almost sounded like the wheels were about to come off, though they never did. This added to the ragged and dangerous feel of the underscore.

I loved the experience. Aurelien Baguerre, Ubisoft's music director from Montpellier, flew out for the sessions. He helped produce from the booth while I conducted on the sound stage. It was glorious, my first big-time video game score as a freelancer and everything was turning out wonderfully.

AFTERMATH

The score from *Peter Jackson's King Kong* was an unmitigated success. Award nominations started piling up. Messages of appreciation started coming in from gamers and musicians all over the world. Press reviews of the game universally raved about the music. Although irritatingly, many in the press assumed that the music was pulled directly from James Newton-Howard's movie score. That was annoying to me, since my entire *King Kong* score had been composed, recorded, mixed, and delivered long before Newton-Howard wrote a single note for the film. But it was also flattering. James Newton-Howard has always been one of my top music scoring idols.

With the success of the score, it felt like I had arrived. When *Kong's Theme* won Best Instrumental at the Game Audio Network Guild Awards, it was like icing on the cake. I thought big titles would start flowing my way in an uninterrupted stream of never-ending success for the rest of my career. In the age-old parlance of show business, I thought I had made it big. Or, in a nod to the name of my company HUGEsound, I thought I had made it HUGE.

But that is not what happened. I was naïve, deceived by my own wishful thinking. Oh, the foolishness of the nouveau riche! After basking in the success of *Kong*, I passed through one of the most perplexing and frustrating down times of my career. I could not get companies to hire me. Could not get audio directors to call me. If I had been a criminal, I could not even get arrested.

Mid-career blues I have come to call it. Made a big splash, but I had not yet developed enough reliable connections, enough deep friendships, or enough of an overwhelming track record to keep the big titles rolling in. I got depressed. It was a dark time. After *King Kong*, I knew I had the talent, skills, and experience to take on any project of any complexity and size. But since none of the big publishers would bite, I went back to what I had always done before, scratching, clawing, hustling my way to anything I could find.

Fortunately, even in the dark, you can occasionally stumble upon a bit of treasure.

To watch videos and hear music from Peter Jackson's King Kong *video game, as described in this chapter, please visit: HUGEsoundRecords.com/ Memoir-04*

CHAPTER 5

Left Behind

TROY LYNDON IMMEDIATELY CAME across as charming and connected. He had been playing *King Kong* and was impressed with the music. He tracked down my contact information and cold-called me with a proposal. How would I like to be part of the world's first blockbuster Christian video game? *The Los Angeles Times* was chomping at the bit to do a feature story. He said investors were falling over themselves to pour money into development.

Jerry Jenkins and Tim LaHaye, authors of a popular Christian book series entitled, *Left Behind*, had signed over their gaming rights to Lyndon, and he envisioned a video game franchise that would sweep the Christian community and spill over into the mainstream marketplace. He said my music score would make a difference and propel the game to heights he had only dreamed of.

At the time, I really needed work. When Troy promised a decent music budget for the score, I hoped this was more than just blue sky. He asked if I would be interested in learning more about his company, Left Behind Games (LBG), before committing to score the game.

Lyndon arranged for me to be flown to John Wayne Airport in Orange County, California. There, a driver picked me up in a black Lincoln Town Car and whisked me away to LBG's corporate offices. So far, so good.

The offices were sparsely decorated, a far cry from the over-the-top décor of most game development studios. But this was a brand new company pursuing a different audience. That is what I told myself. Troy Lyndon came out from his office and welcomed me with a big smile and outstretched

DOI: 10.1201/9781003199311-6

hand. He introduced me to several employees, members of his marketing team, sales team, and PR team, respectively. I asked about developers or producers, but there were not any there.

I sat down with the group and listened to Troy and others wax poetic about the untapped Christian market for video games, and the high-value name recognition *Left Behind* possessed inside that market. I heard about cross-marketing opportunities and launch parties and press. But so far, no one was talking about making a good video game.

I pressed the relevant questions, what kind of game were they making? What kind of music score did they envision? And more importantly, who was actually making this game? They said their first product would be a strategy game, *Left Behind: Eternal Forces*. Troy had sourced a game development team in Romania to build the game. They hoped for a music score that would adapt to gameplay and sound good. That was about the extent of their direction. I asked if there were any primary game states beyond the usual three found in strategy games – exploration, questing, and combat. They said they did not think so.

Troy and I then huddled for a discussion about the budget. He switched his focus to being a small startup and needing to watch his pennies. OK, that is like any businessman trying to lower expectations as a contract negotiation begins. But the speed at which he switched from world-beater to bean-counter made my head spin. How much budget had he allocated for music? He said he actually did not know yet, but had a round of fundraising coming up and would know more after that. Could I come to the fundraiser, play some live music, and mingle with the investors?

Interesting. I told him about the performing Pamela and I had once done on cruise ships, and suggested that he bring us both out. We agreed on a price for the live gig, which was very fair, and several weeks later Pamela and I flew to John Wayne Airport together. We were picked up by the same black Lincoln Town Car, and whisked away to a winery somewhere in Temecula, California.

White tent tops covered the grounds, filled with white tables and chairs. Caterers were running around like busy ants. We set up our little stage area, and watched the well-dressed people arrive and mingle. Troy seemed to be in his element walking around, greeting newcomers with a big smile and a hug. Pamela and I played our part and enjoyed the evening together. Everyone was smiling and toasting each other. It seemed like a very successful fundraiser. Troy said he would call me later, and we returned home.

COMPOSITION MAP, PART 1

As I waited for Troy's next call, my mind started wrapping around the problem and potential of building an adaptive music system suited to a strategy game. Modular systems had been done before, some of them by me, and such systems were moderately successful in providing decent emotional narrative for video games. But they required a significant amount of programming support. From Troy's description of the Romanian dev team, I imagined four guys with laptops siting around a card table in an efficiency apartment. If I was going to create a successful adaptive music system for this game, it would have to be simple to implement, without taxing the software engineering team. I would need to do most of the heavy lifting from my side.

I rolled the problem over and over in my mind a hundred different ways. If I built a modular system, it would require too many callbacks to the game engine and dozens of music files that needed starting, cross-fading, and stopping, potentially hundreds of times throughout the game levels. That is a lot of code. I needed something different, something elegant, something simple. I needed to turn this problem on its head. And that is when the lightbulb moment happened for me.

Traditional music score supports drama as it unfolds across time. Imagine a very simple music score laid out horizontally with a beginning, middle, and conclusion. Now what if that timeline was turned on its side, so that the beginning, middle, and conclusion were now stacked on top of each other? That opened my mind to a brand new idea. I could compose three different pieces of music, each representing exploration, questing, and combat, respectively, using shared measure numbers, shared harmonic progressions, shared time signatures, and the like. I could invent a composition map to use as a guide for my writing.

Such a map would ensure that each piece of music conformed to shared harmonic progressions, dynamics, melodic constructs, and sync-able tempi. Locking these key musical variables would enable instant cross-fading between one piece of music and the next, so that moving through the various pieces of music would sound like a single, through-composed section of score.[1]

Seamless, instantaneous, anytime music transitioning.

All that would be required of the programming team was to call a cross-fade at each game state change. This approach would solve all of our problems. Jackpot.

CONTRACT NEGOTIATIONS

After a few weeks, Troy called and we discussed how much music would likely be needed for the game and what kind of quality bar we hoped to achieve. I also hinted at the music system idea I had been brainstorming. He blurted out how much he had budgeted for the music score. But it would not be nearly enough to hit all of those targets. I pressed for more budget using a few negotiating techniques I had been studying recently, but it was like negotiating with a stone wall. There was no movement whatsoever. None.

At moments like these, a composer has to decide what matters most in this particular transaction. The best way to figure it out is with questions. Where is the composer at in their career? How does their bank account balance look? What financial obligations do they have? What reputation do they have and what reputation are they trying to build? Are there things besides cash that can be negotiated for? What do they want to do as an artist, a creator, a business? These are some of the questions that raced through my mind as I was on the phone negotiating with Troy Lyndon.

We needed a minimum amount of music to make the score functional, about 45 minutes. For such a deeply involved music design, I should be charging at least $1,500 per minute. But that would dwarf the music budget Troy was offering. Even billing at $1,000 per minute would consume most of the budget, and I wanted to be sure we had enough money for live production. I was trying to further my reputation as a composer who produced live orchestral scores. I needed money for an orchestra, and for the studio and engineers required for the recording.

No matter how much I reasonably discounted my creative fee, there would never be enough budget for a full orchestra. I had to get more creative in my thinking. Violins and trumpets are the most difficult parts of an orchestra to render virtually. Everything else could be pulled off adequately with digital samples. I decided I would hire a violin section and a trumpet section. I could also hire Rich Dixon to lay down a bunch of guitar tracks, with Daron Bradford overdubbing live woodwind parts (clarinet, oboe, flute, English horn). With that combo, I hoped to save money and deliver a convincing sound in the score.

This would still slightly overrun the budget, so I offered to cut back on my finished minute rate even more in exchange for the publishing rights for the music. Troy was insistent on owning everything in the game. As a compromise, he offered company stock instead, and we finally settled on $50,000 cash and 50,000 shares of stock. A tremendous amount of up-front work would be required for the composition map-based music design, so I required a 50% nonrefundable deposit. That was non-negotiable from my perspective. We shook hands over the phone, and I drew up the agreement.

Now it was time to see if this crazy composition map I envisioned would actually work.

COMPOSITION MAP, PART 2

The first problem was tempo. Exploration, questing, and combat all happen at different tempi. They are completely unconvincing otherwise. But this first problem also offered an obvious solution. If the exploration song is at 60 bpm, I could write a questing song at 120 bpm, and a combat track at 180 bpm. With each song playing at a perfect multiple of the other, the game engine could maintain synch alignment across the entire duration of all three pieces. That solved multiple problems right off the bat.

The next thing I realized was that duplicating chord progressions in each song aligned by time and related tempi allowed for seamless cross-fading between songs at any time. But even duplicate chord progressions could carry vastly different orchestration colors, thus allowing for an illusion of diversity. Not only that, but selecting different instruments for melody in each song, and even composing different but complimentary melodies in each song furthered the illusion of a single, evolving music cue. When the music cross-faded, it sounded like the score was simply trading counter parts rather than conflicting melodies.

For example, let us examine the first music package I delivered for the first level of the game. The level exploratory song was at 60 bpm and featured lots of arco whole notes in the strings and supporting lower brass. The melody was played on the clarinet, and there was no percussion. The song was about five-minutes long.

The level questing song was 120 bpm and featured marcato strings playing a marching kind of cadence, supported by timpani and Taiko drums. The melody, which was different from the exploratory piece, alternated between French horns and violins. Of course, since this song was also built on the exploratory song map, the harmonies, dynamics, and beats were all aligned. This was critical for keeping the music in sync as it looped.

The level combat song was 180 bpm and featured lots of brass stabs, heavy and frenetic percussion, marcato strings in double time, and melody on a lead guitar. This song too was built on the same composition map as the other two songs.

Here is how it would work. When the level loaded, the three songs were all loaded and began playing simultaneously. However, the quest and combat songs were initially muted, so only the exploratory song was heard. As players began exploring the world, they would eventually come across instructions for a quest. Once they received their quest, the game engine would perform a cross-fade, bringing down the exploratory song while simultaneously fading up the questing song.

But because all the songs in that level were built on the same composition map, the game engine could make that transition at any point in time, I mean ANY point in time, and it would always sound like the music had naturally intensified to a more intentional score for the questing game state. As if it were a single, through-composed piece of music. If the player abandoned or finished their quest, the music would cross-fade in reverse, bringing down the questing song and fading back into the exploratory song seamlessly, as if it were somehow magically following the player's actions. The same mechanic occurred when transitioning to and from combat music.

Seamless, anytime music transitioning, based on changing game states. That was a big deal. And it worked brilliantly.

I will admit though, this required a ridiculous amount of work on my end. Each of the three songs in the music package for each level had to feel different enough from each other to be convincing as a single evolving score. I had to run tests for days on each group to make sure there were no inadvertent train wrecks hiding in one of the songs, waiting for an ill-timed cross-fade to reveal its awaiting mayhem.

But wow, when I finished designing and composing the main part of the score, with all of the three-song music packages working perfectly in sync, it felt like a huge victory. This was an evolutionary leap in game music design, and I had done it all by myself sitting in my home studio, with minimal software support. Wise and Fmod were not even around yet, or at least I did not know about them. It was a tremendous feeling of achievement. Of course, none of the live instruments had been tracked yet. I wondered if the imprecision inherent in live recordings might ruffle the edges of the system.

PRODUCTION

I recorded the violin sections first against the virtual tracks. It was strange being in a room with 24 violins without the rest of the string choir. We progressed through the recording sessions level by level, recording first the exploratory song for a given level, followed by its questing song, and then its combat song. Then we would move to the next level and repeat the process. Keeping track of which sheet music went with which layer, and which level they matched in the game, sort of exploded my mind a few times. But copyist Paul Taylor helped me figure out a system while preparing the sheet music that (mostly) kept us out of trouble.

As the remaining live sessions came and went, I was very satisfied with the sound of this score. While not as lush or explosive as the *King Kong* score that grabbed Troy's attention in the first place, this *Left Behind: Eternal Forces* score was being produced at a fraction of the cost and still sounded really good. The guitar tracks Rich Dixon laid down were a particular highlight.

Allow me a quick sidebar to talk about how Rich and I usually worked together. While composing, orchestrating, and arranging my music, I always play in the guitar parts using digital samples. When Rich arrives, I have generally prepared sheet music with the chord chart and the melody notes I want him to perform. There is a small amount of room for improvisation here and there, but for the most part, he focuses on how to best deliver the lines I have already written. We also spend time working on the sound. Between takes, I may sometimes sing an idea to him, demonstrating additional articulation and dynamic information that never found its way to the chart. He is so quick, he picks up on the changes instantly, and usually plays it back just as I have sung it. It is such a pleasure working with someone who can be so flexible, fast, and artistically articulate.

We recorded everything in Alpine, Utah, at Soularium Recording Studio. Dan Carlisle engineered the sessions and mixed the score. I submitted the wav files to Troy and he quickly sent me a check for the balance due on our contract.

Almost immediately afterward, Troy called and said, "I need to send you some more money. There's another thing we're doing that needs music." He wanted to open the game with a new cinematic cut scene. He sent me a story board and put me in touch with his marketing director to work out the details. We decided to score the trailer with a heavily foreboding orchestral version of a classic Christian anthem. This was going to be so cool.

Tata Vega

I scored the trailer with a dark and unsettling orchestral version of *Amazing Grace*. I always envisioned a deeply soulful vocalist singing the song, but no one in my normal stable of singers fit the bill. The marketing director suggested a few names to me, and I researched them online. The one who really stood out was Tata Vega.

Tata had a ferociously soulful voice, with deep resonances and fiery chops. I thought her voice could put this score right over the top. We reached out and she was a sweetheart, easy to talk with, and affordable too. We booked a session to record her vocals at Eargasm Studios in Santa Monica, California, and I prepped the tracks.

When the day came, I was excited and felt totally prepared. I had double-checked her actual range against the assumed range written into my track. A perfect match. I brought redundant copies of the Pro Tools session on two different drives, and had CDs for backup burns afterward. Not only that, I put on extra deodorant and had breath mints in my pocket. Like I said, totally prepared.

Tata came into the studio exuding star charisma. Everyone melted in her presence. I was no exception, but tried to maintain some professional objectivity as the producer. We got her comfortably situated in the recording studio and warmed up her voice. I initially worked with her from the piano. She was not sounding anything like I envisioned yet, but I figured we would get there soon enough. I decided to play the track, and have her sing along. She loved the track, but was not really feeling the rhythm and flow. Her stylistic approach was not working either, and I continued to offer suggestions, supportive comments, and whatever else I could think of to nudge her into the sweet spot.

The session was droning on and on and we did not have anything keepable yet. I was running out of advice to offer and adjectives to suggest. We took a brief recess, and I consulted with the engineer and the marketing director, who had come along to the session. Everyone was drawing a blank. Tata was gracious and eager to please, but just was not getting it.

When we came back after the break I said, "Tata, I'd like for you to close your eyes and just listen to the playback of the track one more time. Clear your mind of everything we've done up to this point, and just think about the words of the song. Then let's do a take of you singing whatever you're genuinely feeling at that point."

Tata did close her eyes, and as the music washed over her, a different countenance began to glow from her face. When we started over and recorded her singing, she sang the entire song in one take, one glorious take, with a chilling passion that sent shivers through our souls. Nothing like this had come out of her all evening, and suddenly it was perfect. And I mean PERFECT. There was nothing we replaced or edited from that final take.

What made the difference? I do not even know. But at some point, great artists find a voice, they discover a through-thread and bring art to thrilling life. That is what Tata Vega did for *Amazing Grace* and it still gives me chills to this day. Apparently, I was not alone. That rendition of *Amazing Grace* was ultimately nominated for a Game Audio Network Guild award in the Best Vocal Song Performance category.

AFTERMATH

I was getting more and more excited for the release of the game. The promised *Los Angeles Times* article materialized, followed by a flood of other high-profile publicity. I was interviewed in *PC Gamer* and *IGN* regarding the music score. The stock price was rising. Buzz was building.

And then I received my pre-release copy of the game.

In my opinion, it was terrible. I mean, parts of the game were completely unplayable. The game was incredibly buggy. It did not look good, the SFX and VO were not especially well done – it seemed to me as if the game had been built by four guys in Romania sitting around a card table with laptops in an efficiency apartment, rather than by a talented, experienced, and well-funded game development group. The music system worked well enough, but was overshadowed by a glaring range of deficits in the gameplay. When the press finally got their hands on the game, they crucified it.[2] The Metacritic rating landed at 38 out of 100, with user ratings about the same.[3] I was so disappointed.

Obviously, the game did not sell well, even among the Christian audience it was targeted to. The stock tanked, dropping from a high of eight-ish dollars per share, down to fractions of a penny. My stock was restricted to a sales blackout stretching out many weeks after the release of the game. By the time the blackout expired, the stock was completely worthless. I could pick up a dead leaf in one hand and hold the stock certificate in the other hand. Take your pick, the value was about the same.

Allegations of fraud and misrepresentation began surfacing.[4] The SEC filed a lawsuit.[5] I think many investors wondered where all their money had gone. Company employees bailed from the sinking ship and found jobs elsewhere in and out of the industry. I lost track of Troy and went on to other pursuits. I never knew quite what to think of the whole ordeal.

I'm still not sure I know today.

To listen to music from Left Behind: Eternal Forces, *as described in this chapter, please visit: HUGEsoundRecords.com/Memoir-05*

NOTES

1 Chance Thomas, *Composing Music for Games: The Art, Technology and Business of Video Game Scoring,* pp. 111–112; Boca Raton: CRC Press, 2016.
2 https://www.gamesradar.com/left-behind-eternal-forces-review/, https://www.gamespot.com/reviews/left-behind-eternal-forces-review/1900–6162370/, https://www.gamechronicles.com/reviews/pc/left-behind/eternalforces.htm
3 https://www.metacritic.com/game/pc/left-behind-eternal-forces
4 https://variety.com/2013/biz/games/left-behind-games-charged-with-fraudulently-propping-up-company-revenue-1200668566/
5 https://www.christianitytoday.com/news/2013/october/left-behind-games-charged-with-fraud-sec.html

CHAPTER 6

Academy Award

M ANY CONSIDER THE ACADEMY Award the most prestigious acco-
lade in all of entertainment. The famously bald, slender, golden
statuette forever-after confers Hollywood gild upon its recipients. Oscar
winner implies craft mastery and peer acclaim at the highest level. It is
exclusively a film industry honor, awarded annually by the Academy of
Motion Picture Arts and Sciences.

Knowing such facts, you might wonder how a composer like myself,
most widely known for scoring video games, came to be referred to as an
Oscar winner in the press? Stretching as far back as March 2003, several
articles began circulating around the Internet, which refer to me in that
way. Is there any truth in it? If so, let's examine the details. If not, let's talk
about why it has persisted in the press.

First, let us settle the question. Have I ever won an Academy Award?

I have never won an Academy Award for Best Music in a film. However,
it was my fabulous good fortune to be a crucial member of a small team
that won an Oscar together at the 75th Annual Academy Awards. The victory was Best Animated Short Film for *The ChubbChubbs!*, released by
Columbia Pictures and produced by Sony Pictures Imageworks. For this
film I composed, orchestrated, and conducted the original score. I also
arranged and produced the R&B songs. Finally, I contracted the sound
design and Foley services through my company HUGEsound. I even added
a character voice to the final dialog track. Though I was not singled out for
a personal Academy Award, I contributed substantially to the team win.

DOI: 10.1201/9781003199311-7

In fact, working on *The ChubbChubbs!* was a watershed professional undertaking, loaded with important career lessons and interesting stories. Let us explore the whole experience.

KEN RALSTON

Ken Ralston was a pioneering wizard in the world of visual effects. He created effects for the original *Star Wars* film trilogy – *A New Hope, The Empire Strikes Back,* and *Return of the Jedi.* He was a VFX genius, winning five Oscars for *Forrest Gump, Who Framed Roger Rabbit, Return of the Jedi, Cocoon,* and *Death Becomes Her.* Ken sprinkled his magic across so many motion pictures that I love – *The Rocketeer, Contact, Back to the Future, Cast Away,* and several early *Star Trek* films. He worked at Industrial Light & Magic for twenty years and then became president of Sony Pictures Imageworks. He is a legend in the VFX business and an extraordinary talent by any measure.

By the turn of Y2K, Ken and his wife Robin had bought a horse ranch near Ahwahnee, California, a small town whose eastern border adjoins the city limits of Oakhurst. When the Ralstons came up from Los Angeles to spend time at their ranch, Robin would often drive into Oakhurst to attend activities at the local church. It was at one such activity that Robin met my wife Pamela, and the two became friends.

I had met Robin a few times myself and enjoyed her sarcastic wit and kindly disposition, an unexpected personality pairing she carried without paradox. Robin loved horses, an equestrian to the core, and seemed happiest when riding on horseback through the woods or caring for her stable brood. She was also a budding fingerstyle guitarist, which intrigued me as a musician. But I knew nothing of her husband or his film industry achievements. Robin was just another friendly face at church, one of Pamela's newfound acquaintances.

As Robin and Pamela spent more time together, Ken and I eventually came up in their conversations. You can imagine how the dialog may have unfolded.

Robin: "So tell me about your husband."
Pamela: "Oh, he's an up-and-coming composer, mostly writing music for video games. What about yours?"
Robin: "Oh, he's a five-time Oscar winner, multi-millionaire, lord-of-all-he-surveys, genius filmmaker."

Professional contacts can come from anywhere, and I have never been picky, let them come from wherever they may. But I was especially thrilled to discover these unexpected details about Ken Ralston. Even better, Pamela had given Robin a copy of my *Quest for Glory V: Dragon Fire* soundtrack on CD.

In time, Robin and Ken both listened to *Quest for Glory V* and truly enjoyed it. With a genuine and positive reaction to my music, plus a little encouragement from Robin, Ken invited me to Culver City, California, to show me around Sony Pictures Imageworks, a vast enterprise he managed as VFX Supervisor and company president.

Ken Ralston strikes an imposing figure. It's not that he is overly tall, ripped, or dauntingly handsome. But he can come across as slightly aloof and markedly superior – much like Khan does in *Star Trek: Into Darkness*, but with better hair and a well-trimmed beard.

I was relieved when Ken hailed me with a welcoming smile upon my arrival. We had lunch together on the Sony Pictures lot, then walked around Imageworks to meet some of the artists, producers, and coordinators who worked there. Everyone was warm and friendly, and not just because their boss was making the introduction. I sensed a genuine atmosphere of merriment, imagination, and frolic in the air. Many had that Doc Brown wild-genius look in their eyes. It was intoxicating. I felt like I had stumbled into a dream factory.

When I left Imageworks that day, I left hoping, yearning really, for any possible opportunity to collaborate with these creative people on anything they might set their hands to.

Weeks passed. Then, on a sweltering summer afternoon, my phone lit up with an incoming call from Culver City. A gregarious Welshwoman named Jacquie Barnbrook was on the line and greeted me by name. She was calling on Ken's recommendation and had a proposition for me. Imageworks was gearing up to produce its first feature-length animated movie. But first they planned to produce an animated short film, as a way to test their production pipeline. Would I be interested in auditioning to compose the score?

I could hardly believe my ears. Where do I sign up?

Yes, yes, absolutely yes!

THE CHUBBCHUBBS!

Jacquie asked if I would return to Culver City before submitting a demo so I could meet the team. No problem, I drove down immediately and met with director Eric Armstrong (*Stuart Little, Harry Potter*), writer Jeff Wolverton (*Spider-Man, Star Trek*), production designer Yarrow Cheney (*Iron Giant, Treasure Planet*), editor Robert Gordon (*Toy Story*), and coordinator Brad Simonsen (*Encanto, Zootopia*). Each one seemed like an industry titan to me. Graciously, they welcomed me with open arms. We talked about our creative influences, our ambitions for the project, and smart ways we could manage a successful collaboration. It was inspiring to connect with such good-natured, smart, and talented artists.

Jacquie soon became my favorite member of the team. She was outspoken, funny, and loved people. She also had expertise in every facet of production. Jacquie knew her way around a budget and was fearless in the way that actors can be fearless. She regularly outworked everyone else on the team. If I needed anything, Jacquie was the go-to source. She and I became collaborators, cohorts, and perpetual friends.

She was excited to show me an early story concept the team had just assembled into an animatic (an animated storyboard). As the frames whizzed by, I thought the main character was hilarious and instantly endearing. The production design was creative and colorful. I loved the team's ideas and imagined music in my mind almost immediately. This was going to be so much fun.

The film would be called, *The ChubbChubbs!*

I returned home and went right to work. I put a sixteenth-note motif in the strings, a madcap counter-melody in the woodwinds, offbeat stabs from the brass, marimba and timpani accented with piatti. It took two days to turn the music demo around. Meeting with the team and discussing their vision had been incredibly insightful. Not surprisingly, the music I submitted resonated with everyone.

Jacquie soon called with good news. Imageworks would like to offer me a scoring contract for *The ChubbChubbs!* I thanked her profusely, and told her how happy and grateful I was to work on this film. Hoping to strike twice while the iron was hot, I also mentioned that my company HUGEsound offered sound design, Foley, and song production. She said the team would need all of those services and asked me to send over a comprehensive bid.

That was great news, the best possible scenario. But what financial ballpark should I be bidding in? This was not a video game project. Nor was it a feature film. This was a production pipeline test. What financial space does that live in anyway? There were no standards for such media, but I had to start somewhere. I began by laying out the production costs. The first line item was for live orchestra and rhythm section, then additional costs for recording studios and mixing engineers. Next I put in money for sheet music prep and musician contracting, then added amounts for sound design and Foley services. Finally, I added travel expenses and a small buffer for contingencies.

I had everything figured out except my own creative fee. I was still facing the same quandary – what amount would be appropriate for a production pipeline test at a major animation studio? I had no idea.

In pondering the question, I remembered my old friend, Angelique DeGoulette, and her bold advice about playing the piano at the Utah Governor's mansion. "Double your rate and then double it again," she had told me. Would it be feasible to try that approach in preparing my bid for *The ChubbChubbs*?

As I hesitated, another flashback came to my mind, some excellent advice I had once shared with fellow composer Jason Hayes. "Don't decide no for the person you're negotiating with. They can say no all by themselves; you don't have to make that decision for them."

My decision crystallized. Since negotiations usually play out with reasonable give and take, I could always retreat by degrees if needed. Why not go for it? I doubled my normal creative fee, and then doubled it again. I wrote everything up in a formal proposal and submitted the bid. Jacquie did not even blink. The deal went through without a hitch. Sometimes money is no obstacle, at least not the obstacle we fear it might be.

SCORING THE FILM

The time-locked movie files arrived and I transferred them to my video drive. The excitement was palpable as I booted up the system. Each file synched perfectly inside the Digital Performer template I had prepared. But when I pressed play, a totally different film unfolded before my eyes, much different than the one I had auditioned for. The story, the setting, the antagonist, the peripheral characters – everything from the original animatic had been abandoned and replaced with new elements. Only the main character remained, and even he was thrust into a completely different role.

"Stay nimble," I told myself.

The new story cast our hero as a bar janitor working at the Ale-E-Inn, a watering hole on a distant planet for quirky characters from science fiction movies. The film opens up with the camera panning across a crowded bar. We see Darth Vader arm wrestling with Yoda, Xenomorph sucking down a Midori Sour, Robby the Robot dancing with B-9, and Gort chugging a can of motor oil. It was a terrific opening scene, capped by a three-breasted diva belting out Aretha Franklin's *Respect* from a brightly-lit karaoke stage.

Our hero the janitor fancies himself a karaoke star too, and drifts away into sweet daydreams while mopping near an electric outlet. That is when all the trouble breaks loose. One thing leads to another, Jar-Jar Binks makes an appearance, and E.T. takes a flying bicycle ride off planet. A flurry of dominoed action leads to a script-flipping plot twist I never saw coming. It was delightful.

The new film featured two classic R&B songs, *Respect* and *Why Can't We Be Friends*, part of the karaoke comedy bit underpinning the story. Jacquie had licensed the rights to each composition, but could not secure sync licenses for the original recordings. Thus, I was tasked with producing remakes of each song, broken into several segments, scattered throughout the film. These remakes had to be frame-accurate duplicates of the originals, since the team had built their animations in sync with the original recordings.

I was unaware of any automatic beat-sensing software at the time, so I manually input each beat subdivision, building the scoring maps one sixteenth note at a time, in sync with the original songs. It was drudgingly tedious, but I did not know any other way to clone the timeline. I did learn something fascinating and useful during the process. Though subtle, I discovered that each drummer pushed the tempo a little faster going into the choruses, and backed off a bit in the verses. You would never notice such minor changes to the groove while listening casually, the music just felt right. But in the process of beat-mapping each tune, those subtle tempo changes jumped right off the page.

I lifted the arrangements verbatim, including the lead and background vocal parts. Horn sections, guitar parts, bass, everything was transcribed to sheet music and mocked up with virtual samples in prep for the live recording sessions.

Once the R&B songs were fleshed out, I started composing the original orchestral underscore. Each day I would compose music for a small segment of the film, sending a time-coded mockup over to Imageworks. The first two days flew by like a honeymoon, music came quickly and the team loved everything I sent. The main motif was campy and foreboding, setting just the right tone. It was also memorable enough to serve as an effective theme. The main motif makes its first appearance with the opening frame, as the Imageworks logo zooms into view. It repeats each time a menacing storm cloud draws near. The project was off to a great start and everyone was happy.

Then I ran into a roadblock. For the next two days, nothing I wrote hit the target. I knew the team was getting worried when I received a call from Tim Sarnoff, Imageworks' vice president and general manager. Sarnoff was the number two guy at the company, just under Ken. I wondered if he had been dispatched to fire me, but soon learned that he was just passionate about music and wanted to help me along.

Working with Sarnoff was a great experience. I would sing an idea over the phone and he would respond with feedback in real time. We did this every day for a few days, and the interaction helped get me back on track. As it turned out, the team wanted more Mickey-Mousing in this part of the film than I had imagined. Mickey-Mousing is a scoring approach where the music tightly mimics the animated action. Karl Stallings did it best, brilliantly even, in the classic Looney Tunes cartoon scores. Any composer besides Stallings who has ever tried the technique has generally been far less brilliant. But I think Sarnoff helped me find the right balance for this particular film. After we sorted out the middle part of the score, composing the rest of the film's music came together quickly, with smooth sailing to the finish line.

PRODUCTION

I tracked the rhythm section for each R&B song at Maximus Media, a storied recording studio on the northeast side of Fresno, California. We booked talent from the local jazz scene and they were terrific. These guys did not get many opportunities to do session work, and they came in ready to throw down. The Fresno players did not disappoint.

We next tracked vocals at one of Sony's sound studios in Culver City, California. Jacquie contracted Dorian Holley and Darryl Phinnessee to sing the vocals in *Why Can't We Be Friends*. They were superstars to me, having sung with Michael Jackson, Stevie Wonder, Lionel Ritchie, and many more top recording acts. Both arrived with plenty of swagger, charisma, and drop-dead drip. They looked like they sounded great before I ever heard a single note.

On the other hand, my look at the time could generously be described as bland and artless. Imagine a typical IT guy wandering out of his cave – glasses, short hair, clean shaven, dressed in jeans and a starched shirt. That was me. Standing beside the two singers, I was essentially invisible as they jawed with Jacquie about the project. Eventually, Holley asked, "So where's the music producer?" I answered, "I'm right here," and they took notice of me for the first time. Each sized me up and down, hands on their hips, eyebrows raised. "You?" Phinnessee offered, incredulously. I reached out and shook their hands, "Yes, I'm Chance Thomas, composer of the film's original score and music producer for the songs in this project." I continued, "Let's take a look at your parts," and passed around some sheet music. They looked at the charts, glanced at each other, then looked back at me in disbelief. "Man, we knew those guys from War. They were all drunk when they recorded this song. They didn't use no sheet music."

Humor can be a great lubricant for tense or awkward situations. I really wish I would have reached for humor in that moment and said something funny. But instead I was all business, "That's fine, our job is to duplicate what they did, drunk or not, nothing more. I've transcribed exactly what they sang on the recording, divided out into parts, note for note. If you don't mind, I'd like to start rehearsing the parts." I did not win any friends that day, but everyone was professional and we got what we needed.

Jacquie also booked Mortonette Jenkins and Marlena Jeter, another pair of studio vocal royalty, to record the lead and background parts for *Respect*. These women had million-dollar pipes and world-class chops. I felt completely overwhelmed by their talent. I could barely produce the session objectively, I was too busy gushing at every take. None of that mattered, they mostly produced themselves and the tracks sounded terrific.

With the songs completed, I next turned to recording the original score. I booked the Utah Film Orchestra in Salt Lake City, Utah, just a few weeks after they had recorded with John Williams for the 2002 Winter Olympics. They were still on their A-game and performed wonderfully, by far the best orchestral tracking session I had experienced up to that point. The strings, brass, and woodwinds all sounded fabulous, with very little editing.

When the score was finished, I hired sound designer Tim Larkin to create the film's sound effects and ambiences. We booked Jana Vance to tackle the Foley work. Although Tim and I were newcomers to the film industry, everyone at Imageworks treated us with tremendous respect. Both Jacquie and director Eric Armstrong were incredibly open-minded to lessons learned from our game industry experiences, and their leadership style encouraged a spirit of collaboration between us and the rest of the creative team.[1]

SONY MAFIA

With all parts of the R&B songs, original score, dialog, Foley, and sound effects in the can, Jacquie scheduled the film's final audio mix at a dub stage on the Sony lot. Tim and I were both invited, and stoked to see how the big boys did things.

When we arrived, we first held a meeting with a Sony audio manager to find out where our assigned dub stage was, and learn the lay of the land. Oddly, he treated us with gruff suspicion, lecturing us on the evils of non-union talent (we were nonunion talent), and behaving boorishly. He told us his job was to protect the interests of LA's local union base, and he was dismissive of Tim and I and our video game industry work. I finally cut into his rant and asked him to please just tell us where the dub stage was. He grudgingly sent us on our way.

Tim and I brought our audio files on Pro Tools sessions. But when we arrived at the dub stage, the re-recording mixers told us we had to transfer our tracks to Tascam DA-88 digital tape. That was a shocker. DA-88 tape seemed like ancient tech to me. Pro Tools was a completely fluid digital audio editing format, and they wanted our tracks on tape? We were surprised, but complied.

We spent a long time getting the mix just right. Tim Sarnoff was there, along with Eric and Jacquie. Everyone was really happy with the final audio. But a few days later, when Jacquie held a screening at the Burt Lancaster Theater, the mix had seemingly been sabotaged. The levels had been flattened, the surrounds were not firing, and all the magic we had crafted through hours on the dub stage had disappeared. Jacquie literally spent all that night at the theater re-mixing the tracks herself, trying to salvage the film's sound. We never knew exactly what happened, but Tim and I suspected that somehow, Sony's pro-union audio manager had torpedoed our mix. After that strange experience, I always thought of them as the Sony Mafia.

RELEASE(S)

The ChubbChubbs! was first released on July 3, 2002, under the Columbia Pictures banner. It received its first worldwide theatrical run attached to the front of *Men in Black 2*. Audiences enjoyed it so much that Sony added another theatrical run with *Stuart Little 2* later that year. On April 11, 2003, *The ChubbChubbs!* was given its own DVD release with "Oscar-winner" added to the cover. At a running time of 5 minutes 37 seconds, it may have been the shortest DVD ever published.[2] On October 9, 2007, *The ChubbChubbs!* also received a Blu-ray release as a bonus feature on *Surf's Up.*

I attended the film's theatrical premier in Hollywood at Grauman's Chinese Theater. It was the opening night of *Men in Black 2* and the place was packed. Wow, as soon as *The ChubbChubbs!* came on, I was literally holding my breath. You never know how an uninvested public will respond to your work. But when the opening notes of the score began playing over the state-of-the-art sound system in that historic theater, I felt chills. I was hearing my music score and song productions, Tim's sounds, and Jana's Foley. The big screen was radiant with animations created by my friends at Imageworks. The audience was laughing in all the right places, and I knew we had delivered a winner. It was so much fun to be there in that place, on that night, with the Imageworks team.

During this entire project, I had been motivated to vindicate the trust Ken Ralston extended by recommending me to his team. I had worked as hard as I knew how, pushing for excellence in every facet of the process. I hoped everyone would be pleased with my work, but especially Ken. A few weeks following the premier, I came across this quote from Ken in the press: "Chance Thomas' music for *The ChubbChubbs!* is fantastic. I first heard Chance's work when my wife recommended I listen to the compositions for a computer game called *Quest for Glory V.* It had a terrific motion picture feel to it, and seemed Chance would be the perfect choice for Sony's first all computer graphic mini-movie. Chance did some wild renditions of some well known songs for *ChubbChubbs*, plus a wonderful musical score. We couldn't be happier."[3]

Neither could I.

ACADEMY AWARD

Since *The ChubbChubbs!* had received a wide theatrical release, it qualified for submission to the Academy Awards in the animated short film category. I never thought Sony would actually submit it. After all, this was just a pipeline test to prepare Imageworks for future feature animation production. It was never intended to be a serious piece of entertainment in its own right. Nevertheless, a submission was made, and we entered the Oscar competition that year squaring off against *Mike's New Car* from Pixar, and a host of other animated shorts.

On the night of the 75th Annual Academy Awards, March 23, 2003, Eric and Jacquie and many from the team gathered in the Kodak Theater in Hollywood, California, for the festivities. When the announcement was made, Eric strode to the podium to accept the award on behalf of us all. I was serving as a Latter-day Saint bishop at the time and typical of a bishop, I was at a youth event that night, cheering on the young men and young women from my congregation in an extravagant musical production. It was not until much later, in the wee hours of the morning, that I learned *The ChubbChubbs!* had beaten all odds and won the Oscar for Best Animated Short Film.

With that astonishing success, I officially became part of an Oscar-winning victory.

We return now to the original quandary. Many articles came out in the media immediately after the win, particularly in the game industry press, which referred to me as an Oscar-winning composer. I wrote to errant reporters and editors to correct the mistake, but rarely heard anything back. Most ignored me and left their articles as they were. I can only attribute this persistent error to click baiting. For the record, I have never personally claimed to be an Oscar-winning composer. And I do not condone any knowing misrepresentations by the press.

But if George Lucas and Steven Spielberg are right, if music and sound are truly 50% of the movie experience, then I will absolutely stake my claim to a suitable chunk of that famously bald, slender, golden statuette. No doubt the original score, song remakes, and sound design added tremendous support to the animation, helping transform *The ChubbChubbs!* into the delightful, endearing, and Oscar-winning piece of movie magic that charmed the Academy. I will claim that much.

EPILOGUE

If you ever come to my home and visit my studio, you will see a photograph of me holding *The ChubbChubbs'* Oscar statue in front of *The ChubbChubbs'* official movie poster. The poster has my name displayed on it prominently, in the same font size and style as the director and producer.

When visitors ask me about the photo, I proudly tell them I belonged to the creative team that produced an Oscar-winning animated short film. But some respond with a disappointed look on their face, and ask me, "Well, where's the statue? You mean you didn't win an Academy Award yourself?"

I get a little frustrated with that. Sometimes I want to tell them: "You know what? I made extensive and vital contributions to an Oscar-winning film. We did fantastic work and I was right there in the thick of it. We even beat Pixar that year." Sheesh. Aretha said it first and said it best, "All I'm asking for is a little respect."

But I never say anything like that out loud. I just take a deep breath, recalibrate, and express what a wonderful part of my career it was to work on *The ChubbChubbs!*

I do not have a golden Oscar statuette sitting on my shelf. But I do have the vivid memories and the precious friendships.

Surely that is the best kind of gold anyway.

To watch The ChubbChubbs! *Oscar-winning animated short film, as described in this chapter, please visit: HUGEsoundRecords.com/Memoir-06*

NOTES

1 https://worthplaying.com/article/2002/7/4/news/4569-mib2-opens-with-music-by-chance-thomas-quest-for-glory-v/
2 https://en.wikipedia.org/wiki/The_ChubbChubbs!
3 https://www.soundtrack.net/news/article/?id=370

CHAPTER 7

The Lord of the Rings, Part Two

I WAS STANDING NEARLY 9,000 feet above sea level, summitting one of planet Earth's most iconic granite peaks. I was not alone either, Craig Alexander was by my side. A guest in my home that weekend, Craig was one of several winded participants braving the 2007 edition of the annual HUGEsound HALF DOME Conquest. Not for the faint-hearted, this summit was the apex of a 16-mile horizontal, by 3-mile vertical, round-trip hike through the heart of Yosemite National Park.

It was a gloriously clear, sunny day. We soaked up endless magnificent views from the crest of Half Dome, resting our wobbly legs for a good hour or so.

Eventually, Craig and I pulled out our cell phones. While I was calling my wife to share the moment, Craig got on the phone with Turbine Entertainment and received some exhilarating news. There on that peak, Craig accepted a job offer to manage all of Turbine's MMO operations. The new job included oversight of the company's online games, including their crowning jewel, *The Lord of the Rings Online*. After Craig ended the call and gave me the gist of it, we burst into spontaneous celebration, joyful voices carried heavenward by the brisk, mountaintop breeze.

There was so much karma in that shared moment! After all, it was Craig who originated the license to build video games based on *The Lord of the Rings* literature in the first place. A Tolkien MMO had always been Craig's

DOI: 10.1201/9781003199311-8

prescient vision. Meanwhile, I was the one who originated the Tolkien Music Style Guide and Tolkien Franchise Themes, both of which were disseminated across all of Vivendi-Universal's *LOTR* games, including *The Lord of the Rings Online.* But after laying our respective *LOTR* foundations, Craig and I were both displaced from the franchise by bad business decisions outside of our control. Seeing Craig return full circle was a magical moment.

Adding to the magic was the fact that we were in Yosemite. We both loved the park, having visited many times during our respective tenures at Sierra. Looking down from Half Dome's peak, I could see the Yosemite Valley where Craig and his wide Sandi were married in the Valley Chapel just a few years prior. I attended their wedding and remained in close contact with Craig over the ensuing years, never imagining how prominently our friendship would figure in my professional career.

Summiting that day with Craig, cheering his return to *The Lord of the Rings,* was sweet karma indeed. I wondered if my own return to Middle-earth might be approaching too – perhaps just around the next bend in the road.

MINES OF MORIA

Several months came and went. I started a full-time job at EA Games in Salt Lake City as Studio Audio Director. During the job application process, I had secured a critical caveat from EA executive Vance Cook, negotiating the right to continue composing music for existing clients on my own time. Such an exemption was unheard of for EA employees. But Vance was building an audio department for the first time, and part of my leverage was leasing my own fully equipped audio studio to EA at a discount for the duration of my employment.

That caveat proved profitable, as I was able to keep a healthy side hustle going during my tenure there. It proved providential when Craig Alexander came calling.

Turbine Entertainment, now owned by Warner Brothers, was developing a massive new expansion for *LOTRO* called *Mines of Moria.* Craig wanted me to compose an original new score for the expansion, and reconnected me with audio director Geoff Scott to flesh out the details.

Like many audio directors I had once worked with on Vivendi-Universal's Tolkien franchise, Geoff knew me pretty well. He called and immediately set the hook with the right bait, *"Mines of Moria,* baby! It's gotta be SO epic. HUGE orchestra and choir, all live recording, right up your alley!" He continued in that vein with great enthusiasm for several minutes. All music to my ears. This was the kind of return to Tolkien I could only dream about. I felt so grateful to be given this incredible opportunity.

I had moved to Utah for the EA Games job, but my family was still in California waiting for our home to sell. I had nothing on my hands but time, and I filled all that time with work. I would give a full day at EA, grab a quick bite of dinner from the microwave, then compose all night for *Moria*. It was wonderful. I was in vigorous health and back on *LOTRO* making new music for one of the most epic locations in all of Middle-earth.

Can I paint you a quick picture of my composing space? The entire EA dev team was on the fifth floor except for me. The company had leased several hundred square feet on the fourth floor for future expansion, and I built out a single large office there with acoustic treatment for my audio studio. No one else was in that fourth-floor space. During the entire time I worked on *Mines of Moria*, I was completely alone. When I composed at night, I turned off all the lights. Total darkness, total isolation – it was the perfect setting for scoring the long dark of Moria.

Let us take a look at four of the cues I composed for the score.

Moria

Passing through the Elven Door of Hollin and into the bowels of Caradhras, Boromir mutters under his breath, "Who will lead us now in this deadly dark?"[1]

Deadly dark, indeed! Hidden dangers lurked beyond every step. Broken cracks and fissures in the floors, deep wells and treacherous chasms, halls and stairs sprawling in all directions. Orcs and Goblins lay in wait, not to mention Gandalf's warning, "There are older and fouler things than Orcs in the deep places of the world."[2] Moria was an endless, daunting maze of such enormity, it puts Minos' Labyrinth at Knossos to pitiable shame.

In ages past, there had been untold wealth and grandeur in Moria. Under its mountainous dome, the great realm and city of Dwarrodelf had once shone "full of light and splendor ... in many-pillared halls of stone with golden roof and silver floor."[3] A thriving populace once filled each cavern, hall, and vein with hearty industry, merriment, and vigor. But the glory days of Moria were long past, mere shadows casting gloom in a vast cemetery.

Such were my ruminations, rolling a pencil between my fingers, doodling on an empty page, wondering how to frame this monument with music. When players entered Moria for the first time, I wanted the music to express foreboding, heaviness, anxiousness for the journey, joined with grandeur, honor, and reverence for the Dwarves' gloried history.

I imagined a sustained swell of men's choir, joined by tightly voiced chords in the low brass and strings. The harmony would expand in unsettling modulations, changing colors as voicings opened, inverted, and joined new instruments in the orchestra. Occasional booms of timpani and gran casa, buried in long-throw reverb, would add to the atmosphere.

In the middle of the song, the orchestra would pause to gather itself, then swell into a glorious and emotional thematic statement, calling to mind the grandeur of Moria's yesteryears. Then, at the height of the theme, as if telegraphing Dwarrodelf's calamitous end, the music would abruptly diminish, modulating dissonantly, slowly descending into thick and powerful clusters of tubas, bass trombones, and tenor trombones. The harmonies would march forward in an unsettling upward circle, finally coming to rest on the tonic in an open voiced minor chord, spread across the full orchestral spectrum.

As I listened to my completed mockup, there in that dark studio, I experienced a satisfying resonance with the source material. The music felt right all the way down to the bone. I imagined the old professor himself, clenched pipe in his teeth, looking down at me with a slight upturn at each corner of his mouth, tossing me a wink and a nod for good measure.

Drums in the Deep

Michael James Greene was a recording and mixing engineer who I had long wanted to work with. Two of my admired composer friends, Sam Cardon and Kurt Bestor, both praised his exceptional skills behind a recording console. Knowing that *Mines of Moria* was a particularly important project for me, I wanted the very best mixer I could afford. I booked Greene far in advance and was jazzed to have him on board.

Imagine my disappointment and surprise when, just three weeks prior to our scheduled sessions, Greene informed me that he would not be able to mix the *Moria* score after all. He told me that "an important client from Nashville" was coming to town the same week as my mix, and he would need to cancel his sessions with me so he could be with this Nashville client. He suggested that I call another mixing engineer named Mike Roskelley and ask if he might be available to work on my project. I had never heard of Mike Roskelley and I was not happy.

But it is funny how life can work sometimes. Although I had no idea at the time, Greene had just handed me the most fortuitous peer referral of my professional career.

Mike Roskelley turned out to be a brilliant collaborator and technical virtuoso, a kindred creative spirit, and eventually a life-long friend. Over the ensuing years, Roskelley and I became like mad scientists working unsupervised in a chemistry lab, or frenzied kids in a candy store free-for-all.

Our experience with *Drums in the Deep* is illustrative. Roskelley had wrangled the mix into decent shape by the time I came in for my review. As I listened back, my attention was drawn to the strings. The sound was unfocused, a little too warm and cuddly. I wanted to hear the rosin biting into each stroke, like Orc claws scratching splintery doors at Durin's Chamber of Records. I described this to Roskelley and he said, "I know just what to do." He quickly worked over the EQ settings on the strings' direct mic tracks. He adjusted levels, fingers dancing with precision and meaning. He switched up reverb sends and early reflection specs. Suddenly, each voice sharpened into focus. I could now hear cellos scurrying like rats on hardened concrete, violas grinding back and forth like Goblin teeth, violins scratching ever closer, ever higher. The sound was exactly what I had hoped for. The music had come alive, ripping its way through each crescendo.

Next, we focused on the choir. Mike had carved out a nice placement for the choir just up and over the orchestra. The SATB blend was lush and smooth. It worked well for most of the track. But near the end of the song, I wanted more choral urgency and dynamic as we reached the climax. Mike said, "I know just what to do." He worked his magic on the choral blend and placement, giving the women a moment to shine high above the orchestra, then morphing basses and baritones to the front of the mix, barking a fearless Dwarvish chant with presence and power.

We continued on like this for another two hours, building volume curves, carving frequencies, massaging effects, highlighting instruments upon their entrances, and tweaking the mix to our hearts' content. This set a pattern for all future projects we would ever work on together.

As the *Drums in the Deep* mixing session concluded, I slipped into Mike's chair to listen to the final result, surrounded by five massive ATC speakers and a sub, absolutely pinned to the seat. A huge Cheshire Cat grin plastered all over my face said it all. The hard work and attention to detail had paid off. This was a celebration of fine-tuning, a victory of crafted excellence over good enough. A fruitful creative collaboration had been born in the process.

The Hollin Gate

Most composers are inspired by great visuals, and I am no exception. Turbine's art team had created a gorgeous rendering of the Hollin Gate, which I downloaded and opened as wide as possible on my largest monitor. I remember sitting there in the dark for two hours one night, staring at the screen, imagining the magic of that place while trying out different musical motifs in my mind. Somehow, the music had to blend the ethereal nature of the Elves with the heaviness and relentless character of the Dwarves.

My scoring template for *Mines of Moria* was built for Dwarves, using the palette instruments outlined in the Tolkien Music Style Guide. But this track needed Elven instruments too. I pulled in a classical harp sample, additional violin sections, and some flutes.

A staggered arpeggio on the harp felt like a good start. Undulating triplets set up a hypnotic tuple feel. The flutes joined in, raising the stakes. But it felt like straight fantasy and I needed something unsettling in the music. After all, the Watcher in the Water was merely a stone's throw away. So I added violins on a downward arpeggio, but in double time against the triplets. It did just the trick! The violins' entrance disorients the listener in a really cool way, pulling away from the tuple feel. Soon the violin-feel dominates.

Now I needed to foreshadow the other side of the door, the opening into Moria. Enter the double basses. Swelling up and down with the violins, these additions signaled a great mingling of Elf and Dwarf in music. But all of this is just the introduction.

After the intro, the trumpets and violas join in a brief exposition of a wistful Dwarven theme, then hand back to the violins to tell a sad Elven tale. The harp keeps rolling. Moments of suspense intersperse brief motific statements leading to further exposition of the theme against a triplet feel. Finally, it comes home on a high suspended note in the violins and fades away.

Ages of the Golden Wood

For many years, singer Jenny Jordan has been an integral part of my sound, as much as anyone I ever worked with. Hers was the voice of the dancing Dryads in *Quest for Glory V: Dragon Fire*, the voice of death in *Peter Jackson's King Kong*, the frolicking tween-girl vocalist in *Littlest Pet Shop: Friends*, and lead singer on many other commercial, film, and game projects I composed over the years. Among other gifts, Jenny brought to the table a fabulous sounding instrument, a Stradivarius among voices. She also possessed an encyclopedic command of styles, making her an effortless vocal chameleon. Add to that a mastery of music theory, perfect pitch, great work ethic, can-do attitude at recording sessions… I was very lucky to be able to work with her.

Lothlorien's music needed the voice of an angel, or nearly so. I needed the voice of a high Elf, a queen among Elves, a voice worthy of Galdriel. Jenny had already recorded a soaring Elven vocal for the Tolkien Franchise Themes a few years earlier, so bringing her back was a no-brainer.

This particular track, *Ages of the Golden Wood*, would accompany players' first entrance into and discovery of Lothlorien, a magical and most welcome reprieve after the horrors of Moria and Khazad-dûm. Galadriel's beneficent influence is ever present but often out of sight in Lothlorien, floating among the tree tops, breathing life into the forest, watchful and protective without calling attention to herself. I wanted listeners to feel Jenny's voice more than be dominated by it. Thus, you catch glimpses of her vocal soaring high above the orchestration among the flutes, and among the first violins. Yet there are times, most magical and transformative, when one comes face-to-face with the Elven Queen. Those are the moments in the song where the voice is brought to the foreground. The strings swell, the harps gliss, the harmony modulates unexpectedly, and when Jenny's voice comes forward, you can feel the power and magic of the elves, the emotion and wonder rises in the heart!

Parents are not supposed to have favorite children and composers are not supposed to have favorite cues. But I'll break that rule for *Ages of the Golden Wood*.

Mines of Moria was a big hit for Turbine Entertainment and the original music score was well-received by fans and critics alike. Turbine rode the wave of that success for several years. Other, lesser expansions came and went in the meantime, including *Siege of Mirkwood* and *Rise of Isengard*. But I was not involved with the music for either of those. Turbine had an in-house audio department staffed with talented people, including composer Stephen DiGregorio, who took over as audio director when Geoff Scott unexpectedly left the company. Stephen handled the music for those expansions personally.

RIDERS OF ROHAN

Do you think contract negotiations can be fun? Negotiating contracts may sound like anathema to my composer friends. But I believe that the creativity and tenacity required to compose music transfers organically to negotiating. With enough training and practice, negotiation can become a powerful and enjoyable part of any composer's skill set.

Four years after I composed the score for *Mines of Moria*, Craig Alexander called on me again. Turbine was gearing up for another expansion even bigger than *Moria* called *Riders of Rohan*. They wanted an original music score on a scale far beyond anything I had done for *LOTRO* in the past. But we quickly got bogged down in negotiations. The cost for composing so much music, along with the required production to match or surpass *Moria*'s sound quality, would cost much more than they were willing to pay.

Enter creative negotiation. Thinking outside the box, a skill composers are well acquainted with.

I should tell you that *LOTRO* was not the only attractive franchise in Turbine's portfolio. They also had *Dungeons & Dragons Online (DDO)*. I had been aware of *DDO* for a long time, but never made any headway getting a music contract with them. When the negotiations for *Rohan* bogged down, I saw an opportunity. What if I piggybacked a new score for *DDO* on the deal, and recorded both scores simultaneously? We could gain economies of scale by recording the scores back to back – lower studio costs, lower contracting costs, lower musician costs. And if I could pick up the extra work to score both expansions, it made sense for me to offer a discount on the scoring rate we had just been haggling over.

All sides saw the benefits to such an approach. Thinking outside the box had yielded a successful negotiation gambit. Just as we were about to shake hands, I decided to try one more negotiating technique. I dropped a "nibble." A nibble in negotiations is an unexpected and relatively small request that comes after all of the big issues have been resolved. My nibble was asking for the release of a *Riders of Rohan* soundtrack. Turbine was owned by Warner Brothers, after all. Who better to get my music out into the world than WB?

Turbine had never released any of my music commercially, and there was resistance when I brought it up. Soundtracks rarely benefit a game company. For that matter, they rarely benefit composers, at least financially. But I had seen the potential in game soundtracks when I promoted the score for *Quest for Glory V: Dragon Fire* (more than 50,000 units sold) back in 1998. So I ventured the nibble.

Turbine agreed to run it up the flagpole at Warner Brothers. I asked for a name at WB so I could follow up with them personally. If there is one thing I know about the corporate world, it is this – everyone is overburdened. If you really want something outside the norm to happen, you need to shepherd the whole process yourself.

One thing led to another, and between my nibble at Turbine, my new contact at WB, and a little nudge from my friends at Middle-earth Enterprises, WB agreed to release the *Riders of Rohan* score under their Water Tower Records label. Although this concession would not affect my bottom line until royalties began to accumulate, it still felt like a huge win.

Now, I could sign the contract.

So much effort and creativity had been expended just getting to yes, it was hard to believe I had not written a single note yet. I was reminded that contract negotiation can also be part of the creative process. Still, I could hardly wait to get started writing the score.

Style Guide Update

As it turned out, Turbine added a nibble of their own at the last minute. In order to provide continuity for potential future expansion work done by their in-house team, Turbine requested that I update the Tolkien Music Style Guide by adding a specific section for Rohan. This was actually fortuitous, because it helped crystallize my own thinking about the score in a comprehensive way right from the start of the project. It sent me back to the fountain again, digging back into the literature for new treasures, like a seasoned art collector revisiting the old masters.

I was surprised at the fresh insights that came during this new reading of the literature. Rohan was clearly modeled on Old England, and I leaned heavily into those music traditions while expanding the Style Guide – prominent use of melodic appoggiatura, rhythmic triplets, bass recorder and uillean pipes, Bodhrán and horse whips, mandolin and baritone guitars. And above all else, the fiddle, lots of glorious solo fiddle. These all found their place in the new Rohan extension of the Tolkien Music Style Guide.

Each region of Rohan had to be shaded differently as well, depending on its politics, its place in the story, its lore, and its topography. All of these myriad influences had to be sourced, sorted out, and defined in musical terms to generate authentic guidelines. By the time I was finished, the Rohan extension to the Tolkien Music Style Guide had added another fourteen pages of instruction divvied up across Amon Hen, The Wold, Norcrofts, Sutcrofts, Fangorn, and the Entwash Vale. I was almost ready to start composing.

See It, Score It

I mentioned earlier that visual stimuli is always a catalyst for my composing creativity. But since I was starting on the score much earlier in the development process than usual, Turbine did not have game levels available for me to wander through for inspiration. Instead, I relied heavily on Turbine's art director, Todd DeMelle, to send me as much concept art as possible. And just as I had done when starting on the *King Kong* score, I printed up dozens of images and plastered them all over the walls of my studio. Each time I entered the studio to compose, I first walked around the room, staring intently at each image, recalling passages in the literature, matching impressions to the new Style Guide notes, and imagining music before I ever sat down to being writing.

And then fortunately, the music came.

Shadow of the Argonath

This was the first music cue for the new score. Although it underscores a game instance occurring late in the expansion at Amon Hen, in the far southeastern quadrant of Rohan, I thought this was a good place to test the connectivity between my new palette for Rohan and the older themes for Gondor and the Shire.

The music begins with a slow and unfocused version of the Gondor theme played on French horns and uilleann pipes, representing an erosion of Gondor's vision and leadership among the men of the West.

The theme wants to rise in nobility, power, might and strength. You can hear it reaching, stretching, striving, even striking a stout cadence for a moment. But it cannot sustain. Stewards alone can never muster the stateliness required to bear off the world of men in full splendor. Uilleann Pipes echo off into the distance, suggesting the untimely fall of Boromir and the corroded irrelevance of Denathor.

But afterward, there comes an injection of hope. We get a second rendition of Gondor's theme that is a little more focused, a little purer, played on penny whistle and uillean pipes. The penny whistle represents Frodo. Frodo brings hope! The pipes represent the past glories of Gondor's kings, embodied anew by Aragorn. The two instruments interlace and support one another, symbolic of how the fates of the two men are now inexorably intertwined.

There is a gentle climactic rise toward hope, but then doubt returns with the pipes and penny whistle echoing away into an unknown future. And lest we forget that there are perils along the East Wall, the bass recorder brings us back to present dangers, entering with a low drum and slightly dissonant strings.

At the end, the horn and whistle rise together one last time in unity and understanding, ultimately continuing apart as the whistle (Frodo) quietly disappears and the horn (Aragorn) carries on resolutely toward Rohan. Did you ever imagine that so much dramatic coordination went into writing a single piece of music for a video game?

Theme for Rohan

I will never forget my first hearing of the Rohan refrain composed by Howard Shore for 2002s *The Two Towers*. As the Hardanger melody rang out across the theater, I was completely mesmerized. This was the Rohan of my dreams, suddenly given voice in melody! It was stunningly, intuitively perfect. Of all the themes to be found running through Peter Jackson's trilogy, this one resonated most with me.

Ten years later, it was my turn to create a new theme for Rohan. It seemed impossible. Shore's theme was so perfect for the film. The only way I could approach the task was to block Peter Jackson's Rohan from my mind, immerse myself once again in the literature, and find my own way to the heart of Tolkien's Rohan.

How does one broadly define Rohan? A storied nation in decline? A land simmering on the verge of all-out war? Anglo-Saxon reference with Medieval overtones? Hardy people, individual and family tenderness, triumph and tragedy, crops and kinships, determined men and women, wary and weary nobles, hope, sadness, and uncertainty? Yes, yes, yes, and yes! All of those intangibles had to be woven somehow into a new theme for Rohan.

I decided to introduce the theme on classical violin played in a fiddling style. The initial modality is minor, setting up a somber tone. The melody moves on hooks of appoggiatura, so prevalent in Old English music. This places the theme squarely in the Northwestern European tradition, tying it tightly to Tolkien's Anglo-Saxon source material. Other endemic instruments join the theme, including European whistle, bass recorder, and uillean pipes.

All of these colors come from Northwestern Europe of centuries past, clueing that the theme is contemporary to the rise of Anglo-Saxon culture. The progressing harmonies alternate between minor and major tonalities, suggesting the ongoing struggle of the Rohirrim. Triplet melodies against a 6/4 meter further reinforce the cultural resonance. As the theme approaches its apex, there is a triumphant modulation toward ultimate victory. And yet the resolve, though major, is a weak resolve (adding a suspension to the chord) leaving a fragile uncertainty hanging in the air. That was my approach to crafting a new theme for Rohan.

Let us take a sidebar to share a very special highlight about this song. Long after *Theme for Rohan* was composed, recorded, and released into the world, I was asked to conduct a concert premier of this piece with the Utah Symphony at Abravanel Hall in Salt Lake City, Utah. The concert series Video Games Live! (VGL) was coming to town, and *Theme for Rohan* was going to be featured prominently on the program. My old friend Tommy Tallarico, founder and host of VGL, asked if I would like to conduct it.

I rarely conduct my own music in the recording studio because I generally offer more value to my clients by producing sessions from the control room. In that pristine listening environment, there is no detail that escapes my discriminating ear, and I am in a better position to direct the recording over the headphones, giving direction on dynamics, bowings, correcting errors, inspiring passion, and the like. Because of that, I had simply never acquired much conducting experience.

Theme for Rohan is mostly written in 6/8, though there are occasional measures of 5/8 and 7/8 scattered throughout the piece. A live VGL concert unfolds against a master click track, running through the breadth of the show. I delivered my click reference for *Theme for Rohan* in 6/8, 5/8, and 7/8, respectively.

Tommy had reserved enough time for me to run through my song with the symphony once, maybe twice at a rehearsal before the first show. When it was my turn, I stepped up quickly to the podium, raised my baton, and started listening for the click. There were two measures free at the top, then the piece would begin. Wow! Those 6/8 clicks came fast, and the emphasis on beat one was difficult to discern. I got lost and missed the downbeat. No problem, we reset and started over. The second time I hit the opening measure correctly. But when the first 5/8 measure came, I could not differentiate the downbeat and got lost again. We had to start over. And again I got lost in the music, this time after a 7/8 measure. After the fifth failure to get through the piece *even one time*, I shrunk from the podium and asked

Emmanuel Fratianni, the outstanding conductor who traveled with the tour, if he would conduct the song for me. He agreed, and said he would run through it at the end of the rehearsal, if there was time.

I slunk away feeling completely defeated, expecting someone from the orchestra to ask facetiously, "You did *write* this piece of music, didn't you?" Mercifully, no one said anything. In fact, no one from the orchestra even looked at me as I disappeared into the darkness offstage. Totally humiliating.

Pamela had been there in the concert hall during the rehearsal, and asked me what happened. I tried to explain to her how I kept getting lost in the endless flow of eighth note clicks. Tommy came over and expressed some concern too. "What about conducting in two, rather than 6/8?" he offered. "Could you build a click track from quarter notes?" Honestly, I was feeling so embarrassed I was unsure if I wanted to be seen by that orchestra again. But Pamela encouraging me to try one last time. I appreciated the support and drew some renewed strength from her.

"Go solve the problem," I thought, "Rise above your emotions."

Tommy had a spare laptop set up backstage, so I found my way there and tapped out a new click track using quarter notes, except for the occasional oddly metered measures. Those I kept as eighth notes. I practiced against an mp3 of the song, and discovered that it was much easier to keep my place in the score when conducting in two. Maybe this could work out after all.

I returned to the stage just as Emmanuel was preparing to conduct *Theme for Rohan,* at the very end of the orchestra's rehearsal. I walked across the front of the stage to the conductor's podium and tapped Emmanuel on the arm. "I'd like to try this one more time." He looked at me with both compassion and skepticism. "Are you sure? I can do this for you. Besides, we're really out of time. We can't afford a single restart."

From somewhere, I do not know from where, I forced a feeling of rapt determination. "No, I can do this, I need to do this." He stood there unmoved, still skeptical, so I raised my voice just a bit. "I've GOT this." Emmanuel handed me the baton, and relinquished the podium.

The musicians were surprised to see me standing in front of them again. Surprised, but also nervous. I noticed a couple of them checking their watches. But once the clicks came on, I never missed a beat. Much easier to conduct in two than in six. I conducted a complete run-through performance of the song flawlessly. The musicians even clapped when we were done. I felt relieved, and grateful to Tommy and Pamela for encouraging me to fight through my inexperience and find a successful path. I was proud of myself for stepping up when all I wanted was to hide away in an obscure corner.

Later that night at the concert, *Theme for Rohan* was the first song performed after the intermission. Tommy brought me out in front of the audience to introduce me. I was wearing an expensive and flashy tuxedo (which I rented), and Tommy announced that, in all the years he had been doing VGL, I was the first person to ever wear a tuxedo on stage. I took the mic and told the audience, "I wanted to clean up nice for my home town crowd!" The audience loved it, erupting in cheers and applause.

Tommy reclaimed the mic and announced, "Ladies and gentlemen, give it up for Chance Thomas, conducting his very own *Theme For Rohan* from *The Lord of the Rings Online!*" The applause was thunderous and we had yet to play a single note. I rose to the podium, lifted my baton, and together with the symphony gave the audience a stunningly beautiful rendition of the song. When the French horns joined the violins for the concluding statement of the main motif, the climax was spectacular. It was glorious. The crowd went nuts, as I turned around and took my bow with deep gratitude and relief.

Reliving the experience as I write these words makes me want to offer encouragement to every person reading this book. I can promise that you will experience times when you shrink or wilt because of an error, a lack of experience, a clash of subjective tastes, or any number of flameouts that can crush your confidence. When that happens, please picture my drooping shoulders and fallen countenance shuffling pitifully off that stage early in the rehearsal. I was beaten, embarrassed, wilted. Then picture again, if you can, the radiance of basking in the adulation of a huge concert crowd, cheering and clapping, on their feet, as I took in the fruits of an eventual victory. Realize that I am not an extraordinary aberration. If anything I am spectacularly average, well within the broad central span of the Bell Curve. If I can recover from a humiliation like this, so can you. You've GOT this. You can find your solution, dissect and resolve your problem, overcome the negative emotions that would otherwise push you down and hold you back. You are not alone. You are powerful. You are evolvable. You can rise up and break through.

Learning to Ride

Learning to Ride accompanies the player's first attempt at horseback riding in the game. It is basically a tutorial tune. Thus the gentle beginning, the gradually climbing harmonies, the simple arrangement, and the eventual tapering off at the end.

It also marks our first introduction to Rohan's riding motif. The riding motif is typically played on the strings in the lower registers. It is a signature rhythmic riff that repeats like a chorus in this song and throughout other parts of the score. The idea was to convey a lively sense of galloping motion. The choice of low strings is due to the organic nature of the instruments. Their hollow wooden bodies resonate with a rich, natural energy in the lower registers. Not to mention the drawing of actual horse hair bows across the strings.

To complement the strings, two differing sizes of Bohdran were added to the percussion ensemble, one with a 12″ diameter and a tightly drawn head. The other is much larger, approximately 22″ in diameter with a more loosely drawn head. Also unique to Rohan's equine percussion ensemble are a horse whip and leather strapping sounds.

The fiddle takes on a prominent melodic role. The percussion and strings are loose and rustic. The brass adds girth to steady the arrangement. When the song transitions from the timidity of learning to the joy of roaming freely, the baritone guitar and mandolin join the orchestra.

All of these elements work together to help players perceive an ongoing sense of forward momentum, pulling them off of the couch and into the saddle of their own fiery, Rohirric steed.

The Eored

Tales of the American West often include a reference to cavalry coming over the hill. In Rohan, that cavalry would be the Eored.

Tolkien's Eoreds were groups of battle-ready horsemen – armed, armored, and trained for war. They rode hard and fast into battle, fighting with ferocious intensity. Various references place their numbers at between 120 and 200 riders per group.

This music track was written to accompany a player's own furious foray into full-tilt mounted combat. We are talking about full gallop with weapons brandished. Timid souls need not apply!

The driving tempo and aggressive marcato strings kick the piece off with an intense immediacy. The choir joins in, menacing and rugged at first, other times epic and regal. There are brass, percussion, and woodwinds in the orchestra too, but their roles are generally supportive.

In the tongue of Old English, the choir sings of battle glory, death, and freedom, "*Gewinn arë, déap, fréot!*" Then they conclude with the Eored's signature refrain, "We are bold, we are mighty." In the Old English tongue, *"We sindon bald, we sindon strang."*

As a happy side note, this song was nominated for Best Original Choral Song at the Game Audio Network Guild Awards in 2013.

LOTRO Legacy

Included in my contract for *Rohan,* but outside the proper score for *Rohan*, was a new track for the main menu. Since the launch of *Shadows of Angmar* in 2009, *LOTRO* had used a music track by Stephen DiGregorio for its login/main menu theme. The players loved it, but after so many years the dev team was ready for a refresh.

I wanted to honor Stephen's original theme, so I entitled the track *LOTRO Legacy*, and kicked it off with a nod to Stephen's classic menu track. I dressed it up in full orchestral splendor, then segued into an updated orchestral version of my own classic, *The House of Tom Bombadil.* After the Bombadil interlude, I wanted to get back to something epic, so the next segment is a reworking of the Gondor theme composed for VUG's original Tolkien Franchise Themes. It wraps up with a remake of the opening measures of *The Hollin Gate*, from the *Mines of Moria* score. The whole tune is a trip down memory lane, and the players really enjoyed it.

Petition

Released in October of 2012, *Riders of Rohan* was a galloping critical success with fans and media alike. And while it generated rave reviews, it did not bring the financial bonanza Warner Brothers expected. Compared to *Call of Duty: Black Ops 2,* which raked in $500 million on its first day[4] (also released in 2012), *Riders of Rohan* was merely a whimper in the marketplace. Cutbacks in dev budgets followed, which included money for "frivolous" expenses like orchestras, choirs, and a certain composer we all know and love. Expansions for Helm's Deep and Gondor came and went without me, which was heartbreaking after my re-immersion in Tolkien for *Riders of Rohan.*

It upset me to be sidelined again, watching Turbine's in-house composers carry on the music scoring without me. I would sometimes lurk around the *LOTRO* forums, and I regularly stumbled upon appeals to the company to bring me back for more music. That support was gratifying. And while the players' appeals fell on deaf ears at WB, their generous comments went straight to my heart.

Around this time, a young British *LOTRO* player named Patrick Palmer started a petition on Change.org titled, *Return Chance Thomas to LOTRO.* On the petition's main page, Patrick wrote the following introduction:

> "The music produced in-house by Turbine has failed to hit the high standards set by Chance Thomas and have lessened the immersion and experience of recent major in-game events, such as the Battle of Helm's Deep and the entry into Gondor. With further major events surely in the pipeline in terms of in-game releases, such as Minas Tirith and Central Gondor, this petition asks that Turbine acknowledge the impact Chance Thomas has had on the LOTRO franchise and asks him back to fulfill his Middle-earth musical brilliance until the franchise ends."

Following Patrick's introduction, hundreds added their votes and dozens more added their comments. What composer would not be moved to tears by such a show of love and support? I certainly was.

WINDS OF CHANGE

Years later, after an unexpected corporate implosion, Turbine Entertainment was disbanded. The developers reformed into a new group called Standing Stone Games (SSG), acquiring the rights to the *LOTR* license, the game, and all of its assets. SSG also signed a publishing deal with Daybreak Game Company to continue supporting *LOTRO,* which by then was one of the longest running MMO's in the business. This brought about wholesale changes in the back office, so to speak, but it was mostly invisible to the players.

From my perspective, the most important back-office change was a new opportunity to discuss music rights. When Turbine was owned by Universal, then later by Warner Brothers, the company was under the control of businesses with record companies under their umbrellas. Both had kept LOTRO's music rights under lock and key, which was why none of my music from *Shadows of Angmar* or *Mines of Moria* was ever commercially released.

Daybreak, on the other hand, was not in the record business. I sensed an opportunity.

LOTRO 10

While Patrick's petition did not immediately bring a new scoring opportunity, it did spark a passion project I was holding in my heart for many years. But first, some back story…

One reason I decided to pursue music as a career was because, early in my life, I was deeply impacted by music I heard from many inspiring artists. I actually became a composer to create music that would give that same kind of experience to others.

Some of the best music I had written in my life was for *LOTRO*, but no one outside the game's own ecosystem had ever heard my work. I wanted to change that, distributing the music into the wide world so that it could find an audience, connect with people for whom the music would resonate on its own terms.

LOTRO's tenth anniversary was coming up quickly, and I suggested to Daybreak and SSG that one way to celebrate was to release some of the game's best music from the past ten years.

I had recently organized a new record company called HUGEsound Records, under the umbrella of HUGEsound Post Production (see Chapter 15). HUGEsound Records presented a formal proposal to produce, promote, and distribute a tenth anniversary soundtrack for *LOTRO*. This would be a double album filed with the best music I had composed for *Shadows of Angmar, Mines of Moria,* and *Riders of Rohan.*

No offense was intended against Geoff Scott, Stephen DiGregorio, or others who had also composed music for *LOTRO*. Their music was not included. This was a business decision. If HUGEsound was going to foot the bill for production, promotion, and distribution, I needed to skew the profits back my way. Music is a tough business in the 21st century, grosses are low and margins are thin. This was the only way it made financial sense to pursue.

I engaged in negotiations between Daybreak Game Company, Tolkien Enterprises, and SSG to flesh out the details. They agreed to license to HUGEsound Records the right to create a new soundtrack album called *The Lord of the Rings Online: Tenth Anniversary Commemorative Soundtrack (LOTRO 10).* The license included perpetual distribution rights for the soundtrack, including both digital and physical releases, with five years of exclusivity. In return, HUGEsound Records would pay a 5% royalty on gross revenues.

On June 1, 2017, HUGEsound Records released *LOTRO 10* as a double CD album with 26 songs. We also released it as a digital download. It did good business, and has remained an evergreen product in all the intervening years. To this day *LOTRO 10* is my top-selling soundtrack.

MORDOR

I had long admired *LOTRO*'s Art Director Todd DeMelle from afar. His work in managing so many artists and assets in this massive online game, while maintaining a high degree of quality control, had always impressed me. But I did not really know him.

That was about to change. Todd cold-called me one day. He said the *LOTRO* team was working on a *Mordor* expansion and he wondered what it would take to bring me back to create an original orchestral score for the game. By the way, when someone asks you "what it would take," that is a signal that you already have the upper hand in a business negotiation.

I negotiated for my highest per-minute scoring rate, plus *Mordor* soundtrack rights for HUGEsound Records, and budget to record and mix an 85-piece orchestra and choir. It was a very favorable deal.

After the financial terms were agreed upon, we dug into the real work of creative development. The team already had the expansion fleshed out. Soon I was pouring over detailed design docs and creative briefs.

Mordor would force me to confront a gripping darkness in music I had never explored before. The heart and soul of *Mordor* was the dark Lord Sauron, one-time servant of Morgath. Tracing evil back to its lore origins, one discovers the first introduction of evil coming into the world through music, Melkor's dissonant music. To be authentic, the score I composed for *Mordor* must flow from an origin of eviscerating dissonance, in the blackest of hues.

Nevertheless, even *Mordor* was still Tolkien. Even within such a forbidding and oppressive score, I needed to convey a sense of reaching for light beneath the overwhelming shadow, threads of beauty and strength amidst oppressive darkness and decay. Hope is the very essence of Tolkien.

I recorded the *Mordor* score with the Utah Film Orchestra, the same group that performed the original scores for *Riders of Rohan*, *Mines of Moria*, and *Shadows of Angmar*. Featured performers on the *Mordor* soundtrack included David Osmond on vocals, Aaron Ashton on fiddle, Jeannine Goeckeritz on flutes, Daron Bradford on penny whistle, Nicole Pinnell on cello, Rich Dixon on guitars, and the Utah Film Choir. The score was recorded at HUGEsound Post Production in Salt Lake City, Utah. Michael James Greene engineered and mixed the recordings.

After the Fall

One of the first areas players encounter after passing through the imposing Black Gate of Mordor is Dor Amarth. It is a wide-open wasteland, with active steam vents, scattered rock fragments, broken down battlements, and strewn wreckage from Sauron's demolished war machinery. In creating the score, I thought texturally first. I was searching for an element of eeriness within an airy and open ambience. None of the ambient or granular synth patches in my arsenal conjured the right feeling, so I opted for an organic solution. I booked flutist Jeannine Goeckeritz into the studio and asked her to bring two bass flutes and an alto flute. For two hours, we experimented with her playing low pedal tones, overblows, and various other effects on each flute. Each flute was recorded on a separate track and I retained every take. This was exactly the source material I needed.

Jeannine is another collaborator with whom I have had the pleasure of working again and again over the years. Her golden flute (rose gold, actually) has graced most of my music scores from *Riders of Rohan* onward. Sometimes when a session concludes, you just know you have captured magic. Jeannine hit a home run with these tracks.

After the session, my plan was to search for the coolest bits and pieces from each individual track. But when I sat down to begin the sifting process, all three tracks were unmuted. When pushing play, I unexpectedly heard the tracks play back *together*, the alto flute playing alongside both bass flutes. It was unearthly! I thought the sounds were incredible already when recorded one at a time. But playing them back in a polytonal texture was terrifying and beautiful. I began editing the best combinations together, sending each track through an LCR delay echoing into long-throw reverbs. The music was almost visible, a ghost-like morphing of overtones and undertones dueling and dancing in the air.

Such an incredible texture, perfect to scatter across the regions of Dor Amarth. But beyond texture, the region needed to impose a powerful exploratory theme, marching players resolutely through the stifling darkness and imposing horrors of Dor Amarth. I selected mighty double basses and cellos for the initial introduction of the theme, then added truly crushing percussion, sampled from a variety of wrecking ball industrial noises. I had it now – otherworldly texture, formidable theme, and colossal percussion. Now players could enter this game world properly.[5]

Lhaereth of Seregost

Deep in the heart of Mordor lies the stronghold of Seregost, the castle dwelling of Lhaereth the sorceress, rising high above the poisoned and decaying filth of Agarnaith. Tolkien lore tells us that Lhaereth sought union with Sauron in wicked matrimony to form an evil power couple, spreading their collective shadow over all of Middle-earth. Tragically for her, two little hobbits and a gangly river creature found their way to Mount Doom and ruined her wedding plans (among many other things).

As I imagined how to score this part of the game world, I envisioned Seregost as a sort of anti-Rivendell. To me, Lhaereth's fortress of malevolence was the antithesis to Elrond's house of light, love, and healing. In preparation for writing, I returned to Rivendell to study my theme from the original Franchise overture, picturing what a negative-exposure, mirror version might sound like – as if taking a darker reflection of Rivendell in my bare hands, twisting and warping it mercilessly, then dragging it through a sewer.[6]

Keep in mind, the essence of Tolkien is reaching for light, through the oppressiveness of darkness. Even a sadistic sorceress could be a tragic character when viewed from a certain vantage point. Out of the filth and despair of Seregost, I needed a theme erupting with longing and lost love, bleeding with heart-rending passion.

Distant metal clanging and claustrophobic ambience set the stage. Double basses growl and threaten far below, hinting at the theme momentarily, then vanish into the shadows. High above the murk, sordino violins and violas rise in minor clouds, a tonal haze hanging stiffly in the air. The cellos hint at the theme again, then join the basses in a melancholy foreshadowing of its opening phrases. But they fail to complete the task, fading again into oblivion. Then comes the quiet lull before the storm, and suddenly, with a modulation and suspended cymbal, the full theme explodes in dark and wailing splendor.

With the theme concluded, the song recedes back into darkness. Double basses come again carrying a processed coupling an octave below. Oh, the gravity! At the conclusion of the piece, a delicate theme restatement on arco violins frames a vulnerable children's choir, wringing the last full measure of poignancy from the piece - a tragically dramatic addition to *Mordor's* original music score.

Coronation of Aragorn

In the midst of SSG's game design for exploring and conquering Mordor, the dev team inserted an instance of Aragorn ascending to the throne of Gondor. This comes complete with all the Middle-earth pomp and circumstance you would expect. Originally, this struck me as an arbitrary "meanwhile, back at the ranch" moment – both out of place and oddly unnecessary. But as I delved further into the expansion, I realized just how desperately players would need to emerge from Mordor now and again, just to catch a breath of fresh air. *Mordor* is an exceptionally dark, depressing, and menacing experience compared to everything else in the game world. Players would likely embrace the Aragorn ascension instance like coal miners embracing an open sky after long hours in deep tunnels.

During the coronation instance, the king is dutifully and enthusiastically celebrated. But what truly touches the heart is the way the Hobbits are held up in high esteem and given their moment to shine. Appropriately too, since it was the endurance and heroism of Hobbits that made the rise of Gondor possible again. Hail to the Hobbits, long live the Hobbits!

I thought it would be fitting and deliciously fun to intertwine the regal theme of Gondor with the Shire theme of the Hobbits. Both motifs trace their origins to the original Franchise Themes I penned nearly twenty years prior. Pulling the old themes out for this uplifting intertwining was very satisfying.

Similar to its role in the game, the track *Coronation of Aragorn* has a refreshing function in the *Mordor* soundtrack album. The major harmonies, bright colors, and noble melodies offer a welcome reprieve from the draining sonic tapestry underscoring the rest of *Mordor* with such menace and dread. I suspect that soundtrack listeners will enjoy the exploration of darkness in the *Mordor* score, but probably wait with optimistic anticipation for this particular cue.

Ever On

The song *Ever On* is an unabashed love letter to the players of *LOTRO* and to all fans of *Lord of the Rings* across the globe. But why stop there? In its broadest sense, this song celebrates the adventurer in all of us. I think that may have been what the old professor had in mind when he penned these collectively relatable lyrics:

The Road goes ever on and on,
Down from the door where it began,
Now far ahead the Road has gone,
And I must follow if I can,
Ever On! Ever On![7]

I set these words to music for the first time back in 1998, while trying to find the right voice to score *J.R.R. Tolkien's Middle-earth Online* for Sierra. It was a miserable failure, dreadfully unlistenable. But I kept chipping away at the task off and on, determined to find a melody, accompaniment, instrumentation, and singer that would properly celebrate the rustic spirit of adventure that rises in my breast each time I read those evocative lyrics.

One hot California day, during August of 2000, I was refinishing a Redwood deck under the blistering summer sun, when a melodic idea came into my mind for the opening line of the song. I tried singing it, and found a mutual fit between the song lyric and the lilting rise and fall of the melody. It was a good opening line, but I struggled to find my way through the rest of the tune.

Two years later, I was driving home from GDC late at night and decided to revisit the old walking song again. This time I managed to work out the melody for each verse heading south on I-5, but got hung up on the chorus. Suddenly, as if the muses themselves had grown weary of my endless unfinished attempts, a fully fleshed chorus downloaded directly into my mind. I can still recall with perfect clarity the stretch of highway in central California where it happened.

Ever on! Ever on!

The soaring vocal bespoke the wild abandon of freedom, while a descending orchestra played like passing cobblestones under a wagon, or swift waters rushing under Brandywine bridge. Again and again I played the song over in my mind, singing loudly, pounding out the Bodhrán rhythms between each palm and finger against the steering wheel, with ferocious fiddling and fretwork filling the arrangement.

A day or two after returning home, I took a shot at sequencing the arrangement, just as I had imagined during the drive home. When I finished, listening back to my work, I thought, "Well, this is perfectly adequate," which meant it was utterly unacceptable. I returned to tinker with the arrangement again from time to time, but I never uncovered the magic I had felt in the car during that late night drive home. Sigh.

Life flew by. *Ever On* was lost in a flurry of yesterdays and discarded old computers. I was unsure if it would ever see the light of day. But when the *Mordor* expansion happened, and the game team told me that *Mordor* was a capstone to the game's long and winding road, the thought sparked in my mind to venture one last attempt at capturing *Ever On* in an original song.

This time the arrangement came together quickly, with an intuition informed by years of daydreaming and experimentation. Also, since I had money and client expectations riding on the outcome… let's be honest, those can always stir extra motivation into the recipe!

One of the things I always hoped to achieve in the song's music was the same duple resonance found in the lyrics. The words convey a universal message about the thrill of grand adventures juxtaposed with the simplicity and purity of a Hobbit simply stepping outside his door. Who can tell what will befall a Bilbo, a Frodo, or you and I, when we take those first halting steps away from the familiar and into the vast unknown? It is a brilliant rendering in the books, and I yearned to find some comparable framework within my music.

The song had to begin unassumingly. An acoustic guitar, a small Bodhrán, and a single, unprocessed voice. A fiddle could join along the journey, maybe a penny whistle too. And when the chorus arrives, the song could open up wide with an orchestra and soaring vocals. But then, it should return to its rustic beginnings with the fiddle and penny whistle. I liked those ideas. Maybe I could add an instrumental bridge too. The song needed it, and an instrumental break would be nice to showcase the terrific fiddle playing of Aaron Ashton, who had given so much of himself and his talent to the earlier *Riders of Rohan* score. I brought my old friend Rich Dixon along to record all of the fretwork in the song.

One struggle I wrestled with in the past was finding the right singer for the song. This time was no easier. Several great studio singers auditioned for the part, but none quite delivered the vibe I was hoping for. When David Osmond expressed an interest, I was skeptical. I thought his voice was too fresh-sounding, too smooth for an adequate rendering or reflection of unpolished Hobbit culture. But when I heard him singing the chorus, sailing effortlessly and free like a skyboard riding the blue expanse, I was totally inspired. I brought David into the studio and we did several takes of the entire song, dialing in this line, adding harmonies to that line, tweaking here and there. I thought it turned out great. I only have one small regret. I wish we could have made the first two lines sound a bit more rustic. But everything else sounds fantastic. Overall, Osmond delivered a knock-out punch.

Ever on! Ever on!

This is the final song on the *Mordor* soundtrack. As it turns out, it was also the final song of my *LOTR* career. After *Mordor,* SSG doubled down on its budget-saving approach to music production, relying solely on their in-house team to deliver each ensuing score.

Since then, I have retired from composing. Looking back, *Ever On!* seems like an especially serendipitous capstone to my long years of personal and professional adventures in Middle-earth.

Thank you J.R.R. Tolkien for creating such a magnificent playground.

Thank you to the game developers whose intelligence and creativity built so many epic fantasy worlds on Tolkien's framework. Thank you to the executives who hired me, and to the musicians, singers, and engineers whose talents grace each music score. Finally, I say thank you to the players of every game, and to the fans of every soundtrack – none of this would have been possible without people playing the games and enjoying the music. For more than twenty years this has been an epic creative journey, a grand and glorious adventure, which I shall never forget.

Ever on indeed.

To listen to music from Mines of Moria *and watch music videos from* Riders of Rohan *and* Mordor, *as described in this chapter, please visit:* HUGEsoundRecords.com/Memoir-07

NOTES

1 J.R.R. Tolkien, *The Lord of the Rings Part One: The Fellowship of the Ring*, p. 369; New York: Ballantine Books, 1982.

2 Ibid.

3 Ibid, p. 376.

4 https://www.engadget.com/2012-11-16-call-of-duty-black-ops-2–500-million-24-hours.html?guccounter=1&guce_referrer=aHR0cHM6Ly93d3cuZ29vZ2xlLmNvbS88&guce_referrer_sig=AQAAALicbJxQRoEuq5p5lc93Ik1-Enw5Vs8Tu_WOscsynL0N51bQ3XmUxa0KxiQtf5m09hlDoO7Wh_E_LA2IIu_xAX-LQShlvnIK6m1MaihBasBhuMSXJejv97bNjtjLM-JKEZ58mnfsHYfhQGz2MErnq_Jlp0-XxZpYo2EzUvYILyrD
5 https://www.mmobomb.com/ten-years-making-middle-earth-music-interview-lotro-composer-chance-thomas
6 Ibid.
7 J.R.R. Tolkien, *The Lord of the Rings Part One: The Fellowship of the Ring*, p. 58; New York: Ballantine Books, 1982.

CHAPTER 8

EA Games

CAREER CURRENTS CAN SHIFT unexpectedly, altering shape and trajectory in surprising ways. Catalysts can arise from a variety of motivations, both internal and external.

For example, consider my sojourn as studio audio director with EA Games. In 2007, my family and I were still living near Yosemite National Park, in the foothills of the Sierra National Forest. It was a beautiful spot. But my daughter Tia was approaching high school age, and the local home-schooling resources at our disposal were nearing their apogee. We recognized that Tia needed a richer and more challenging experience in high school, so we began to look elsewhere.

Meanwhile, HUGEsound was in feast and famine mode, enjoying incredible peaks of success interspersed with frustrating stretches of desert. I was not opposed to seeking greener pastures for a while. Around this time, I discovered a job posting for EA's new studio in Salt Lake City, Utah. We had lived in SLC before, and I knew many people in the music business there. Pamela located a charter academy, the Academy for Math, Engineering, and Science, which seemed like a perfect fit for Tia's aptitudes. All of these motivations and circumstances converged to motivate my application for EA's studio audio director position.

I was no shoo-in. This would be a highly competitive application process. EA Games was a juggernaut in the industry. Nintendo's Wii was the hottest thing in gaming, and the market for casual games was taking off like a rocket. EA's new Salt Lake City studio had recently signed a partnership to build casual games for Nintendo's Wii and DS systems, all based on

DOI: 10.1201/9781003199311-9

Hasbro properties. It was an exciting time, and EA Salt Lake was set up to take advantage of it. I determined to put my best foot forward, especially since I knew that rivalry for the job would be stiff.

In my application, I chose to focus on many of the peripheral skills I describe in Chapter 11, rather than emphasizing my composing experience. I also highlighted my team leadership experiences as senior music producer at Sierra, audio director at Tektonic Studios, franchise music director for Vivendi-Universal Games, and even my volunteer service as a Latter-day Saint bishop, which involved a wide range of leadership responsibilities. I shined a spotlight on every relevant skill. The resume was solid.

Of course, there is a natural part of me that thinks I will win every pitch or application I pursue. Confidence is a good thing. But life sometimes unfolds differently than how we envision. I have learned to be OK with a certain degree of ambivalence. Still, I was happy when Jessica called from EA Salt Lake with an invitation to fly out for an interview.

INTERVIEW

How do you feel when you approach a job interview? Are you self-assured, nervous, terrified? I have felt all of those emotions and more during a lifetime of interview experiences. But I have not always controlled them. Once, while being interviewed by an eight-person committee at a game development studio, a programmer and I nearly came to blows. I was prideful and defensive, while he was arrogant and combative. Of course, he was the one with the job, while I was merely the applicant. Instead of reacting smartly with technical answers or redirected questions, I became belligerent toward his entrapment questions filled with code-speak. I almost shouted at him. No surprise, I never got a chance to work with that developer. After how I had behaved in the interview, I did not deserve to.

I wanted things to be different with my interview at EA. No matter how the conversation went, no matter what kinds of technical problems, mental brain-teasers, thinly veiled entrapments, or organizational quandaries they threw at me, I was going to keep my head and respond with intelligence, consideration, and maybe even some humor. That was the plan.

As it turned out, most of the people at EA Salt Lake were gracious, friendly, deferential, and fun. I met with several individually, and then with a small group. My experience meeting Art Director Matt Peterson is illustrative. As I walked across the tile floor to shake his hand, he said, "You had me at *Hobbit*!"

General Manager Vance Cook was the only hard-hitter in the bunch. Vance had owned the company before selling to EA. He had a programming and business background, and I was expecting lots of technical and budget-related questions. I had prepared thoroughly in both areas. He tossed me some tough ones, but my preparation paid off. EA Games was starting an audio department for the first time, and Vance hoped to keep it small. I reassured him that my broad range of skills could get the ball rolling, while also laying the groundwork for building out a small team.

I felt good about the interviews that day. As I looked out the window during my flight back to California, I couldn't help but notice how beautiful Salt Lake City looked at night.

NEGOTIATION

The hoped-for call arrived bringing good news. EA Games offered me the studio audio director job in Salt Lake City. But I was not ready to celebrate just yet. A significant deficit existed between what they were offering and what I needed, before uprooting my family from California and moving them to the Rocky Mountains. I tried unsuccessfully to resolve the gap with HR, but they had limited pocketbook authority. I would have to speak with whoever held the real power at the studio. For EA Salt Lake, that person was Vance Cook. It was time to escalate the negotiation. I made an appointment with Vance to discuss the financial details of my potential employment.

Let us pause this story for an instructive sidebar about negotiation. In any business deal, no one ever gets what they deserve. Each side only gets what they negotiate. A sense of fairness may be part of the negotiation, but you can never count on it.

Very early in my career, I discovered a book entitled, *You Can Have Anything You Want: But You Have to Do More Than Ask*. Studying that negotiating book became a game changer for me, opening my eyes to a transformative way of thinking about transactions. The more I practiced the principles in that book, the more frequently I could extract favorable outcomes from my business dealings.

Next, I read another negotiation book called, *Getting to Yes*. This was a more substantial academic work on the subject. It deepened my understanding of the psychological motivations, which underpin people's tendencies, especially when forced into difficult corners. Some of those insights have been helpful in allowing me to think around counterpart's objections, often well before they revealed them.

Finally, I studied a third book, *Never Split the Difference*, written by a successful FBI negotiator. Its contents gave me several new and additional practical tools for my negotiating toolkit. All of them have proven helpful.

I will go out on a limb and say that no other business skill will impact your bottom line as much as the skill of negotiation. I highly recommend investing as much effort as possible into studying and practicing negotiation in all aspects of your career.

The three books cited earlier are excellent resources. There is also a chapter in my textbook, which specifically addresses negotiating video game music contracts – creative fees, copyrights, licenses, package deals, deliverables, schedules, approvals, revisions, expenses, indemnification, payment methods, additional compensation, performing rights, ancillary usages, scripting your negotiation, etc. This is valuable and immediately actionable information for video game composers. You might consider checking out each of these books from your local library, or adding them to your permanent reference collection.

Now let us return to the story of my negotiation with EA's Vance Cook and see how things played out.

This was a delicate time, because I was far from the only fish in the sea. Although the interviewing teams had preferred me among the finalists, at this early stage of the game there was minimal investment of time, energy, or emotion in my candidacy. I needed to step very carefully in order to preserve any initial trust and build this budding relationship. But I also needed to lean EA gently toward meeting the objectives that were important to me.

Here were my two sticking points:

First, we were at least $15,000 apart on salary terms. I wanted more money than they had budgeted for the position. And it was important to me that I try negotiating to capture some or all of that difference.

Second, EA Games prohibited employees from working on any games besides their own. I had built up too many valuable clients in the video game industry to simply walk away from them. Besides, Craig Alexander and I were already talking about a new music score for *LOTRO*'s expansion, *Mines of Moria*. Composing that score would be a dream gig for me. Somehow, I needed to obtain an exemption from EA to continue scoring video games as a side hustle.

Vance and I began talking about the money first. His initial point was that he had never paid for audio before, nor had he ever created games like the casual games they were embarking on. This was new to him, and as GM, he needed to ensure sufficient budget to cover all aspects of game development, without putting any part of it in jeopardy. He also had limited funds allocated from EA corporate for his employees, and was fiscally constrained by their position policies and restrictions. He presented a compelling rationale to buckle and say, "Sure, I'll take your original offer."

But I'm just not that guy.

Instead, I countered by pointing out that, as EA Salt Lake's sole initial audio hire, I would be carrying an inordinately heavy load – not only in generating audio designs, building pipelines, creating assets, and overseeing implementation, but in building out reasonably equipped audio studios and searching for the next hire(s). In those days, EA stratified its hires into numbered categories. Vance had been approved to hire me at category II, and I persuaded him to submit a request to hire me at the next highest strata. That would add another $5k to the starting salary. But we were still at least $10k apart. That's when I made my move to not only find the other $10k, but also lay the groundwork for getting an outside work exemption approved.

I told Vance that equipping audio studios was a very expensive undertaking. I showed him the costs of a Pro Tools system, SFX libraries, mixing boards, speakers and amps, sequencing software, and virtual instruments. It was a significant amount of money. Then I pointed out that, as a freelancer for many years, I already owned all of that equipment. What if EA leased my equipment and libraries during the day at a discounted rate, in exchange for my use of the gear for personal projects at night? I presented the scenario as a big win for us both. This arrangement would save Vance a major capital expense up front, handing EA a full suite of tools I was already efficient with, while also giving me everything I needed to make the relocation decision.

Vance agreed, and we set the lease amount at $1k per month. The deficit in EA's offer had been eliminated, and the seed had been planted to allow my use of equipment after hours for personal projects. Now I just needed to specify that some of those personal projects happened to be video games.

Bringing up outside video games triggered a strong negative reaction from Vance. But with methodical explanations, I was able to successfully demonstrate that none of the outside games in my side hustle cue would compete in any way with EA Salt Lake's games. As a result, we were able to draft an addendum to my employment contract, which specifically listed all of my existing clients and upcoming contracts, and protected them under an exemption from EA's prohibition policy. Negotiation complete.

With those issues resolved, I officially became an employee of EA Games, Salt Lake City's audio employee number one.

SETTING UP SHOP

On my first day of work, I discovered that there was no place in EA's existing office space that would work for an audio studio. Audio recording and mixing require ample listening space, sonic isolation, acoustic neutrality, and room enough for the equipment. My rig consisted of two connected Yamaha 02R digital mixing consoles sitting in a nine-foot-wide oak mixing desk. Plus two Mac Pro towers, two Dell PC towers, two Dell widescreen monitors, one Dell oversized CRT monitor, two Genelec 1031-A powered speakers, and several racks filled with mounted outboard gear. Not to mention several boxes for my SFX libraries on CD's, plus microphones and stands. I needed a large built-in room, and only cubicles were available in their existing fifth-floor office space.

Not to worry, Vance was a forward thinker and had already made arrangements to lease additional space on the fourth floor. He envisioned growing new dev teams into this space as the partnership with Hasbro expanded. Since no one else was there yet, he asked me to pick out the most suitable space for my own audio studio, and also for those of future hires.

First choice of prime real estate is a huge perk. I did not let that go unnoticed or unappreciated. Vance's goodness toward me was fueling an ever-growing drive to do exceptional work, and take on more tasks than I should before offloading to contractors or other employees. This demonstrates how a great leader can win loyalty and deepen commitment by empowering people with everything they need to be successful. Vance was already showing that kind of leadership in his early dealings with me.

I selected a large isolated office on the north wall, with wide windows opening toward the Ogden finger of the Wasatch mountain range. The size and layout of the room were a perfect fit for the dimensions of my mixing desk. For sonic treatment, I placed acoustic panels and bass traps in targeted spaces around the room, and stuffed thick insulation above the ceiling tiles. When completed, the studio was functional, comfortable, sonically competent, and reasonably isolated. I loved it, and was ready to get to work.

EA Salt Lake had two teams working on Hasbro-themed casual games. One team was figuring out how to build a game around *Nerf Blasters*. The other team was figuring out how to build games based on *Littlest Pet Shop*. Neither was ready for audio assets yet, but they were both getting close.

I met with producers and programming leads from each team to sketch out audio production and implementation pipelines. We sorted out which software engineers would handle audio implementation tasks, what audio software would plug into the game engine, how would we track version control, how would we connect audio to animations, and so on. Those were the kinds of foundational pieces you have to figure out when setting up a framework for audio production in games.

The next step was to take a stab at audio designs for each game in pre-production. The *Nerf* team was struggling to build a viable game design, so I went through many iterations with them. Audio is always at the down-stream mercy of game design. On the other hand, the *Littlest Pet Shop* team had cemented their design, and were building five different versions of their DS game, one for each season of the year, and a fifth game for the Wii. Wrangling each of those products around a compatible audio design required many meetings and a fair amount of compromise. But we got there.

With those pieces in place, I began to generate audio assets. It did not take many months to realize I could not carry the load alone. Contractors could help with specific tasks in a stopgap way. But to crank out the amount of audio needed for all these games, I would have to grow the audio depart-ment a little sooner than originally anticipated. I recommended bringing two additional audio artists onboard, one assigned to each franchise. I would continue to produce assets for each team, and manage the audio development between them. I hired Victor Crews, who had been working as a sound designer since leaving Sierra, and Jeff Meacham, a strong-arm recommendation from one of the producers. Both proved to be excellent hires. They hit the ground running and helped me provide each team with a growing flow of exceptional audio assets. It was also rewarding to be part of an audio team again, just like at Sierra.

Let me close out this chapter with a few stories specific to each game franchise.

NERF

What kid doesn't love *Nerf Blasters*? Heck, I was in my 40s and I loved them! Making a video game built around these iconic toys sounded like so much fun. Hasbro had partnered with Nintendo to create a special *Nerf Blaster* that could switch out a dart canister for a Wii controller. That meant you could fire the Wii in the game simply by pointing and pulling a trigger on your custom *Nerf Blaster*. When finished with the game, you could switch out the Wii controller and slip the dart canister back in to shoot real darts. This had the potential to be a huge success.

My audio team spent a lot of time perfecting the sound of firing the various Blasters. We started by making recordings of each Nerf Blaster specifically featured in the game. And although the recordings gave us the iconic "fffttt" sound, we needed something more. I give credit to Victor Crews for completely transforming the Nerf sounds, blending live recordings with effects such as jet rockets and diesel trucks, synth whooshes and sword swipes.

My sons loved the fact that I was working on this game, and I often brought them to the office for playtesting the game with me. Besides, *Nerf Blasters* could always be found lying around the studio, and impromptu battles often sprung up between us without warning. Devs were as likely to join in as my sons were. It made for a fun, light-hearted atmosphere at work. Eventually, the producers invited the employees to take most of the Blasters home. My family ended up with two or three *Mavericks*, a *Long-Shot* (my favorite), a *Switch-Shot*, and a *Vulcan*, complete with a 25-dart ammunition belt. Oh the battles we had around the house!

Nerf N-Strike was the title given to the release version of the game. Each game box included one custom *Nerf Blaster* called a *Switch-Shot* for the Wii controller. I have to say, *Nerf N-Strike* was one of the most fun video games I ever worked on. I thought it was going to be a huge hit. While sales numbers were respectable at just over a million units worldwide, it never hit the blockbuster heights I had hoped for or even expected.

Nevertheless, an *N-Strike* sequel was in the works when I left EA.

LITTLEST PET SHOP

Honestly, this was one part of the EA gig that I was not initially excited about. Audio Director for *The Littlest Pet Shop*? Hardly the resume builder I dreamed of while working on *King Kong, Marvel*, and *Lord of the Rings* games. But every cloud has its silver lining, and *Littlest Pet Shop* (*LPS*) was no exception.

During my time at EA, I worked on six *LPS* games. The first five were customized versions of the first release – DS games split out into each of the four seasons plus a Wii version. Gameplay revolved around tending your pets and building points through mini-games. The mini-games turned out to be slightly addictive and totally fun. I even found myself playing mini-games for my own entertainment, beyond what was required for the job.

Producing audio assets for these first five games was fairly straight-forward. We created random vocalizations for the dozens of animals in the game, designed sound effects for mini-games, and licensed some cute music tracks to loop in the background.

But for the sixth *LPS* game, a distinctive new game design inspired a bleeding-edge audio innovation that I am still proud of today.

The sixth *LPS* game was story-driven. Newly hired game designer, Amy Adkins, was writing thousands of lines of dialog among the animals to drive the story forward. Since the animals were swappable, each line of dialog could be recited by any one of potentially 20 different animals. Recording that many lines of specific animal dialog would cost a fortune, since EA had recently become signatory to the SAG-AFTRA contract. The memory footprint for that much dialog would also exceed the available space on any DS disc.

I needed an innovative solution. As I pondered how to approach this problem, I realized that all of Amy's script could be roughly grouped into four broad categories – declarations, descriptions, exclamations, and questions, with each sorted by three levels of emotional intensity. That meant 12 conversation states could cover her entire script.

What if the animals in the game made vocalizations, rather than words? Could I use vocalizations to convey the intent of the script in each of those 12 conversation states? And if so, could I limit the number of vocalizations to a reasonable number? This would require some research.

I began to study up on English phonemes, which are the distinct sounds we cobble together to make words in our language. There are 44 phonemes in English, but I did not need to make actual words. I only needed to convey general meaning, offering the illusion of conversation. I also studied the melody of conversation, how our voices lilt up and down as we communicate various kinds of meaning to one another.

Reverse engineering spoken language yielded fascinating insights, some of which had immediate application for solving the hard problem of generating endless animal language in this game.

I began experimenting by recording short vocalizations and stitching them together in various ways to create the illusion of words and sentences. By the end of my research and experimentation, I had identified 16 different phoneme vocalizations that we would need to make this work – sentence starters, sentence enders, sounds for emphasis, connective sounds, throwaway sounds, and a few others. Moreover, I contrived formulas for stringing those vocalizations together, so that they would convey the intended meaning in each of Amy's 12 states of script sentences.

All I needed to record was 16 vocalized phonemes for each animal, and we could cover any conversation possibility in the entire game. That was a massive reduction compared to recording 50,000–60,000 individual lines of dialog!

The illusion of complexity derived from carefully crafted simplicity.

Sixteen vocalizations for each animal, and 12 formulas could convey the meaning of any sentence. It was affordable too, costing only a fraction of the amount needed to record the whole script.

I discussed all of this with Amy, and she agreed to tag each sentence in her script with a marker for one of the 12 formulas. Those markers would trigger programming calls to assemble the audio files in proper order, as outlined in each formula.

The team leadership approved the system, and I began auditioning voice actors for each of the 20 different animals. It was an interesting ask for the actors, having them imagine the sound of a giraffe talking, or a peacock, and then submitting an audition. Voice acting pays well, so I received dozens of auditions. Screening the submissions was an adventure for my ears, and in time the auditions were whittled down to a single voice actor for each animal. The talent was drawn from the Bay Area, so I flew out to EA's Redwood Shores studios near San Francisco, California, to do the recording.

Without question, these were the most unusual recording sessions I had ever produced. For each animal, the selected voice actor would come into the studio and vocalize each of the 16 phonemes. Of course, there were multiple takes of each vocalization. They had to follow specific lilts, deliver precise lengths, and sound convincing as each respective animal. Lots of laughter between takes! You would have enjoyed being a fly on that wall.

I returned from San Francisco with perhaps the most bizarre collection of human noises ever assembled on a single hard drive. Yet, at the conclusion of my editing, it was as if the animals were actually speaking, each in their own "native" tongue, conveying generalized meaning that any English-speaking person could easily understand. So far, so good.

But I had forgotten one critical element of the system. What about animations? Could I convince the animation department to create a library of animations to match our 16 different phonemes? I presented the idea to the team, and the animation manager was not in favor of it. Fortunately, two of the junior animators on the team saw the potential and jumped at the chance to innovate. They each took personal time after hours to create animations matching each phoneme. When we tested it with the Toucan, the results were staggeringly compelling, absolutely sensational. The 12 conversation-state formulas now stitched both audio files *and* animation files together in real time, rendering a convincing illusion of actual words and sentences. Not only had we had made a Toucan talk using Toucan-like sounds, but it was as if the animal was conveying real meaning in English. To see it and hear it was incredibly compelling.

This was coming together brilliantly.

As a final step, I approached the programming team to commit resources to hook up the formula tags which Amy had added to each sentence in her script (1–12) to trigger the audio and matching animation sequences. Unfortunately, that is where things finally fell apart. The assigned programmer procrastinated, pushing this task to his back burner. By the time he started working on it, our development window was drawing to a close. He balked at the amount of work he now realized would be required of him. Skipping completely over Amy's tags and the 12 formulas, he simply coded random calls for both audio and animation. Now the vocalizations and animations were not sequencing in the right order, neither were they matched to one another. This was not acceptable to me, but he pulled a political end around, gaining support from the producer and general manager for his shortcut.

Normally, this was a battle I would fight with all my faculties. But I had just won an audition to score the *Avatar* video game (see Chapter 9), and my attention was now split between trying to ramp up for *Avatar* and tying up loose ends with EA. The *LPS* animal language system I had poured so much intelligence and energy into was going to be a casualty. The programmer won the battle, but in my opinion, lost the war. There had been so much magic in hearing and seeing those animals speak, with the audio and animations aligned together according to the formulas. But a programmer who procrastinated, and did not want to put in extra work short-circuited the magic, delivering a watered-down, dumbed-down, thumbs-down version of the animal language system instead.

Meanwhile, I had bigger problems to address.

AVATAR

Vance Cook was leaving EA and had recruited a new general manager to take his place, bringing in Jon Dean from EA's Florida office. Jon did not approve of my contract exemption, which allowed outside freelancing, and was actively working with EA headquarters to quash my addendum. Meanwhile, *LPS* and *Nerf* projects were screaming toward their respective finish lines, and there was still lots of audio work to be done. Finally, Ubisoft was laying down strict security regulations for everyone working on *Avatar*, and soon that would include me. They would not allow me to start working with them until I had disconnected from EA Games' network and had a privately keyed lock on my door.

I put a proposal on the table to resolve every concern. I would stay at EA until the current games shipped, helping both teams get their audio to the finish line. I would work for EA during the day, then work on *Avatar* at night and on Saturdays. I would disconnect from EA's internal network, have the locks changed on my office door, and get a separate, private Internet hookup. After the current EA games shipped, I would resign from EA and relocate my studio to a converted bedroom in my home. I could even assist in locating a new studio audio director to take my place at EA.

It was a solid proposal, a well-crafted win–win, successfully addressing the needs at both EA and Ubisoft. But Jon Dean was having none of it. It seemed there was only one issue for him. If I decided to work on *Avatar*, I would have to leave EA. That was his ultimatum.

Avatar was everything *LPS* was not. Not only that, the creative fee for scoring *Avatar* was double my annual EA salary. There was no way I was letting that go. My proposal had been fair, productive, and timely. But ultimatums can make any situation untenable.

I tendered my two-week notice.

To watch video from Nerf N-Strike *and hear music from* The Littlest Pet Shop *as described in this chapter, please visit: HUGEsoundRecords.com/ Memoir-08*

CHAPTER 9

Avatar

I WAS ON MY WAY home from San Francisco, having just attended the 2009 Game Developers Conference. Suddenly, my phone began to vibrate. It was a number from Canada.

Music agent Noemie Dupuy, always smart and lively, was on the line. "Chance! I have brilliant news. Ubisoft wants you to pitch for a top-secret new game they're developing. The game is called *Avatar...* and it's from James Cameron!"

I had no idea what *Avatar* meant. But I definitely knew about James Cameron. Any possibility of working with one of Hollywood's most successful and innovative directors was an opportunity to be seized with vigor. Count me in.

Only problem was, I had a full-time gig. I was a studio audio director for EA Games. We were in crunch mode preparing to ship two new titles. One of the titles featured a complex AI voice generator for animated creatures based on English phonemes. I had invented this voice generating system from the ground up and was deep into fixing bugs. You may recall that story from the last chapter.

Point is, my plate was full and the *Avatar* demo was due in two weeks. I was unsure if I could make the submission cutoff, but I asked Noemie to send over the pitch materials anyway. Just in case.

THE PITCH

Most pitch packages contain a detailed overview of the game design, plus video capture, screenshots, and other relevant goodies. Not this one.

DOI: 10.1201/9781003199311-10

Avatar's pitch package offered only a flimsy game description that boiled down to something like this:

> Explorers from Earth mine alien jungle planet.
> Conflict ensues.

Now here is the funny thing. Thin as that description was, I instinctively knew what it sounded like. As it says in *Composing Music for Games*, "Music scoring is a language ... where predictable expectations exist for how music conveys specified meaning and context."[1] Because of such predictable expectations, even those few words gave me everything I needed to envision a fitting demo for the game. I decided to go for it.

How would you approach a demo pitch like that? What instruments would you use? How much music would you send? Which processing would you apply to the tracks? Lots of questions to explore and resolve!

The approach I took may not surprise you. In an all-night composing session, I created an exotic original theme that underscored exploration, questing, and combat modes. I streamlined the demo to a single piece of music, about three-minutes long, progressing like a story through each represented game state. The motif repeated again and again with variations throughout. I hoped this theme would bedevil listeners long after the demo was over.

I selected a native American flute to sing the melody, processed by sending a L/R ping-pong delay into deep reverb. The rhythm sprang to life with spirited hand percussion bouncing over giant tribal drums. A standard orchestral palette played along underneath, warm and wide. Dissonant electronic pads and pulses brought additional color and flavor to the sound.

The all-nighter was a success and the demo came together just before dawn. Off it went to Montreal, into the infamous and indeterminate black hole of anxious waiting, which every pitching composer knows all too well.

This time the wait was mercifully short. Five or six days after receiving my demo, Noemie called again. She said that James Cameron's brother David, along with key members of the game team, had reviewed the submissions and selected me for the project. I was thrilled!

But then came an unexpected caveat. They only wanted me for one half of the score. They wanted me to create music for the indigenous species (Na'vi) part of the game. A second composer's demo had more fully captured the essence of the military industrial complex (RDA) in his music. The team wanted the other composer to do the RDA half of the score.

I love my fellow composers in the game industry, I really do. And I admire their work. But this situation created a problem for me. EA Games was changing management at my studio, and the new GM would not let me keep my job while simultaneously scoring *Avatar*. If I wanted to work on *Avatar* at all, I would have to resign from EA. But since this contract offer from Ubisoft was for only half of a score. I could not afford the financial risk.

After stewing about this overnight, I decided to try a very bold move. I decided to make a play for the whole score. I made my pitch to Noemie, and she gently floated the idea to the team. They did not like it at all. They worried that a single composer would never complete the score in time. Nor did they think that both Na'vi and RDA musical styles could come from a single voice.

THE NEGOTIATION

It is always risky to rock the boat. Especially in a profession like composing, where supply far outweighs demand. There are ALWAYS plenty of other composers lined up behind you, ready to take your spot at a moment's notice. Unless I backed down, there was a good chance I would blow this whole thing.

But I was in a tough spot. I wanted to score *Avatar* but could not afford to quit EA for half of a music scoring contract.

I decided to write a letter to the *Avatar* team directly addressing their concerns. I would need to come across as confident and passionate, but not greedy or arrogant. I needed to be persuasive but not overbearing. And I needed to send it within just a few hours. No pressure.

This is what I wrote to the team (excerpts from the letter):

> Regarding the tight schedule and large amount of music needed:
> We are more likely to rise to great achievement in the face of great challenge. We are more likely to find profound inspiration in the face of profound difficulty. By our very human natures, we are more naturally rallied to our finest efforts by a daunting task. The simple, the easy, the ordinary – these lack the power to reach the deepest part of our natures, therefore failing to draw out the superlative that lies within us. Only by extending our grasp to the very apex can we reach and deliver the otherwise unreachable.
> A case in point is James Horner's experience in scoring the final climactic scene of *Aliens* for James Cameron. In the insanity of all the reshooting and re-editing that took place because of Cameron's

intense focus on details (another hallmark of greatness), Horner had only three weeks to create the entire score. I've never forgotten the interview where Horner describes pushing himself to all extremes, detailing a thirty-six-hour straight composing session where he scores the final scene. Not surprisingly, it's the music from that very scene that producer Gale Ann Hurd says is "the signature cue from the film" and has found a resonance far beyond the film, being used in countless action film trailers to this day.

My team and I thrive on intensity. I once scored thirteen commercials for an international client in sixteen hours. The haunting and award-winning game theme from *King Kong* was created during a single intense all-nighter, with the Montpellier team waiting across the ocean. We do amazing things under a deadline.

Regarding the two very different styles of music required to underscore the Na'vi and the RDA:

Great veteran composers, like great veteran actors, possess tremendous range. Consider the actress Meryl Streep, and her performances in two recent films, *Doubt* and *Mamma Mia*. They couldn't have been more diverse roles. Neither could she have delivered more perfectly for each film. Great veteran composers also do this. Consider James Newton Howard. His scores for *The Sixth Sense, Dinosaur* and *Snow Falling on Cedars* couldn't have been more dissimilar, yet each is perfectly on target.

Likewise, my own range of voices is expertly diverse. Consider the scores from *Lord of the Rings Online, King Kong, The ChubbChubbs, Left Behind, Quest for Glory* and *Inspire: The Chicago Spire Art Film*. A more diverse collection of music may be difficult to find! But each delivers the right musical voice, and each delivered award-winning scores in every case.

The Montreal team faces an important and exciting decision. I hope these thoughts will offer encouragement to the team, and build their confidence in entrusting the [full] *Avatar* score to my veteran experience. There's nothing I would like more than to dive deeply with them – and deliver an *Avatar* game score that surpasses everyone's hope and ambitions. I look forward to the team's decision.

Somehow that long letter did the trick. It allayed the team's concerns and gave them enough confidence in my skillset and passion to hand me the full contract.

And what an empowering lesson that taught me!

I learned how essential it is to ask for what you really want. I learned that it is important to be polite and persuasive when making a point. It is also useful to have a representative who can buffer the discussion. Agent Noemie Dupuy did that for me. She sent up the trial balloon about using just one composer, and then gave me the team's feedback. She let the team know I would be sending a letter. But at the end of the day, I was still the one who had to write that letter. I was still the one who had to find arguments that would address the team's concerns, persuading them that I was proposing a leap forward rather than a stumble backward.

Yes, we need to be very clear about what we want in a negotiation, and maybe even in life. We need to seek our goals in a respectful and professional way. We can all benefit from developing the skill of persuasion. It was a very empowering lesson for me.

The fully executed *Avatar* contract arrived on a sunny afternoon in late April. I tendered my two-week resignation notice to EA Games the same day.

INTO THE FIRE

That is how I secured the *Avatar* gig. Turns out, getting the gig was the easy part.

The music design called for nearly four and a half hours of music tracks. The schedule allowed just 70 days to compose the score, plus another month or so to produce it. What had I gotten myself into?

Complicating matters, I wanted to harmonize my video game score with the film score. Earlier in my career, I scored several games that were tied to film IP, but I never had access to the corresponding film music. That disconnect always seemed counterintuitive to me, and I wanted this project to be different. I approached Cameron's producer Jon Landau and suggested that he connect me with film composer James Horner. I wanted to understand Horner's approach from the ground up, enabling me to reflect his film score sensibilities in the game music. I thought that would bring a strong sense of kinship to our respective projects. Landau said he would look into it.

Meanwhile, the development team flooded me with content, tons of screenshots, cut scenes, and gameplay capture. This would be the world's first stereoscopic 3D video game and it looked incredible. *Avatar* had the potential to be a runaway hit.

Days were ticking by with no reply from Landau about a Horner meeting. I had to start writing three or four minutes of new music daily to stay on schedule. I wrote like crazy, lots of action beds, leaving room to hopefully work in a film theme once I was exposed to it.

Still, the call didn't come. Twenty-five percent of the game's score was written. Then 45% of the score was written. Then 60% of the score was written. Would I ever get a chance to hear the film music and coordinate the two scores? Finally, the call came. Landau had arranged for me to meet with James Horner. I was heading to Malibu, California.

JAMES HORNER

At the end of a long winding driveway, in the foothills outside Malibu, sits a stationary guard house just left of a tall wrought-iron gate. I pulled up to the gate, driving a modest rental car. Simon Landry, a music supervisor from Ubisoft's Montreal studio, was sitting next to me in the passenger seat. A heavy-set man emerged from the guardhouse wearing dark sunglasses and a security vest. Definitely packing a sidearm. He got right to business, "What's your name? Why are you here?"

I told him our names, and he scanned a clipboard, then made a checkmark about half way down the page. "Go ahead." As the gate opened, a relaxed-looking figure emerged from the rambling ranch house and walked toward us. It was Simon Rhodes, Horner's long-time engineer.

We exchanged pleasantries, and he motioned us into the house, offering to give us a quick tour. The interior was elegant, with beautiful woodwork, expensive flooring, and modern lighting. Everything was well-cared for.

The highlight of the tour was seeing the dining room. Not your ordinary table and chairs. In fact, there was no table and there were no chairs. Instead, there stood a nine-foot grand piano, lid raised, surrounded by an array of expensive Neumann microphones. I commented to Rhodes, "Wow, I love Horner's home." He gave me a cockeyed look and said, "Home? You think this is Horner's home?" He laughed and then continued, "This isn't his home. This is the flat they rented for him to write the film score."

There are moments that come along in life, which shatter your paradigm about how the world works. This was one of those moments. My payday for composing and producing *Avatar*'s video game music was in the healthy six figure range, enough to pay off a mortgage and invest some cash for a rainy day. By far the most money I had ever made from a music score, *Avatar* had elevated me to the top of the game music business. And yet, in the blink of an eye, I felt like the lofty pinnacles of video game music were merely an ant on the boot of the blockbuster film music business.

My mind circled back to the thought again, like maybe I had misunderstood it the first time. "This is the place they *rented* for him to write the score?" I was incredulous, but Rhodes and Landry were already heading up the stairs. I followed behind, wondering what other shocks to the system would greet us on the second floor.

We walked down a long hallway, toward a large and brightly lit room packed with audio gear. Hunched over a keyboard when we entered the room was James Horner.

Horner straightened himself, and turned to face us. He smiled, and held out his hand, "Hi, I'm Jim." This was my first clue that maybe the preconceived notions I had harbored about top film composers was wrong. I thought he would treat me as an irritant. I thought he would begrudge the time. I imagined him to be vain, filled with his own magnificence, looking down his nose at me like… well, like an ant on his boot.

I was completely, embarrassingly wrong.

The man was gracious, engaging, solicitous. He was humble, interested, and interesting. He treated us as peers, equals in the grand adventure of music-making.

He was also brilliant. As he played cue after cue, describing elements of palette, harmonic language, theme, color, and texture, I was enthralled, feverishly taking notes, soaking up every detail.

Time flew by, and Horner was about to play the last piece for us. This was a new cue he would premier for James Cameron later that afternoon. As he prepared to play the tune, he paused and began offering a series of disclaimers, "Now we haven't mixed it yet, and the percussion samples are only temporary, and I'm not sure about the vocal harmony we tried on measure 14, and, and, and …"

As he trailed off, I thought to myself, "Dude, don't you know who you are? You're JAMES HORNER! You're the musical voice of *The Rocketeer, The Wrath of Khan, Braveheart, Titanic!*" And yet, here he was, frantically trying to lower our expectations before playing a brand-new cue.

In that very moment I realized that, in some ways, he is just like the rest of us. Making disclaimers before we play new music for someone. Always nervous about how a freshly composed track will be received. I have done that a hundred times myself. For just one moment, in that moment, I felt that James Horner and I were truly peers.

And then he pushed play.

A gorgeous, anthemic, celebratory song began to emerge from the speakers. On the screen, a small group of Na'vi figures climbed up twisted vines hanging from a floating pod of Hallelujah Mountains. As they scrambled ever higher, passing a waterfall, soaring Banshees swept past, reaching heavenward. Music entwined with picture in perfect symbiosis. The orchestra was a fluid motion, the nasal chanting swirled effortlessly. I was completely mesmerized. This track, *Climbing Up Iknumaya - The Path to Heaven,* is one of the world's great moments in film music. And I heard it first in a rented writing house, introduced with a flurry of disclaimers, from a humble master of the craft, nervous about how two video game guys might react.

James Horner taught me so much, and not just about music. He taught me that brilliance can come coupled with grace. Success does not have to breed arrogance. And at some level, all humans are peers. Even if just for a moment.

PRODUCTION

I returned from Malibu, California, to my writing studio in Bountiful, Utah, totally invigorated. Horner had sent me home with his entire work-in-progress film score. I had every cue in its raw state. I also had copious notes from his mentoring on how he approached *Avatar*'s film music. I was ready to rumble.

First order of business was integrating what I had learned into my own score, particularly the movie's main theme. Within a week, I had written several new cues, faithfully reflecting his scoring approach. I also worked his theme into several of my existing cues. Off they went to the team in Montreal.

Days later I got an unexpected call from the developers asking about the new music. "What is this?" I was asked with a heavy French-Canadian accent. I explained that I had integrated Horner's scoring language and movie theme into some of the new and existing cues. "We don't like it," came the shocking reply. "It's too much nice. It needs more drums," they added.

Too much nice?

More Drums???

I was stunned. And upset. My desire to create a close integration between the film score and the game score was disintegrating. What went wrong? It took me a minute to realize that, for all its action and adventure, the *Avatar* movie was basically a love story. The game, on the other hand, was wall-to-wall search and destroy. Light bulb moment – I could probably use Horner's instrumental palette, harmonic foundation, and parallel textures in my score. But the tenderness, the reaching, the lofty mysticism, and above all the gorgeous love theme – any of those elements from the film would have to be expunged from my game score. Well, mostly expunged. I still found a few relevant moments to secretly weave them in.

Meanwhile, I was running out of time. Recording sessions were already booked in Los Angeles, Seattle, and Salt Lake City. Thirty-five percent of the score was still unwritten. Those were tough days, long days! I would compose all day and into the night. My head would drop heavily down on the keyboard while I mustered just enough energy to write a little more. The process continued until I was slumped on the keyboard far longer than I was writing. At that point, I would slide out of my chair onto the floor, curl up in a sleeping bag, and crash for a couple of hours.

This continued for days on end, week after week, with only Sundays to spare me. I never worked on Sundays, which probably saved my health. As a side note, the "no Sunday" practice arose from both a religious conviction and a survival instinct. I have carried that practice throughout my career.

Los Angeles

One of the things I negotiated for in this gig was a big production budget. Maybe not a blockbuster film-sized production budget, but big enough to track the best brass players in the world, the studio brass players in Los Angeles. One of my composer friends asked me what sort of brass parts I was going to write for the score. I told him, "Whatever I want. When you record the top brass players in the world, there's nothing they can't play!"

Still, I was nervous walking into the Newman building on the Fox lot. So much breathtaking film music had been made in that place, literal film music history! I was still carrying the stigma of being "just a video game composer" and I did not know how these world-class session musicians were going to react to me, or to my music. I was about to find out.

John Rodd was the chief engineer on this session. I hand-picked John based on his years of experience engineering in that very room. Plus, he was a regular at GDC and I liked him. A few minutes after I arrived, John suggested that we walk out onto the sound stage where the musicians were setting up. I bashfully followed him in, where he introduced me to everyone. I began telling them how honored I was to be there, and that I felt a little intimidated, when trumpeter Rick Baptist climbed down from his third level riser, and walked straight up to me. Rick is a pretty big guy, even bigger with his arms wide open in a loud Hawaiian shirt. He had an ear-to-ear grin on his face. "Welcome to LA!", he bellowed, and gave me a big bear hug. Everyone was smiling. They all seemed so eager to be in the studio. Rick set me instantly at ease and ignited incredible positive energy for the session.

Paul Taylor was there too. Paul is an in-demand orchestrator who was living in Southern California. We started working together in 2005 when he did the sheet music prep work for my *King Kong* score. He is an excellent conductor too. I hired him for both roles on *Avatar*. He was excited to be there, looking forward to hearing people like Rick (trumpet), Wayne Bergeron (trumpet), Steve Becknell (French horn), Phil Teele (bass trombone), and Alex Iles (tenor trombone) blow this score right off the page.

Oh man, did they ever! Hour after hour they played – bright, tight, punchy, in tune, on time, just the right phrasing, just the right tone. Killer licks, monster blats, enormous swells… it was glorious. Glorious!

Seattle

I had arranged to record strings in Seattle, Washington at Bastyr Chapel. As is my custom, I arrived early enough to meet the engineering team and introduce myself to some of the musicians. Quite the opposite experience from the sunny dispositions I encountered in LA, these musicians were all dark clouds and cold shoulders. For whatever reason, none were interested in making my acquaintance or hearing anything about the score they were about to record. I was a little rattled by their indifference. And definitely disappointed.

This was not my first time in Seattle for a recording session. I had recorded *King Kong* at Studio X years earlier and had a terrific experience. But that was back in the day. The musicians seemed so excited to do session work back then. But on this day, the day of my *Avatar* session, for whatever reason, they seemed indifferent and maybe even a little put out.

Regardless, the show must go on. You have to make the best of whatever situation you find yourself in. I gave a pep talk to start the session and we began cranking through the charts. Everything turned out just fine. The musicians performed well and we got all the tracks we needed. It just was not as magical as recording in LA.

Salt Lake City

I had tracked percussion, woodwinds, and soloists in Salt Lake City before going to LA. Now I was back in Utah, heading into the home stretch. We were screaming toward the finish line, with enormous amounts of music to edit and mix. Mixing artist Mike Roskelley set up two editing rigs for me in his attic. I hired a local editor to assist, and split my time between editing tracks in Roskelley's attic, and running downstairs to guide the mixing process in the mixing suite. I eventually had to hire a third editor, Richie Nieto, who worked long distance for us from Toronto, Canada. All four of us were going around the clock for days. It was brutal.

I would like to say something important here about the editing process. After you finish tracking, and before you mix, it is critically important to go through all the takes and splice together the very best parts. You may also need to slide part of a phrase here or slip part of a note there, just to make sure everything hits right in the pocket. Dynamics can be pushed and pulled to create more impactful phrasing. The editing phase takes your tracks from good to fabulous.

The mix is important too. I think most people realize that. Of course, the magic has to be in the tracks already, but a great mix can shine a white-hot spotlight on all the best parts. No one does that better for my music than Mike Roskelley. Our collaboration reached new heights during the *Avatar* mix.

Mike had a massive monitor hanging up on the wall, about 12 feet in front of his mixing chair. Pro Tools was displayed there, and I would stand next to the monitor while we mixed, pointing my finger at various tracks, tracing lines for volume curves, FX sends, slight timing adjustments, EQ, whatever I was hearing in my head. He would dial it in perfectly, transparently. Other times, I would lay on the couch at the back of the room and describe something in very nebulous, esoteric terms. He would say, "I know just what we need," and pull out some wild effect, or carve the perfect EQ notch, or really whatever was needed. So often he was spot on.

But we are also human, and not the *same* human. Occasionally, we did not exactly share a Vulcan mind-meld. That was especially true during the mixing of a track called, *Aerial Combat Acrobatics*. This piece was a barn-burner, a climactic action track bristling with brass riffs and sizzling with string runs. Plus plenty of thundering percussion throughout. I really wanted this one to shine. I remember when Mike played me his initial draft, the strings were murky and the brass placement felt odd. We talked about it. We worked at it. But it was not coming together. I described what I wanted to hear differently, and Mike said he would take another shot at it.

The next day he played a second version of the mix for me. This time the strings were slightly brittle and the brass sounded small. We worked at it again, and hit a dead end. I came back the next day, but once again, the mix was not hitting the target.

That was a tough conversation. After I described where the mix still fell short of my expectations, Mike was not happy with me. He is a real artist in his own right, and one of my favorite collaborators. But none of that changes the fact that he had not hit this particular target yet. Good enough was not good enough for this music score. It had to sound great.

We took a break, then came back and worked at it one more time. He invented some new process and it finally locked the brass into perfect placement. That opened up more space for the strings, which now also fell into place. The whole track was beginning to mesh. I slipped out to grab some lunch for us, and when I returned to preview the mix, it was smokin' hot. Every instrument had found its own tightly defined sonic space and the colors were dialed in to perfection. So good!

REFLECTION

One hundred and ten days passed from the time I wrote the first note until the final cues were delivered to the team. In spite of the "great challenge" and "profound difficulty" predicted in my letter, everything ultimately came together. The dev team was ecstatic with the music. Na'vi tracks sounded tribal, atmospheric, and other-worldly. RDA music was militant, earthy, and action-oriented. The score's high fidelity attracted several music award nominations, including Music of the Year and Best Video Game Score. The whole experience was a win–win–win across the board for all parties involved, a best-case scenario.

At the Game Developers Conference following the game's release, I presented a postmortem lecture on my *Avatar* experience. The talk was well-attended by a gracious audience. It must have resonated with the crowd, because a few weeks later I received GDC's Ace of Spades Award for the highest rated talk of the conference. It was the first and only time an audio talk has won the award.

To listen to excerpts from the Avatar video game score, as described in this chapter, please visit: HUGEsoundRecords.com/Memoir-09

NOTE

1 Chance Thomas, *Composing Music for Games: The Art, Technology and Business of Video Game Scoring*, p. 3; Boca Raton: CRC Press, 2016.

CHAPTER 10

G.A.N.G., GDC, and GSC

THERE I SAT, RIFFING on the piano, singing my heart out in Tommy Tallarico's living room. It was an impromptu performance of *Point of Know Return* by Kansas, given to a room filled with composers and sound designers. Everyone was taking their turn on the ivories, and there was so much talent. This was my posse.

I was attending my second Game Developers Conference (GDC), meeting scores of interesting, intelligent, and creative people. I met them in workshops and at restaurants. I met them inside the conference center, lingering in the hallways or sitting outside on the steps. I met them at Tommy's house and at the airport. We talked of our individual past and collective future. We traded war stories and ambitions. These were my professional peers, my music tribe. I finally felt as if I was settling into the right corner of the entertainment world.

GDC became an annual touchstone for me. It was a place where I had a platform, where I could speak out at workshops to evangelize live orchestras and studio musicians in video game music. I could promote joining the Grammy Awards campaign. I could give postmortems and share important lessons I had learned the hard way, so that the next generation of composers could step on my shoulders and move the industry toward a better future.

It was also a place to learn and connect. I gave workshops but also attended them. I shared ideas with my peers but also collected ideas from them. GDC happened once each year, and it was an important ritual for me to remain connected to this thriving, professional community.

DOI: 10.1201/9781003199311-11

Back to *Point of Know Return*. After a long day of GDC talks and work-shops, Tommy had invited me and several other game audio folks to his home in San Luis Obispo, California. As I introduced myself to some of the other guests, I was surprised at the spontaneous camaraderie blossom-ing between us. It was so natural. It would be so great if we could keep this going throughout the year.

G.A.N.G.

That may have been what Tommy was asking himself too. Later that same year in Austin, Texas at George Sanger's Bar-B-Que audio retreat, Tommy proposed founding a guild for game audio professionals. He sug-gested the name, Game Audio Network Guild (G.A.N.G.), and proposed providing the seed money to launch the org himself.

I had not been able to attend, but after Bar-B-Que, Tommy called me to share the idea. I loved it. We could build a community of game audio pro-fessionals with online forums for connecting and sharing throughout the year, a leadership group to influence audio education, and even our own awards program. Why wait for the Grammy Awards? We could honor our peers all by ourselves.

Tommy invited me to join the newly forming Board of Directors, and we began meeting regularly to flesh out the purposes and means of build-ing the organization. We decided to launch the guild at the upcoming GDC in 2002. I suggested we pass out T-shirts with the G.A.N.G. logo on the front, and we added this phrase to the back:

The G.A.N.G.'s all here!
Are You?

Today I have almost 20 years of retrospect to look back on this. With that perspective, I can say without equivocation that I believe G.A.N.G. did more to create the rare, mutually supportive game audio culture enjoyed by people in this industry today, than any other effort by any other individual or group. The camaraderie we share, the open collabo-ration, the ubiquitous encouragement, the mutual cheering even for a competitor ... this culture is rare. Let me tell you a story, which illus-trates just how rare it is.

Many years ago, after spending the day at the Electronic Entertainment Expo (E3) in Los Angeles, I was having dinner with a large group of game music composers at a restaurant not far from the convention center. We were talking about our latest projects, complimenting each other's latest work, discussing new insights and ideas, and sharing contacts with each other. None of that was out of the ordinary for us.

After a time, I noticed a sharply dressed man sitting alone at a far table continually watching us. He seemed curious, puzzled, wanting to come over, but not quite able to muster the will. Finally, I think his curiosity got the better of him.

He walked straight up to my table, looked me in the eyes, and said, "Who ARE you guys?"

I told him we were all professional composers working in the video game industry. He seemed dumbfounded. He stared at us without speaking for an uncomfortably long time. "But ... why are you hanging out with *each other*?" he eventually blurted out. I told him we loved being together and loved learning from one another. We were peers, fierce competitors even, but we were also friends. He was stunned. "Well, I'm a film composer, and you will never see anything like this among film composers." He described his corner of the industry as a tussle of rampant opportunism, backstabbing, dishonesty, and other sordid practices. His description called to mind the words of San Francisco Examiner columnist Hunter S. Thompson, who wrote about the record industry in the 1980s: "The music business is a cruel and shallow money trench, a long plastic hallway where thieves and pimps run free, and good men die like dogs. There's also a negative side." We invited our new film composer friend to join us and try out a different experience.

A full story of G.A.N.G. is well beyond the scope of this chapter, and believe me, there is much to tell! I will share just a few stories with you here.

Early in G.A.N.G.'s history, George Sanger was serving with me on the Board of Directors. He brought forward accusations of financial malfeasance at one of our Board meetings. He raised other concerns too, such as G.A.N.G.'s endorsement of commercial products in return for donations to the guild. None of us were attorneys, we were all composers or sound designers, so George's concerns led to a higher level of legal scrutiny in our dealings. That was a good thing, helping us to tighten the focus of the guild's efforts.

G.A.N.G. shed many peripheral forays, and relocated its energy among three primary efforts – (1) supporting and empowering connectivity between members of the game audio community, (2) guiding the audio track at GDC, and (3) the G.A.N.G. Awards.

G.A.N.G. AWARDS

As G.A.N.G.'s Board developed an approach to nominating and judging award-worthy content, I championed the importance of having a completely transparent awards process. I wanted an awards program where every entry had an equal chance to be thoroughly considered. Tommy suggested a system where anyone could nominate their own work, with no entry fee, thus encouraging the broadest possible outreach.

We decided that the Board of Directors would initially screen entries and vote for five top selections in each category, thus distilling the many entries to five Finalists. Tommy and his brother Mike set up a spreadsheet for the Board, with every submission linked so we could simply click–listen–judge and vote, submission by submission. With this process, every submission had a chance to be heard by everyone on the Board, with an equal chance to be among the Finalists. I liked that.

The Finalists, selected by the Board in each category, were then presented to the general membership in a straightforward, democratic awards selection process. Each Finalist was uploaded to a website with its own public link. G.A.N.G. members could progress from category to category, listening for themselves to each and every Finalist, and vote their conscience. There would be no special interests controlling the vote. Winners would be selected based on the merit of listening. I loved the purity of it.

Sigh… I was so naïve. Within a few short years, the mass of submissions had completely overwhelmed the 12 members of our Board. It got so bad I only had time to screen music submissions (not dialog or SFX). Even then, on my first pass I only listened to the first 30 seconds or so. From that initial listening, I would narrow my review to 10 or 15 finalists, and then listen to those again for the first minute. Then I would cast a vote for my top five in each of the music categories. I learned that other members of the Board were doing even less, some simply relying on the popularity of a title to render their votes. Submissions had ballooned to so many entries across so many categories that the time commitment was completely out of hand.

I reasoned that at least the members would take time to listen to five Finalists before making their selections. But as it turned out, very few Finalists were listened to by the general membership at all. We could track how many files were accessed on the voting site and the numbers were paltry. I also discovered that the biggest companies were wielding undue influence on the voting process. For example, one year while I was working in-house for EA Games, I received a blanket email from one of the senior audio directors at the company "instructing" all EA audio employees to vote for one particular EA title. I was incensed! That completely violated G.A.N.G.'s ideal of merit-driven awards. Similarly, I was told that Sony audio teams regularly voted in block.

This was anathema to everything I believed in, everything I had worked for in supporting and promoting these awards.

After many years, I took it upon myself, as a senior member of the Board of Directors, to insure that at least the Finalist selections were purely merit-based, as much as possible. At one of our board meetings, I raised my concerns and volunteered to lead the music selection process for the foreseeable future.

I recruited 32 screeners, organized into two committees of 16 people each – carefully selected from a broad cross section of experienced composers, music directors, music press, and even music students – and divided the several music categories between them. This would scatter the burden of screening submissions across many shoulders, making the process doable, enjoyable, and as objective as possible. I was very pleased with how things turned out that first year. Every submission received significant listening from all 32 committee members in their relative categories, and the Finalists reflected *the merits* of the submissions, not their well-known-ness. This was a huge victory for me, and for all the members of our guild.

Unfortunately, the following year, some members of my music committees ghosted their responsibilities, and a handful of submissions were not reviewed thoroughly. I became upset and disillusioned, resigning from my leadership role over the music awards. Later that year, I also resigned from the Board of Directors. After 17 years at my post, I reasoned it was time to invite new blood into our leadership group, to wield a fresh perspective and influence the future of the guild. The pure meritocracy I had long envisioned for the awards never fully materialized. But we did get very close one year.

GDC

In my textbook, *Composing Music for Games: The Art, Technology and Business of Video Game Scoring*, I make the point that vanguards and experts win. In other words, those who are among the first and those who are among the best in a particular market are generally the most successful.

Combining the success of *Quest for Glory V: Dragon Fire*, one of the first live orchestral scores in gaming, with my push for a game music Grammy category, I seemingly became both expert and vanguard overnight. Thus, I became a desirable candidate to speak at GDC early in my game music career. The first year I spoke about producing a live orchestra. The next year, I spoke about the Grammy Awards campaign.

For the next 15 or 16 years, I spoke annually at the conference in one form or another. A couple of highlights are worth mentioning.

For 12 years, I served as a panelist for the Music Demo Derby. This is how the Derby worked. Composers would submit a one-minute original music track, as if they were submitting a scoring demo to a potential client. Members of the panel would listen to the track, and then respond spontaneously, riffing in real time, making comments about each submission. I loved hearing the variety and originality of music submitted each year, then offering my encouragement and sometimes constructive criticism. There were always four members of the panel, and each year I would share the table with superstars like Chuck Doud, Paul Lipson, Jason Hayes, and many more. Composers such as Sean Beeson, Wilbert Roget, Anastasia Devana, and others had their first real exposure to the industry during these GDC Demo Derbies. I always enjoyed the process. I felt like this was one way to give back and encourage the rising generation.

One year at GDC, I had the great honor of interviewing Nobuo Uematsu (*Final Fantasy, Chrono Trigger*) for a special session of the conference. The room was packed, of course. Uematsu-san was in high spirits and cherry picked a number of inspiring, educational, and entertaining stories to share with us. For example, when asked about writing music for early game systems (limited to three-note polyphony), he described the experience as liberating. Instead of cramping his creativity, it shifted his focus to writing adventurous melodies, rather than relying on production. He also shared his idea to adapt rock music from the 60s and 70s for live orchestra, leading to his most famous composition, *One-Winged Angel*. Uematsu-san was gracious, engaging, and laughed easily and often throughout our interview. One funny anecdote he told on himself was that he occasionally took off his pants to compose, dancing around the house in his underwear. Other times, he would soak in his bathtub for inspiration. Truly, he was one-of-a-kind!

Another year, I gave a talk about composing and producing the video game score for *James Cameron's Avatar*, entitled "Avatar Game Score Postmortem: High-Stake Challenges and Universal Takeaways." The room was packed. Tommy Tallarico introduced the talk in his typically flamboyant style. Recording engineer and mixer John Rodd shared the stage with me and played all the audio clips. I had worked hard preparing and practicing what I believed would be an inspirational and educational talk. I hoped it would resonate with the audience in all the right ways.

Sometimes you hit on all cylinders. I cannot explain why some moments come together more magically than others, but this was one of those moments. It felt like the audience was hanging on every word. The room seemed to be filled with friends cheering me on from start to finish.

After that conference, I received a surprise present. GDC's executive team gifted a customized deck of cards to each of the top 52 speakers at the conference, those who received the highest ratings that year. Each card was backed with the photo of a conference speaker. The highest rated speaker was placed on the Ace of Spades card. I flipped the Ace of Spades over and was shocked to see my photo there. I was the Ace of Spades! The *Avatar* game score postmortem had received the highest rating of any talk at the conference that year. Not bad, not bad at all.

After winning the Ace of Spades, I was invited to join GDC's Audio Advisory Board. My role was to assist in vetting submissions to speak in the audio track of the conference. I also assisted in advising and mentoring selected speakers with the preparation of their talks. That was a wonderful experience, and I served on the Audio Advisory Board for seven productive years.

My involvement at GDC gave a tremendous boost to my career. Several music contracts trace their origins directly to GDC, including *DOTA 2, Faeria, Roguebook*, and *Lego Star Wars III* – all of which you can read about later in this book. I nearly sold my business because of a meeting at GDC in 2013, giving me a dress rehearsal for the actual sale of my business three years later. The textbook I authored for CRC Press got its first jump start at GDC. I received awards and handed out awards at GDC. Friendships were formed and forged there. GDC was an annually important touchstone for me, professionally and personally. I would encourage anyone who is serious about a career in video game music to attend and participate regularly.

GSC

GameSoundCon (GSC) was launched by Brian Schmidt in 2009, in part to create a second annual gathering for the game audio community at large. The first two GSC conferences were held in San Francisco, California. Thereafter, the conference has been held annually in Los Angeles, California, at the downtown Biltmore Hotel.

Brian asked me to give the first GSC keynote address. In thinking about what to say, I remembered a favorite story about persistence and creative determination from music agent Bob Rice. If there is anything young composers and sound designers need, it is persistence and creative determination! In giving this keynote, I wanted to involve more than just the ears of the audience. Studies in neuroscience show that the greater number of senses involved in an experience, the more memorable it tends to be. A key piece of Bob's persistence story revolved around donuts, so I began looking for a donut shop shortly after arriving in San Francisco. Wouldn't it be fun to involve the audience's sense of taste, touch, and smell while I shared Bob's story?

I was on foot, and in those prehistoric times, there was no map or navigator on my phone. I did a lot of asking around for a donut shop, and the locals were helpful, pointing me this way and that until I found my way. The smell of sugary dough told me I was getting close long before I saw the sign. I stepped into the shop and ordered 120 donuts from the black-haired Asian woman behind the counter, ten boxes of a dozen donuts each. My plan was to begin the keynote by passing boxes of donuts around to everyone in the audience. But I had not considered the logistics of getting the donuts back to the conference center. It was an awkward juggle carrying ten boxes of donuts down the streets of San Francisco, hoofing it back to the conference center in the hot sun.

I was a sweaty mess when I arrived, and was due on stage within minutes. I ducked into the public restroom to splash some water on my face, cool off, and compose myself before going out to speak. I took a deep breath, gathered my materials, and strode into the room.

As I began handing out donuts to the audience, I told them Bob's story. Bob had been a record executive for GRT corporation, and was seeking an appointment with Leon Hartstone, president of Wherehouse Records. Bob had called often, leaving a slew of messages, but Leon never returned any of his calls. Finally, Bob drove over to Hartstone's office with a bag of donuts and a mug of coffee. He also brought a pillow and a newspaper.

Bob entered the building and asked Hartstone's secretary if he was available for a meeting. She asked if Bob had an appointment and he said, "No, he hasn't returned any of my calls for an appointment. But I'll just sit here on the couch and wait until he has five minutes to meet with me." The secretary said, "I don't know if Mr. Hartstone will be able to see you today." To which Bob replied, and this is the great lesson about persistence, "That's okay. I'm prepared to sit here for several days until Leon can see me. I don't care if it takes all week, I'll just sit here quietly until he is available."

Of course, you can imagine how the story turned out. After about five hours, Hartstone's curiosity got the better of him, and he came downstairs to see this unusually persistent man. Bob's five-minute request turned into a two-hour meeting, and a long and mutually profitable business relationship was born in the process.

I loved telling that story, and relished watching everyone in the audience caught up in the experience. For a moment, I stopped talking to survey the situation – sticky fingers rubbing back and forth, jaws chomping up and down, sweet sugar rushing through tastebuds and into bloodstreams, nostrils taking in that classic glazed scent, all eyes forward and ears tuned in to this inspiring story. Each of the five senses were active as I shared Bob's tale of persistence and creative determination. Maybe that would increase the odds of people recalling the story when faced with their own stubborn career circumstance. Persistence and creative determination are traits that successful composers cannot thrive without.

I also told another important story during that keynote. Although it did not evoke as many senses, the second story was riveting in its own way.

I told the audience about my long and winding journey to win the Tolkien Music Director contract for Universal Studios' game division (Chapter 3). I spoke of the deep preparation I undertook, which included years of researching the literature, during which time I dug up every reference and inference to music, song, sound, voices, instruments – literally ferreting out every detail that had any connection to music.

To drive the point home, I reached down into a bag and pulled out four ragged and worn copies of *The Lord of the Rings* and *The Hobbit* in paperback. Each book was filled with yellow stick notes poking out on all sides, marking my discoveries. I described many of the details I had unearthed about how J.R.R. Tolkien envisioned and described music in his fantasy world, backed up with page numbers and quotes from the literature.

This was my way of encouraging deep research and thorough preparation. Deep research and preparation are part of becoming an expert. And as I've indicated earlier, vanguards and experts win. After winning the position of Tolkien Music Director for Universal Studios (later Vivendi-Universal Games), I was told that it was the deep research and thorough preparation I had undertaken that really pushed my application over the top, bypassing other talented applicants.

Here is one last story from GSC. Fast forward to 2015. Brian again invited me to give the conference keynote. I felt it was important to deliver another message about persistence and determination, as I had come to believe that persistence and determination were critical and predictive factors in composers achieving success.

During the 2015 keynote, I told the audience a fable about Socrates. I asked if there was a volunteer who would come forward and assist me. Andy Forsberg, a recent graduate from Berklee College of Music and a newly hired composer at Hexany Audio, raised his hand. I called him to the stage and began to unfold the tale.

According to legend, Socrates was once approached by an exceedingly earnest student who asked, "Master teacher, what is the secret to finding success in my life's work?" Socrates asked the young student to follow him, and they walked across the city without saying a word. They arrived at a neighborhood in Athens with many fountains and pools of cool water. Socrates settled down on an outcropping next to one pool in particular. "I would like for you to look deeply into the water here." Eagerly, the student knelt down at the edge of the pool, grasping the rough stone edge in each hand, and leaned forward. His excited eyes pierced the surface to plumb what depths of wisdom Socrates must have hidden in this special spot.

As I spoke, I motioned for Andy to stand in front of a table next to me. On that table sat a large "something" hidden by a thick linen tablecloth. I asked Andy to pull back the cloth and show the audience what was hidden. As he pulled back the cloth, he revealed a large, semi-transparent, rectangular plastic tub filled with water. I told the audience this represented the pool of water in Athens where Socrates and his student were gathered.

"Let's act this out, shall we?" I instructed, "I'll be Socrates, you be the student." Andy flashed a worried smile to the audience.

I continued, "OK, now where were we? Ah yes, Socrates instructed the student to look deeply into the pool of water. Andy, you go ahead and do that, look deeply down into this tub of water and we'll pretend it's a beautiful pool in Athens." Andy complied, bending his head over and staring at the surface of the water.

I continued, "And this is what Socrates did next …" That's when I grabbed Andy with both of my hands, plunging his head deeply into the water with a huge splash, washing over the edges of the tub, all over the table, and spilling out onto the stage.

I held his head underwater as I casually continued my story.

After the initial shock of Socrates' unexpected action, the student began to think. "What is Socrates trying to teach me?" The student felt the teacher's strong hands on his head and puzzled. "What is the lesson here?" Do I need to place myself trustingly in a teacher's hands without question? Must I submerge myself completely in my craft in order to succeed? Must I experience the cold rush of surprise and handle it deftly along the path? Was there some great truth hidden in these waters?

The young student's mind raced to discover the great mystery!

But soon, his mind stopped wondering about great insights and began panicking for lack of breath. He tried to lift his head up, but Socrates increased his resistance. He waited another moment, but then began to feel desperate. He tried turning his head one way and then the next, only to be thwarted by the remarkably strong grip of the old master teacher. Now the situation was becoming frantic. He twisted himself with great power now, violently wrenching his head around, arching his back, using every muscle to free himself from this wicked old man's grip. At long last, with every ounce of strength and energy he possessed, he lurched his head out of the pool, gasping for breath.

Andy played along as I narrated the story, fighting against my hold, twisting and turning, ultimately bursting free from the water and gasping for breath. People in the audience were shocked, and poor Brian nearly had a heart attack, wondering what kind of sadist was giving his keynote that night. It made quite a powerful impression. I continued the story.

The student spun around, accusing the man he once revered, "How could you do that to me? I came to you for wisdom, and you tried to drown me!"

The old master smiled a gentle smile and shrugged his shoulders. Then placing his hands on the student's trembling arms and looking deeply into his eyes, Socrates could now reveal the lesson this young man had come seeking. "When you muster all of your focus, energy, and strength for success – the same intensity, the same single minded motivation you marshaled for saving breath – then, my young friend, nothing can keep you from the success you seek."

Of course, everything with Andy had been pre-arranged. We had rehearsed the part earlier in the day. Andy was young and healthy, and took a deep breath at my signal before dunking his head in the water. When I gave him the next signal, he began thrashing around, and then when the time was right, I simply pulled him out. Brian was still a little shaken afterward, but I assured him, everything was safely planned. I am pretty sure no one in attendance will ever forget that keynote.

Go HUGE or go home.

If you are in a position to make an impression to a large audience, do your best to knock it out of the park. Make it memorable. A little bit of showmanship can go a long way. After all, we are in the entertainment business. I tried to keep that in mind both times I was granted the privilege and honor of inspiring my peers at GSC. I hope those moments proved helpful to some who were in attendance.

GSC was helpful for my career too. I made important contacts there for my work in virtual reality, for my textbook, and especially for my forays into Hollywood.

Your own story will be different from mine in many ways. But one benefit of reading my memoirs is the positive transformation that can occur as you invite my life lessons to merge with your own. I have experienced that too. Early in my career, I read many biographies and memoirs of successful people. Over time, the accumulated wisdom, portable principles, and insights I picked up began to crystalize within my own perceptions, habits, and actions. My ability to recognize opportunity sharpened. My success in pursuing opportunity increased. The memoirs I read became part of my extended education. The experiences and wisdom shared by these successful men and women supercharged my progress. The skills they taught became my own.

I was never the most talented, most intelligent, or most creative among my peers. Instead, the keys to my success came from learning how to uncover opportunities, and how to capitalize on them with skill, patience, savvy, and persistence. I played by the rules, never gained any advantage by dishonest, immoral, or illegal means. Reading the memoirs and biographies of other successful people distilled those skills for me. I hope that reading this memoir will likewise be beneficial to you.

CHAPTER 11

Warcraft and Other Peripheral Life Savers

I T STILL HURTS TO REMEMBER how demoralized I was. Down and out. No work, meager money, little hope. Anyone who has lived through extended unemployment knows how depressing and frightening it can be.

It was early 2001. A cold, wet winter had settled over our California mountain community. The days were short and dark. The nights were long and miserable.

I had no scoring projects. No way to earn money to put food on the table. I was getting desperate. In addition to my HUGEsound hunting and gathering efforts, I was starting to dig through "Help Wanted" postings, applying for jobs on the Internet, meeting with job training advisors, crafting resumes, trying just about anything to open some door. Any door.

During an especially dark moment, a kind man from my church congregation, Dean Fletcher, hired me to clean the carpets in his house. I almost broke down and cried, I was so grateful. Still, as I pushed the pink-smelling shampoo vacuum back and forth in long straight lines across the floor, I could not help but wonder why no one wanted to hire me to compose music any more.

I was still creating original demos and pitching for projects. I was still cultivating new and old friends in the game industry. I was reaching out to film and television contacts, and keeping in touch with old clients from

DOI: 10.1201/9781003199311-12

the ad business. But nothing was coming back to me. The radio silence was carving deep, cavernous fractures in my soul.

Perhaps only composers and actors can relate to the experience of auditioning again and again, putting out such an intimately personal expression of yourself with all your heart, all your hope ... only to meet with an endless treadmill of rejection. It is profoundly, desperately agonizing.

WARCRAFT

But churning milk does eventually turn to butter.

My old friend from Sierra, Jason Hayes, called and asked if I would help him produce a live orchestral recording for an upcoming *Warcraft III* trailer. He even had a small budget for my services. Hallelujah! *Warcraft* was becoming a huge franchise, and I would have been thrilled to do anything on it. I would have shined Jason's shoes and sharpened his pencils. As it turned out, this was Jason's first time to record an orchestra, so he needed help locating a sound stage for the recording, contracting an orchestra, and booking an engineer.

I was ecstatic, relieved to be working on a music project again, even if it was someone else's music. I booked Jason's session at the large chapel at LA East Studios. We brought in 25 string players and ten brass players to perform the score, which Jason conducted. Between takes, I would occasionally offer an idea or observation through the headset. About half way through, we ran into problems with a viola part. Fortunately, I was able to fix the part and transcribe it back to sheet music during a break. There is always something unexpected that comes up in the heat of a session.

Though my involvement was small, I cannot begin to tell you how meaningful it was to me. Finally, I was working on a music scoring project again! With a dear friend who recognized that I still had something valuable to offer. The money I earned from that gig was negligible, but the impact it had on my rattled spirit was HUGE. It returned a degree of self-respect to this shaken man. It put a little spring back in my step.

EARTH AND BEYOND

The next small project that helped me stay afloat during a downturn came from Craig Alexander, my former boss at Sierra. Craig could be intimidating and aloof, but as I spent time getting to know him on a personal level, I discovered a man who was caring, whip smart, efficient, and loyal to those he believed in.

After Sierra's California studio was destroyed by fraud a few rungs up the corporate ladder, Craig found work at Westwood Studios in Las Vegas, Nevada. Westwood was well known as the dev group behind the *Command & Conquer* games. After Craig settled in to his new position, he was handed the reins to *Earth and Beyond*, an expansive MMO set in outer space. Most of the music had already been produced by audio director Paul Mudra and his crew. But when a new quadrant opened up for expansion, Craig wanted to give me a shot at it. He made arrangements for me to come to Vegas and meet the key members of his team.

Flying to Las Vegas often fills passengers with eager anticipation, and I was no exception. Though my anticipation was of a different flavor than the rollicking vacationers reveling in the seats around me. I needed work, and was chomping at the bit to sink my teeth into a new music score. But I was nervous too. Craig was still new at Westwood and was sticking his neck out for me. I did not want to do anything that would reflect poorly on him. That thought troubled me during much of my flight.

Upon my arrival, Craig dispatched producer Rade Stojsavljevic to pick me up at the airport. Rade was tall, dark, and strong, but his most striking feature was a delightfully dry and spontaneous sense of humor. He dispensed wry commentary every two or three minutes during the entire drive to the studio, rolling in like planes at JFK. This was going to be fun.

We arrived at Westwood and immediately went to visit Craig. It was so good to see him again. Craig got right to business and walked me down the hall to meet Christopher Klug, a designer overseeing the new quadrants in *Earth and Beyond*. Craig may have been the alpha dog, but Chris was clearly the smartest guy in the room. Chris struck me as a guy who did calculus problems at night for relaxation. He started to explain the game's software system, but quickly realized that he needed to dumb it down for me. No problem, he was gracious and accommodating. He transitioned quickly, telling me about the new alien races inhabiting the expansion, the galaxy quadrants they were vying for, and all the cool gameplay features. This was the sort of lore and game state information I needed before starting a new score. I was on the edge of my seat.

Last stop of the day was a meeting with audio leads Paul Mudra and Dwight Okahara. It is always easy to hang with fellow music and audio peeps, and I felt an instant connection with them both. Perhaps it is the way musicians' brains are wired. Before long they were both regaling me with old war stories – fighting the absurd limitations of early game audio tech, keeping cool during the Vegas summers, sweet collaborations with fellow composers Frank Klepacki and David Arkenstone. By the time I left Westwood, I felt provisionally welcomed onto the team, and had begun formulating the first few strains of new quadrant music in my mind.

Composing an original score again, even for a small expansion, was like reconnecting me to essential oxygen. Laying down a pulsing synth bass beneath otherworldly symphonic harmonies and ambient effects felt exhilarating, invigorating, transportive. Composers in the heart of their careers need to be busy writing music to feel fully alive. I think every music maker can relate to that. Creative people at the peak of their powers can feel incapacitated when disenfranchised from work. Extended dry spells can be gut wrenching, crippling, debilitating. Cranking out music again was life-affirming for me. It also put a little jingle in my pocket, added some thickness to my wallet. All to the good.

LEGO STAR WARS III

During another drought, I made a trip to the Game Developers Conference to shake the bushes. During the conference, I met with Jesse Harlin, a rounded, scruffy looking young composer ("*Who's scruffy looking?*") with a razor-sharp mind, wit, and radiant talent. I do not recall many details of our meeting, but I do remember that I had a friendship with someone Jesse wanted to connect with. Or maybe I had information about an upcoming project he was interested in. Either way, I agreed to open the right doors for him, but ended the conversation with an "I'll help you and you help me," pitch.

It was not long afterward that Jesse reciprocated, requesting assistance on a big music editing job for *Lego Star Wars III*. Again, here was a game for which I was not the composer. The main theme was of course, John Williams' iconic masterpiece. The rest of the score was the excellent work of Kevin Kiner, composer for *Star Wars: The Clone Wars* TV series. The editing job entailed going through Kevin's entire catalog of *Clone Wars* music, culling out cues that could work under each of the game's levels, menus, and cinematics. I told Jesse, "I would love to do this job for you. When do I start?"

One little wrinkle cropped up in the contract negotiation I had never seen before. Jesse told me that LucasArts required all of its contractors to purchase indemnity insurance. I could understand this better if they were hiring me to compose an original score. But for a contract music editor position? I was surprised, but found an insurance agent in Chicago, Illinois, who would sell me the required insurance at a reasonable cost.

Fortunately, I was able to fold that cost back into the contract price, so the expense did not cut into my fees.

Once we finalized the contract, Jesses sent me every episode of *The Clone Wars* TV show, along with DVDs of all the music. I loved hearing Kevin's work. Kevin had a knack for Williams-sounding orchestrations, but added his own rhythmic and synth-savvy voice, which set the work apart in a cool way.

To build music for the game levels, I made note of potentially complimentary cues that could be fused together to make longer suites. It took days of careful listening and classifying to discover and codify potential matches from among the endless cues. After that, the assembly came together rather smoothly.

On the other hand, the game's cinematics required a lot more Frankensteining. Due to their dramatic nature, cinematics are succinctly timed, but I found very little in Kevin's body of work that would sync with the cinematics successfully. I supplemented his music by composing new original segments that fit the pacing. This helped the edited pieces blend together under the action.

I needed the money from this gig and was glad to have the work. I was thankful that I owned the equipment and possessed the editing know-how for the job. But as an extra benefit, I also received a free copy of the game. My oldest son Dietrich was a huge fan of *Star Wars* at the time, and he passed many hours sitting on the family room floor, playing *Lego Star Wars III* with deep satisfaction. He thought it was cool that his dad had a role in the vast *Star Wars* universe.

X-MEN: THE OFFICIAL GAME

Composer Josh Aker once coined the term "sacred pairs" to refer to people like George Lucas and John Williams, Tim Burton and Danny Elfman, Christopher Nolan and Hans Zimmer – creative duos who collaborate again and again, generating successful artistry in every project. In describing his own collaboration with Donald Mustard (*Infinity Blade* series), Josh said, "We grew up together. We create together. We know what to expect from each other and we value our relationship."[1]

I loved that perspective, and wondered if my own creative pairing might be developing with Craig Alexander. After his stint at Westwood, Craig was hired by Activision to run their team in San Jose, California. They were just putting the finishing touches on *X-Men: The Official Game*, and needed some last-minute help. Craig invited me to San Jose and introduced me to Activision's local audio director Nick Peck.

Nick's day job was directing audio for Activision, but he gigged at night as a keyboard player in a rock band. I had been a rock band keyboard player myself during college and high school, and we quickly found common ground. Nick was a big guy with a large, broad face. He wore Clark Kent glasses, and sported a thick coiffe of well-styled brown hair. He was whip smart about music and audio technology. There were no dead spots in his skill set. Yet he did not overlord people with his know-how. There was a genuine sweetness to Nick that reminded me a lot of James Horner.

As Nick showed me the game, he pointed out places where they still needed help. There were a couple of game levels that did not have music yet, including the climactic boss battle against Sabretooth. Most of the game's cinematic cutscenes also needed music. A large batch of cutscenes had been delayed until the end of production, and Nick had no other resources available. I was more than happy to jump into the fray. I had been a genuine fan of the first *X-Men* film, and had a pretty good feel for the style of music that would work well in the game.

A word about composing music for cinematic cutscenes. Each one is like a miniature movie. Scoring a cut scene is not terribly different than scoring a short film like *The ChubbChubbs*. Everything that happens at scale for large format entertainment, like a feature film or AAA game score, also happens in microcosm for a cutscene. The composer's music has to set the right mood, heighten the emotion, propel the action forward, provide contextual clues to the audience, enhance the aesthetic, and contribute to the structural unity of the scene.[2]

Nick was happy with our collaboration and really appreciated how well the music turned out. The audio lead was relieved to find that each delivered file had been topped and tailed with sample-accurate precision, and that all delivery formats were correct. Craig was pleased that I had delivered everything on time and within our budget. This was the reputation I wanted to build and it was a conscious decision. With each project I hoped to leave in my wake well-composed music that always fit the purpose, high-quality production, accurate files, happy collaborators, and satisfied producers who knew that I hit their targets.

MARVEL: ULTIMATE ALLIANCE

As a good business practice, I believe in making friends with as many people in the industry as possible, across all disciplines. I have friends who are programmers, friends who are producers, friends who work in marketing and public relations, friends who design game levels, and friends who make art. During my career, I also managed to befriend a few music agents, such as Bob Rice. We served together on the Board of Directors for the Game Audio Network Guild and became good friends. I loved hearing his deep, crusty baritone spin tall tales from his colorful past. He really did work with Journey, you know.

During one of the slow seasons in my career, Bob told me about a new Activision game on the horizon called *Marvel: Ultimate Alliance*. He asked if he could submit my name on a short list of potential composers. I cannot remember if I sent examples of my prior work or submitted a custom demo, but the dev team selected me to work on the music score, along with two other video game composers, Mark Grisky and Chris Velasco. This would be my first experience creating a music score hand-in-hand with other composers and I was excited at the prospect.

Shortly after signing the composing agreement, I was contacted by Ellen Lurie, the enthusiastic young audio lead from Raven Software who would be working with the composers. Ellen loved games and audio, and exuded gusto for the gig nearly every time we communicated. She was fun to work with, and owns the unique distinction of being the only client to ever give me a Green Bay Packers Cheese-Head hat as a gift (Raven Software is in Wisconsin). I had regular contact with producer Michael Abel as well, who offered much appreciated encouragement.

Marvel: Ultimate Alliance was a brawler, with each player picking a team of four Marvel heroes to play at a time. Personally, one of my favorite groupings was Iron Man, Captain America, Spider Man, and Wolverine. That was a powerhouse alliance! For a guy like me who grew up reading *Avengers* and *X-Men* comics, making music for this game was nothing short of surreal.

The areas in the game I was assigned to score were Atlantis, Niffelheim, and the Shi-ar Starship. Several cinematics were also assigned to me for scoring, including encounters with Dr. Doom, Loki, and Nick Fury's Helicarrier. This was almost too cool to be true! I especially enjoyed creating the music for Atlantis. I sent an early version of the track to Griskey for his feedback, and he was encouraging and complimentary. Honestly, we could not believe how lucky we were to be writing music for such incredible, iconic, fantasy settings. Griskey and I ended up sending music files back and forth to each other during production, cheering each other on. Velasco mostly kept to himself, but I enjoyed hearing his music once it was implemented in the game.

MONOPOLY STREETS

Even after resigning from EA Games to score *Avatar: The Game*, I kept up the relationships I made there. I would occasionally meet for lunch with Jon Dean, chat with Vance Cook who still lived in my neighborhood, and interact on social media with Matt Peterson, Dustin Hansen, Matt Copeland, and others.

Every healthy relationship enriches your life, so there is intrinsic value in keeping in touch with good people. As an added bonus, some of those relationships may also benefit your composing business. That was certainly the case when, over lunch one afternoon, Jon Dean asked if I would be interested in auditioning to score an upcoming new collaboration between Hasbro and EA Games called *Monopoly Streets*.

I was intrigued. A video game version of *Monopoly*? I had always loved the board game. I definitely wanted to learn more.

Jon introduced me to Neil Melville, the game designer recently hired to lead development on the project. He also reconnected me with Kelly Mondragon and Jeff Peters, two Hasbro-product producers I had met while working in-house. As an audition, Neil and Kelly asked me to submit an original instrumental theme that "sounds like *Monopoly*." They further instructed me that the theme needed to be "hooky and memorable."

First things first. How do you come up with a melody that is hooky and memorable? I have a secret weapon for that! Years ago, I discovered that writing memorable themes was easier if I made up dummy lyrics to compose to first. For example:

> *I love to play Monopoly,*
> *You love to play it with me,*
> *We love to play Monopoly,*
> *Let's make some money!*

Silly lyrics, I know. But that is not really the point. The lyrics were never meant to be recorded. They were a composing tool, a scaffolding upon which I could try out different melodic ideas. The words had the grammar of a typical pop music chorus. As such, they implied phrasing, meter, vector, syllabic breakdown, rise and fall, question and answer – all musical constructs a composer can attach meaningful notes to. It was like building myself a musical paint-by-numbers template for making memorable themes.

I experimented with melody after melody using the dummy lyrics, riffing away until I found a sequence of bouncy, rising motifs that stitched together in a hooky and memorable way.

The technique worked wonders. Not only did the technique generate a contract-winning pitch, but the resulting *Monopoly* theme sticks with people many years after playing the game. For example, one recent day while working on this book, an email arrived from an unknown address in Switzerland. Here is what it said:

> Dear Mr. Thomas. In my past time I enjoy listening to Monopoly Streets. After several years of not having played this game, I still sometimes find myself humming the melody of the main board theme. Thank you for your time and for your music!

Many such messages have crossed my desk. The theme just sticks with people. It's memorable. It's hooky. And the technique works. Writing to dummy lyrics is a highly effective tool for generating memorable themes. I invite composers everywhere to give it a try.

Now what about style, arrangement, and production? What about creating music that "sounds like *Monopoly*." How would you solve that problem? How would you communicate the *Monopoly* experience in music? Would you go street smart and gritty with hip-hop or blues? Would you try industrial rock or suburban pop? Country twang? Epic opera?

Distilling the key ideas you want to communicate to your audience will suggest specific musical grammar, syntax, and idioms for your composition.

Here is how I approached the distillation process. First, people from all walks of life have played *Monopoly*. The game has been played for generations. Its scoring language should have broad, cross-generational appeal. That suggests a hybrid idiom like jazz, pop, or classical music. Second, *Monopoly* has the potential to chew up many long hours, sometimes bridging across several days. *Monopoly* can easily become *monotony* for some. People know this about the game, so I wanted to counteract that preconception with overwhelming energy and excitement in the score. That suggests a syntax of short phrases, and the grammatic structure of an overture or montage.

My final solution was to spread a big band overlay across a wide range of stylistic underpinnings – jazz, rockabilly, hip-hop, corporate orchestral, and others. The tempo was 108 bpm, with a syncopated triplet rhythm to drive the tune along. A three-piece brass section (trumpet, saxophone, and trombone) was recorded live, with Chris Heins sampled brass fleshing out the big band sound. Guitars and clarinet were also tracked live. I played the piano, with drum machines and synth bass rounding out the production. The music was a big hit, resonating with a broad spectrum of audiences, generating plenty of excitement to play the game.

I should also mention something about the music design. Game play in *Monopoly* includes several special circumstances such as rolling doubles, going to jail, landing on Community Chest, paying taxes, passing Go, and more. We decided on signature stingers for each event. The goal was to magnify the emotional high or low associated with each circumstance. For example, landing on Free Parking sounds like a party. Community Chest has a civic, hopeful ring to it. Going to jail is a cartoony downer. Rolling doubles is a quick shot of adrenaline. All the pieces work so well together.

Being a fan of the original board game, I found great satisfaction in helping the team at EA bring the *Monopoly* experience to the console gaming world. And each time I hear from people who still find themselves humming my "hooky" theme, it puts a smile on my face all over again.

CYTUS

Throughout my composing career, patience has been more than a virtue. It has been a lifeline.

Cytus is an entertaining Taiwanese game that is not especially well known in the United States. Players follow a story and generate points by tapping on animated music notation that matches notes in the music score. When Shota Nakama called and asked me to submit music for a couple of levels, I was stoked. But you should know that this invitation was more than a decade in the making. Here is the backstory of how we arrived at that point.

In 2005, Shota Nakama was a student at Berklee College of Music in Boston, Massachusetts. While studying music composition and guitar, he met another like-minded student named Filippo Beck Peccoz, also studying composition and guitar. The catalyst that supercharged their connection was video game music. They both loved video game music. So much so, they launched a video game music club at Berklee and became its co-presidents.

As the club grew, they expanded their activities beyond gaming tournaments and listening sessions. Eventually they persuaded the administration to start bringing video game composers to the campus to give Master classes on composing music for video games.

I was their first guest lecture.

My meeting with the students covered music design, world-building, and orchestration. Most examples were pulled from my recent video game scores for *Peter Jackson's King Kong* and Universal's *Lord of the Rings* franchise. One segment that Shota and Filippo especially enjoyed was called, Orchestrating Great Reviews. It was a discussion of descriptive words typically used by the media when responding to specific orchestration techniques. Pulling from press clippings about my *King Kong* score, we built the following table.[3]

What The Media Said	What It Means Musically
Exciting	Rapid contrapuntal lines
Sumptuous	Added sevenths and ninths in the string choir
Atmospheric	*Sul tasto*, polychords, clusters
Menacing	Sharp dynamics in the low brass
Eerie	*Sul Ponticello*, tremolo
Foreboding	Suspensions, low brass, low strings
Sweeping	Arpeggiated strings, unison lines, glissandi
Expressive	Effective dynamics and typecasting
Relentless	Repetitive lines against changes
Epic	French horns and classical choir

With each term and explanation, I played a corresponding track from the *King Kong* score for the students, so they could hear the correlation.

After the presentation, Shota and Filippo took me out for Sushi and we talked for hours. It was the start of a friendship, originally based on professional respect, but eventually growing into layers of personal connection.

I kept in touch with Shota off and on for years. I followed him on social media and congratulated him on his graduation, his first professional opportunities, and the many expanding successes he was having in business. Shota was building contacts and contracts in the United States and abroad. It was fun to see him fly.

That is how I came to receive the phone call about *Cytus*. We had kept in touch. I had followed and applauded his career, and he had done the same for mine. Our mutual support and friendship had grown. When he had an opportunity to bring in another composer for the *Cytus* project, he thought of me.

My contract was for two songs, about three minutes each. I would compose and arrange the tunes, record the virtual tracks into Pro Tools, then send Shota the sessions. He would overdub guitars and take care of the mix. I negotiated for my normal scoring rate at the time, $1,200 per finished minute. It was a small gig, but another one of those peripheral projects that came during a lull and kept me alive to fight another day.

GUARDIANS OF DAVID AND CHAMPIONS OF CANAAN

One of the original team members from Legend Entertainment's *Unreal 2* development group (see Chapter 15) on the east coast was James Parkman. James and I had only remained loosely in touch, so I was surprised when he called me from Austin, Texas. He had recently relocated, accepting a lead role at a Christian game company called Kingdom Games. Their design team was raiding Old Testament lore for fresh gaming ideas. They found their mark in the history of King David.

James was producing a strategy/combat game called *FIVE: Guardians of David*, where players take on the role of the king's guardian, one of five available player characters, each with unique abilities. Composer Alexander Brandon, one of my old HUGEsound Network buddies, had been hired to create the music score. But he was unable to take on the full project and kindly recommended me for the balance of the score. Of course, my name resonated with James Parkman, and he reached out personally to invite me onboard the project.

Kingdom Games was funded on a shoestring, so I discounted my rate down to $1,000 per finished minute. However, I also negotiated to retain the copyrights for both the music and the recordings. Kingdom Games would retain a license to use the music in any of their games, and on any promotional media publicizing their games. But copyrights would remain vested with me.

Alex and I quickly found a style we liked, a blend between iconic Middle-eastern modal music and epic fantasy game scoring. We did our homework and selected a number of indigenous instruments to use in our scores. I think we each delivered six different looping tracks, each about four or five minutes long. Almost everything was produced with digital samples, though I did hire an experienced studio singer for the main theme. It all sounded pretty sweet.

The game was moderately successful, enough that the company sprung for a sequel. *Champions of Canaan* would not only extend the story, but would also include several new gameplay features to enrich the experience.

James flew me out to Austin to meet with the team about the new project, but I did not see Alex in the meetings. Whether he was tied up with another gig, or simply uninvited from the project, I never knew. But James offered the full music score for *Champions of Canaan* to me.

I took a calculated risk in negotiating this deal. Not only did I still request the same copyrights/license arrangement of our prior deal, but I also requested $1,500 per minute, explaining that I had accepted a reduced rate on the earlier game as a favor, helping an upstart company get their first game out the door. Now that they had experienced some success, it was time to charge my normal rate. Of course, I was planning to handle all aspects of production personally, so there would not be any add-on costs for contract musicians, engineers, editors, or mixing artists. James agreed to my terms and we signed the deal.

Although it was a sequel, in many ways the devs were treating *Champions of Canaan* as its own new game. The graphic design had a splashy new look, and many of the gameplay features had evolved substantially. In addition, the team asked me to compose a brand-new main theme, in addition to new level music for the game. I developed the new theme as an overture, a blend of memorable statements and variations – rousing action motifs and exploratory themes, all orchestrated with exotic sounding ethnic elements.

Incidentally, all of this music was composed and produced in 2013 and 2014. Retaining the copyrights proved to be an especially smart move, since both scores were priced into the eventual sale of my business in 2016.

DUNGEONS & DRAGONS ONLINE

Dungeons & Dragons Online (*DDO*) had a broad player base, but the game had never featured an epic original score. By 2012, it was long overdue for the full orchestral treatment. For the game's first foray into Forgotten Realms lore, the 2012 expansion, *Menace of the Underdark*, I contracted with game developer Turbine Entertainment for a new original score with all the bells and whistles – large live orchestra, 24-voice SATB choir, small acoustic ensemble, and a few featured soloists. Such a large-scale production was a composer's playground and I was thrilled with the opportunity.

To get started, I covered my studio walls with screenshots from the game world, and drew on that inspiration for the score. The main theme was Medieval, or rather a modern orchestral interpretation of Medieval ideas. Martial and heroic, the theme took grand leaps in the melody – up a sixth, up a seventh, with stepwise movements in between. French horns and trombones in unison powered the melody, with grand heroic statements. The stout theme breaks away for a bridge/interlude in the string choir. Lush and emotional, suspensions tug and resolve, leading up to a spartan restatement of the martial theme in the men's chorus. I think most composers love writing and recording epic sounding music like this.

There is quite a range of stylistic diversity in the breadth of this *DDO* score. The Old English village *Evening Star* called for lutes and guitars, Irish flute, and solo cello. That part of the score is rustic, honorable, and homey, with just enough tugging at the heart strings, but not too much. At the other extreme we have the Drow city of Schindylryn, the oppressive dungeon far beneath the surface, filled with menacing contrabass singers, low strings and brass, hugely resonant percussion, and morphing ephemeral textures in sordino strings and synth pads.

One of my favorite tracks in the game score is called *Dark Elf Defense*. Beginning like a typical trope of video game combat music, it soon finds its way into a full-on fugue between the five string parts, as one group and then the other attack their strings in aggressive waves, like ranks of swordsmen leaping into the fray. Lively and sophisticated, this technique brought yet another colorful flavor to this rich and lively score.

While the *DDO* contract spared no expense on its production, and paid me a generous creative fee, the quantity of music was relatively small. I composed just over 30 minutes of music for this score.

Incidentally, the license for *Dungeons & Dragons* was controlled by Wizards of the Coast (WOTC), based near Seattle, Washington. *Magic: The Gathering* was another valuable WOTC property. After scoring *DDO*, I made a trip to Seattle to explore the possibility of scoring an upcoming *Magic: The Gathering* video game. I had an inside track, since my sister, graphic artist Nene Tina Thomas, was one of the first artists to create original artwork for Magic Cards. Some of her original cards now sell for a small fortune. Though my pitch gained some initial traction, it fizzled out in subsequent months. You just can't win them all.

THE VOID

The VOID was an immersive, location-based, 3D virtual reality (VR) experience. For a time, it seemed like *The VOID* was going to take the world of entertainment by storm, forever transforming the way we amused ourselves. It certainly began that way. Sadly, infighting and mismanagement eventually sunk this promising venture.

But we are getting ahead of ourselves. Let me first introduce you to *The VOID* properly, and explain how I got involved.

Remember Jon Dean from EA Games? When EA Games eventually shut down their Salt Lake City, Utah office, Jon launched a pair of new ventures. One of those ventures was the Utah Digital Entertainment Network (UDEN). UDEN's goal was to foster growth among all aspects of digital entertainment within the state of Utah through meetups, web-based job postings, resource databases, and ongoing networking. I joined the organization to support Jon and meet new people in the business.

At the second or third meeting, Jon's special guest was Curtis Hickman, a working Las Vegas magician who had recently relocated to Utah to develop a new kind of VR experience. He described a VR venue similar to a movie multiplex, where people could choose from various attractions – Ancient Mayan Temple, Alien Starship, Vampire Grotto, Atlantis – and buy tickets to that attraction, then walk into the corresponding "theater" to have that particular VR experience.

A key selling point for the VOID was that their virtual worlds were mapped on top of actual physical staging and props. Thus, your interactions took place in a hybrid combination of physical and virtual inputs. It sounded incredible as I listened to Curtis describe the experiences they were already building. After the meeting I introduced myself to Curtis and asked if I could stop by his office to learn more. He gave me a business card and invited me to call him up sometime.

I did not wait very long. After a brief and pleasant phone conversation, Curtis invited me to stop by The VOID's test facility and see what they were cooking up. The first VOID experience he showed me was the Ancient Mayan Temple, and it completely blew my mind. Let me share my walk-through experience with you.

I began by stepping into a small booth lined with sound foam. The foam was gray and divided into small rectangles, reminiscent of the Sonnex acoustic foam that once covered the walls of my Sierra studio. Inside the booth, I was greeted by a live assistant who helped me put on a VR helmet and light backpack filled with computing gear. Once I put on the helmet, my eyes were covered up with goggles holding tiny screens broadcasting the virtual images. Interestingly, I saw the same little sound foam rectangles on screen that I had just seen with my natural eyes. Implication? What I see in the goggles is real. I reached out to touch the wall and felt it. Illusion complete.

The helmet included headphones, so now my ears were also covered. The live assistant spoke to me through a microphone, and I heard him just fine. Second subliminal message – what you hear through the headphones is coming from a real person. Very smart.

Suddenly, a portal appeared, opening inside one of the foam-covered walls. I reached out to touch it, and my hand went all the way through. That was another reality suspender, because just moments earlier, I had been touching the solid wall. Now I was looking into the opening and could see the courtyard of an ancient stone structure covered with vines. I heard the voice of the assistant, encouraging me to go through the portal. As soon as I stepped through the portal and looked around, the portal closed and a stone wall appeared in its place. I stretch out my fingers to touch it, and sure enough, the portal I just stepped through was gone and I felt a solid wall in its place. Freaky!

In my goggles, I could see an ancient throne. I walked over to it and reached out to touch the throne and sure enough, I could feel it with my hands. In fact, I even sat down on it. This was awesome. I noticed a torch on a far wall, and the assistant's voice encouraged me to go pick it up. I did so, and felt the torch firmly in my hand. Then, everywhere I pointed it, that part of the temple would light up, as if from the very torch in my hand.

On and on the experience went, crashing through a stone wall, turning tumblers on a stone puzzle, walking across a narrow bridge with endless chasms on either side, and riding a rickety elevator up to a windy and sunny exterior. My mind was totally blown. This would transform entertainment as we knew it. I wanted to be part of it in a big way.

I met with Curtis after going through the Mayan Temple experience and could not stop gushing. He said they were close to finalizing the experience and would soon be ready for post-production polish. In fact, *The VOID* had been invited to build a temporary version of their Mayan Temple experience at an upcoming TED conference. Steven Spielberg and Harrison Ford were expected to be at the conference and were reportedly interested in trying out the experience. I asked if Curtis would give me the opportunity to bid on the audio when the time came, and he agreed.

It was not long before Curtis reached out again. He needed a voice actor to record their script, very similar to what the live assistant had spoken to me when I did my walk through. He also needed sound effects for everything from the portal opening, to stone works moving, to a final scene where the temple starts to break apart and tumbles down around you. And he wanted a little bit of music, though music would be the smallest part of the gig.

No problem. My company HUGEsound could provide all of those services, and I hoped it would cement a relationship between us, opening opportunities for future music and sound work as the company grew.

Britani Underwood was selected for the voice over. She would play the role of the guest's partner, radioing in and giving instructions, warnings, and lore hints as the person moved through the temple. We booked one of the small rooms at LA East for the session, and everything went smoothly. I did all the editing myself, and designed a number of optional effects chains, which transformed her luscious-sounding voice into crackling radio talk. These were skills I had picked up working on *Littlest Pet Shop* for EA Games (see Chapter 8), and they came in handy.

For the sound effects, I reached out to Michael McDonough, one of the original HUGEsound Network affiliates from the late 90s. For all our attempts to collaborate over the years, and the many times I had referred him to work for others, this would be the first time I was able to hire him personally for sound design work.

During the project, McDonough would submit work-in-progress sounds and I would offer ideas to help tweak them for a better fit inside the experience. When the final files arrived, everything was exceptional.

The last part of the contract was the music. Though it was mostly ambient, there were a few places where I brought some epic underscore to the soundscape.

I say music was the last piece, but that is not actually true. The last piece was the implementation. After all the assets were produced, I spent a few days sitting with programmers at *The VOID* overseeing the creation of audio hooks in the code, mix settings, and spatialization. They spent enough time to get it right, and I cannot tell you how thrilling it was to walk through the experience a final time with all the high-fidelity, properly implemented audio working perfectly.

I have not talked about the contract yet, so let me touch on that. Curtis offered to pay Brittany separately, so my contract covered dialog editing and effects (including the recording studio), sound design, music, and implementation oversight. I sent McDonough the SFX list and asked him for a bid. I took his bid and added my time for producing, plus a 10% markup. With the VO script in hand, it was easy to estimate how many hours of studio time we would need for recording the dialog. I entered those costs, and added my time for producing the session. For the music, I bid at $1,500 per finished minute. Then I added a 5% buffer for potential negotiating room.

As I recall, Curtis pushed back at the overall cost. I expected that, and after some haggling over a few details, I offered to cut the bid by 4%. He was very happy with that and we signed the deal. I was glad the initial bid included a 5% buffer.

Harrison Ford and Steven Spielberg did go through *The VOID*'s Mayan Temple experience at the TED conference, as expected. The ear-to-ear grins on their faces, showing up in photos all over the Internet, said it all. They loved it, and spoke glowingly to the press about their impressions. *The VOID* had delivered a sensational combination of aesthetic and technology. I was convinced it would take off like a rocket.

At some point after the TED conference, Disney bought a controlling interest in *The VOID* and directed development toward experiences based on their movie franchises. They also leased venues in popular locations including Times Square, downtown Tokyo, and other prime spots. The first Disney-influenced experience was based on *Ghostbusters* and by then, they had full-time audio in-house, so I was not involved.

The *Ghostbusters* experience was well received, and soon afterward they began developing a new experience based on *Jumanji*. I did get a call for that one. They needed someone to transcribe some of Henry Jackman's film score and recreate it digitally. Some new soundalike music would also be needed. I bid the whole project at a reduced scoring rate of $1,200 per finished minute, plus my studio rate of $125/hour, plus third-party mixing costs. No back and forth, they simply agreed and we went to work.

It had been a long time since I transcribed another composer's work. Pulling Jackman's music apart was both educational and entertaining. Educational because I learned some interesting nuances from his woodwind voicings, and entertaining because they were just fun cues. The process involved figuring out all the individual parts, playing them into my sequence, and finding good virtual sounds to replicate different parts of the orchestra. I hired Mike Roskelley for the mix.

Sadly, shortly after releasing their *Jumanji* experience, *The VOID* imploded. I never heard any official details, but word on the street painted the picture of a promising company that had been mismanaged and flea bitten ever since Disney took the reins. Such a shame. *The VOID*'s adventures remain the most vivid and memorable entertainment experiences of my lifetime.

OTHER LIFE SAVERS

It is surprising to look back at how many little projects like these came along during large and small lulls in my career. There is no room to include them all, but there were many others – *Marvel's Champions*

Online, Disney's Ghosts of Mistwood, Driven in Detroit, Paraworld (trailer), Bakery Story 2, and more. There was also music I composed for advertising campaigns and music libraries. All of these filled holes when I was seeking for more substantial scoring work. And while many of these filler contracts were music composition gigs, many of them were not. Just like the *Warcraft III* trailer, *Lego Star Wars III*, and *The VOID*, some of these projects required other skills.

I mention this because young composers are likely to face down times in their careers. Some lessons drawn from my experiences in this chapter could be helpful. They are probably self-evident, but let me summarize three takeaways to underscore the obvious.

First, it is important to cultivate a broad skillset. Jason Hayes did not call me to write music for the *Warcraft III* trailer. Instead, he needed help with some of the peripherals. Because I had those skills, experiences, and connections, I was useful to him and his project. Those peripheral skills got me the gig.

Second, beware of pride. If I was willing to clean carpets in a man's house to make a few dollars, then I could certainly help *The VOID* with editing dialog, or cut up Kevin Kiner's TV scores to make video game level music. I have met some struggling composers who would never "stoop" to work on something that was outside of composing their own original music. I suppose if they were independently wealthy (they were not), or had blazed a trail of never-ending blockbusters (nope), then they needn't worry. Instead, they have continued to struggle needlessly. Please do not let pride keep you from accepting projects that will put food on your table, buy clothes for your kids, or provide a nice dinner date for you and your partner. Working keeps us productive and learning, keeps our momentum from dying, and allows us make new friends and clients in the industry.

Finally, I learned that staying active during down times kept me from completely falling off a cliff emotionally. I kept busy in my hunting and gathering efforts. I remained active in my family and spiritual life. And I stayed vigilant with my health. All of those efforts built a buttress around me for times when emotional resiliency was wavering.

I do not want to soft pedal this in any way. It can be absolutely soul crushing to miss out on gigs you need to thrive. You will undoubtedly feel desperate and afraid during times when you cannot find work. But it can be a life-saving relief if peripheral projects can plug some of those holes, even something small like a *Warcraft III* trailer contracting gig.

To watch videos from Marvel: Ultimate Alliance *and* Monopoly Streets, *and to hear music from* X-Men: The Official Game, Marvel: Ultimate Alliance, Champions of Canaan, *and* Dungeons and Dragons Online, *as described in this chapter, please visit: HUGEsoundRecords.com/Memoir-11*

NOTES

1 Chance Thomas, *Composing Music for Games: The Art, Technology and Business of Video Game Scoring*, p. 232; Boca Raton: CRC Press, 2016.
2 Chance Thomas, *Composing Music for Games: The Art, Technology and Business of Video Game Scoring*, Chapter 1; Boca Raton: CRC Press, 2016.
3 Chance Thomas, *Composing Music for Games: The Art, Technology and Business of Video Game Scoring*, p. 34; Boca Raton: CRC Press, 2016.

CHAPTER 12

DOTA 2

G DC 2013 WAS APPROACHING fast and I was wrestling with a universal dilemma facing all composers. How do I get potential clients to listen to my music? And more importantly, how do I present my music in its best possible light?

Music was available on my website, of course, and also on Apple Music, Amazon Music, and the like. I would typically include those links in my email signature file. But I wondered, did audio directors and game designers ever tap those links? And if they did, which tracks would they pick to listen to? And even if they picked a great track, how would they listen to it? Were they listening from their cell phone, or from tinny speakers on a laptop or tablet? None of those scenarios appealed to me.

I needed to figure out how to get potential clients to hear the best possible examples of my music in the best possible listening environment. And I wanted to figure it out in time for GDC 2013.

Everything was booked. Meetings had already been arranged with several potential clients. But I had not solved the listening predicament yet. I kept the problem marinating on the back burner of my brain.

One night, I was listening to music through a nice set of Sony studio headphones. "Man, I wish I could give a set of these away with my demos. Getting some free headphones would encourage people to listen, and it would sound terrific." While I was not prepared to spend $150 per demo on a headphone gamble, the idea had started the wheels turning.

I wondered if there might be a new headphone manufacturer who would love an inside track in the video game industry? I researched the market and discovered an upstart company in Denmark named AIAIAI. They had just released a new set of wireless headphones, and their website portrayed them as eager new kids on the block. I reached out and connected with their US marketing team. I asked if they might be interested in getting their headphones on the ears of influential audio directors in video game development. Of course, they were interested. "But who are you again?" asked the marketing manager, "And what exactly is your plan?"

"Google me, composer Chance Thomas," I suggested while we were on the phone. A few prominent credits and awards came up as he did a quick search. "Impressive," he said, "I see you've got some cred in that industry. Now, what's your plan and what do you need from us?"

I told him about the Game Developers Conference, and explained that I had scheduled appointments with audio directors at EA, Sony, Valve, and other heavy hitters. If AIAIAI would give me a dozen of their new wireless headphones, I would hand them personally to a dozen industry insiders. He agreed to ship me a dozen of their top headphones within the week at no cost to me.

This was great news, and I was stoked. But what delivery system would I connect them with? How would I host my music? Vinyl had not made a comeback yet, CDs were out of date, and most composers were handing out music demos on thumb drives. I needed something extra, something with more appeal and better logistics.

At the time, vintage iPod Shuffles were selling on eBay for $15–$20 each. Since the headphones were arriving for free, an outlay of $15–$20 for each demo was well within my budget. I snatched up a dozen colorful iPods and loaded them with my best demos.

When the headphones arrived, each one was packaged in its own elegant and stylish box. Inside each box was just enough room to insert an iPod and a HUGEsound promotional pamphlet. The presentation looked chic and impressive. I departed for GDC with 12 classy demo packages in tow.

Among my first GDC appointments was a meeting with Mike Morasky from Valve. I had been introduced to Mike by Tim Larkin at a G.A.N.G. Awards show two years earlier. Tim worked at Valve too, but had not extended any potential freelance opportunities to me yet. I figured it wouldn't hurt to give Mike a try.

Mike and I had a great meeting, talking about music, games, skiing, kids, interactivity, and seemingly a hundred other things. He finally asked about the box I kept fiddling with. "Oh yes, this is for you," I said, handing him the shiny package, "This is my new demo." Unwrapping the box,

Mike's eyes lit up at the wireless headphones and colorful iPod. He slid the printed booklet out and started thumbing through the pages. He picked up the iPod and admired its shiny surface, then pulled the headphones out and tried them on his head. A moment later he gushed, "This is the coolest demo I've ever received. I can't wait to listen." I knew he would. And I knew it was going to sound great.

TI4

Months passed and one morning Mike Morasky's number lit up my phone. I greeted Mike enthusiastically, and he mentioned that he had been listening to my demo (I knew he would) and that the music sounded great (I knew it would). The AIAIAI headphones and iPod had turned the key, solving every composer's listening quandary.

But Mike was calling with more than just compliments. He had an unexpected proposition for me related to Valve's new worldwide blockbuster, *DOTA 2*. Visual reskins had become immensely popular with gamers and were a growing source of revenue for Valve. Mike had begun to champion the idea of developing custom music scores as yet another way to reskin their games. Discussions had progressed, and Valve wanted a test case to see how it would work. Mike suggested they try it first with *DOTA 2*.

By 2014, *DOTA 2* had become a video gaming juggernaut, approaching eight million monthly players.[1] Mike proposed that I compose an all-new music score for *DOTA 2*, a musical reskin to be included in a bundle of game upgrades and add-ons for the player community. Called the *Battle Pass*, Valve would sell this bundle as a way to fund a generous prize pool for the upcoming TI4 International tournament. The tournament would decide the top *DOTA 2* team in all the world.

This sounded like a deliriously exciting opportunity. Mike hit me with the full pitch and asked, "You wanna give it a shot?"

I loved the idea, but suddenly found myself hesitating. My friend Tim Larkin had been the composer for *DOTA 2* since its inception. Would he be OK with this? Would he agree to having me step in and rescore his baby? Mike assured me that Tim was onboard, and even asked Tim to call me later to confirm his support. Tim did call with his support, and added more to the conversation by saying that, if this experiment worked out seamlessly, Valve could propagate music packs across their other games, opening up new scoring opportunities for many more composers. I liked the sound of that and agreed to move forward with negotiations.

I worked closely with Mike Morasky to hammer out the contract details. My first request was generous funding for a large orchestra and choir. Creative fees were proposed at three different rates, based on the asset type. Layered tracks with three intensity levels would be billed at $2,500 per finished minute. Stingers and tags would cost $500 each. Linear and looping tracks were budgeted at $1,500 per finished minute. Breaking down the creative fees like this brought transparency to the pricing discussions and clarity to our contract negotiations. There was very little negotiation, as Mike approved my full budget as proposed.

With a contract in place, Tim provided me with an overview of the music design architecture and sent over his original music files. They offered an adaptive template I could compose to, and connected me to a system I could plug into for testing. Plug and play was the objective. At the end of the gig, we wanted to simply swap out Tim's music files with mine – same file names, same gameplay function, but different compositions and recordings.

I was itching with anticipation, wondering what musical style would light a fire for the players. I downloaded and played the game, visited forums, watched gameplay videos, and listened repeatedly to Tim's original score. Tim had crafted a hybrid middle eastern, contemporary western orchestral score, with lots of Duduk and ethnic percussion. I wanted to keep a contemporary flair, but decided to take the score in a bold new direction.

My imagination was running wild, envisioning a glorious collision of high fantasy game music and Monday Night Football. I wanted screaming trumpet riffs and epic choral chanting, bristling synth lines, and a full live orchestra. The first cue I composed morphed all of those elements into one heroic barn-burner. I sent the mockup to Tim for review. "Sounds great to me," he said. Mike was onboard too, "Full speed ahead!" They cut me loose, and cues came together like wildfire. I had rarely written music so quickly, and I was enjoying the style immensely.

My digital orchestral library was robust, but my virtual synth collection was a little weak. One of my composer friends, Or Kribos, connected me with Hybrid Two's CEO, who supplied complimentary copies of two riveting virtual instruments, Project Alpha and Project Bravo. I used them both generously throughout the new score.

Once the music was composed and approved, I hired a 48-piece orchestra and a 24-voice choir, hoping to bring the score to vibrant life. The orchestra performed fabulously. The choral singing was so epic! The recording sessions were among the best I had ever produced, the rare project where every performance lands in the sweet spot. All of the recordings were crisp and clean. When I left the studio, I knew I had gold in those tracks.

But I soon received unsettling news. Mike Roskelley, my longtime mixing collaborator, abruptly announced that he was taking an unplanned sabbatical from mixing music. He was leaving the very week I planned to mix the *DOTA 2* score. As an olive branch, he offered to let me use his studio while he was away, and encouraged me to mix the score myself. After the successful recording sessions, I may have been riding too high on a cloud of endorphins. Against my usual better judgment, I decided to tackle the mix personally.

It was during this mix that I encountered one of the strangest and most disturbing phenomena I had ever experienced in a studio. I had booked a week to mix the score, and found myself going at it pretty much around the clock. The music was complex, with multiple layers, and there was a lot of it. I was having a tough time wrangling all the tracks into shape, and time was evaporating quickly. When exhaustion would completely overcome me, I would pull three chairs together and lie down across them to snatch a few hours of sleep. I would set a phone alarm for two or three hours, then rise and get after it again.

Toward the end of the week, probably Thursday afternoon, I became frustrated. I was trying to blend some sampled strings in with the live string tracks. But everything sounded distorted. No matter what I dialed back – EQ, effects, levels, etc. – nothing removed the distortion. I rebooted the system, checked the amplifier and speaker thresholds, soloed tracks, everything I could think of to troubleshoot. No good. I knew those tracks were clean because I had listened to them critically during the recording sessions and afterward while editing. Still, the distortion persisted.

And then, something truly alarming happened. I accidentally knocked a note pad from the desk onto the floor and it sounded distorted. Everything in my mind ground to a halt. I was trying to make sense of what my ears had just told me. I snapped my fingers. Distorted. I clapped my hands. Distorted. I made several other noises in the room on various surfaces. All fuzzy and distorted.

I called Pamela. Her voice sounded fuzzy and distorted. By now I started focusing on a feeling within my ears. They felt swollen on the inside. Somehow, I had bludgeoned my hearing so relentlessly for those days and nights of mixing that every sound coming through that mechanism was distorting.

I returned home to my own bed for a full night of comfortable, silent sleep. I felt enough improvement by the following morning to return to the studio and finish the mix. I had never experienced anything like that in my life. I hope to never experience anything like it again.[2]

Delivery of the score had been hotly anticipated, and the files plugged in as seamlessly as we had hoped. The new music completely transformed the aesthetic of the game, but it left the function unchanged, hitting all of Valve's technical and artistic goals. That elicited a universally positive reception from the dev team. But the real test would be the players. No one knew how they would to react to a "music reskin." As *Battle Passes* went on sale and began flying off the shelf, we held our collective breath. In a trickle at first, players began installing the new music. A buzz started spreading across the community and soon the installation numbers swelled. The players were embracing the new music pack wholeheartedly! Enthusiastic comments started arriving from all over the world. Sweet success.

Later that year, Tim invited me to Seattle for Valve's championship *DOTA 2* tournament, The International TI4. The tournament was held inside Key Arena, where I had once watched the NBA's Seattle Sonics play my hometown Utah Jazz. Now it was filled to the nosebleed seats with MOBA gamers screaming and cheering maniacally during each match. Worldwide, more than 20 million people tuned in to watch the tournament.[3] It was surreal to me, seeing video gameplay displayed on massive arena screens, with all the pomp and circumstance of an Olympics or Super Bowl. The winning team was from China (Newbee), who took home more than $5 million in prize money, from a total pool of nearly $11 million.[4] When I returned home from Seattle, I scolded my children for doing homework and told them to start playing *DOTA 2*.

TI8

From time to time, Tim Larkin would call up and invite me to join him on a fishing expedition in Alaska, a hike through Banf, or some other outdoor adventure. In January of 2018, he called again and I assumed he had another adventurous invitation up his sleeve. Turns out he did, just not the kind I was anticipating. He cut right to the chase:

> "We hired Mick Gordon to do the score for TI8, but something has come up. Things aren't working out and we're running out of

time. You did our first music pack back in 2014, so you know the drill. Think you could whip up another new *DOTA 2* score for us by March?"

Yes, yes, absolutely yes!

Every composer learns that most clients want their music good, fast, and cheap. But generally, they can only pick two. The music can be fast and cheap, but the quality won't be as high. Or the music can be good and cheap, but it will take longer to deliver (fill the cracks between higher paying clients, farm out the work to contractors, etc.). This is a good rule of thumb to remember: good, fast, and cheap – pick any two.

Valve was up against a tight and immovable deadline, so the fast turn-around was a given. For a blockbuster like *DOTA 2*, the quality bar had to be high. So, we now had good and fast, those were nonnegotiable. Since cheap had to drop by the wayside, I hit Valve with a big bid. But it surprised me when Tim said they did not want to pay for a live orchestra or choir this time around. He only offered to pay my creative fee. I pushed back, knowing how critically important those live components were to my production approach. But let's face it, an orchestra costs a lot of money. So does a large choir. For the TI4 music score, I had hired a total of 72 musicians and singers, each earning at least $50/hour for several hours. Add recording studio time and engineers, and you can see how the costs multiply. For TI8, Valve just was not willing to go that deep. Maybe because they had already lost money with the previous composer? I did not know the cause, but every push for live orchestra money hit a brick wall. At the end, Tim bumped up the budget enough to cover a couple of studio soloists and a third-party mixing artist, but that was it.

Good-ish, fast, and cheap-ish. It wasn't optimum, but we had a deal.

Now here is a question. If this was your project, how would you come up with innovative new music for a game you had already scored once before? Where could you find fresh and relevant influences? I asked myself the same question. And I found an answer in the absolute spectacle of attending the *DOTA 2* International tournament. I had been inside Key Arena when it overflowed with *DOTA 2* players and fans. I had felt the intensity of competition as the final teams battled it out for a multimillion-dollar purse. The ravenous energy, the larger-than-life eSports phenomenon, plus my personal reaction to it all – this was a fresh well I could draw renewed inspiration from, enough to invigorate my imagination for another run.

But production limitations may also dictate the type of score you compose. That was certainly the case with this one. With a fractional production budget, I only had enough money to hire two studio soloists for a few hours each. I had to think carefully about what flavors were available within that limitation to bring extra spice to the score. If I veered toward a hybrid orchestral-rock score, I could probably get away with building the orchestral part of the arrangement from digital samples. The heavy guitars would skew the style, and sampled orchestra tracks might work well within the genre. Big drums and cool synths could make an appearance too. It would not be as epic as TI4, but maybe I could still deliver a screamin' score.

Resolved – at least one of the two soloists would be a rock guitarist.

Serendipitously, after wrapping up recording sessions for an unrelated film score, I found myself discussing the TI8 music with a group of orchestral musicians who played on the TI4 score years earlier. Among them was principal cellist Nicole Pinnell, who described a guitarist she had recently worked with while on tour with singer David Archuletta. The guitarist's name was Nick Petty. Nicole could not say enough good things about his chops, intonation, and timing. She gave Nick her highest recommendation.

That was enough for me to pick up the phone and make a call. Nicole and I had collaborated on so many projects together. I knew her judgment was uncompromising and her taste was impeccable. That kind of trust cuts both ways. You will find people in your careers that win your trust like Nicole had won mine, people who can offer conduits to new talent and creativity. Such referrals can benefit the quality of your music and the breadth of your reach. On the other hand, you may find yourself in a position to help others who have come to trust your good judgment too. You may be in a position to recommend valuable pieces for their creative puzzles. Never hesitate to share great resources where they can help others succeed, even your competitors. Helping other people create fabulous content benefits us all in the end, bringing good karma to givers and gracious receivers alike.

I did call Nick, and he was terrific. Taking a page from my favorite 70s rock band Kansas, I composed a rapid-fire rhythmic guitar riff to drive the score into a frenzy. The riff had to be played with precision and passion. Nick plugged into the vibe right away and killed the execution. But we had to work on the sound. I was looking for a violently muted sound, with a massive transient hit and quick release. It had to be that way, otherwise the quick riffs would get buried under muddy sustain. We first tried fastening an eraser to the top of the fingerboard, but the effect was too much like a capo. After a couple of other misfires, we draped a small towel across the top of the strings, and that did the trick. Nick could dig into the strings with his pick and deliver the huge transient I wanted. But the towel would quickly dampen the ringing, keeping the riff sounding exceptionally and organically trimmed. Nick was a great sport through it all, and every session with him was a pleasure.

As the overall score came into focus, I felt that a female vocal would add another layer of fantasy sheen to the hybrid orchestral-rock sound I had developed. Since stretching beyond my normal stable to find a new guitar player worked out so well, I likewise cast a wider net for the female vocal role. I auditioned five different singers by having them improvise on the main theme. Each one sizzled in their own way. But Jenny Jordan, whom I had worked with many times before, delivered head and shoulders above the rest. As mentioned earlier in this book, Jenny has sprinkled her immense talents like magic dust across so many of my scores. Her range, gorgeous sound, stylistic versatility, and consummate professionalism in the studio made it easy to call on her repeatedly. She always brought what was needed, and reliably created a signature sound that was unique to each music score. Such a dazzling and versatile instrument.

In spite of our long history together, Jenny was not offended nor prideful when I asked her to audition for this part. Some talent might be miffed if a longtime collaborator asked them to submit a custom audition. Not Jenny, she was humble and eager to come in and compete for the job. That is one trait that separates a true professional from a diva. Jenny got the gig.

The vocal parts I imagined would require two different types of vocalizing. For the main theme, I needed Jenny to sing a thematic melody, searing hot and strong, as if her voice was another weapon in our rock-and-roll arsenal. We worked out the part together, experimenting with different placements of the voice in her head, her throat, and her chest. The approach that ultimately worked the best was a throaty belting of vowel singing, which we processed through reverse reverb and double-tap echo, then bounced over into a flanger. If you can imagine that in your mind's ear, you know that is one trippy sound!

The other type of singing was specifically for a track called, *One Foot in the Grave*. For this track I needed a highly mysterious, ethereally wispy voice, delicate, but also foreboding. Jenny switched her delivery to a breathy head voice that gave us the creeps, in the best sense of the word. Her solo track was cool, but I asked her to also improvise some higher harmony parts, so we could hear how they might add to the atmosphere of the score.

I must say. One of my favorite things about collaborating with other talented creatives is the surprise and delight that occurs when you stumble onto something truly magical. When Jenny's new harmonies started floating into the score – playing off her original solo vocal, drifting through the guitar moans and creaking percussion parts – it was absolutely spine-tingling. I never imagined that effect while I was composing the score. It took another creative talent to bring that extra tingle to the party.

Such versatility and musical intuition are what make the best talent worth their weight in gold. As a composer, you will recognize that quality in the smart and talented people who become a reliable part of your stable. Just as your clients will recognize that quality in you. They will come to trust you because your musical instincts will be right for their project. Your voices will align, and by doing that, your music will amplify their vision and add immense value to their creation. Seek clients and collaborators with whom you can experience this kind of creative magic repeatedly, and your career will progress with valuable contributions to the artistic fabric of the world.

The score was completed on time and within Valve's budget. The new music pack was gobbled up by the *DOTA 2* community, and we received an outpouring of props and appreciation from players across the globe.

POST SCRIPT

Looking back in retrospect at these stories, it strikes me how many interconnected pieces had to fall into place for this to work. T18 came to me because I did a good job scoring T14. T14 came to me because I devised a clever package to get Mike Morasky to hear my music in a controlled listening environment. That package became a possibility when I persuaded AIAIAI to donate headphones to my cause, making it their cause. And the idea was catalyzed because I was attending GDC and needed an innovative solution to an age-old problem. Just look at how all the dominoes fell. Or to use another metaphor, how the dots aligned.

As the late Steve Jobs taught us, we can rarely connect the dots looking forward. But looking back today, everything is crystal clear.

To listen to music from DOTA 2 TI4 and DOTA 2 TI8, as described in this chapter, please visit: HUGEsoundRecords.com/Memoir-12

NOTES

1 https://venturebeat.com/games/*dota-2*-grows-larger-than-world-of-war-craft-but-league-of-legends-still-crushes-both/
2 Chance Thomas, *Composing Music for Games: The Art, Technology and Business of Video Game Scoring*, pp. 280–281; Boca Raton: CRC Press, 2016.
3 https://www.polygon.com/2014/7/29/5949773/*dota-2*-the-international-tournament-20-million-viewers
4 https://bleacherreport.com/articles/2136697-*dota-2*-international-2014-grand-finals-results-and-updated-prize-money-pool

CHAPTER 13

Faeria and *Roguebook*

W HEN ASPIRING COMPOSERS ASK my advice about music scoring for video games, I always mention attending the Game Developers Conference (GDC) in San Francisco. And here is why. Not only is it a great place to learn about game audio development from the best in the business, but it is also an unduplicatable melting pot of game developers from all across the world. Some of those developers are in desperate need of music services. In such cases, it might as well be your music that solves their need.

Or in the case of the charming Belgian game *Faeria*, it might as well be my music.

It was the first day of GDC in 2015. I wanted to get a jump on the competition, so I was walking the expo floor as soon as they opened the doors. One of the first booths I encountered was a display of games from several Italian game development studios. I handed out a bunch of my business cards and collected several more, but none of their games really grabbed me.

That is another thing I learned at GDC. Take time to search for the games that really grab you. That way your enthusiasm can shine through effortlessly.

FAERIA

After wandering a bit more, I spotted a large poster with the word *FAERIA* printed on it, surrounded by beautiful characters and gorgeous settings. It was clearly a fantasy game, my favorite genre. Nothing else on the expo floor existed for me at that point, I had closed the mechanism and became 100% focused on this potential target in front of me.

 DOI: 10.1201/9781003199311-14

As I entered the staging area, I began pouring over all of the displays, searching their info, getting a feel for the fantasy world, and imagining music. I caught the eye of Martin Pierlot, the game's art director, and we began to chat. I gushed about the artwork, genuinely, and wanted to know everything about the game. It was early in the day, so he was still fresh from his coffee and happy to tell me all about it. I listened like a sponge, responding with enthusiasm and curiosity in the right places. Eventually, the conversation turned to music.

He said they did not have a composer under contract yet, but had some people they were considering. I told him I was already getting musical inspiration about his game, and sang him a couple of ideas on the spot. I also described the composition map music system I had designed for *Left Behind* and suggested that model as a possible approach for his game. Everything was resonating with Martin, and we agreed to follow up with each other the following week.

I asked if there was anyone else on the team I should meet, and Martin introduced me to two other key people at the company, Jean-Michel Vilain, the programming lead, and Olivier Griffet, the director of business development. This gave me the opportunity to learn even more about the game and share my enthusiasm and lightbulb moments with other people in decision-making positions. I had one chance to deliver a strong first impression and I wanted to make the most of it.

Once I felt I had made just enough of an impression, without over-staying my welcome, I left them with business cards, and arranged for a call the following week. Then I walked away and continued exploring the expo floor.

But *Faeria* remained on my mind.

The following week, as arranged, we connected on a Skype call and explored the design of their game. *Faeria* was a strategy deck-builder with the same three-state game play as *Left Behind*. I explained the benefits of a music system based on composition maps – (1) seamless, anytime music transitioning based on changing game states, (2) very low programming overheard, (3) budget savings. I suggested that such an approach might work well for *Faeria*.

Meanwhile, key members of the leadership team had visited the links on my business card and listened to music samples from *Quest for Glory V: Dragon Fire*, *The Lord of the Rings Online*, and *Peter Jackson's King Kong*. Between the chemistry we felt at the first meeting, the music design conversation on the Skype call, and their appreciation for my past work, they offered me an initial contract to compose and produce a main theme for their game.

My instincts are good, but not always perfectly aligned with those of a particular dev team. For the main theme, I created a waltzing piano fantasia, nearly four minutes long, which began delicately, morphed into a bold and aggressive second movement, then returned to the original delicate motif. It was the kind of song I could envision piano teachers buying as sheet music for their game-loving students for an upcoming recital. I was so excited to send it over.

However, this music was not what the team envisioned, which generated another Skype call. Even a miss like this can be a good thing if it brings clarifying direction from your client. That is exactly what happened here. As a result of my misfire, the team put a video together with many images from their game world. The video conjured a totally different feel from what I had composed in the blind. Now it was clear that the theme should begin with a feeling of danger and suspense, then morph into an invitation to discovery, wrapped around a world percolating with wonder.

Faeria was a more organic world than I originally understood. I would need the resonance of solo wooden instruments in this score. The recorder, the Irish flute, and the cello could bring those flavors. They were difficult to counterfeit in my digital mockup, but the virtual samples got "close enough" to convey my ideas to the team. They heard the new theme and loved it.

In my contract, I had budgeted a modest amount for live production. I always bring that up and negotiate for it, though not every time successfully. Having even a small amount of money budgeted for live production gives composers options they would not have otherwise.

I would like to share something serendipitous that happened during one of my live recording sessions for *Faeria*. This was a cello session with Nicole Pinnell, an extraordinarily talented, passionate, and skilled musician. She had recorded all of the cello parts successfully for the *Faeria* theme, and we still had 15 minutes left on her call time. Instead of sending her home early, we decided to experiment with her instrument and record a variety of unusual sounds for potential future use.

One sound in particular stood out above all others. Nicole put a tremendous amount of rosin on her bow, and placed the bow on her low C string, near the bridge on the instrument and near the frog on her bow. Then she pressed down on the bow as hard as she could, and nudged it slightly forward. The bow gripped tight to the string and refused to move until the last possible second. When it did move, it only moved the tiniest distance, but uttered a shockingly loud transient, an otherworldly guttural grunt. I had never heard anything like it. While I found no use for it in the *Faeria* score, I squirreled it away inside my personal sample library. Later, I was able to utilize that sound in the score for *The Lord of the Rings Online: Mordor* as a signature for the land of Lhingris. Mixed with an EQ emphasis around 100 Hz and again at 7 kHz, echoing into a deep and dark reverb, that guttural cello grunt sound is SO creepy and foreboding. I mention this to encourage healthy experimentation when you have a little extra time with musicians in the studio. They know their instruments better than you do, and may have discovered unexpected sounds or techniques they can share with you. Surprising bonuses can come when you turn them loose and experiment together.

The main *Faeria* theme instantly generated a spike of positive online buzz for the game, which charged up the dev team. Soon we began discussing a contract to score the rest of the game. The primary score for the game would be built on a composition map design, such as I had previously discussed. But the game would also require components from traditional game music design, including loops, tags, stingers, and transitions.

The budget was limited, but getting all of these music cues to play nice with each other would require a lot of design work on my side. I negotiated a higher rate for my personal services, as well as retaining all the copyrights, which cut out any additional money for live production. Sometimes you just can't get it all.

The score turned out well, every component handing off nicely to the others according to the various state changes in the game. *Faeria* became a sleeper hit in deck-building circles. The game generated great reviews from a surprised and impressed gaming press, and terrific word-of-mouth buzz from players. I was thrilled for the team and happy for my own tangential success. Reactions to the music were extremely positive, and my rapport with the game team had been excellent.

It is always disappointing when a great team breaks up, but especially so when the game has been successful. I was saddened to learn that Abrakham Entertainment went through a painful reorganization after *Faeria*'s success.

Life carried us away on disparate currents, and I lost track of my Belgian friends.

ROGUEBOOK

Many years later, I was pleasantly surprised to receive a message from Jean-Michel Vilain. After all the dust settled, he had secured the rights to *Faeria* and taken ownership of the company outright. He was now developing a sequel called *Roguebook,* which expanded the *Faeria* fantasy world into new domains and added updated gameplay. Bolstering his hand was the addition of Richard Garfield to the design team. Richard brought serious cred as the original designer of *Magic: The Gathering.*

Jean-Michel asked me, "Would you be interested in scoring our new game?"

There was something magically enticing about the *Faeria* fantasy world created by Jean-Michel and his friends. I am unable to put it into words, but somehow the music captures it. That is one of the wonderful things about music, right? Music can convey some impressions that evade written language.

At the time I was stretched pretty thin with other projects, but I knew if I could get a good budget, I could pull together a score for *Roguebook* that harked back to the magic we had all discovered with *Faeria.* I pitched an orchestral score with hybrid elements, produced with digitally sampled instruments and a few live overdubs. He liked that idea, because he knew that would keep production costs down. But what should I charge for my creative fee?

I knew I needed more than usual. I was stretched thin and would have to bring on additional talent to take some of the busy work off my plate. At the time, my base rate was $1,500 per finished minute. I decided to double the rate and submit the bid, expecting to engage in a few rounds of negotiations before landing on a mutually agreeable number. But there was no negotiating, Jean-Michel accepted my bid without reservation.

I next proposed retaining the copyrights in all compositions and recordings, so that I could sell the *Roguebook* soundtrack at HUGEsound Records and distribute it digitally. Again, Jean-Michel agreed to my terms. That is a rare moment, when a client agrees without equivocation to all of your contract requests. After signing the deal, I indulged in a little celebration, probably took Pamela out for dinner at a nice restaurant. But Jean-Michel may have been celebrating too. Offering me such favorable contract terms riveted my full attention on his music score, even nudging me into a mindset to overdeliver. So, while I was celebrating the favorable terms of this deal, perhaps Jean-Michel was doing the same thing, though for very different reasons.

As I began composing, I realized anew the need for organic wooden resonances in this fantasy world. I recalled seeing a video months before posted by woodwind specialist Kristin Naigus, playing what she called the Native American Super Bass Flute. It looked like it was carved from a hollow bamboo trunk and made the most gently haunting, woody sound. At the time, I made a mental note of the sound for future notice, and now recognized that *Roguebook* would be a perfect fit for the instrument. I tracked Kristin down and learned everything I could about the Native American Super Bass Flute, especially about its range and how it spoke through each part of its range. I decided to use the instrument to introduce the old *Faeria* theme in the opening cue, *Unearthing the Roguebook*, which brings players into the new layers of *Faeria* explored in *Roguebook*.

Kristin had another instrument that I wanted to record in the score too, that was the Quenacho. This is a tunable Peruvian flute, often made from Ashwood, which delivers another flavor of haunting resonance. The sound is hard to describe, but I will try. Imagine a sound reverberating from the back of the throat, being pushed out through the nose. I know, that makes no sense as I write it. But if you listen to the opening statement in track eight, *Under the Vast Oversky*, from the *Roguebook* OST, you will probably agree that is exactly what it sounds like.

I also found a place for bass recorder in the score, with its famously muted timbre, which opens track six, *Pages of Hidden Secrets*.

Of course, one of the most resonant and woody instruments ever constructed is the cello, particularly as played by Nicole Pinnell. Nicole's playing is scattered throughout the entire score, though I really love her work on *Pages of Hidden Secrets*, beginning just under a minute into the cue.

I also brought Jeannine Goeckeritz onboard to scatter some classical flute, alto flute, and orchestral bass flute across the score. These bits of sonic spice are like a chef's secret ingredient, transforming an otherwise pedestrian virtual soundscape into moments of refreshing ear candy.

Composer J Scott Rakozy lent a hand with some terrific additional music for the score, helping me through a tough squeeze in the production schedule.

The final touch was hiring mixing artist Mike Roskelley. He and I have always worked so well together, and getting in the mixing trenches with Roskelley added a higher level of polish to the score. He is always that good.

After delivery, Jean-Michel let me know that he was thrilled with the sound of the score and with how well it worked inside the game. Knowing that he was once again a happy and satisfied client did my heart good.

Happy clients will benefit your business again and again. Even if they do not return to you directly, which many will, happy clients are your best advertising since they tend to tell other decision makers about the great experiences they had working with you. Treat all of your clients like gold.

To watch videos and listen to music from Faeria *and* Roguebook, *as described in this chapter, please visit: HUGEsoundRecords.com/Memoir-13*

CHAPTER 14

Might and Magic
and *Combat of Giants*

H*EROES OF* M*IGHT AND* *Magic* has a long and storied history in video games. I first caught wind of the franchise in the late 90s, while working on the score for *Quest for Glory V: Dragon Fire* at Sierra. Among my co-workers at Sierra, *Heroes of Might and Magic* was always discussed in hushed and reverential tones, especially by the fantasy genre faithful. I was intrigued, but always from a distance. I had no connections to anyone working on the games at New World Computing, nor later at 3DO. Even after the franchise was sold to Ubisoft, I could never discover any inroads. Sometimes, all one needs is a little patience.

You may recall Aurelien Baguerre from the account of *King Kong* in Chapter 4. Aurelien was an intuitive and inspiring music director. I loved working with him, and the score turned out so well under his guidance. After such a tremendous collaborative experience, I had hoped to work with him again. But shortly after *King Kong* shipped, Aurelien left Ubisoft's Montpellier studio and I lost track of him for a time.

When he resurfaced a few years later, Aurelien had moved from Montpellier, France to Quebec, Canada. He had taken a new position with Ubisoft, appointed audio director over an upstart dev team with an innovative mandate – produce a compelling deck-builder game infused with the rich fantasy lore of the *Might & Magic* universe. Aurelien had been given a small budget to produce a main theme, and wanted to talk with me about the prospect.

DOI: 10.1201/9781003199311-15

I was reminded again that personal connections to satisfied clients and friends in key places are everything in this business. Maybe everything in any business.

Aurelien was embarrassed that the music budget was so small, but offered to pay my full rate to compose a three-minute main theme. We would produce the theme virtually, with no live elements. I nibbled a few more dollars for a contract mixing artist. Ubisoft would retain the copyright, but they would allow me to freely promote the music and my involvement in the game. They also agreed to pay me a 50% nonrefundable deposit up front. We had our agreement.

The first game was called *Duel of Champions*. The game producer, Stephane Jankowski, loaded me up with lots of beautiful concept art and game lore documents. As I immersed myself in this fantastical world, the inspiration came for a dark, martial theme, marching forward on relentless marcato strings and heavy percussion. Contrabass choir samples and gritty brass stabs reinforced the oppressive march, interspersed with brush strokes of fantasy colors from a soprano chorus, first and second violins, and high woodwinds. For a completely synthetic rendering of an orchestral/choral composition, the final result was compelling.

The game was a surprise success, and Ubisoft authorized a more robust sequel.

FORGOTTEN WARS

Aurelien wanted to pull out all the stops for the sequel, *Forgotten Wars*. I pitched a 52-piece live orchestra and a 24-voice SATB choir, with overdubs from several ethnic instrumental soloists. Additional budget was included for sheet music prep, musician contracting, conductors, recording engineers, and my favorite mixing artist. I reduced my creative fee to $1,200 per finished minute, but proposed a license carve-out to retain the soundtrack rights.

Costs for such a score can skyrocket without careful packaging and management. For years I had been refining a music production sweet spot in Salt Lake City, Utah. Here I could bring together a larger orchestra, a larger choir, a great sounding studio, and exceptional engineering talent for a lower price than any of my competitors could in Seattle, Nashville, Los Angeles, or London. And while there were two popular Eastern European options that could successfully undercut me on cost, I did not love the sound of any recording coming from those places. My packaging in Utah was getting great results and saving my clients money. It was a real competitive advantage.

Aurelien accepted my bid, but Ubisoft would not agree to the soundtrack carve-out. Everything else was approved.

The folklore for *Might & Magic*: *Forgotten Wars* drew its inspiration from ancient Egypt, and I was eager to explore new and exotic flavors from that part of the world. It was fascinating to research the sounds and ranges of the oud, bouzouki, Middle Eastern fiddle, Persian flute, and duduk. Each instrument conjured a cultural resonance in my imagination of great Pharaohs, oceans of bitter sand, and mysterious dark arts. I would find room for every one of these instruments in this new music score, woven in among the orchestra and choir.

Meanwhile, a young composer from Israel named Or Kribos had built a friendship with me. I was taking on a small mentoring role in his career, and I invited him to sit in during the live recording sessions for this game. There is simply no way to understand the unique pressures of a live orchestral recording session without being in the control room, watching it go down. Live sessions provide singular lessons about the raw collision of artistic vision, time pressure, budgetary constraints, and human limitations. All of these stresses converge as clients, engineers, musicians, and singers look collectively to the composer for artistic direction, problem resolution, and split-second decisions. Watching veterans handle such pressures deftly and with composure teaches volumes. This kind of mentoring experience offers lightbulb moments and nuances of insight to students and young composers, which a classroom or home studio can never provide.[1] I wanted Or to have that experience.

A lightbulb moment occurred while recording flute overdubs. One phrase, in particular, sounded too generic, too lifeless. I needed the musicians to deliver the line with more exotic flair. As I tried explaining the articulation to the classical musicians booked for the session, I was not making much headway. Dynamic markings were not helping. Phrasing suggestions were not helping. Things were becoming a little tense.

Aurelien looked toward me to resolve the situation and get us back on schedule. As I rose from my seat to walk onto the sound stage and talk with the players face-to-face, Or suddenly blurted out an idea of his own. You could have heard a pin drop as everyone in the room wondered why this student guest had broken protocol and advanced his own idea, especially at such a tense moment. But here is the thing, it was a really good idea. He suggested that the musicians overblow two of the notes in the phrase, the same notes I had been trying to emphasize with accents or staccato markings. I turned to Or and thanked him. Then glancing around the control room, I added, "I don't care where the good ideas come from. The important thing is to grab them, and get them into our score." I gave Or's suggestion to the flute players, and within just a couple of takes, they delivered the flavor I was searching for.

I could have been prideful in that situation. I could have told Or to mind his place and remember that he was a guest invited only to observe. But how would that have helped my client? With persistence, I would have eventually led the flute players to the right take. But that would have wasted precious time and money.

As a composer, you do not have to have all the good ideas. But you must have the good judgment to recognize good ideas and capture them. Your client is hiring you to produce a great sounding score, no matter how you get there. That was a potent lesson for us all that day.

We finished recording, mixing, and editing the score. Aurelien forwarded the finished tracks to his boss in Quebec. I will never forget the look of pride on his face as he uploaded the files and pushed send. The glow of satisfaction from a happy client is like the shine of gold bars in your personal Fort Knox. Client goodwill has reliable staying power and always grows in value over time.

When Aurelien came to Utah for the *Forgotten Wars* sessions, I invited him to add one extra day to his travel schedule. I used to host annual hiking trips to the top of Half Dome (see Chapter 15) when I lived in California near Yosemite National Park. Those hiking trips had been wonderful life experiences and paid big dividends for my business. Now that I was in Utah, I offered to take Aurelien hiking in Bryce Canyon National Park. If you are unfamiliar with Bryce Canyon, take a moment for a quick Internet search. The canyon is truly spectacular, unique in all the natural world.

With a successfully completed score still playing in our heads, we hopped into my car and made the drive down to Bryce Canyon. What a glorious day! Being out in nature opens people up, especially after they have spent an intense week inside recording and mixing studios. Aurelien and I talked incessantly, took loads of photos, hiked several trails in the park, and deepened our friendship in the shadows of Bryce's majestic Hoodoos. I also brought my youngest son Preston along, and his vibrant personality only added to the charm of the day.

Let me pose a question. All other things being equal, who do you think a client would rather work with on their next music score? Someone they know only from their music? Or someone they have also laughed with, shared personal life stories and spectacular experiences with – a peer, a colleague, and a friend?

When you spend time with clients outside of the studio – especially sharing highly memorable experiences in remarkable places – it bonds you together in profound and durable ways. Seeking for such opportunities with your own clients can augment your personal recipe for success in business and greater abundance in life.

COMBAT OF GIANTS

Several months after our trip to Bryce Canyon, Aurelien called and invited me to join him in Quebec City for talks about music for another new Ubisoft franchise. He made arrangements for me to fly in a day early, so he could show me the St. Lawrence River front, the Chateau Frontenac, and other local highlights.

As my flight gradually descended toward the Quebec City airport, I spotted hundreds of tiny blue swimming pools dotting backyards, as far as I could see in every direction. A quick Google search revealed that Quebec has over 300,000 backyard pools. Even California does not match Quebec in its number of pools per capita. I never imagined such a cultural signature in a place like this, so far north.

Aurelien met me at the airport, and treated me to a day on the town. Quebec City is a walled city, another trait I had not expected. The St. Laurence River cuts through the heart of the capital, with a daunting Citadel rising high above the water. Aurelien and I wandered around the Citadel, discussing philosophy and history, catching up on our families, and comparing notes on the latest cool audio tech. He showed me several other highlights of the city, and as daylight began to ebb, we saw the famous Chateau Frontenac lighting up for the night.

Now this is the important part. Spending stress-free time together like this made it easy to deepen our friendship. We had dinner at his home, where Aurelien introduced me to his talented wife, Celia – not only an excellent cook but a freelance photographer with the eye of a true artist. I met their son Paul, and we all laughed and played together after dinner. When clients become friends, everything about the experience is enhanced. I returned to my hotel room that night a richer man.

The next day, it was time to pursue riches of another kind.

Ubisoft was launching a new franchise, and Aurelien said they had plans for video games, toys, animated cartoons for television, maybe even animated films. He wanted to bring me in on the ground floor, and I was excited and grateful. The franchise was *Combat of Giants*, and its first product would be a video game for Nintendo's DS. The game would be called *Dinosaurs*.

Aurelien cited our *King Kong* score as a good initial reference point. He also cited James Newton Howard's *Dinosaur* score as another reference. The game design called for an arcade-style fighting game between increasingly potent dinosaurs, acquired by players as they progressed through the levels. Aurelien's proposed music design was simple – each level had a musical introduction, a fighting loop, and two stingers for victory or defeat. There would also be a main theme that played during the menu, and a scored opening cinematic. The music budget was fixed and these were all the assets we could squeeze out of it. That meant only a single combat loop per level, which I thought would be problematic.

Here was the problem I envisioned. Players would have many battles in the same level before moving on. With only one loop, hearing the same music in every battle would quickly become tiring, and eventually annoying. When players get annoyed by the music, they shut it off. Game over for the music team!

But then I had a lightbulb moment. I proposed a minor adjustment to Aurelien's music design. Neuroscience teaches us that the brain gives priority attention to new stimuli, such as when music *first* begins playing. If we could vary what players heard first when the combat music started, that would significantly reduce the risk of listener fatigue.

I offered to divide each music loop into four interchangeable segments. The programming team would need to insert a shuffle mode into their playback system, selecting any one of the four segments first, then stitching together each subsequent segment randomly. This would convey the illusion of more variety than we actually had, giving us more bang for the buck. In each level, players would hear something completely different the first four times they began fighting, effectively creating the illusion of more variety.

It was a simple solution to increase the perceived reach of my client's music budget, and Aurelien loved it. Of course, it meant I needed to compose each music loop carefully, so that each segment split sounded like a natural beginning, flowing seamlessly into whatever segment came next. It took some extra work, but the final result delivered an elegant solution to a hard problem. All without impacting the budget.

Aurelien and his team embraced the idea wholeheartedly, and we began negotiating our agreement. I wanted to produce the score with a live orchestra. I wanted to retain copyrights in the compositions and sound recordings. I wanted $1,500 per finished minute.

The Rolling Stones once famously sang, "You don't always get what you want … but you just might get what you need."

Ubisoft nixed the live orchestra for this score, but agreed to a small production budget so I could hire a mixing artist. Ubisoft would not relinquish the music copyrights. But they did agree to produce and release a soundtrack album, paying me a royalty on all sales. They would not go as high as $1,500 per minute for this score, but they did agree to pay $1,200 per minute. If I remember correctly, the contract called for about an hour of music.

Aurelien's reference scores were my own *King Kong* and James Newton Howard's *Dinosaur* – both epic, live orchestral soundtracks. I worried that it would be difficult to convey the raw orchestral firepower of those scores using only digital samples, especially considering the aging samples I owned. I needed to beef up my arsenal, so I researched the newer orchestral and percussion virtual instrument libraries, and selected those with the most aggressive and realistic sound I could find.

In any score, the composer is always looking for a signature. I tend to build my score signatures around themes and colors. But as I began working on the *Dinosaurs* score, for some reason my high school marching band percussion experience came to mind. During one year of high school, I had a brief stint playing the tri-toms in our marching band. Our percussion section was unusually aggressive, with several drummers who had played for many years. Although most of my drumming experience had come from sitting behind a drum set, I could hold my own on the tri-toms. Our explosive cadences and drum fills came to my mind as I began thinking about the rhythm of giant dinosaurs battling each other arcade style. Some of that flavor began finding its way into the percussion tracks underlying the score. That became part of the signature sound.

As the score took shape and found its voice, I slipped into the zone day after day, week and week. Most composers know this feeling – your fingers are flying over the keyboard, compositions are pouring effortlessly from your mind, orchestrations come naturally, time flies by. You cannot wait to get into the studio each day and you hate to leave at night. It is a great feeling, one you can hardly describe as working. Many of you have been there. It is rare, but when it happens it is a state of mind to be treasured.

Since the score was 100% virtual, I tracked all the parts at my home studio. The parts were generated from Digital Performer triggering dozens of digital instruments in Kontakt and Play. I recorded the instruments into Pro Tools, eight stereo tracks at a time. Synchronization was a challenge because DP was hosted on one Mac Pro tower while Pro Tools was hosted on a second Mac Pro tower. I used an Avid MasterSync to keep them aligned. Occasionally, for no reason I was ever able to discern, the two computers would slip out of sync and I would have to edit the recorded tracks back into alignment. A ghost in the machine or something. Except for those rare times, it was a sample-accurate solution.

I delivered the Pro Tools sessions to mixing artist Mike Roskelley, and he returned stereo mixes to me at 48 kHz 24 bits. I brought the stereo mixes back into Pro Tools and cut the battle loops into four sample-accurate segments for each level. All of the tags and transitions were topped and tailed, meaning that any silence at the beginning or end of the files were eliminated, and I sent the full music package up to Aurelien and his team in Quebec City.

I was surprised when Aurelien called me weeks later and asked if I could send him sheet music for the main theme. "Yes, I can generate that for you. What's the plan, what is the intended use?" He told me he had squeezed just enough extra budget from his producer to record the main theme with a live orchestra in Prague for a 3DS version of the game called *Dinosaurs 3D*. I was never excited about recording in Eastern Europe, but Aurelien was insistent that he wanted to try it. I sent the score, and he made the recording without me.

When he returned to me with the results, my reaction was mixed. There was definitely a difference between the new live tracks and my original virtual version, but it was not always a good difference. I did not like the sound they captured, and there were several places where the orchestra was badly out of tune. We tried to mix the live and virtual versions together, and ended up with a final blend that sounded "OK." But neither one of us ever loved it.

Without fabulous source material, the old adage "fix it in the mix" can only take you so far.

To watch video from Might & Magic *and hear music from* Might & Magic *and* Combat of Giants, *as described in this chapter, please visit:* HUGEsoundRecords.com/Memoir-14

NOTE

1 Chance Thomas, *Composing Music for Games: The Art, Technology and Business of Video Game Scoring*, p. 335; Boca Raton: CRC Press, 2016.

CHAPTER 15

Rise and Fall of HUGEsound

To uncover the origins of this dramatic story, we need to rewind the clock to 1999, and return to Yosemite National Park in northern California.

I had been working on *J.R.R. Tolkien's Middle-earth Online* as an employee of Sierra Online when massive fraud brought the parent company to its knees. Sierra shuttered the California development studio and changed my status from employee to contractor (see Chapter 2). The brief security I had experienced working for a large company tumbled like a house of cards.

As I sometimes did during times of uncertainty or stress, I drove into Yosemite National Park and climbed to the top of Sentinel Dome. There I sat, high above the noise, surrounded by an unbroken circular view of the entire park, contemplating my future. Amidst ancient natural temples – El Capitan, Half Dome, Yosemite Falls, and Cloud's Rest – my mind began racing, imagining a new and ambitious path forward.

I could build my own company. I could focus on world-class original music for video games. My live orchestral score for *Quest for Glory V: Dragon Fire* had made quite a splash, suggesting a possible focus. I could also embrace other aspects of audio as the company grew. I would seek the highest profile games, the most intelligent and creative designers, the biggest budgets, and the most talented collaborators. All of these would become my targets.

DOI: 10.1201/9781003199311-16

For a person who had just lost their job, the idea was oversized and absurdly arrogant. Like Yosemite itself, it was audacious, enormous, aspirational, HUGE.

Yes!

There on that mountaintop, I settled on a name and direction for my new business. I would call the company HUGEsound, fund it personally, and launch it out of my home in Oakhurst, California. I would begin by pitching game companies in Los Angeles and San Francisco, both within four hours' driving distance. It felt good, it felt right. I climbed down from the summit with a new spiring in my step. I drove home invigorated, and immediately set to work.

I built a small studio in my home, adding a reinforced wall to seal off a second-story loft, making a functional workspace. The studio overlooked a sunny atrium on the east, and opened to a Redwood deck on the south, overlooking acres of tall pines and mighty oaks. I wedged my equipment racks underneath a wide oak mixing console, with two sets of monitors and reference speakers perched on top. An old business desk and assorted office equipment lined the west wall. Modest in ways and inspiring in others, this little room was the original home of HUGEsound.

However, I never posted a single photo of this space. It was not the aspirational image I wanted to present to potential clients. If I was going to promote myself to the outside world – and let's face it, as a new business that was exactly what I needed to do – I wanted to convey oversized ambition, HUGE success, and projects on the grandest scale. I began obsessing about branding, turning ideas over and over in my mind. Until one day, it suddenly seemed so obvious. I needed images from the site of my original inspiration. I needed a photo shoot on top of Sentinel Dome in Yosemite National Park.

One dark and frigid Spring morning, way too early for most creative types, a small group of friends joined me in lugging props, camera gear, costumes, and even a Korg Trinity keyboard, up to the summit of Sentinel Dome for a sunrise photo shoot. Graphic designer/photographer Mark Aro was our visual maestro, tasked with turning this mountaintop excursion into marketable assets. He staged several imaginative shots, including two designed specifically for the upcoming sunrise. Capturing the sunrise was not just aesthetically desirable; it was also a symbolic statement.

For the first sunrise shot, Aro positioned me at the silver Trinity keyboard in a flowing, ankle-length black duster, fingers dancing across the keys. My head leaned in slightly, as if unconsciously carried away by the unheard music. The stage was a wide expanse of wind-swept granite, just north of Sentinel Dome's highest point. The camera was positioned about 30 feet away. Pine needle scent spiked the frosty air. My fingers were numb from the cold. Aro framed the shot with Half Dome rising boldly, even arrogantly, behind me to the left. We were poised and ready for the sunrise.

Just as the sun broke over the top of Iron Mountain far to the right, Aro snapped the photo. It was perfectly iconic, exactly the image I hoped to convey to the world.

By the way, for my *Lord of the Rings* friends, that was no misprint. The name of the summit marking our sunrise was in fact, Iron Mountain. Dwarves take note!

The second sunrise shot had to be prepped in advance for a near-simultaneous shoot. We did not want the sun getting away from us, climbing too high in the sky. One of my friends put on a black tuxedo with tails and stood on a large granite boulder, music stand raised high in front, holding a baton in his right hand. Both arms were lifted skyward. The camera was placed about ten feet behind him, facing east. As soon as we finished the keyboard shot, we ran over and snapped photos of the second shot, conducting the sunrise peeking over the distant mountains. It was glorious!

We had so much fun that morning, framing all manner of evocative images – scribbling away on sheet music under an ancient snag, holding a guitar facing Yosemite Falls, the obligatory leather jacket + shades pic, staring off into the distance, and many more. By the time we hiked down, laughter and chatter mingled with the sweet songs of Mountain Jays, we had captured a formidable arsenal of images. Each juxtaposed against Northern California's grandest scenery. The imagery was audacious, enormous, aspirational... HUGE!

I hired Aro again to design a logo for my company, and began constructing a website, www.HUGEsound.com. I filled the site with images from our Yosemite photo shoot. The new custom logo sat atop every page, with music samples and press clippings featured throughout. I bought a year of web hosting, and officially opened for business.

HUGEsound's first contract was with Sierra Online, composing original music for *J.R.R. Tolkien's Middle-earth Online*.

MARKETING

As GDC approached, my number one goal was exposing HUGEsound to as many industry insiders as possible. I designed and printed up a brochure, and the Sentinel Dome photos looked terrific inside it. But I began wondering how much the brochure would really hold people's attention. Capturing mind share at a busy conference such as GDC is a tall order for any marketing effort, let alone for a freelance composer swimming in a vast sea of a thousand other composers.

I needed more than a nice brochure. I needed something sticky, some ingredient I was still missing. Maybe a call to action, but not necessarily a sales pitch. I could not quite put my finger on it.

Then it occurred to me. If I really want to cement the connection between HUGEsound and Yosemite, why not host an event at the Park itself? The idea rolled around in my mind, as I absentmindedly picked up the brochure and started thumbing through its pages. A photo of Half Dome seemed to jump off the inner panel. Bam! What if HUGEsound hosted a hike to the top of Half Dome? Half Dome was iconic and widely known. It was visually bold, and the hike would provide a genuine challenge. That would be memorable.

Yes, that was it. A Half Dome event would provide the missing ingredient in my marketing pitch. I just needed to brand it the right way. It needed a name that was bold, cool, with some gaming flavor mixed in, clearly connected to my company. I decided to christen the event, the ***HUGEsound HALF DOME Conquest***.

I employed my meager design skills at creating an invitation, which fit nicely between the bottom folds of the brochure. Now I was ready for GDC.

It was my hope that distributing invitations to the HUGEsound HALF DOME Conquest would cause a splash, and they did. Whenever I spoke about my new company, I also mentioned the Half Dome event. I passed out brochures and invitations left and right. A few people inquired about music demos, which I also carried at the ready. By the end of the conference, there was palpable buzz about HUGEsound and the upcoming HALF DOME Conquest event. Mission accomplished!

I do not recall how many people signed up that first year. But I will never forget this: they spent the entire day with me. I played them carefully curated excerpts of my original music during the 90-minute drive up to the trailhead. We talked openly about their respective needs for music and sound. Who would not want an opportunity like that with potential clients? And of course, conversations splintered into a hundred different directions totally unrelated to business. That was part of the joy and genius of it.

I hosted the HUGEsound HALF DOME Conquest annually for eight years, forging lifelong relationships and building the HUGEsound brand. At least seven prominent scoring contracts trace back directly to relationships I built or strengthened during those hikes. Those scores generated more than a million dollars in income for my business. Considering my costs were minuscule – printing a few invitations, filling my car with gas for the trip, and providing food and drinks along the way – the return on investment was staggering.

Please consider this. As you think creatively about your own business, consider what actions you might take that could connect your brand to something larger than yourself. What imaging or events might you conjure up that could capture the imagination of your target audience? Try to be as creative in your branding as you are in your music.

I think this is particularly important for a lone composer attempting to build a successful career. These kinds of questions and their implications are worth pondering. Imaginative answers may lead you to unexpected and highly profitable results.

EARLY YEARS

None of this should lead anyone to believe that the early years of HUGEsound were easy. They were not easy. The early years were filled with relentless activity and aggressive hard work. Most efforts felt like planting seeds and cultivating dirt without much harvest. I felt the brand growing intangibly, but I was impatient for concrete opportunities. And of course, opportunities did come, even in the early going. But it was no flood of success. More like intermittent light rain.

I had to fight against discouragement and exasperation. It took many years and much effort to build a fledgling business into a successful company. There was nothing to do but press forward.

During a few early pitches, some developers asked if HUGEsound also offered sound design and voice services. I had not personally developed those skills yet, so I recruited peers who had them. Sound designers, voice casting agents, composers with different competencies than mine – these I invited to join what I termed the HUGEsound *Network*. The Network was a cooperative, rather than a partnership or corporation, with each member voluntarily promoting the other's work, calling on fellow members as projects required additional services. With the Network in place, sound design, VO, and expanded composition services were added to my company's growing offerings.

This arsenal helped secure my first contract with EA Games, providing music and sound effects for a *Frogger* clone called *Bunny Luv*. Another contract came through Network composer, Alexander Brandon, who steered me to Epic Games and Legend Entertainment for the game, *Unreal II*. Overseas contacts in the Network helped secure a music scoring and sound design contract for the *Paraworld* trailer. HUGEsound was growing and the Network was fueling some of that growth.

In the midst of this video game work, an unexpected film-scoring opportunity arose with Sony Pictures Imageworks. That exciting story was detailed in Chapter 6. Here I just want to point out that, while music scoring services won the Imageworks contract, additional audio services from the HUGEsound Network bolstered the bottom line. Access to other service providers made for good business.

Perhaps the brightest highlight from HUGEsound's early years was the score for *Peter Jackson's King Kong*, published by Ubisoft. I will just mention that the score for *King Kong* received substantial critical and popular acclaim, pouring in from all across the world. With such high praise, I thought HUGEsound had arrived. No more feast and famine; perpetual success was certain from this point on. *King Kong* would provide more than enough profile and momentum to send HUGEsound into orbit for years to come.

I was so naïve.

King Kong proved to be no more than a lofty transient in HUGEsound's early growth. After that, business inexplicably fell off a cliff. I could not get anything going. During one especially difficult year, my total income was about $13,000. That was crushing financially, but also crushing to my sense of self-worth. I wrestled with depression, cynicism, and apathy. Dark times, for sure.

But I kept serving in the industry. I served on boards for the Game Audio Network Guild, the Academy of Interactive Arts and Sciences, and the Game Developers Conference. I spoke at universities and colleges about composing music for games. And I kept coming back to my faith – faith in a better future, faith in our Creator, faith in the benefits of hard work and tenacity. My wife Pamela continually encouraged me during the lean times, which was a tremendous source of strength. Eventually business started to pick up again. HUGEsound began to enjoy another season of success.

MID YEARS

While the early years benefited from the expanded resources in the HUGEsound Network, demand for extra audio services tapered off during the middle years. By now, most of my contracts called for epic-sounding orchestral scores. Potential clients narrowed their interest in HUGEsound to my personal music scoring, primarily in fantasy and science-fiction genres. Most large developers I pursued had in-house audio resources anyway, so nonmusic production needs were taken care of.

These mid years became a time for bulking up my composing credits, adding new titles such as *Champions Online, X-Men: The Official Game, Marvel: Ultimate Alliance, The Lord of the Rings Online: Shadows of Angmar, Inspire: The Chicago Spire Art Film, The Lord of the Rings Online: Mines of Moria,* and *The Ninth Domain.*

In late 2007, I had an opportunity to join EA Games' new development studio in Salt Lake City, Utah. They hired me to launch and manage their audio department (Chapter 8). During the hiring process, I negotiated with the general manager for clearance to keep HUGEsound open for moonlighting opportunities, as long as it did not undermine my work for EA. It proved to be a fortuitous perk. After-work evenings soon bustled with activity as HUGEsound kept chugging along.

I also began licensing music for movie trailers and television shows like: *Pawn Stars, Swamp Men, The Bachelorette, America's Most Wanted,* and many more. With a full-time gig at EA Games, and a side hustle purring at HUGEsound, my career seemed to be firing on all cylinders.

But no one knows what may be coming around the next bend in the road. On my way home from GDC that year, I received a surprise phone call about a top secret new James Cameron project (Chapter 9).

Avatar turned my world upside down. The *Avatar* audio team needed four hours of music tracks on a screaming schedule. I hoped to begin my work on that contract while remaining at EA, but a new GM had recently taken over who offered none of the flexibility of his predecessor. I tendered my two-week notice and returned to HUGEsound full time. It was the right decision, as the next several years brought some of the highest profile, most lucrative, and creatively rewarding scores of my profession.

James Cameron's Avatar: The Game, was followed by other sensational titles including *Dungeons and Dragons Online, Might and Magic: Duel of Champions, The Lord of the Rings Online: Riders of Rohan, Might & Magic: Forgotten Wars, Combat of Giants: Dinosaurs 3D, Monopoly Streets, Champions of Canaan, DOTA 2 TI4,* and so many others. HUGEsound had finally come into its own as a truly successful business.

GAYLEN RUST

On a hot August day in 2016, I received a phone call from sound designer Michael McDonough. McDonough was a prolific sound designer, one of the first contractors I recruited for the HUGEsound Network. I had connected him with *WildStar*'s game development team, where he provided sound services for many years. I also hired McDonough to design sound effects for one of my contracts with *The VOID*. We had a good history together.

During this August phone call, McDonough excitedly told me that an investment company had purchased a large media building in downtown Salt Lake City. The president of the company wanted to turn it into a successful entertainment business. McDonough had already accepted a full-time position with the new venture. He invited me to meet with him, along with the president of the investment company, for lunch and brainstorming.

A few days later, I sat down with McDonough to a healthy meal of blackened salmon and kale salad, where he introduced me to the investment firm's president, Gaylen Rust.

Gaylen was a thick man with dark glasses and a wide nose, soft rounded shoulders, and a bowl haircut. All of those features blurred out of focus when he flashed his brilliant white smile, his eyes dancing with delight. Gaylen had an excitable personality, and it seemed he was always excited about something. A self-described entrepreneur-philanthropist, Gaylen boasted that he took over his father's small coin shop and turned it into a prominent national powerhouse. From there, he had branched out into real estate, race horses, and charitable giving. He even dabbled in the music business. With millions available to invest, he wanted to jump into the entertainment business in a big way.

McDonough and I were a captive audience.

After finishing lunch, we drove to the nearby media building Gaylen had purchased. It was a sprawling complex of studios and offices, about 16,000 square feet total. Wandering through each room, we brainstormed about trends in entertainment, market location, local and regional demand, and growth potential. I offered my opinion about how a well-funded media business could dominate the local scene and become a viable competitor in the regional marketplace, even snatching national work from the West Coast. I also floated blue sky ideas ripe for pursuit, such as spatialized music mixing for headphones, a VR piano learning system, and capturing the market for live orchestral video game scores.

We passed several hours together discussing big dreams and grand schemes. As we prepared to say our goodbyes, Gaylen asked if I would consider joining his new entertainment venture full-time. He stressed that his financial muscle could fuel all the dream ideas we had just been discussing. He reminded me that McDonough was already onboard. For a moment, it seemed like the opportunity of a lifetime.

Still, I needed to think about it. Things were going great at HUGEsound, just not at the stratospheric level I had been imagining with Gaylen. I called McDonough and we talked at length about the potential of joining forces. He waxed enthusiastic about Gaylen and the energetic commitment he had already demonstrated for the new enterprise. McDonough encouraged me to join with him, and I was almost persuaded.

What would you do? Imagine that your personal business is thriving, and then unexpectedly you are presented with a new opportunity that could scale your services to a level you may never achieve as an independent. What factors would you weigh and appraise in making such a decision? Financial, creative, lifestyle, social, political, etc.?

I weighed all those factors and more. While I did not like the idea of walking away from HUGEsound, I was enticed by the possibilities of the new venture. Was there any way I could join the new venture and keep my old business too? It dawned on me that there might be a way. It would require a risky proposal and deft negotiation, but maybe I could get the best of both worlds. Gaylen had been emailing me, asking about my decision. It was time to unveil my proposal. We agreed to meet.

We sat down kitty-corner from each other at a long white table inside the new building. I told Gaylen that my company had grown a sterling reputation and amassed many loyal clients in the skyrocketing video game industry. My business was thriving and it did not make sense to walk away from that. What if we could integrate my company into the new venture? What if Gaylen's investment firm purchased HUGEsound outright, including the business name, equipment, copyrights, URL, and other business property? He could then hire me at a VP level to assist in guiding, building, and running the new company.

Gaylen was not only open to the proposal, he loved it.

We spent the rest of the afternoon working out a purchase agreement for my business, including scope of assets, purchase price, time frame for closing the deal, and payment terms. We also discussed my salary and terms of a guaranteed employment contract. We shook hands at the end of our lengthy negotiating session, with a detailed agreement in principle. Gaylen's investment company would buy HUGEsound, and I would come to work as VP of Creative Development and Music.

During my career, I have always done my own legal work. Business law was one of my favorite classes during college, and in subsequent years

I read voraciously about music contracts. But selling my business? That was on a different level. I needed an experienced lawyer in my corner. I reached out to attorney Jim Charne, former president of the Academy of Interactive Arts and Sciences. Jim specialized in entertainment law and he agreed to draw up contracts for the sale and purchase of my business. Believe me, Jim earned every penny. The agreements he drew up were iron clad, and the advice he offered was rock solid. I knew my interests in the transaction were secure.

Everything was on track. But a few days before signing the agreement, something foreboding occurred, although I did not know it was foreboding at the time. Gaylen came to speak with me and suggested that, instead of paying for HUGEsound in cash, he could pay me with equivalent shares from his investment company's silver pool. He contended that the gains I would accrue from his silver pool investment would far outstrip anything I would achieve using cash in other ways. He claimed he had a formula figured out that generated extraordinary gains.

I thought about his offer. Gaylen was very persuasive, hammering home the idea that my money would grow exponentially through his silver buying and selling formula. But I had experienced my own significant returns in real estate and stocks, and preferred the idea of having more direct control over my investments. "No thank you," I said finally, "I'll take cash money please." He pushed the silver pool idea again, just prior to our signing date. Again I declined to participate.

"Cash money, please."

We signed the deal a few days later. It was a bittersweet moment, selling a business I had started almost 20 years prior. But many young entrepreneurs launch a business for this very purpose, to grow its value over time, and redeem the increased value through an eventual sale or merger. Some might say it is one version of the American Dream.

GETTING READY FOR PRIME TIME

McDonough had opened talks with a Hollywood television editor named Michael Fox, who wanted to relocate to Utah. He pitched Gaylen with the idea of adding a picture editing/finishing division to the company. This would be a massive expansion beyond our original business plan, but seemed to offer great upside potential. Gaylen agreed to bring Fox onboard at a VP level, and instructed us to integrate an editing division into the venture.

We now had our VP leadership team in place. I would run the music division, McDonough would oversee sound, and Fox would build a television editing business. We agreed to call the new company, **HUGEsound Post Production – Picture | Music | Sound**.

Gaylen hired his son Curt Rust to oversee building maintenance and repair. Jenn Sprague joined us from Warner-Chappell, where she assisted in producing their vast music library, and handled musician contracting. Jenn was a bright and shining star, with a radiant smile and infectious laugh that quickly disarmed anyone in her presence. She had a strong work ethic and genuinely cared about people, winning friends and respect at every turn. McDonough recruited recordist/mixing artist Michael James Greene to join the team as chief audio engineer.

Payroll was already swelling, and the building was nowhere near ready for business. We needed equipment, technical infrastructure, acoustic treatment, structural reconstruction, signage, furniture, landscaping, and a coolness factor to match our ambitions. We divided up the responsibilities between us.

My first duties were ensuring the sound integrity of each studio space, and overseeing a complete visual makeover.

The building contained a dozen large and small rooms, suitable for a variety of audio and video suites and studios. The bones of the facility were generally good, but significant sonic work was needed to improve internal sound dispersion and secure external sonic separation. I called Sound Design International to help, inviting them to render a full sonic assessment of each room, recommending acoustic enhancements and structural remodeling, as required to meet our professional studio specs. Hugh Park, a building contractor with experience from Gaylen's other properties, handled the construction.

It took months of work, but the results were generally outstanding. Each room was dialed to near acoustic neutrality, with a high degree of sonic isolation. The sound stage had a nice live feel to it, with thick theatrical curtains we could pull around for dampening, as needed. Everyone could crank up the speakers in their respective studios without rattling the rest of the building.

I especially loved the sound of my new composing suite. Bass traps, edge traps, and a carefully calculated positioning of assorted acoustic panels had created an ideal listening environment. The air itself sounded perfect in that room, a magical blend of frequency color, reflection, and dampening.

Next up was the task of reimagining the look and feel of the building. To guide me in that process, I set two overarching goals: (1) crossing the threshold into HUGEsound should feel like entering a magical workshop of imagination, a creative playground where anything was possible and (2) promotional decor in the building should build confidence, reinforcing the exceptionalism of our team. Clients should see tasteful reminders that they were in excellent hands.

The intersection of these two goals required a very particular visual recipe. Professional and playful. Trendy and timeless. Sophisticated and loose. Confidant and solicitous.

I interviewed a number of design consultants and selected Kristina Weaver of Lisman Studios to assist with the interior design. Kristina was terrific. She would bring in stacks of ideas, spreading out options across temporary tables for review. I would pour over color schemes, lighting fixtures, furniture styles and materials, art, set pieces, signage, plants, flooring, pillows, trash cans, ping-pong tables, you name it. Before taking on this role, I had no idea what a comprehensive and sprawling undertaking I had signed up for. Creating the right cohesive look and feel for our facility was an enormous job.

The current condition of the building did not offer much by way of inspiration. The core color scheme was dark and bland, with a few oddities leftover from the prior design. For example, the front doors opened into a large lobby, abruptly blocked by a 28-foot-high wall. Rather than greeting people with warmth and possibility, visitors were stopped dead in their tracks, a welcoming aesthetic right up there with the Black Gates of Mordor. Even worse, a one-way security mirror (like a police interrogation room) overlooked the lobby, creating the impression that visitors were being spied on.

It all had to go.

We tore down the wall and opened up the entrance, revealing beautiful skylights overhead. This change created an atrium flooded with glorious natural light. An airy new color scheme brightened the dark walls with fresh paint. We mounted a large, custom art installation against the back lobby wall. It became a signature, its curved, jewel tone sculpture panels morphing in endless light and dark hues from pinks and purples, to aquas and blues. High above the art installation was our logo, HUGEsound Post Production, with three divisional headings hanging underneath, PICTURE | MUSIC | SOUND. We set up a glass reception desk on the left side of the lobby, backed by a tall, white leather chair. A semicircular sectional with jewel tone pillows was placed on the right, framed by three huge Fiddle-Leaf Fig trees. A large TV monitor showcased a looping sizzle reel, mounted on the south wall. Posters of our highest profile work hung throughout the building in sleek black frames – *Avatar: The Game, The Last Ship, Pentatonix, King Kong, Almost Human, DOTA 2,* and others.

In the back of the building, we installed a break room and play area, with large soft couches, a foosball table, a ping-pong table, a full kitchen, high-top tables and chairs, and bright lighting. Classic film posters on canvas stretched across wooden frames surrounded the space – *Ben Hur, Wizard of Oz, Sunset Boulevard, It's a Wonderful Life* and more. Pinpoint lights hung in curved arrays from the ceiling, cutting slow arcs of light up and down each hallway, a visual metaphor for sound waves and unspooled film.

Each studio was outfitted with comfortable couches and chairs for clients, colorful rugs and coffee tables, lamps, overhead track lighting, and prominent displays for prestigious award statues and certificates. Team members all had their own workstations, desks, and Herman-Miller Aeron chairs. Curt Rust was my right-hand man throughout the whole remodeling process, lending his good taste and boots-on-the-ground assistance. McDonough jumped in too, enlisting his wife's aid to bring some finishing touches to the bathrooms.

The entire place now looked and sounded sensational. As I crossed the front threshold and wandering through the facility, I felt a profound sense of satisfaction and wonder. HUGEsound Post Production struck me like a fresh Hollywood transplant. Truly, this had become a world-class creative playground, a workshop of imagination where anything was possible!

McDonough had overseen the internal connectivity between all the rooms, and contracted wiring technicians to assist with the design and installation. He also upgraded the Foley pits, and managed the purchase of new gear to outfit his sound design studio. He also outfitted a secondary sound design/VO space.

Fox had been equipping an entire wing of video editing suites, while building a video server that was fast and secure enough for network television work.

Greene went shopping for a Neve console, managing its installation, wiring, and calibration. He also made sure the sound stage was abundantly equipped with mics, mic stands, music stands, chairs, headphones, splitter boxes, and interfaces for any kind of recording session we might host – live orchestra, rock band, film shoot, choir, soloists, whatever.

Prior to opening, I submitted a request to Gaylen for an additional team member, a VP of Sales and Marketing to bring high-level clients through the door. Oddly, Gaylen declined this position with some vehemence. He insisted that we each do our own sales and marketing. I had been doing that my entire career, but I still worried that we might be hamstrung without a seasoned VP of Sales and Marketing to hunt the big game.

In another pre-opening move, I asked Gaylen to outline an organizational hierarchy for the company. I thought we could use some managerial clarity within and among our team. He responded that he was CEO of HUGEsound, responsible for all financial decisions and high-level vision. But he wanted the rest of us to work as a committee, without any defined authority or reporting levels. He said he hoped to pit us against each other in a positively competitive way, each championing ideas, seeking allies, and winning consensus, striving to make decisions in the best interests of the overall company. I was naïve to running a larger business, but I was skeptical about the effectiveness of such a management approach. I shrugged my shoulders and went back to work.

It was a cold and sunny December morning when the crane from Allied Sign arrived to install a newly polished, curved silver, HUGEsound Post Production electric sign, hanging high above the front entrance. This was a day of celebration. It was like putting the cherry on top of a sprawling, 16,000 square foot banana split. We were almost ready to open the doors.

We spent the next month tying up all remaining loose ends, clarifying our marketing strategy, preparing promotional materials, and building buzz for the grand opening. HUGEsound Post Production had all the glitzy vibe and cutting-edge technology of the best studios along the West Coast. That should be enough to dazzle the local market. But how could we set ourselves apart even more? What could we offer that would also draw clients away from Los Angeles, San Francisco, or Seattle and bring them here?

PRODUCT, PRICE, AND PROMOTION

Pricing was one issue we debated hotly. In a vivid realization of Gaylen's competitive committee idea, I pushed for pricing that was higher than the local market, but below rates in the coastal cities. Others pushed for pricing that matched local studios, in order to better compete for the home-grown market. Fox and I were not as concerned about the local market, taking the position that HUGEsound was built to pursue more lucrative targets. Besides, I reasoned, we should position ourselves as the premium option for local business. But Greene, McDonough, and Jenn fought hard for us to match local pricing. In the end, they prevailed.

A strategic proposal I championed was adding a Utah-adventure element to our marketing. Just as I had discovered success in positioning HUGEsound and Yosemite together to build the brand in the beginning, I suggested wrapping HUGEsound Post Production around a Utah-adventure experience. We could take visiting clients snowmobiling, dog sledding, hiking through Utah's National Parks, and the like. This was something no other studio was offering, and it hit a resonant chord with the team. We decided to include this in our pitch for lucrative clients.

As a final lure, we leased two rooms at a luxury apartment complex next to the studio to provide out-of-state clients with complimentary housing while they worked with us.

The combination was formidable. Award-winning team, Hollywood vibe, cutting-edge tech, passionate talent pool, small market pricing, complimentary housing, all wrapped around a Utah-adventure experience. We had our pitch, our pricing, and our place. We were ready for the world.

OPEN FOR BUSINESS

On February 3, 2017, HUGEsound Post Production opened its doors to the public. Curious visitors and invited guests streamed through the building from early morning until late at night. People were amazed that such a facility and gathering of top talent could exist in Utah. I eagerly ushered group after group through the building, chatting people up, showing off each studio, bragging about Fox, McDonough, and Greene, and all the brilliant work they had done. I would pause for a few minutes in my own studio too, playing music samples from *The Lord of the Rings Online*, *DOTA 2, Avatar*, or other titles as visitors expressed interest. It was an exhausting but invigorating day.

Driving home late that night, I knew we had a hit on our hands.

Months flew by in a flurry of activities. I eagerly promoted all divisions of the company, inviting filmmakers, video game creators, VR developers, media executives, and others to come and explore our offerings. I took key prospects snowmobiling and dog sledding, dined with them, and escorted an endless parade of tours through the studio. I talked about how our picture, music, and sound teams could successfully and affordably meet their needs. They were dazzled, and why not? The potential synergies were extraordinary.

In those early days, I sought to help each division of the company to flourish. I brought my existing clients to other divisions as a way to build business and expand relationships. But this approach did not produce the results I had envisioned. In fact, it failed to secure several opportunities, which I brought to the table. For example, two of my music score clients came looking for sound design services. I handed them both to our sound division, but they failed to capitalize on either opportunity. Similar things happened with potential VR projects from Los Angeles, San Francisco, New York, and Boston. Maybe it boiled down to our pricing or location. But I wondered if in-house corporate provincialism was to blame. Perhaps I had simply invited too many cooks into the kitchen. Over time, I learned that my efforts were best spent when focused on selling our orchestral recording package and my own music scoring services.

With this narrowed emphasis, I began bringing many West Coast friends and peers to record scores at HUGEsound – Billy Martin, Nick Peck, Matthew Carl Earl, Peter McConnell, Jason Walsh, Tim Larkin, Vinicius Barbosa Pippa, Maclaine Diemer, and others. I loved pitching our orchestral recording package because I truly believed it was the best orchestral recording solution in America. I pitched the passion and expertise of our musicians, the great sound of our scoring stage, our vintage mic collection, the veteran experience of our engineering team, our best-in-the-nation pricing, the complimentary luxury accommodations next door, all wrapped around an unforgettable Utah-adventure experience. Pitching that package was a lot like fishing a fully stocked pond. I would bait the hook, cast the line, and reel them in, slipping clients carefully into Jenn's fabulous customer service net. Jenn made our clients feel celebrated, indulged, and right at home. She was a client-care champion.

Meanwhile, my scoring services were in high demand. Exciting opportunities came to compose and produce many new scores, including: *DOTA 2 TI8, Kingdom Maker, The Lord of the Rings Online: Mordor, Curse of the Serpent's Eye, Tales of a Time Traveler, Rime of the Ancient Mariner, Warhammer: Chaosbane,* and a dozen smaller projects for local clients. I also arranged music for recording artists and produced albums. I launched a record company under the HUGEsound umbrella and began laying the groundwork for a commercial music library. It was a wildly productive season and the music division was buzzing.

McDonough was thriving too. He was often booked on an IMAX film or TV show, building sounds for a live event, recording Foley, or editing dialog. He regularly brought potential clients into the building. I was proud of his creative efforts and bankable results. He generated high revenues, often comparable to mine. We needed every bit of it. Success depending on all of us making it rain.

Greene had a nice bevy of clientele too, keeping a steady stream of recording and mixing projects coming through. His totals may not have been eye popping, but every dollar mattered. The steadiness of his revenue stream was like a gift that kept on giving to the bottom line.

Unfortunately, Fox was another story. He was a phenomenal film editor, a true artist in his craft, and I adored his work. He was also the coolest guy in the building. No one cast a Hollywood vibe like Fox. But he wasn't a salesman. His division would have benefited from a sales and marketing executive, like I had proposed prior to opening. Picture editing and finishing is an especially expensive medium, so his division hit the balance sheet with a vengeance.

VR PIANO AND SPHERE

While the music division was percolating, I also wanted to pursue revolutionary (or at least evolutionary) products in the VR space. One of those products was a VR piano keyboard learning system. The idea was simple enough, build a VR piano for Oculus, HTC, and Sony and combine it with a didactic system for learning how to play. The hook was that a person could use the virtual piano anytime, anywhere – sitting on a beach, laying down in bed, standing on a mountain top – playing the virtual piano (literally) in the air in front of them. All the components were worked out, piano samples to use, modular piano lessons, haptic gloves with motion and distance sensors, additional keyboard sounds for fun and variety.

I took my ideas to the University of Utah's GApp development lab, meeting with director Roger Altizer and a small team tasked with evaluating the viability of potential VR projects. We white boarded everything – the concept, design possibilities, development options, market, pricing models, competition, distribution, life cycle. This was the most thorough product vetting I had ever participated in, and the process was stimulating. However, by the end of the evaluation, Altizer and his team rendered a "not-viable-candidate" verdict. I carried the results back and discussed them with Gaylen. We decided not to pursue the VR piano learning system.

But I had another blue sky idea, a more grandiose and thrilling idea, one that hatched while attending GameSoundCon that year. Mike Henein from VisiSonics had been showcasing spatial audio technology for gaming at the conference. As I listened to the demo, it totally blew my mind. This was the first time a 3D audio technology had managed to impress me with *clearly discernable* sound directionality, both inside and outside my head space, using stereo headphones only. I could distinctly hear sounds behind me. I could hear sounds above me. Sound was discernable below me, to the right and to the left, and centralized deep inside my head. VisiSonics had crafted a superior system for placing sound effects and ambiences around a truly spatialized soundstage.

I was duly impressed. And of course I wondered... What if their technology could be applied to spatialized music mixing? Oh, my imagination went wild! Envision a kick drum pounding in my chest, a bass riff dancing at my feet, a filter-sweeping synth rising far behind me, edging closer and closer, finally leaping high overhead and swooping down far in front of me, shooting out rapidly to the right and left horizons, while an onslaught of guitars exploded in the center of my skull. The possibilities set my mind on fire.

The word SPHERE kept tickling my brain. It perfectly described the soundstage for this kind of music. It also suggested an all-encompassing business model. I quickly envisioned a complete development pipeline, from recording studio tools and techniques, to professional mixing plug-ins, to consumer apps for decoding and conforming, to artists who would record, mix, and release spatialized music through our HUGEsound Records label.

A quick sidebar on consumer apps. The plan was to develop two consumer apps: (1) A premium SPHERE product consumers could use to hear top-to-bottom SPHERE projects, exclusively recorded, mixed, and released through our studio and label system. This would be a high-fidelity decoder app, delivering the kind of mind-blowing, hi-res, outstretching music experience I imagining so vividly at GSC. (2) A budget music conforming app that would take existing music and pseudo-spatialize it, approximating the SPHERE soundstage experience for millions of existing songs mixed in stereo. This could put HUGEsound on the map at an enormous scale.

After returning home from GSC, I wrote everything up and pitched it to Gaylen. Simultaneously, I also pitched it to VisiSonics. The proposal caught fire on all fronts. Everyone was ready to sketch out next steps.

I drafted an initial development plan, which outlined legal, financial, developmental, and logistical milestones. I began recruiting smart people who knew spatial audio like Nick LaMartina from Magic Leap and Tom Todia from Full Sail. I began reaching out directly and indirectly to stimulating recording artists including Gingger Shankar, Zoe Keating, and Kaskade. We began roughing out specs for a SPHERE mixing plugin called Boundless that could enable engineers to create a positionally dynamic, completely spherical music experience delivered through stereo headphones.

Things picked up steam after meeting in person with VisiSonics' president Ramani Duraiswami at the 2017 CES show in Las Vegas. I sketched out an initial agreement between VisiSonics and HUGEsound, between Duraiswami and Gaylen, which both signed. This put us on the road to figuring out one of the most exciting and evolutionary leaps in music technology history.

Weeks later, VisiSonics sent Mike Henein to Salt Lake City as a next step in laying additional groundwork for our companies to work together. During Henein's visit, something happened between him and Gaylen, something I neither witnessed, nor ever received a clear explanation about. But once Henein left, Gaylen told me that he no longer trusted VisiSonics. Furthermore, he was unwilling to move forward with the SPHERE program. On the spot, he mothballed our development. Unilaterally kaput. Just like that.

I was angry and disappointed. More than anything else we were doing at HUGEsound, this partnership with VisiSonics had the most potential for mass market, billion-dollar success. I never understood why Gaylen threw it away so abruptly and definitively. I circled back to him again with a variety of different angles, but he quickly dismissed them all. Nothing rekindled his interest in the project. It was a tough loss for me, hard to let this one go.

It still stings. But life goes on.

GIVING BACK

Shortly after HUGEsound Post Production launched, I began opening my composing studio for job shadowing experiences on Friday afternoons. Young composers were invited to hang out with me while I composed, edited, mixed, evangelized, did troubleshooting – whatever was on the agenda for the day. I would talk about business, work–life balance, and answer questions as they came up. It was all free.

You might describe it as educational jazz. Without a formal mentoring system in place, we took each session as it came, improvising each situation and playing off each another in real time. Whatever I was doing that afternoon, wherever the work led, that is where we would go. Over the course of six months I welcomed 19 different composers into the program. I remember every one of them –Joshua Sohn, Rachel Robinson, DeAndre Allen-Toole, Caleb Cuzner, Christopher Escalante, Karina Pardus, Dallas

Crane, Bryan Atkinson, Kristina Austin Bishoff, Tyler Olsen, Matt Janovsky, Katelyn Limber, Rob Tinney, Luke Wickman, Monique Shang, James Egbert, Benjamin Cole, Peter Murray, and Isabelle Ruegner. What a terrific and talented group. Eager to learn, ambitious, curious, imaginative, gracious. Many have excelled creatively and are thriving in exciting careers.

But eventually, I had to acknowledge an uncomfortable drawback. Having people watch me work, *changed* my work. It was unsettling. Perhaps you can relate. Imagine yourself sitting at your keyboard or workstation, laboring over a piece of music while someone listens to every note. Or picture yourself drafting a contract while a stranger watches you think and type. Or imagine taking a client call and having your side of the conversation scrutinized. I tried to convince myself that it was not impacting my work, but I knew that it was. Unfortunately, with people watching me compose, it altered my creative process. I often had to go back and replace music I had written during job shadowing sessions. Eventually, I called it quits. It was not right for my clients to be negatively impacted, even for the sake of future composers. Still, I am glad I did it for six months, and I have remained a fan of all the talented young composers who came through.

McDonough and Greene sometimes welcomed interns and job shadowers into their workflows as well. I think we were all trying to be good citizens in our respective industries. For a while, everything felt right in the world.

OVERGROWN

McDonough and I were the first two VPs hired, and we had some nuanced differences in philosophy about business. Those nuanced difference were mostly a good thing, as they were generally complimentary. But there was one area where we sharply diverged. While we both wanted growth, we held very different viewpoints regarding how to achieve it. My position was that, after starting with a critical core team, we should only add full-time personnel after they could be supported by existing revenue. Meanwhile, we could fill necessary stopgaps with contractors. On the other hand, McDonough believed in hiring full-time personnel first, which he thought would lead to profitable revenue growth in the future.

Gaylen followed McDonough's recommendations and our payroll ballooned out of control. The picture division added Mark Nelson as a second video editor, Crash Carlucci as a colorist, and eventually Denice Angelo as a sales agent. The sound division added Luis Morales, J Scott Rakozy, and Joe Belliston as additional editors. I was not completely innocent either, dabbling with the possibility of hiring composer Jason Hayes to bolster our game music reach.

The corporate accountant regularly showed me the books, and I was startled to see how much our payroll had mushroomed without compensatory revenues. This was unsustainable.

About this time, Gaylen also hired a business consultant to render an evaluation of the company. The consultant was Derek Marquis, former CEO and managing director of BYU Broadcasting. Derek was thin and unassuming, but spoke with great precision and persuasiveness. He wanted to assess us and determine how to make HUGEsound profitable. I am not sure what Derek charged for his service, but in my ornery way, I could have given Gaylen the answer for free: cut the overgrown payroll and light a fire in underperforming employees. I felt that we needed every key employee to bring in the equivalent of their own salary plus overhead and profit. I was doing that and the music division was thriving. Two or three others were mostly pulling their weight too. But the rest of the team was not. I had seen the books, and I knew. Most were taking plenty of money out without bringing much in. The company was drowning in red ink.

Derek took several weeks and went through his evaluation of the business. He held frequent company meetings where we explored a wide variety of potential business directions – from developing original screenplays, to servicing corporate clients at Silicon Slopes, with lots of other ideas in between. It was an interesting exercise, though I believed the core team already knew their markets. We just needed to work them harder and smarter.

Derek concluded that the company was generally focused correctly, but suggested that the picture division needed additional investment to grow into its potential. He proposed that Gaylen also hire a company president to offer strategic leadership. He further recommended that we change our company name from HUGEsound to HUGE Studios, in order to avoid alienating potential picture clients.

Gaylen agreed with Derek's conclusions. He beefed up his investment in the picture division, elevated Derek to the new full-time position of company president, and changed the name of our company to HUGE Studios.

I could not see how any of those changes would help our bottom line. In fact, I feared just the opposite.

I redoubled my efforts in evangelizing our music scoring and orchestral recording services. What else could I do?

Shortly after Derek became company president, he called me in for a meeting. He greeted me warmly, smiled, and invited me to sit down. He then suggested I was making too much money. He asked if I would agree to a salary reduction. It was a surprising request, since the music division was generating more revenue at that time than any other part of the company. From a financial, managerial, and PR perspective, I was definitely pulling my weight. I liked Derek, but I told him if he wanted to trim the fat at the company, he needed to look elsewhere. Besides, Gaylen had signed an employment contract, which guaranteed my current salary for three full years. That was a key concession I had secured before agreeing to sell HUGEsound and join his venture. I excused myself to grab a copy of the employment agreement, and soon returned, setting it down on Derek's desk. He was not happy, but he knew I was right.

Soon afterward, Derek was called to serve as a mission president in Australia for the Church of Jesus Christ of Latter-day Saints, a three-year, full-time commitment. Derek would be leaving soon.

After Derek's departure, Gaylen hired Jenny Latchman-Atkins (Jenny LA), a former producer at KUER public television, to serve as our new president. She was joined in the corporate hierarchy by another new full-time officer, Anna Maidon, hired as CEO over all of Gaylen's entertainment-related businesses. I was stunned by this latest new hire. How could we become profitable by adding even more management layers to the payroll? To my simple business mind, it made no sense at all. I put my head down and buried my energies in music scoring work.

At least Jenny LA was a hard worker, smart, and good with people. I was unsure about her strategic vision or financial acumen, but she was definitely helpful with clients and prospects. Over time, I believed she could develop new business for us. She reminded me a lot of Jenn Sprague, who everyone loved.

On the other hand, Anna Maidon was a mixed bag. She was bright and driven, yes. But when she stepped in and began exercising her leadership role over our individual divisions, her actions seemed haphazard and clumsy, often stirring up controversy where none had existed before, generating hard feelings without benefit. It was difficult to see what improvement she was bringing. I wondered if the company was unraveling. I tried to share my concerns, but Gaylen had become distant and distracted. Again, I put my head down and buried myself in music scoring work.

THE BOTTOM FALLS OUT

The date was November 22, 2018. McDonough was laying back audio for a new TV series. Fox was cutting an indie film project. Jenny LA was hosting visitors from out of state. I was at a nearby mixing studio working with a contracted mixing artist.

Near the end of the day, I swung by HUGE to drop off a drive. Jenn Sprague met me at the door with a troubled look on her face. "There are a bunch of attorneys and police here," she whispered. "They want to see you in the conference room right away."

Never had I imagined such a phrase being spoken to me in all my life. It sent a cold shiver down my spine.

I found my way to the conference room, where a pair of young attorneys acknowledged my arrival. One quickly escorted me to my scoring suite. He sat me down and shut the door.

The FBI had filed charges against Gaylen's investment firm. The charges alleged a $200 million Ponzi scheme going back at least ten years. The court had authorized a local law firm acting as a receiver to take possession of all downstream businesses and assets, including HUGE Studios. Gaylen was being taken into custody.

I was stunned. Speechless.

After gathering my wits, I finally asked the attorney, "What does this mean for our employees, and for our clients and contractors?" There were projects in the pipeline, musicians, singers, conductors, music prep, and mixing under contract. We had made commitments. The attorney responded by telling me to continue with business as usual, "Just keep things rolling and think of the court as your new business owner."

But it did not play out that way. Four days later, the studio was shuttered. All employees were terminated without warning, pay, or benefits. We were locked out of the building. Everyone was told to file any outstanding financial claims with the court, including clients and contractors. My equipment was gone, locked in the studio. My copyrights were gone, tied up in court proceedings. My music distribution agreements, all painstakingly negotiated, were stuck in the mess. I was supposed to be mixing the *Warhammer: Chaosbane* score.

Anger began boiling up from inside me. I felt like a rip saw had been thrust into my chest. How could Gaylen have done this? Not just to me, and to the HUGEsound team and contractors, but allegedly to hundreds of duped investors? Gaylen's wife and oldest son had also been implicated. I was beside myself.

But it occurred to me that I had a choice about my anger. If I remained incensed and embittered, it would be like shoving the rip saw deeper and deeper into my chest. Dwelling on my hurt and anger was only pulling the saw back and forth, back and forth, continually shredding the fabric of my soul. How would that help me? On the other hand, if I chose forgiveness, that would be like gripping the saw firmly with both hands, pulling it out of my chest, throwing it to the ground, and walking away. Maybe then real healing could occur.

As the legal system ran its course, Gaylen was duly convicted and sentenced to 19 years in prison. Terrible choices had been made, awful acts had been committed. Damage was done to me and hundreds of other innocent people. Nevertheless, I had a choice whether to let his actions damage me further or not. I could forgive him. And with forgiveness, I could be free.

Ultimately, that's what I did. I chose forgiveness. I will not presume to speak for anyone else whose savings were plundered, or whose livelihoods were ruined. But for me, for the health and resonance of my own personal creative soul, I forgave Gaylen and all others whose criminal actions had destroyed our studio, put people out on the street, and caused me to start over in the twilight of my career.

Yes, forgiveness made a huge difference. In fact, it made all the difference. I soon felt at peace. I carried no festering wounds. It was as if a terrible storm had furiously enveloped me, then passed quietly away. The sun was shining again and the air was clear and free. My future was still unwritten, and I could yet compose new chapters going forward. Forgiveness freed me from a terrible cancer of bitterness and vengeance.

Please consider this. If someone has done you wrong, hurt you, marginalized you, bullied you, whatever – I encourage you to first remove yourself from any situation that continues to harm you. Then once you are safely removed and securely planted out of harm's way, consider forgiveness. Forgiveness can heal your wounds and set you free in a way nothing else can.

AFTERMATH

By the time the dust settled, we had all scattered and gone our separate ways. McDonough, Mark Nelson, and Joe Belliston continued independently with some of the contracts they had started at HUGE. Greene went to work for Funk Studios, a previous client and competitor. Fox and Crash picked up TV editing and coloring work in Hollywood. J Scott Rakozy and Luis Morales set up small studios in their homes. Jenn Sprague and Anna Maidon went to work for live event companies, and Jenny LA started doing freelance work for BYU-TV. Gratefully, everyone landed more or less on their feet.

As for me, I secured two new scoring projects, but did not have any equipment or a place to work yet. I needed to gear up, but at this late stage in my career, it did not make sense to spend a ton of cash on brand new equipment. I began calling around to friends in the business, "Do you have any old gear you've retired that I can buy from you?" Several people came through, offering old computers, monitors, interfaces, software, and virtual instruments. In the most spectacular case, Troels Foelman, founder of 8-DIO virtual instruments, graciously allowed me to take my pick from among his vast arsenal of sample libraries. I was overwhelmed by Foelman's generosity, and thrilled with the sound of these new virtual instruments! With the help of these good friends, I managed to outfit a lean DAW system and built a small basement studio. It was a far cry from my composing suite at HUGEsound, but I was back in business.

Lucrative music scoring projects began arriving in short order, bringing an unexpected financial windfall, including *Warhammer: Tomb Kings*, *Unseen Universe*, *Jumanji: Reverse the Curse*, *Roguebook*, *The Settlers: New Allies*, and many smaller projects. It was a surprisingly prosperous season.

So much generosity had been showered on me by Troels and others as I was starting over. I wanted to find a way to pay it forward. The opportunity presented itself during the COVID-19 pandemic. At a time when many musicians, performers, and engineers were out of work, I was able to pour over $80,000 into local music economies – hiring musicians, editors, engineers, mixers, and more. It felt wonderful to be on the giving end.

Meanwhile, the court appointed receiver asked me to assist in finding a buyer for the former HUGEsound facility. Clearly hope springs eternal, as I began dreaming of saving the building and resurrecting the company. I agreed to help the receiver seek a buyer for the building. I was especially on the lookout for someone who might want to relaunch some version of our entertainment business. Several well-heeled, smart, and ambitious prospects came to take a look. I gave them comprehensive tours of the studio and opened the company books. Without exception, potential buyers were dazzled by the facility, but astonished by the bloated overhead compared to the revenues. After seeing the books, they generally declined any further exploration.

But one media business owner and her financial partner saw the potential in relaunching HUGEsound with a leaner business model. They tendered the highest bid among all of the offers collected by the receiver. Their purchase package was two-third cash and one-third financed. They presented a solid business plan and recruited me to help restart the company. In the end however, the receiver elected to sell the building to a commercial property developer from New York City, who tendered a lower overall offer (though it was all cash). That was hard to swallow, one more bitter pill.

From this process, a small silver lining emerged for me personally. After working so closely with the receiver, I was allowed to negotiate fair terms and eventually extricate HUGEsound Records from the receivership. This included repurchasing several music copyrights, distribution agreements, logos, and other HUGEsound website materials. Most valuable among them was my music from *The Lord of the Rings Online.*

The process took 23 months, but on March 1, 2021, HUGEsound Records rose again from the ashes as a boutique music gallery, showcasing several of my film and video game soundtracks, including *The Lord of the Rings Online.* The gallery also includes photos, interviews, BTS videos, and inspiring quotes about the positive impact and power of music. It also hosts all of the bonus content for this book.

EPILOGUE

I recently drove to the old address of HUGEsound Post Production to reminisce. The building was gone. There was nothing left but a huge hole in the ground, excavation for a new high-rise apartment building. If I was looking for closure, that would certainly be definitive.

During a keynote speech at GameSoundCon in 2015, I told the assembled audience that vanguards and experts win. I still believe that is true today. But it is also true that resilience wins. A perpetually resurgent individual is never out of the game for long. Resilient people eventually and inevitably will their way back to success.

Life is shambolic. No one can predict what lurks around the next corner. You may lose things that are of great value to you. People you care about may get hurt. Poor business decisions made by others may shrink your bottom line. None of it is fair.

A video game career can be especially volatile. The game industry is an endlessly mutating swarm of ambition, creativity, boom and bust, brilliance, greed, transience, charisma, geekiness, innovation, passion, expertise, and guesswork. Frankly, the asymmetrical nature and chaotic energy are part of what kept me interested and involved for so long. But it can be a wild ride.

Hopefully this chapter, chronicling the rise and fall of HUGEsound, will encourage you to rise again when your own building gets knocked down.

When your dreams are destroyed and opportunities evaporate, you may need a brief respite to lick your wounds. You may need to recalibrate from time to time. That is OK. Being resilient does not mean you do not have emotions, or that you will not endure suffering. But being resilient does mean you will always get up and try again, no matter what. Resilience wins.

In business and in life, resilience always wins.

I leave you with a few reflective verses I penned on a day of licking my own wounds and doing some recalibrating of my own. For your times of struggle:

COBBLESTONES

Sometimes you feel defeated. Broken. Empty. Hopeless.
Why bother? I can almost hear you say it.
Please don't give up.
Don't give in to the illusion of temporary defeat.
Nor to the mirage of easy success.
The road to lasting happiness is paved with cobblestones,
From a thousand broken attempts.
Get up. Try again. Gather your strength. Muster your courage.
Every effort adds another tiny piece to the sprawling puzzle.
Pain is inevitable.
But so is success, given enough time and evolving efforts.

The relentless make their way.
You are resourceful, imaginative, creative, part of a resilient race.
Rest on your sword for a moment. Then rise and return to battle.
The world needs your gifts!

To see video from HUGEsound Post Production, and photos of HUGEsound and HUGEsound Post Production, as described in this chapter, please visit: HUGEsoundRecords.com/Memoir-15

CHAPTER **16**

Warhammer

T HIS IS A TALE of defeat and resilience that somehow found a way, even
in the face of seemingly insurmountable odds.

The last chapter chronicled the court-ordered shut down of HUGE-
sound Post Production. I was in the midst of producing the original music
score for *Warhammer: Chaosbane* when that happened. The files and equipment were seized, assets were frozen, agreements were suspended, and I
was fired without warning and without pay. I will tell you the story of how
I navigated the court-ordered shutdown and its fallout. And I will give you
a proper postmortem on the music score itself, from the initial pitch to post
production.

But first, I need to retrace my steps back to a pair of formative events
that set everything in motion.

FMX CONFERENCE

In April 2016, I attended the FMX Animation Conference in Stuttgart,
Germany, as a guest speaker. The conference organizers asked me to give
a presentation about music and sound in *The VOID*. *The VOID* was a location-based virtual reality (VR) experience that had recently made a big
splash when Harrison Ford and Stephen Spielberg raved about it in the
press.

After wrapping up my FMX conference talk about *The VOID*, a gentleman approached me and introduced himself. His name was Vincent
Percevault, and he ran a French entertainment conglomerate named G4F
Productions. G4F had a stable of sound designers on staff and also represented a handful of composers.

DOI: 10.1201/9781003199311-17

Vincent and I hung out. We talked about our respective businesses, we talked about our families, we told some jokes, we had a good time together.

As the afternoon wore on, Vincent offered to represent me into the European marketplace. I was happy about this and felt enthusiasm to do business with him. We negotiated a European representation agreement and I sent him promotional materials for his website.

Two years passed without a peep. Then on May 4, 2018, I received an email from Vincent. He wanted to talk about a potential music scoring project. He wrote, "We are actually working on a new *Warhammer* game where we are pushing hard to have you onboard for the music composition. Can we set up a Skype next week?"

Yes, yes, absolutely yes!

On May 9 I joined Vincent and several sound designers from G4F on a Skype call. They were all enthusiastic and friendly, and shared many details about the new game. They said that if I was interested in pursuing this project, I would need to submit a generally dark, Medieval, fantasy music demo with foreboding undertones. They also asked me to submit a bid.

Can we talk about the demo process again for a moment? Countless times in the past, I had created custom music demos targeted to a specific pitch. But at this point in my career, I had plenty of dark, Medieval, fantasy music in my back catalog. Rather than composing something new, I raided my own archives. The demo package included cinematic themes from *Lord of the Rings Online* and *Dungeons & Dragons Online*, combat music from *Might & Magic* and *LOTRO*, and ambient exploration tracks from *Might & Magic*. I gathered all of the tracks together into a well-organized format and uploaded the pitch to a DropBox folder for the team.

I proposed an all-in budget that included a live orchestra, contrabass choir, conductor, sheet music prep, contracting, studios, engineers, and a creative fee of $1,500 per finished minute. Five days later, I heard back from Vincent. The dev team loved the music samples in my demo package, but they said the price was too high.

What would you do if a potential client loved your work but asked you to cut the price?

Here is one way to handle it. I told them I could work for less if we cut the live orchestra out of the package. Then I sent over MIDI mock-up versions of the demo tracks they loved so much. I told them, "Yes, we can do this for less money and here is what it will sound like. Just compare the MIDI versions to the live versions and let me know what you think." Comparing the two, they obviously preferred the live choir and orchestra. They agreed to spend more money to acquire a higher-quality product, with the caveat that I also produce a soundtrack album from the score.

With a price agreement, you might think we were basically done with the contract. But there were many more details to iron out, including a couple of uncommon wrinkles. For starters, there were several parties to the agreement – HUGEsound Post Production, G4F the agency, the dev studio, and the game publisher. All parties wanted a say in the negotiations. Second, a soundtrack album had been requested, but we needed to sort out copyright ownership and distribution, mechanical rights, and performing rights royalties.

Of course, there were also all the normal things that have to be negotiated in a game-scoring agreement, like indemnity and liability, submissions and approvals, credits, promotional allowances, delivery and payment milestones, agency fees, and many more terms. All of these details had to be resolved.

We began negotiating the contract on May 31. After 67 days of contract negotiations, on August 6, all parties finally agreed to terms. Here are some of the key points from the fully executed contract:

- 50% nonrefundable deposit before any work begins. This clause has always been important to me, but with international clients and working with a foreign agency for the first time, it was more important than ever. Gaining this concession provided a huge safety net, and added a significant financial incentive to all parties to make the relationship successful.

- 50% balance to be paid after delivering the last of the final approved assets.

- HUGEsound would retain authority to make all decisions about talent selection, studio selections for recording and mixing, engineers, etc.

- Several terms in the contract were devoted to revisions and acceptance. In a nutshell, the client had 14 days to submit in writing whatever revisions they wanted. Revisions were limited to three rounds back and forth. If 14 days went by and no revision requests were submitted, then that music was deemed approved. Any revision requests submitted after contractual approval would incur additional costs.

- Publicity notices announcing my connection to Warhammer, both prior to and after the game's release, had preemptory approval.

- The credit clause required that "Music by Chance Thomas" be added everywhere any credit related to the game was listed.

- Indemnity was limited to actual breach, proven in a court, not claimed breach.

We could not agree to terms regarding the OST. I wanted distribution rights, PRO royalties, and mechanicals. But after two months of haggling unsuccessfully, we decided to address the OST rights in a separate agreement.

With a score contract in place, and a 50% deposit sitting in the bank, it was finally time to get to work.

HAPPY TRAILS ACROSS THE OCEAN

The development team was in France. I was in Utah. The publisher was in England. It was important to establish a time and method for regular communication. Being eight hours behind the developer and seven hours behind the publisher, it made sense to schedule our meetings for the end of their day, which corresponded to the beginning of mine. That way, I could receive direction from the developer in the morning, work on music throughout the day, and send the results back to the team. They would have content to review the next morning when they arrived at work. We found that this process worked well.

As a side bar, you will find that most people have a preferred method in which they like to communicate. For example, I once had a client who would never answer a text or an email, but she would always pick up the phone after the first or second ring. Other people like to use Slack or Teams. One of my clients would not answer any form of communication unless I reached out via Skype chat. The *Warhammer* team loved to have video Skype meetings, and would use email as a supplement. So that is how we handled our communications during the project.

We also had to decide what language to communicate in. The publisher and I were both English-speaking. The developer and agency were French-speaking. Although I spoke some French, we ultimately decided to use English for our work communications.

To the reader, this may all seem very tedious – contract negotiation, setting up meeting times, figuring out how to communicate. But it is important because these are the footings that build the foundation of your working relationship. Taking time to set these pieces in place built a solid foundation for our successful creative collaboration.

FRENGLISH

In spite of the solid foundation we built, language differences did become an issue once we got into the details of creative direction, interpretation, and feedback. We hit a major speedbump when I started sending over the first work-in-progress drafts.

The revision notes were a little scary. Responding to one cue, they asked if I could make the music more *"greenish."* In another note, they suggested the music would sound better if it was *"crispy."* Still another revision request asked that I improve the cue by making it more *"clumpy."*

How would you respond to those words of creative direction? Greenish, crispy, and clumpy?

My guess was that these were aesthetic slang words in French that had very clear meanings to them. But when translated into English, they were gibberish. It is important to understand what your client is really looking for. Language barriers can make it difficult, but not impossible. I requested a Skype meeting to seek additional clarification, approaching them with questions like these:

"When you say greenish, should I interpret that as fresh and vibrant? Or stagnant and dissonant?"

"When you say crispy, should I interpret that as distorted? Or clear and present?"

"When you say clumpy, should I interpret that as thickly grouped together? Or slow and plodding?"

Drilling down with the team about the intended meaning of these terms brought clarity, and I was able to make revisions on target without wasting additional time guessing about what they wanted.

WHO'S THE BOSS?

Another issue we ran into was finding consensus on the *Main Theme*. By this time, there were several cooks in the kitchen, several members of the team offering their input. I began to feel a little foggy about which voice I should be paying the most attention to. To help resolve this, we had another Skype call, during which we agreed that the creative director from the dev team would take the official and exclusive role of giving authoritative feedback and approvals. When it comes to revisions and final approvals, a composer needs to know who's the boss.

I was feeling optimistic now. We had sorted out the Frenglish confusion and clarified my source for creative direction. I was locking onto their vision now, delivering tracks they liked, and the music was getting approved. Without major unforeseen roadblocks, the project should proceed smoothly from this point to completion.

FULL SPEED AHEAD

By now, I was cranking out the cues. Most of the score was written and orchestrated in about 30 days. I wrote epic orchestral bombast and tender violin solos. I wrote Russian choral tunes and atmospheric ambience.

For the *Main Theme*, I even designed a new instrument. It was reedy and guttural, with an organically synthy snarl that could make the hair stand up on the back of your neck! It can be heard most easily on track two of the *Warhammer: Chaosbane* soundtrack, snaking around underneath the contrabass choir.

With approvals coming quickly from the client, we moved into sheet music preparation and started booking singers and musicians. For sheet music prep, I typically complete the orchestration myself, then send MIDI files, mp3 stems, and extensive notes on phrasing, articulation, and dynamics to an engraver who uses Finale to produce the final sheet music. For contracting singers and musicians, I turned to Jenn Sprague, our director of production at HUGEsound Post Production, who knew all the best players and singers in town.

On November 5, our recording sessions began. The choir was menacing, the orchestra was an aggressive firestorm. Just as I had hoped, we were sailing along smoothly. On November 12, I started editing. And on November 15, the mixing sessions began.

THE HAMMER FALLS

The date is now November 16, 2023. I spent most of the day at Mike Roskelley's mixing studio, figuring out the sonic signature for the score. We put the first few cues in the can. I stopped by HUGEsound afterward to wrap up some loose ends before heading home.

To my shock and confusion, I found police officers and attorneys posted throughout the building. The attorneys showed me a court order giving complete control of our company to a local law firm acting as a receiver on behalf of the courts. The attorneys described accusations of massive fraud allegedly perpetrated by the parent company of our parent company, to the tune of over $200 million across at least ten years. I was stunned, absolutely stunned. Much of this was outlined in the last chapter. But in this chapter, I will offer a few more details.

November 16 was a Friday. We were told to anticipate "business as usual" going forward, with one exception. The courts would be our new owners. We were warned not to touch any of the computers, until we met again with the attorneys the following week. The courts were sending in forensic experts over the weekend to examine all computing devices.

What would you do if you were thrust into a situation like this? Would you trust that everything would return to normal on Monday, that it would be "business as usual"?

I did not trust that. I immediately identified one of the attorneys who seemed star struck by the studio, and was walking around slowly, staring at posters *of DOTA 2, King Kong*, and *Avatar* up on the wall. I introduced myself as the composer who scored each of those games. As it turned out, he was a big fan. I zeroed in on him and asked, "Can we talk privately?"

We went into my office, and I asked him questions about the receivership procedure, and how things might look going forward. I asked him what kinds of liabilities we might be exposed to. I asked him if he was a gamer, and he said yes. Not only was he an avid gamer, but he was a HUGE fan of *Warhammer* games. I mentioned that I was in the middle of mixing the new score for *Warhammer: Chaosbane*, and asked if I could please make backup copies of the drives containing the *Warhammer* files. His brows sort of pinched together, and he leaned back in his chair and said, "Well, you're not supposed to touch them over the weekend." I gently protested, leaning in just a bit, "But I am mixing over the weekend. I need these files backed up right away."

I let him sit with that for a few minutes while we chatted about other games he enjoyed playing, and some of the other games I had worked on. Eventually, I circled back to my request, pressing the immediacy of the weekend mix and the urgency of having these files backed up. He let out a sigh, leaned forward and said, "OK, go ahead and make backup copies of your files, since you're in the middle of the project and working this weekend." I thanked him, and wrote him an email on the spot, requesting confirmation that he had given me permission. He replied back in the affirmative.

It is always good to have a paper trail.

As soon as the attorney left my office, I backed up everything from all my drives and took the backups offsite. I also cleared out all of my personal belongings that night – awards, books, pictures, anything I had not sold to

Gaylen's investment company or acquired on behalf of the business. Just in case.

Monday morning rolled around, and I broke the news to my *Warhammer* client about what happened to HUGEsound. I assured them that mixes were proceeding offsite at a third-party studio and reassured them that I had backed up all of their files and removed them to a safe and secure location. I promised that I would still assemble all of the required assets and deliver them on time, as agreed. Although they were initially alarmed, by the end of the call their fears had been assuaged, and they were appreciative of the reassurances I had given.

Later that morning I drove to the mixing studio. I told the mixing artist, Mike Roskelley, what had happened Friday. I told him the attorneys had assured us that we should just keeping working on existing projects. "Business as usual, is specifically what they said," I told him. So we kept mixing.

On Tuesday morning, shortly after I arrived at HUGEsound, police officers and attorneys showed up again. All officers and employees of the studio were rounded up and brought into the conference room. We were informed that the court had made a new decision. Instead of continuing in business, we were being shut down immediately. Everyone was terminated without pay. No one could return to their offices without police escort, and then only to gather any obvious personal effects, such as a jacket or purse. Any item potentially in question (like awards or posters) would have to go through a filtering process with the receiver. I was so glad I had removed my personal belongings Friday night. We were instructed to turn over our keys and police escorted us out of the building. I shuddered, hearing the cold clank of a locked door behind me.

The worst news came later. A follow-up memo stated that any existing unpaid financial obligations that the studio had undertaken would not be honored. I think we had just barely paid the singers and musicians who performed on *Warhammer*. But Roskelley had not been paid anything yet for the mix, as he always billed in full after final delivery. What was going to happen to him?

I asked that question, and was told that, because any studio agreements and obligations now fell under the jurisdiction of a fraud case, creditors would have to submit claims to the receiver and get in line behind the jilted investors. With hundreds of millions of dollars in claims already stacked up in a growing line, there was little chance that Roskelley was going to get paid. I needed to tell him.

By Wednesday morning we were half way through the mix. I went to Roskelley's place and told him what I had just learned. Because of the court's changed position, they were no longer going to honor existing financial agreements or obligations. He would have to submit a claim to the court. I admitted that I thought the odds were high that the receiver would run out of money long before they paid his claim. Roskelley and I had a long history together, and I had regularly insured that he was paid very well for his work. So, there was a huge amount of goodwill built up between us. Still, the prospect of asking him to do a full week of work with likely no payment gave us both pause.

But what could I do? One way or another, I had to get the mix finished and delivered to my client. Even though I was no longer legally bound to deliver this score (because of the court's new decision not to honor existing agreements), I absolutely felt ethically responsible to finish the project and deliver the score.

I had to find a way to get it done, regardless of the steel trap that had slammed to the ground around me.

Mike and I talked through the situation. I told him I would pay him a portion of his normal fee from my own pocket, just in case his claim was never paid. At least he would have a portion of his fee to help soften the blow. Thankfully he agreed to my terms, and we finished the mix.

YOU CAN'T PAY US ENOUGH

Once the mixes were finished, I still needed to export and edit all of the stems for the game. I also needed to build tracks for the OST. But I had no equipment. All of my equipment had been included when I sold HUGEsound to Gaylen Rust and his investment company. Now that equipment was locked up with the court proceedings.

I reached out to the receiver and asked if I could rent my equipment back for two weeks, just long enough to finish the *Warhammer* contract. I offered to pay an hourly rate or a daily rate to gain access to my old office and audio equipment. They told me, "No, because it's not worth our while to send one of our $200 per hour attorneys down there to unlock the studio for you, and stick around until you're done. It's just not worth our while."

Pleading to their sense of business integrity, and reminding them I was in the midst of an unfinished project, fell on deaf ears. Wow. What was I going to do now? My equipment was gone. I started reaching out to friends to see if I could scrounge together some kind of affordable stopgap system to finish this *Warhammer* project.

As I was in the midst of this scramble, the lead attorney for the receiver, Joe Covey, called me. I thought he might be calling to say they had reconsidered, that they were going to let me rent the space with my old gear after all. But Covey was a top dog at the firm, floating high above the ground-level attorneys who had been dealing with me. No, he did not know anything about that. Instead, he was calling about something completely different. Someone had contacted the receiver about potentially buying the building, and Covey asked if I would meet him at the studio and give the potential buyer a tour of the facility.

Double wow! They would not unlock the door so I could finish my work on *Warhammer*, but now they want me to show the place to a potential buyer?

How would you react?

I told Covey I would be happy to show their prospective buyer around the studio for a fee. And it would only cost him $200 per hour.

I thought there was some poetic justice in that number.

He agreed to my fee, but then as part of the deal, I also negotiated the right to freely access my old studio room and equipment, for as long as it took to finish the *Warhammer* game score and OST. A little leverage and dealing directly with the top dog can sometimes turn the tables in your favor.

I showed the studio to Covey and his potential buyer, and did a compelling job. So much so that Covey contracted with me to continue showing the studio as needed for the next 15 months. All at $200 per hour. Even today, I feel some warped satisfaction with that ironic turn of events.

But I digress. Let's get back to *Warhammer*. Within a short time, I completed the stem exports and OST editing and delivered every contracted asset to my client.

SWEET SUCCESS

For the *Warhammer: Chaosbane* publisher and development team, everything worked out in the end. The music score was completed at the high-quality bar everyone hoped for. All the music for the game was delivered on time, including special edits for the game's soundtrack album. The developer never had to pay anything above the original contract price. And although the developer and publisher were immediately informed of the studio's shuttering, they were also made to feel secure that their score was never in jeopardy.

To watch videos and listen to music from Warhammer: Chaosbane, *as described in this chapter, please visit: HUGEsoundRecords.com/Memoir-16*

CHAPTER 17

Swinging for the Fences

DURING MY BUSINESS TRAVELS, I once met a music editor who worked for film composer Howard Shore. I will keep his name private, because what I am about to share was surely a violation of his confidentiality agreement.

He was working with a group of music editors on the score for Peter Jackson's *Return of the King*, the triumphant final chapter in the wildly successful *LOTR* film trilogy. One morning we were chatting on the phone when he casually dropped a mind-blowing bombshell. "Yeah, do you have any idea what the music budget is for *Return of the King*?" he said. "The music budget is ten million dollars. Can you believe it? I am not kidding, the music budget is literally TEN MILLION DOLLARS!"

My paradigm had just been shattered into ten million tiny green pieces.

At the time, I was producing a suite of themes for my own *Lord of the Rings* music, suites of themes and supporting cues that would be shared across half a dozen games throughout VUG's Tolkien games franchise (see Chapter 3). My total music budget to create these multi-game thematic overtures was around $105,000, including creative fees and production costs. Honestly, I had been thrilled to secure that much budget at the time.

But when I learned that Howard Shore's music budget for a *single* film was literally *a hundred times greater* than my entire *LOTR* franchise themes music budget, I felt angry, hoodwinked, and naive. My prior thrill with game music money now seemed like the Emperor's new clothes.

I had stumbled upon a dirty little secret. There was an astonishing contrast between the money lavished on blockbuster film music versus the money doled out for video game music. As much as I loved my friends and clients in

DOI: 10.1201/9781003199311-18

gaming, as much as I savored the artistic and technical challenges of game music, I was now aware of a staggeringly more fertile financial pasture.

The grass (and the cash) were MUCH greener on the other side of the fence.

In the remainder of this chapter, I will share my many colorful attempts to scale the barrier between game music and film music. Or to use another analogy, my attempts to go all-in for a home run, swinging for the fences of a Hollywood blockbuster film score.

THE CHUBBCHUBBS!

My first Hollywood nibble came from auditioning to score *The ChubbChubbs!*, then winning the audition and becoming an integral part of the creative team. *The ChubbChubbs! was* produced by Sony Pictures Imageworks and released by Columbia Pictures, both major players in the film industry. The project paid me exceptionally well, celebrated its debut at Grauman's Chinese Theater with *Men in Black 2*, and went on to win an Oscar at the 75th Annual Academy Awards. *The ChubbChubbs!* was released as bonus content with three different films and eventually received its own stand-alone DVD. The full story was chronicled in Chapter 6.

Who could have asked for a better entre into Hollywood? "Chance Thomas has arrived," I thought arrogantly. I just knew my next score would be an animated feature or live-action blockbuster. And yes, a few meetings did open up with powerful people like Monica Zierhut and Kaylin Frank, two VPs of Music at Walt Disney Studios, Yair Landau, founder of Mass Animation, and others. But as I rolled into each meeting, putting my best foot forward professionally and personally, it was painfully obvious that I failed to produce any fireworks with the Hollywood elite, not even a spark of interest. Like a pleasant but unremarkable first date, I simply did not dazzle. I could not get follow-up meetings with any of them, let alone offers to score big-budget films.

Tough crowd! If I was unable to win over established gatekeepers at the top of the food chain, what was I going to do? How could I further my ambitions to grow a presence in the film world? It was sobering, but I was undaunted. I just needed to find another way.

What would you do?

Composer Kurt Bestor had once told me, "It's not what you know, it's who you hug."

There was one small group in Hollywood who felt huggable. Those were the friends I made working on *The ChubbChubbs!* We had remained in touch, and those relationships were growing. It was not long before a new opportunity bubbled up to the surface with them.

INSPIRE: THE CHICAGO SPIRE ART FILM

Jacquie Barnbrook was breathless. She could hardly contain her enthusiasm on the phone. "Santiago Calatrava … [*something, something, something*] … new film … [*something, something, something*] …!"

She was rushing her words and the cell phone reception was not great in Coarsegold, California anyway.

"Wait," I said, "Slow down, I'm having a hard time following you. Can you say it again?"

"Santiago Calatrava! The most celebrated architect in the world! He wants Imageworks to create an animated previz film for his new building in downtown Chicago. I'm producing it! I want you to be part of it. Can you come down to Los Angeles next week and meet the director and the executive producer?"

Yes, yes, absolutely yes!

The following week, I was perched under a shady green awning outside Starbucks in Culver City, California, chatting excitedly with Jacquie Barnbrook, director Sheena Duggal, and executive producer Paul Currie. Sheena hailed from Manchester, England; Jacquie was from Whales; and Paul came from Melbourne, Australia. The charming diversity of accents dancing across the table was delightful.

Sheena was focused on me and curious, peppering me with questions, probing to better understand my dramatic sensibilities, relevant imagination, flexibility, and past experience in music scoring. Paul was quieter, but watched me carefully, observing my interactions with the two women, absorbing and analyzing each answer, occasionally following up with a clarifying question of his own. Jacquie kept things lively and helped moderate the conversation.

The hour flew by in a minute, and all parties felt invigorated by the meeting. We were sensing the loose beginnings of a shared creative vision. And that was exciting for everyone. Finally, a few sparks!

Following additional phone meetings, Jacquie sent over a rough work-in-progress animation showing one extended section of the previz. It looked incredible! This was no typical previz, it looked more like an art film. Floating in the sky, high above Chicago, cottony clouds parted to reveal stunning silver and glass living spaces, towering over the city. A descending Seagull soared into view, steering the camera gracefully around the curvature of the building, where sparkling panels glistened in the sun. It was nothing short of extraordinary.

Sheena had temp-scored the film with Rachmaninov's Piano Concerto #2, and initially asked me to adapt that classic with a new orchestration and recording. But as I sat with the footage, allowing my imagination to embrace the images, a subtle melody began to float across my mind. It was a pure and simple piano motif, expansive and inviting, far more open and airy than the harmonically dense Rachmaninov piece. To my sensibilities, this was a better fit for the "floating-in-the-clouds" vibe I was getting from the visuals.

But it is risky to recommend a wholesale change to any director. I needed to approach her with wisdom. Sheena was anxious to get my reaction, but I asked her for a few days to marinate on it. That allowed time to flesh out the original piece I had imagined, and lay it back against the picture. Only after uploading this rescored version of the animation to Imageworks' FTP site, did I respond to Sheena with my thoughts.

"Rachmaninov was a brilliant composer, and Piano Concerto #2 is a personal favorite," I began. "It definitely conjures up an emotional sense of importance and majesty for the film." Sheena agreed and we spent the next few minutes talking about a possible adaptation. Then I broached the idea of a possible alternative, just for the sake of comparison. "As I've been absorbing the footage, a couple of things keep coming to mind. One is the city-in-the-clouds vibe I get from the visuals. The other is the deeply personal experience it will be for individuals and families to live in this space." She was listening intently, and I continued. "I've had a new, original music idea come to me that highlights those two aspects of the film. I've uploaded a copy of the current previz with this new musical idea synched up." I paused, in case she wanted to voice an objection. Instead, she asked me to continue, "If you get a chance to download the new version and compare the two, see which music best supports your vision. I'm offline this weekend, but let's circle back on Monday and let me know what you think."

It was important to give Sheena an enforced buffer of time before responding to me. Temp love is pervasive across all creative media, and I did not want to be the victim of a knee-jerk rejection. Giving her the weekend, and inviting her to compare the two options, provided space for her to potentially disengage from temp love and give the comparison a fair chance.

It worked. Sheena decided that the new original music was a better fit for the film's purpose, and for the visual aesthetic her art team was creating. I got the green light and went to work.

The score opens with a flourish in the orchestra, grand and colorful, winding down quickly toward a transition to solo grand piano. The bare melody sings alongside the gliding Seagull, joined by supporting warmth in the low brass and string choir. The camera carries us seamlessly inside the Spire, revealing a comfortable living space. Solo clarinet and flute trade gestures, then join together in a dance of intertwining harmony and countermelody. As we drift outside on the ground floor, the camera slowly pans up to reveal the money shot – we now see the entire exterior for the first time. The orchestra swells, deepening and rising simultaneously, joined by the powerful resonance of a 24-voice choir as the full majesty of the Spire ascends into view. The brilliant sky morphs across daylight and into night, with a time lapse panning out to show the Spire nestled along the waterfront, taking its place within Chicago's famous skyline. A children's chorus joins the score, and as the lights of the city sparkle like diamonds in the dark, the orchestra decrescendos, diminishing to a solo violin and a single sustained note from the children. As the screen fades to black, we transition to the Chicago Spire logo, and the orchestra returns in its full splendor, grand piano hammering out a final lift and resolution.

Sheena loved it. So did Jacquie, Paul, and everyone else associated with the project. With high marks from the executive team, I moved into production, recording the grand piano, SATB choir, and International Children's Chorus in Salt Lake City. Later in Seattle, the 70-piece Northwest Sinfonia performed the orchestral parts of the score under my baton, recorded in Bastyr Chapel. Reed Ruddy did the mix. Sheena had come up to Seattle for the sessions and seemed completely enchanted by the process. Happy client, happy life!

The film and score were complete, and invitations arrived for a grand "unveiling" of the construction site in Chicago. Paul Currie came to the forefront of preparations and reached out personally, inviting me to compose a new piece of music which would be performed live by a string quartet at the unveiling ceremony. I had never composed for string quartet, so I took this as an opportunity to try my hand at chamber ensemble writing. The new piece hearkened back to the main motif of the film score, but expanded into its own creative direction. The music was timed to coincide with massive curtains rising in coordination with a light show and other video elements.

At the gala, I had the chance to meet Gerrett Kelleher, the Irish owner of Shelbourne Group Development and CEO of Lightstream Pictures, which co-produced the Spire film. I also briefly met Santiago Calatrava, the famed architect who designed the Spire. However, I spent most of my time at the unveiling with Gabriel Calatrava, Santiago's son, who explained in great detail the mathematics and engineering principles supporting the Fibonacci ratios and twisting design of his father's building. It was a fascinating evening, as I rubbed shoulders with the ultra-rich and brilliant. I felt surprisingly comfortable among them, mostly because I was deeply interested in their stories and hung on every word.

Weeks after the unveiling event in Chicago, our film was entered into the Aurora Awards competition, where it took home Platinum Awards for Best Short Film and Best Original Score.

Sadly, the real estate crash of 2007–2008 pulled the rug out from under the construction project, spurring massive panic among investors. The Chicago Spire lost its funding and the project died a disappointing death. All that remained for years afterwards was a huge hole in the ground, intended for the Spire's foundation and parking garage.

From a business perspective, it is always disappointing when a project you are part of does not quite reach the finish line. But I had negotiated generous creative fees for the film score and the live chamber piece, so the financial component was covered. I also retained ownership of the music copyrights, and have licensed the music in the intervening years. The film itself was beautiful, and the score production had been sumptuous and pristine. I was proud to show the work to friends and potential clients. The Aurora award was a nice touch and still shines from its spot in the studio trophy case. I tried out new things during the process, grew as a composer and as a businessman. But the most valuable part of the whole experience was the relationships. I am still in touch with Jacquie and Sheena, and have enjoyed the business and personal side of those associations for many years. Paul Currie and I became friends too, and would eventually join up in a business venture of our own.

ROBOTA: REIGN OF MACHINES

Some may recall watching the 1999 theatrical trailer for *Star Wars Episode One: The Phantom Menace*. I will never forget my first time – seeing the new characters, hearing the old music, being blown away by the gorgeous and inventive visual designs on the screen. I could tell this was *Star Wars*, but with an added layer of visual sophistication. I did not know it yet, but this was my first exposure to the brilliantly creative mind of Doug Chiang.

Doug had been leading Lucas Film's art department since 1995, and with *Star Wars Episode One: The Phantom Menace*, Doug took on the additional role of Art Design Director. I thought his designs were genius, a blend of Renaissance proportion and sumptuousness, with traditional science fiction, and a sprinkling of Asian influences. Doug would go on to lead the visual design for many other films and television series in the *Star Wars* franchise, including *The Force Awakens, The Last Jedi, The Rise of Skywalker, Solo, The Mandalorian,* and *Obi-Wan Kenobi.* It is no exaggeration to say that Doug Chiang has defined the look of *Star Wars* for nearly 25 years.

But adorning George Lucas' creations with visual splendor was not Doug's only ambition. His vivid imagination had also given rise to a fictional world of his own making, *Robota: Reign of Machines.* The story was fascinating – a man awakens with amnesia, finding himself on a world overrun by robot warriors. He realizes his veiled memories can save the dwindling remnants of the human race and the planet's sentient beast population.[1] But he must do battle with the tyrannical robot leader to rediscover his true identity.[2]

Doug's ambition was to create a new film franchise based on this world, with ancillary video games, books, and action figures. To introduce *Robota* to potential partners and gather interest, he was producing an animated teaser. The character design, creatures, world building, and animation were all coming together brilliantly. But he did not yet have a partner for audio.

Doug had become acquainted with Ken Ralston while working on *Forrest Gump* and *Death Becomes Her.* When Doug mentioned that he needed audio for his teaser, Ken suggested he reach out to me and passed along my contact info. That kind of recommendation is worth more than its weight in gold. It is worth its weight in mithril. This cannot be overstated. The best professional opportunities generally come from people who know you and have had great experiences working with you.

Doug sent me the two-minute teaser, and I instantly fell in love with its style and story. I believed *Robota* could easily become a successful mainstream franchise. My mind quickly flooded with interesting musical ideas for the score. I wrote the score within a day or two, then took an additional day to tweak the orchestration and give it a good mix. Doug was thrilled with it, and especially connected with the theme, which repeats a two-phrase motif throughout the score, much like the hook of a pop song.

All aspects of audio were contracted to HUGEsound. I brought Tim Larkin onboard for the sound design and audio mix. *Robota*'s visuals were already incredible. But the music and sound added a shimmering layer of intrigue, drama, and coolness to the teaser.

Doug produced a second teaser many months later. This one focused on a search and destroy mission leading to intense hand-to-hand combat. Tim and I reprised our respective roles through HUGEsound and delivered another solid soundtrack. Doug was becoming a satisfied client. He was also becoming our friend. I even stayed overnight at his home during a trip to San Francisco. The Chiang's were wonderful hosts.

Although the teasers looked and sounded great, serious interest from major film companies was not forthcoming. We were all puzzled, but some of my Imageworks friends opined that the film Doug had proposed would be exceptionally expensive to make. For many Hollywood pocketbooks, it was just a little too rich.

Meanwhile, author Orson Scott Card had caught wind of *Robota* and offered to write a short story version of the plot. It was a great read. Chronicle Books published the story as a coffee table book, including high-resolution images from Doug's *Robota* designs. I still have my copy of the book, a prized possession.

Shortly after the book was published, Sony signaled some interest in *Robota* as a video game. Rather than building another animated teaser, Doug assembled a small team to build a game level, creating a vertical slice demo for Sony. HUGEsound provided the music and SFX, but I never saw the finished product. Somewhere along the way, the deal fell apart. I do not think Sony ever progressed the project beyond that point.

To me, it was shocking that someone of Doug's pedigree, talent, intelligence, reputation, design and production skills, and stimulating original ideas (so well executed in these teasers) could venture his own swing for the fences without ultimately getting *Robota* made into a movie or video game. I was flabbergasted. Everything about *Robota* was fine-tuned for sci-fi audiences of the day. Produced and marketed well, it could have easily become a flagship franchise. Doug had a flawless reputation. Everyone in the business loved him. If Doug Chiang could not get *Robota* made, who could get anything cool made at all?

Around that time I received a surprising call from Paul Currie.

THE FOURTH MAGI

After the Chicago Spire project went under, Paul Currie and Garrett Kelleher doubled down on their efforts to build a future for their film company, Lightstream Pictures. They would eventually go on to produce and distribute several successful films, including *Hacksaw Ridge*, *The King's Daughter*, *2:22*, *Blacklight*, and others.

When Paul called me in 2009, he sounded uncharacteristically enthusiastic in describing what he hoped would become a flagship title for Lightstream Pictures, *The Fourth Magi*. This was an animated family film in the classic Disney tradition, a Christmas movie highlighting the triumph of generosity over self-interest, a coming-of-age story wrapped around the greatest story ever told. The script was wonderful, the Old World locales and scenery were magnificent. The international reach and evergreen appeal were irresistible.

Paul invited me to his studio in Santa Monica, California, where he handed me several weighty, hand-sculpted maquettes of main characters in the film. I loved feeling the rough-hewn clay in my hands. We leafed through sketches and renderings of Egyptian set pieces and Middle Eastern story settings. I sat back and watched the first teaser trailer for the film on a massive screen, overwhelmed by the scale of this epic story. Completely smitten by such a promising IP and quality pre-production, I wanted nothing more than to score this film. Not only that, but I even felt motivated to roll up my sleeves and help as a producer with the fund raising. I had never raised money for a film before, but the fire inside was already burning.

In my mind, a successful fund-raising pitch required something tangible to hand prospects, so my first step was to put together a hefty promotional book. I authored all the verbiage and formatted the contents, pulling screenshots from the animation and inserting a DVD of the teaser. Paul and I worked out financial projections, including estimated box office with various investment, recoupment, profit, and equity-sharing scenarios to include as well. Each page was printed on gorgeous, glossy card stock, custom stitched into a 10″ × 11″ book. It was bound with elegant calf-skin leather, rich and soft to the touch.

While I was developing the promotional book, a specific target popped into my mind. Bart Warner and his wife Liz ran a nonprofit music foundation funded by Bart's highly successful car and truck dealerships. Pamela and I were friends with the Warner's, and had once performed live at their company Christmas party. When I suggested a meeting to discuss possibly funding an animated feature film, they agreed to see me. The funding target I mentioned to Bart was somewhere in the low to mid seven figures.

When I shared the news with Paul, he got really excited. This was a real prospect, brought to the table by a composer! We eagerly set a date and time for the meeting. I would go to Bart's office. Paul and his Lightstream partner Garrett Kelleher would join 30 minutes later via conference call.

I gave Bart and Liz a copy of the book, and talked them through the story, the characters, the production approach, and the music. I played the teaser for them, and we talked in general terms about costs and payout. I could sense the momentum building. There was growing enthusiasm in their comments. Bart expressed that he was genuinely open to investing in this film, and was ready to dig into the fine print of the deal. It was time for the call with Paul and Garrett.

Paul opened the conversation and bonded with the Warner's instantly. He was polite, gracious, and persuasive, speaking convincingly about the broad appeal of the story, the outstanding creative talent assembled, and innovations, which the technical crew were introducing into the animation pipeline. As Paul was concluding, Garrett took over the call, ostensibly to parse out the financial details. But from what I could hear, he mostly boasted about his development acumen in commercial real estate. He just kept going on and on about it. The meeting headed quickly downhill from there. You could feel the oxygen hissing out of the room. It was painful. When Bart finally interrupted to ask some clarifying questions about the prioritization of payouts to various investor classes, Garrett seemed to ramble on like a drunken man. I am not sure he ever arrived at the point.

By the end of the call, Bart's enthusiasm and interest had fizzled out. The call had been a disaster. The Warner's would not be investing after all, and they apologized to me. They knew the creative side was top notch. But the conversation with Garrett had eroded their confidence in the business end of the deal. I spoke with Paul afterwards, and we bitterly commiserated the loss of the Warner's investment.

I approached a few other people about investing, but never got that close again.

Shortly thereafter, Paul decided to relocate his production company to Australia to take advantage of government programs designed to foster the burgeoning film industry Down Under. Of course, their film commission regulations required a near-unanimity of Aussie talent to secure state funding. That meant my value as an American composer would fall by the wayside. It was a bitter pill watching *The Fourth Magi* sail out of my reach. Sadder still, the film has seemingly sailed beyond anyone's reach. To this day, *The Fourth Magi* that Paul was developing has never been made.

Are you beginning to grasp how gloriously rare it is for a creative project to actually get produced and released to the public? How difficult it is for all the disparate pieces to come together, align, agree, and ultimately gel into a successful commercial product? It is so hard.

There is a depth of grit and motivation required to continually pick yourself up and start over again, year after year, decade after decade, that very few can fathom. And yet, for those who do, the rewards eventually come.

I daresay, only the lionhearted are guaranteed a successful long-term career in this business.

LOST TREASURE HUNT

The Fourth Magi had not worked out for me. But another big swing was coming down the pike. Jacquie Barnbrook, who was becoming a film industry mentor, discovered that a new executive at Sony Animation had graduated from Brigham Young University, my alma mater. When Jacquie called to tell me the news, she had already arranged a lunch for the three of us the following week. Could I come down to Sony for the meeting?

Yes, yes, absolutely yes!

As I approached the sun-drenched courtyard outside Imageworks, I was greeted by Jacquie, who had grabbed a small, round table under a leafy shade tree. She waved me over and introduced Matt Davis, the newly appointed director of Post Production for Sony Animation. At first glance, I thought Matt looked like an intellectual, with his prominent forehead, slightly over-sized jacket, and piercing gray-blue eyes. His stiffly parted brown hair and tense facial expression hinted at a mind always in deep thought or complex calculations. Despite feeling some initial intimidation, Matt's easy nature and clever wit soon set me at ease. It was not long before Jacquie had to slip away for another meeting, but Matt and I continued our conversation throughout the afternoon. Little did I know, he would go on to become Sony's VP of Production, overseeing blockbuster hits such as the Academy Award-winning *Spider Man: Into the Spider-Verse*, *Cloudy with a Chance of Meatballs*, and *Hotel Transylvania*.

Some time after our first meeting, Matt invited me back to LA to discuss the independent production of an animated television series. After a brief greeting in his office, we left the Sony lot for an off-site restaurant. Over lunch, he shared with me the details of a TV series he was producing independently. The series, entitled *Lost Treasure Hunt*, was an action-packed adventure, following secret agents on weekly missions to protect valuable artifacts from cunning thieves and profiteers. The show was unique in its attention to historical accuracy and its focus on real-life relics and storied locations from global history. Imagine *National Treasure* with a focus on Christopher Columbus. And replace Nicholas Cage with a pair of energetic, animated 20-somethings.

Matt had secured funding from the National Endowment for the Humanities and built a top-notch team for the pilot episode. The crew consisted of Richard Bazley (*Iron Giant, Tarzan*), animation director Roque Ballesteros (*Star Wars: Rebels, Happy Tree Friends*), and screenwriter David Rosenberg (*Rugrats, The Wild Thornberrys*). Despite the impressive lineup, one crucial aspect of the show's production was still missing – theme music and underscore. As of yet, Matt had not contracted with a composer.

Matt had taken notice of my music in *The ChubbChubbs!* and again in *The Lord of the Rings Online*. He asked if I would like to audition to score his pilot.

My audition consisted of scoring the opening minute of the show, a ramping-up action montage leading to the show's logo and title screen. The audition would showcase underscore and thematic writing in a single, one-minute combo. The show had a terrific open, and I loved the animation. But loving it was no guarantee I would write a winning track.

The task proved to be more difficult than I expected. I composed three distinct variations in diverse musical genres, and advised Matt that I still lacked sufficient information to determine his preferred style for the show. Matt expressed gratitude for my thorough approach, but unfortunately, none of the three demos I submitted fully met his expectations. He did identify one specific instrument he liked in the third demo, and a certain energy he enjoyed in the second one. Armed with this feedback, I asked if I could present one more final demo, hoping to better align with his vision.

The fourth demo was a resounding success, perfectly capturing Matt's musical vision. He circulated it among the other key players on the team and their enthusiastic responses mirrored Matt's. He immediately extended a contract offer to compose the score for the pilot.

Let us pause for a moment to reflect on these events. Despite three initial failed attempts, I was able to deliver a winning demo on the fourth try. My persistence and determination, coupled with an ability to pivot and adjust the stylistic approach, ultimately paid off. Despite the uncertainty and time investment, I refused to give up and my efforts were ultimately rewarded with the job.

The offered pay was much lower than my normal earnings from video game contracts. Of course, I hoped that the pilot would be successful, and that the show would get funded for a full season, bringing me along for the ride. Still, there was no guarantee. Lots of terrific ideas never get greenlit, as we have seen in this chapter.

To bridge the financial gap, I suggested retaining the copyrights and offered instead a worldwide, unlimited term license for educational television purposes. Despite some initial hesitation, and only after consultations with his entertainment lawyer, Matt agreed to the arrangement. The process took about six weeks to resolve, but we both got what we needed in the end.

The production of the pilot came to a successful conclusion, with a dynamic and thrilling action adventure score adding to the excitement. I loved the final outcome and expressed my admiration for Matt and the team. It was a privilege to be part of such a trailblazing pilot and I had my fingers crossed, hoping the program would get picked up by a major educational TV syndicate for full season production.

Lost Treasure Hunt made its debut on PBS during Columbus Day and the pilot has been aired regularly ever since. Although a full season was never produced, I am pleased to report that the pilot continues to generate a steady stream of recurring royalties year after year.

DISNEY'S *JETS*

Once upon a time, I dreamed of writing music for Pixar films. In pursuit of that dream, I met Kimberly Jorgensen (now Kim Adams), who produced 13 of Pixar's short films (*Moon Mater, Time Travel Mater, Partysaurus Rex,* etc.). In sharing my ambitions with Kim, she connected me with Tom MacDougall, the music director who oversaw music for all Pixar films. I introduced myself via email, and could hardly believe it when Tom responded to me. In gratitude, I sent Kimberly a beautiful bouquet of flowers.

For the next few years, I emailed Tom every six or eight months, just checking in. A couple of times, I told him I was coming to Los Angeles and offered to take him to lunch, but he graciously declined. Somewhere along the line, he was promoted to VP of Music over Pixar and Disney Animation.

Tom was still responding to my occasional emails, and in one response, invited me to send a few examples of my music. He promised to cycle my tracks into an iPod he kept around for listening to new tunes. This was an incredible stroke of good fortune!

What do you send to one of the most powerful film music executives on the planet, when given the opportunity? Oh, how I agonized over that decision! Do I send multiple variations of a singular style, hoping to make an impression with that one style? Should I send a smattering of varied functional scores, demonstrating my ability to cover a full range of dramatic situations? What about overtures, which take the listener on a journey? Which three or four tracks was I going to send to Tom MacDougall?

At length, I decided to send three strong thematic pieces and one action track. I sent him *Theme for Rohan* from *The Lord of the Rings Online,* an evocative track with an historic flair. I included *Ann's Theme* from *King Kong,* a tender and emotional piece. Going outside the box a little, I sent the *Main Theme* from *Faeria,* mainly because people seemed drawn to it, even those who had never heard of the game. Finally, I included an action track, *Aerial Combat Acrobatics* from *Avatar: The Game.* I crossed my fingers and hoped something would resonate.

Weeks passed, and one day I opened Outlook to discover an email from Tom MacDougall. He thanked me for sending the music over, and mentioned how much he had enjoyed listening to one song in particular.

Which one would you guess?

Of all the tracks I sent, *Main Theme* from the little-known deck builder *Faeria* was his favorite. Keep in mind, this was the VP of Music for Pixar and Disney Animation. He did not have to write anything to me at all, let alone send a compliment about a piece of music from an obscure video game. I was over the moon.

As I continued nurturing this relationship, Tom told me that my best opportunity to find a way into the Disney ecosystem would be to score one of the upcoming Pixar shorts. He promised to keep my music in his listening rotation, and when considering an upcoming new short, he would give my music a listen along with the other tracks he had in rotation. I could not have asked for anything more. To have my music in the ears of Tom MacDougall? I thought I was dreaming.

Two more years went by with no change in our relationship. When Tom was promoted to president of Walt Disney Music, I ventured another invitation to lunch. Much to my surprise and delight, this time he agreed. But on my way to Los Angeles, I received word that he needed to cancel our lunch. Instead, he asked if I could meet with him for 30-minutes later the same afternoon.

When I arrived at Tom's office, he greeted me warmly and offered me a seat on the couch. My head was on a swivel, his office a veritable wonderland covered with posters from *Cars, Hercules, Big Hero 6, Lilo and Stitch,* and so many more. Gold records, signed original concept art sketches, *Wreck It Ralph* action figures, it was so impressive.

Tom was laid back, but businesslike. Our conversation bounced across career highlights, admired musicians, professional sports, and family life. These were topics that came naturally to me, and I felt we were building good rapport.

I brought along a gift to thank him for carving out time to see me. He was curious and gracious as I handed him the giftwrapped package. He loosened the bow and peeled back the paper to reveal a white box tied shut with twine, and a black gift card attached to the front with a large gold clip. The gift card had his name written in gold ink, with an expression of gratitude handwritten inside. Next, Tom untied the gift box and lifted the lid to unveil a large brown, soft leather, rectangular messenger bag. He seemed delighted!

"Lift the flap and see what's inside," I suggested. As Tom unsnapped the leather buckles and pulled open the flap, he saw the second part of my gift. Inside were a pair of Sony studio headphones and a new iPod fully loaded with music from several of my best scores. "I'm just updating you on my music," I offered. He smiled and expressed appreciation for the thoughtful gifts. He fingering the leather on the messenger bag, and set the headphones and iPod prominently in the center of his desk, smiling again and expressing his appreciation.

We concluded our meeting, took a couple of selfies together, and parted amicably. I was convinced that the relationship had arrived at a point where I could send him a music pitch for a specific film project and he would listen.

By now I had also connected with Hollywood music agent Randy Gerston. Randy informed me that Disney Animation was producing a sequel to the 2013 animated feature, *Planes*, a tepidly received film that nevertheless won a young audience. The new sequel would be called *Jets*, and Randy shared the story brief with me, capturing my imagination. I decided to compose a suite of themes based on information gleaned from the story brief. If the music turned out well enough, I would send the tracks to Tom MacDougall for his review. I was certain this was finally the right opportunity to lift me into the world of film scoring for feature animation.

I composed and produced six tracks, building from synths and electronic percussion, metal guitars, and digital orchestra. One of the tracks turned out surprisingly well, a tender song for piano and orchestra called *Epiphany*. It was written to underscore one of those classic Disney moments, when the disheartened main character finds new purpose and resolve at an important crossroad in their journey. The "new friends" track, the "evil adversary" track, and the final "save the day" track were solid. But I struggled with the opening theme, which introduces the main character. I wrote and rewrote, orchestrated and reorchestrated, mixed and remixed. Nothing ever sounded just right to me. But I was so determined to pitch for this film, I decided to package everything up and send it to Tom anyway.

He listened through the package, but was not impressed with the opening track. He wrote back in very lukewarm terms, suggesting that he did not really understand the music without my written description. There was none of the praise he had lavished on the *Faeria* theme years before. I feared I had made a critical misstep.

Weeks later I learned that *Jets* had been canceled by Disney anyway. I was told that the script never met muster, and the plug was pulled in order to focus on more promising properties. Even if I had bowled Tom over with my submission, the opportunity would have evaporated anyway.

When I later reached out to Tom about listening to my *Avatar 2* pitch (which was totally awesome by the way, see Chapter 18), he took a stern tone, telling me that Disney does not accept unsolicited material. He never wrote back again after that.

You really can spend years building a bridge in Hollywood, only to tear it down with one critical misstep.

FULL DOME FILMS

Sometimes you will meet a person for the first time and everything just clicks. Even people who seem like polar opposites can unexpectedly discover an instantaneous connection. That is what happened when I met Terence Murtagh.

Terence is a brilliant astronomer, author, and filmmaker from Scotland. He is not especially tall, rounded in the middle, sporting a shock of bright white hair and matching goatee, which offsets his ruddy complexion. A pair of wire-framed glasses, only slightly unstylish, complete the look. Terence could pass for a professor on any college campus, or as a regular at any neighborhood pub. He was in his seventies when we first met, stopping in Salt Lake City, Utah, for a week between trips to the Birr Telescope and Arecibo Observatory, located in Ireland and Puerto Rico, respectively.

Tales of a Time Traveler

Our first meeting was at the newly opened HUGEsound Post Production in early 2017. Sound designer Michael McDonough had arranged for an introduction to discuss Terence's upcoming film, *Tales of a Time Traveler*, which was being produced by Evans & Sutherland's Digital Theater division. McDonough had provided sound design to E&S films for several years, and this meeting offered an opportunity to expand into music scoring.

McDonough asked for details about the new film, and Terence became animated describing the many wrinkles and variations in time he had discovered through research and observations. I will not attempt to describe the science of it here, but I was spellbound listening to Terence recount his many discoveries undergirding the film. The science was fascinating, and the film production held great promise. This would be one of the first films in the world produced and projected in 8K, so the resolution would be phenomenal. That was my cue to begin pitching for comparable quality in the music.

I pitched a big, live orchestral sound for the score, something that could hold its own against the stunning graphics. But Terence had booked *Doctor Who* actor David Tennant for the narrator role, which gobbled up an exorbitant portion of the audio budget. The 8K animations were also bloating production costs. As I tried to negotiate substantial fees for our services and production budget, we came to an impasse. E&S Digital simply did not have enough money available for the kind of score I was pitching.

HUGEsound Post Production had just opened its doors, and we were anxious to show what we could do with our orchestral sound stage, Neve console, and talented team. I finally suggested that we could give his film the music it deserved at a reduced cost in return for two concessions. First, HUGEsound would license the music master sync rights to E&S Digital, but retain copyrights to the music compositions and recordings. Such a license would cover every reasonable need E&S would have for the music, including releasing the film to full dome theaters worldwide. Second, if Terence was pleased with the results of working together on this film, he would agree to fund a substantial audio budget for his next film, which was already in the pipeline.

We had our deal. On the music side my creative fee was negligible. We were pouring most of the score budget into a 61-piece live orchestra with its associated recording and production costs. The copyrights would prove highly profitable in years to come, as we released a successful soundtrack album of the score, and later licensed the music for lucrative music library placements. But I am getting ahead of myself. Let us talk first about composing and producing the score.

Growing up with *Star Trek, Star Wars, Stargate, Independence Day,* and other great science-fiction epics, I had always wanted to score a film set in space. *Tales of a Time Traveler* gave me that opportunity. I think every composer subconsciously references *Planets* by Holst when initially thinking about music for an infinite universe. But as I started scoring each scene, broad romantic themes emerged instead. Not romantic in terms of a love story, but romantic in terms of the romantic period in music history, greatly influenced by the Russian masters. I resisted the urge to go overly far down that road, pulling back tastefully, stirring in subtle elements of seafaring adventure music. Then, lest I completely abandon the formidable science on display, I integrated synths and ambiences to allow the sound-scape to breath with a diversity of colors, not always overwhelming the audience with the weight and drama of conspicuous themes and heavy orchestration.

The film touches on several time periods in Earth's history – the Jurassic period, Stonehenge, ancient Egypt, Meso-America, and others. These scenes offered an opportunity to sprinkle a few indigenous instruments into the score. Expanding the palette with localized spices and hues has always been a hallmark of my scoring approach.

Once I completed composing the *Time Traveler* score, I brought Terence into the studio to hear a full playback of the film with my mocked-up music score playing along. Such review sessions can be nerve-wracking for both composer and director. The director has imagined and cherished the film for so long and is understandably nervous about whether your music will enhance the experience or ruin it. Of course, the composer wants the director to be thrilled, and is nervous about whether their tastes will align. Score reviews can be scary!

But there was nothing to be worried about here. As I mentioned at the outset, Terence and I connected instantly. As one cue handed off to the next, with scenes morphing seamlessly from one to the other, Terence had the look of a man carried away on the current of pleasant dreams. We finished the review without a single revision note and big grins on both of our faces. Bear hugs were probably in order, but we high-fived instead. He was thrilled, which meant I was thrilled. We moved into production.

The substantive content in *Tales of a Time Traveler* inspired one of my more complex orchestral scores. I hired DB Long to prepare the sheet music and went through my usual process with him. I also hired a *second* experienced orchestrator, Nate Hofheins, to do a second pass through the sheet music, looking for any additional enhancements or adjustments.

Nate found a few things to tweak and I was grateful to have another set of eyes on the score before we brought in the orchestra. Nate also conducted the sessions, so I had the ulterior motive of increasing his investment in the score before leading the group.

I do have one funny story from the string sessions to share. Ben Henderson, who has played first chair double bass on my scores since the early 1990s, once joked with me about the "functional" nature of the bass parts I typically orchestrated. He teased me, "I don't see you writing any solos for me like you do for Aaron (violin) or Nicole (cello)." Unbeknown to Ben, I *had* written an ambitious double bass solo into the *Time Traveler* score, about two-thirds of the way into the film. When the cue came up in the recording session, Ben looked like he was having a near-panic attack. Surrounded by 44 other musicians, he was suddenly the only person playing. I told him over the talkback, "Hey, you wanted me to write you a solo … so I wrote you a solo!" I grinned from the control room, but I am not sure that was helpful. We did a few takes of Ben playing alone, and also a few takes with all three bass players attempting the section. It never turned out quite right, which is my one regret about the production of this score. I asked the mixing engineer to craft a convincing blend of Ben's solo with the digitally sampled bass from my mock-up, but it ended up sounding heavy on the mock-up and light on Ben. After the strings session, Ben agreed he would be perfectly happy playing my functional bass parts in the future.

The brass section was another story. In a minor music market like Salt Lake City, there tend to be fewer outstanding studio musicians than in larger music towns like Los Angeles, Nashville, or London. Especially when it comes to brass players, if you don't get the top handful of players, the session may be a little more work. In this case, it was a *lot* more work. Take after take, the brass just were not playing in tune. I had to uncover the source of the problem. I asked the French horn section to play by themselves, and it was glorious. I asked the trumpets to play their part alone, and it sizzled. But when I asked the trombone section to play, it was like Forest Gump's box of chocolates – you never knew what you were going to get. Eventually, I released the entire trombone section from the session. That's also known as firing them. I had to complete the score with a blend of live horns, live trumpets, sampled trombones, and tuba. Once I sent the bones home, the brass sessions flowed smoothly and we recorded some incredible sounding tracks. Just know that many of the chordal trombones you hear in this score are sampled.

The final sessions were with the woodwind section. Gorgeous performances. Everyone was in a great form and great spirits. There was one section of the score which required a flute player to switch quickly to piccolo. When she made the swap, the microphones picked up the noise of her switching instruments. So on the next take, the oboe player (who was free for a few measures) quietly rose up, took her flute away in a handoff, and gave her the piccolo in return. This allowed us to roll through that section in one take without breaking any continuity. Fun little moments like that can stand out during recording sessions, unexpected memories that bring a smile years later.

The film premiered in Houston, Texas, later that year. Terence went down for the event and said the audience loved it. I was happy that he was happy. I was also deeply satisfied with the way our new studio and team had performed. To top it off, Terence reminded me of our agreement, and told me he had already reserved a "vastly expanded music budget" for his next film.

Unseen Universe

It is always a good thing to have a "vastly expanded music budget" for a score. But it was particularly beneficial at the end of 2018. By then, HUGEsound Post Production had been destroyed by fraud (see Chapter 15). I was out on my own, initially without any equipment, and without a studio.

Terence and I met together at E&S Digital to talk about the future. I assured him that I could still compose and produce the *Unseen Universe* film score, drawing from the same talented orchestral musicians who had played on *Tales of a Time Traveler*. I told him we could record and mix the score at LA East Recording Studio instead of HUGEsound, and the music would turn out just as good.

But Terence was nervous. The implosion of HUGEsound had rattled him. Back in early 2017, when he arrived at HUGEsound for the first time, it had been easy to sell Terence on my services. We were meeting in a world-class recording facility, surrounded by luxurious accommodations and prestigious awards. But now all of those trappings were gone, and I was starting over from scratch. It required all my powers of persuasion to convince and reassure Terence that I could still deliver a world-class score without the security blanket of HUGEsound. After long meetings and many reassurances, he decided to take the leap of faith with me.

There was no way I was going to let him down. At my new work-station I posted a John Williams quote to inspire me to keep my foot on the pedal. Williams once said that he works and reworks themes until they sound "inevitable." I wanted to achieve a similar level of accessibility in this new music score. That desire motivated me to craft and refine all of the thematic writing in the film – iterating, testing, revising, scrapping entire cues and starting over. As a result, the *Unseen Universe* score drew out some the loveliest melodic writing I had ever done.

In the end, it all came together. I produced the score with many of the same musicians who performed *Tales of a Time Traveler*. The strings sounded exquisite, the woodwinds were clear and pure, and the brass brought their A-game for a robust, epic flavor. Even the trombones! Glenn Neibaur and the LA East engineering team captured every note in crystal clear, high fidelity. Terence was very happy with the results.

Let me reiterate the importance of negotiations before closing this episode. From a business perspective, after HUGEsound was destroyed, my bank account was in desperate need of a "vastly expanded music budget." I had to set myself up for composing again and finance live production of the new film score. Retaining the copyrights also proved valuable, as many copies of the *Unseen Universe* and *Tales of Time Traveler* soundtracks have been sold from HUGEsound Records' online soundtrack store. I have also licensed those sync rights, which proved profitable, generating royalty streams and substantial fee payments. None of those benefits would have accrued to me without searching for tangible ways to offset a low music budget on the first film.

Too many composers simply agree to low budgets without looking for alternative means for additional compensation. I cannot stress enough how critical it is for composers to be serious about the business side of their composing careers. None of us can foresee what the future will bring, good or bad. I never imagined that HUGEsound would be destroyed by fraud, and that I would be starting over from scratch in the twilight of my career. But best business practices, such as negotiating persuasively for advantageous rights and resources, set me up for success.

DISNEY'S *JUNGLE CRUISE*

Gena Downey was a savvy music executive at Walt Disney Pictures' archive division. She was on a first-name basis with all the key players in the film music group, and met regularly with group president Mitchell Leib.

Gena had taken a shine to my music from *Lord of the Rings Online* and *Peter Jackson's King Kong*. She had a hunch I might be a good fit for Disney's upcoming film, *Jungle Cruise*. Under her guidance I began assembling an audition package of eight music cues, with further tutelage from Hollywood music agent Randy Gerston. The crowning jewel in the package would be an original *Jungle Cruise Main Theme*, lavishly produced with live orchestra.

We discovered that Leib was gathering his team in three weeks to discuss options for the *Jungle Cruise* film score. Gena planned to raise my name at the meeting and deliver my audition personally. All the pieces were falling into place.

We had no draft of the script yet, just a general story idea and some notes about the proposed film style. With that meager information, I composed a rousing, old-time adventure theme.

We booked a full orchestra and recorded the *Jungle Cruise Main Theme* demo at HUGEsound. I brought in mixing artist Mike Roskelley to work his magic on the tracks. Unfortunately, problems surfaced during the mix, delaying the theme's delivery.

With time running out, Randy and Gena wanted to get a feel for the flow of the music. I sent them a mocked-up audition package with all eight cues, substituting the unfinished main theme with a temporary placeholder. The placeholder was an old library cut I had done for Warner-Chappell Production Music with vaguely similar color and timing. Listening to the full package, the flow of music felt so good! All that remained was to swap out the placeholder and plug in the *Jungle Cruise Main Theme*, just as soon as we finished mixing it.

Mike and I doubled our efforts to finish the mix and everything came together just in time for the meeting. But somehow the files did not get switched properly. We unintentionally delivered a demo package that still had the placeholder music imbedded. Disastrously, it was the opening cue of the audition!

Listening to that placeholder, Mitchell Leib was not impressed. "I'll pass," he told Gena, bringing the audition to an abrupt close.

I was not aware of the file mixup until weeks later. But by then, it was too late. James Newton-Howard had been selected for the score. My one shot at scoring *Jungle Cruise* had capsized completely.

What did I learn? Career openings can be razor thin and vanish suddenly. There is no margin for error. I should have never used a placeholder, not in a mocked-up audition package so close to our delivery date. Also, our mix issues should have been resolved in half the time, leaving plenty of space for checking and double checking our submission. Greenhorn mistakes. Costly, very costly mistakes.

Don't get me wrong, I never harbored any naivety about my odds. Chance Thomas vs James Newton-Howard was always going to be a long shot, a David vs Goliath proposition. But at the very least, I would have liked for Leib to hear the *Jungle Cruise Main Theme,* which I composed for the film. That might have kept him listening to the whole package. And who knows where that may have led?

I will never know.

Instead, a rare opportunity slipped through my fumbling fingers, leaving me bereft of Hollywood glory. Only a cautionary tale remains, tattering in the wake.

On the other hand, let us not undervalue this startling fact – Mitchell Leib, President of Music & Soundtracks for The Walt Disney Motion Picture Company, actually sat down and began listening to my submission.

Getting to that beachhead was a HUGE win. No one can be considered unless they are being considered.

I credit Gena Downey and Randy Gerston for making that happen. But I will also allow some credit to myself for pursuing and nurturing those relationships, and for building a career track record that won their confidence.

Unfortunately, we fumbled at the goal line. Instead of hearing my original *Jungle Cruise Main Theme* demo, Leib heard a placeholder track from Warner-Chappell Production Music.

But imagine this. What if he had listened to the right track? The submission package was really good, eight cues totaling about 23 minutes. It was a full suite, offering a wide range of dramatic situations and stylistic nuances relevant to the film – adventure, comedy, romance, danger, action, mystery, even a touch of the supernatural. He might have been impressed enough to explore things further. It is a shame none of those tracks were ever heard.

So, here are some lessons drawn from this experience that might resonate with you:

1. Build a track record throughout your career of outstanding achievement to win the confidence of potential partners.

2. Target career team members and build relationships with people who believe in YOU and have the ability to get your music in front of decision makers. Or at least in front of decision-maker facilitators.

3. Whatever you do, do it all the way. Scaled to the opportunity, and within your range of resources, always take it to 11. You will never regret giving it all you have.

4. Don't fumble at the goal line.

5. Learn from experiences, make course corrections, and move swiftly and confidently to the next chapter.

AVATAR 2

I have one last story to share with you about swinging for the fences. It is the story of my quest to score *Avatar 2*, the film sequel to the highest grossing motion picture of all time, from James Cameron. This was my final, ultra-ambitious, uber-HUGE swing for the fences.

The epic journey of pitching for *Avatar 2* is an epic saga in its own right. Its pursuit has taken me on a long and winding road, populated with the most colorful cast of characters, unexpected synchronicity, and roller coaster of emotions. The pursuit of *Avatar 2* fills its own entire chapter.

Turn the page, and I will tell you the tale.

To watch videos from Inspire: The Chicago Spire Art Film, Robota: Reign of Machines, Lost Treasure Hunt, Tales of a Time Traveler, *and* Unseen Universe, *and to listen to demo submission music from Disney's* Jets *and Disney's* Jungle Cruise, *as described in this chapter, please visit:* HUGEsoundRecords.com/Memoir-17

NOTES

1 https://ariabento.wordpress.com/2018/02/28/robota-doug-chiang/

2 https://www.amazon.com/Robota-Doug-Chiang/dp/048680495X

CHAPTER **18**

Avatar 2

O<small>N</small> J<small>UNE</small> 22, 2015, the music world was stunned by the unexpected death of beloved film composer James Horner.

James died instantly when the single-engine S312 Tucano turboprop he was piloting went down in Los Padros National Forest, just north of Santa Barbara, California. I was devastated by the news. Our music-scoring community went into mourning, along with film music fans from across the globe.

James Horner was too young, too precious. He left too much unwritten music behind, ungiven to the world.

Horner once sheepishly told me that he was the last of the old-school film composers. In a day when most of his contemporaries were handing off large chunks of music to be written by their apprentices, Horner felt an obligation, even a passion, to compose every note himself. He was an artist and a gentleman. The world became poorer the day he went home to heaven.

Months went by. Sadness subsided into numbness. Numbness gave way to fond nostalgia. Life went spinning frantically on its way.

One day, an uncomfortable thought arose in my mind, "I wonder who is going to score *Avatar 2* for James Cameron?" I sort of squirmed in my seat and changed the topic. But after closing my mind to the question, it returned with a surprisingly convicted reply,

"You should do it. And you should do it to honor James Horner. There is no one left on this planet more emotionally attached, more imaginatively immersed, and more musically conversant in the scoring language of *Avatar* than you are. You should absolutely score the next film."

That is the story I told myself.

Still, at many levels, I was ashamed to have thought such a thought. Horner had been kind to me, a mentor to me, lifting the hood on the inner workings of his approach to Pandora's cultural and emotional narrative. He helped guide me in composing music for the first *Avatar* video game, one of my finest scores at the time. How could I think about scoring the film sequel? He had not even been gone a full year.

But the thought was persistent and growing. Perhaps the best way to honor Horner's investment in me was to carry on his legacy, to carry his vision into the new film's score. To mingle my own voice with his in a way that would never diminish his work, but would add appropriate originality to the new film. That felt right to me.

NETWORKING

I decided to reach out to Horner's former agency, Gorfaine-Schwartz, and share my convictions. I called agent Cheryl Tiano, whom I had met at GDC a few years prior. Cheryl represented a few of my friends in the game industry and I thought she could steer me in the right direction.

She listened patiently as I explained my history with Horner, my experiences with *Avatar*, and the conclusion I had recently arrived at. Would she help me find a way to pitch Cameron with the idea? She took a moment to gather herself, and then stated rather flatly, "There is no chance in hell that you are scoring *Avatar 2*."

I tried to persuade her to see my point, but she was unmoved. "No chance. No way. Never." We hung up and never spoke of it again.

Tiano's statement returned to my mind many times in the months and years that followed, "There is no chance in hell that you are scoring *Avatar 2*." Such a terse, castigating response! I was well aware that athletes often use such verbal disses as motivation to prove their naysayers wrong. But to my tender soul, her stinging words felt more like cancer than rocket fuel. I vowed to never throw such poisonous darts at another creative spirit as long as I had breath to live.

Instead, let me say this to every aspiring, striving, hopeful soul. To those who dream big, to those who aim high. It can be daunting to pursue a lofty goal. Other people's cynical remarks can be crippling, deterring your pursuit of greatness. Do not absorb their barbs. Do not immobilize yourself by giving oxygen to such damning thoughts.

Doing nothing is the only guarantee that nothing will happen. Taking action kicks the door wide open to possibility. As Jake Sully famously said, "Sometimes your whole life boils down to one insane move."

I am taking the leap.

I called another agent, Amos Newman. Amos was the head of Music for Visual Media at the William Morris Agency. Back in 2006, my friend Adam Levenson had brought me in to meet Amos with the idea of repping me into the film business. But with existing clients like his dad (Randy Newman) and superstars such as Hans Zimmer and Trent Reznor, Amos didn't exactly see me as a golden goose. Still, I called him to talk about my *Avatar 2* idea and left a message with all the details. He never called me back.

Clearly this was going to be harder than I thought.

Somehow I had to get in front of James Cameron. With my profound connection to Pandora and my deep understanding of the musical language Horner had developed, I knew I could propel the franchise forward, all the while honoring Horner's voice in the process. Surely that was worth a listen. I just needed to connect with Cameron. If the two Hollywood agents I knew would not help me, I would have to find another way.

CASTING A WIDER NET

The paths that I pursued in the ensuing months and years brought me face-to-face with fascinating and powerful people, interesting characters, and unexpected twists and turns. I would not believe it myself if I had not lived through it. In retrospect, it is shocking how determined and resourceful I became in my pursuit of this dream. And while some people cast cutting aspersions on my quest, others offered timely support and assistance along the way.

Six people in particular gave notable assistance to this ambitious pursuit – Sharon Smith Holley, Cathy "Crystal" Curtiss Albrecht, Paula Parisi, Randy Gerston, Gaylen Rust, and Crickett Goodsell Tyacke. Let me touch briefly on each.

SHARON SMITH HOLLEY

Sharon's cascading brown ringlets frame a rosy face radiating endless curiosity and kindness. There is something more there too, a probing intellect that draws clarity from chaos, an aptitude that meticulously organizes order from disarray. Small wonder Sharon found her niche as a VFX editor. For nearly 30 years she has plied her trade in the film industry, also serving as a board member and secretary for the Motion Picture Editors Guild (MPEG).

I first met Sharon in Los Angeles on a clear and sunny Spring afternoon. She was sitting at a bronze-framed glass-top table inside the courtyard of a quaint garden café. Verdant branches twisted overhead, with flowering shrubs and hanging vines surrounding the space. It seemed a fitting locale for my first conversation with this gentle genius.

Sharon had worked for Lightstream Pictures in the past, and currently had an office in the same building as Jon Landau, *Avatar 2's* producer. I thought she might have an inside track, and I arranged for Jacquie Barnbrook, our mutual friend, to introduce us. I had sent Sharon a link to my *Avatar 2* pitch web page prior to our meeting, also bringing along headphones, an iPod Shuffle loaded with the tracks, and a thumb drive, just in case. I wanted to be prepared for any scenario.

We talked about shared interests and mutual acquaintances. Then the conversation turned to the business at hand. I asked, "Have you had a chance to listen to the music I put together for *Avatar 2* yet? Did you like any of it?"

Her reply was playful, but on point, "I'm here, aren't I?" punctuated with a broad smile. "I think the music sounds really good, and might even be a good fit. But who knows? Jim Cameron is his own man."

We discussed several ways she might be able to forward my music up the chain. She concluded that the best approach would be to personally deliver a pitch package to Jon Landau. I said, "That's about as good as it gets," and thanked her liberally. I returned home from the meeting brimming with excitement and immediately wrote a cover letter for the package. I loaded a thumb drive with music from my *Avatar* video game score and sent everything to Sharon, then waited breathlessly for good news as days disappeared into weeks.

Sharon eventually let me know that she had dropped off my package with Jon's secretary. The only response had been that they were not ready to consider music yet. She did not know if anyone had listened to any of the music. I felt a little disappointed at the news, but undaunted. Reconnecting with Sharon, we brainstormed if there might be another avenue. She mentioned Cameron's film editor, Stephen E. Rivkin, an acquaintance she hoped to see at an upcoming Guild event. I put together a second cover letter with another loaded thumb drive, and sent them away to Sharon.

They did see each other at the MPEG meeting, and Sharon gave Rivkin my thumb drive along with her own handwritten note card. She complimented the music and suggested that, if he liked the music and felt that any tracks were appropriate, he could use them as temp music while editing early scenes for the film. I thought the idea was brilliant, and kept my fingers crossed. Unfortunately, Sharon never heard back from Rivkin. Shortly afterward, her own editing schedule picked up and swept her away to distant lands, where exciting projects consumed her time and talents.

CATHY "CRYSTAL" CURTISS ALBRECHT

Cathy was a student of video game music composition at Berklee College of Music, studying through their online learning division. We became acquainted while crossing paths at annual game industry conferences such as GDC and GSC. One evening at a party, we struck up a conversation about *Avatar*. When I mentioned my desire to score the film sequel, she said, "Well, I know Jim and Suzy pretty well. They're customers at the crystal shop where I work in Malibu. I help them with their energy divination items and sometimes give them spiritual advice."

You could have knocked me over with a feather.

Over the next several months, Cathy jumped onboard my campaign to reach Cameron. She often talked with me about Cameron's energy, reaching his higher self, improving my manifestations, and other abstract concepts. But one day she dropped me in my tracks, "I brought your name up to Jim today and reminded him that you did the music for his *Avatar* video game. I asked him what he would think about you scoring his next *Avatar* film."

Mic drop! This was such an unexpected coup, and from such an unexpected source. A direct connection! A personal mention! I could hardly wait to hear more about their conversation.

She continued that Cameron seemed vaguely familiar with my name from the game, but did not light up with any special kind of recognition. She also said his response about the music for *Avatar 2* was a little distancing, as he responded bluntly to her, "I'm not sure what I'm looking for yet." He finished his business and quickly left the store.

Cathy never mentioned him again, and soon relocated from Malibu to Oxnard, circling out from Cameron's orbit. She continued to send me peace, happiness, and harmony in occasional messages. But no further connections to Cameron were forthcoming.

PAULA PARISI

GameSoundCon is an influential annual gathering of audio professionals working in the game industry. It is the ongoing work of Brian Schmidt, one of the brightest stars in our game audio universe. GameSoundCon is well-attended, well-respected, and often offers a boost to people entering the business. For the 2015 conference, Brian had asked me to give the keynote address.

A few hours prior to giving the keynote, I met with journalist Paula Parisi, a sharp and intuitive writer working for *Billboard* magazine. Paula was covering the conference, and I was on her short list of interviews as the keynote speaker. We met in a long hallway, settling into adjacent chairs for a comfortable conversation. She asked me about my history in the business, and about some of game music's more colorful characters, including George "The Fat Man" Sanger, Tommy Tallarico, Bob Rice, and others.

But I soon turned the interview around, asking about Paula's own history in the business. In the process I learned that, among other things, she had written a book called, *James Cameron and the Making of Titanic*. Her book chronicled many of the experiences Cameron had while bringing the award-winning film *Titanic* to life. I could hardly believe the synchronicity of that connection.

We chatted enthusiastically about her book, and she mentioned the name, Randy Gerston, *Titanic's* music supervisor. Randy had worked directly with Cameron and James Horner on the film's score and source music. Currently, Randy was a music agent representing film and video game composers, a partner at Fortress Talent Management. I learned later that he represented two of my friends, Gordy Haab (*Star Wars: Battlefront*) and Neal Acree (*World of Warcraft*). Paula mentioned that she knew Randy personally. This was too good to be true.

Maybe Paula could connect me with Randy Gerston? If Randy thought I had a shot, as a bona fide Hollywood music agent, perhaps he could finally get my music heard by Cameron himself. Graciously, Paula agreed to make the introduction.

I gave Paula a copy of my *Avatar* video game soundtrack. We exchanged contact info and departed as new friends. It had been a very productive interview.

True to her word, Paula reached out to Randy and suggested that a meeting might prove mutually profitable. It was not long before Randy's assistant called to set up the appointment.

RANDY GERSTON

I will admit, I was nervous sitting in the offices of Fortress Management for the first time. Randy Gerston represented Oscar winners Mychael Danna and Howard Shore.

Michael Danna and Howard Shore!

Film-scoring gods among the rest of us mere mortals. But there I was, waiting for my turn to meet with agent of the gods, Randy Gerston.

Based on the recommendation of Paula Parisi (and a secondary nudge from fellow composer Gordy Haab), Randy had agreed to meet with me. He soon came out of his office and waved me in, "Come on in here, have a seat."

Randy struck me as a trimmer, fitter version of singer Stephen Bishop. They could have purchased their wide, thick-rimmed glasses from the same designer. Randy seemed to be riding high that day, laughing easily and enjoying a good barb in the conversation now and again. I introduced myself and we engaged in small talk about our backgrounds and mutual acquaintances. When he mentioned his role as music supervisor for *Titanic*, I grabbed my opening.

"Randy, what I'm really interested in is representation that can get my music in front of Jim Cameron." I told him about my history with *Avatar*, my mentoring experiences under James Horner, and my convictions about the fictional world of Pandora. He immediately turned skeptical, "Jim's a very hard man. He suffers no fools. And you, some white bread kid from Utah? He'll eat you alive."

I had noticed some NFL swag around the office when I first sat down. Judging from Randy's age, and his home in California, I speculated that Randy might be a 49ers fan. I took a deep breath and launched into my reply. "Do you remember the 1990 Super Bowl, when Joe Montana threw a record five touchdown passes? Five touchdowns! Man, that was incredible."

Randy remembered it enthusiastically, but wondered where I was heading. I continued, "Five years after Montana set that record, a white bread kid from Utah led the 49ers to another Super Bowl championship. His name was Steve Young. And in that game, Steve Young broke Montana's touchdown record with six touchdown passes of his own. Six touchdowns! Do you remember?"

Randy was smiling, and nodded his head.

It was time to deliver the punch line, "Never underestimate a white bread kid from Utah."

Randy laughed and admired my pluck. He had also done his homework, researching my background, listening to my music, talking with people in the video game industry about me. But he wanted to see if I could take a punch. I am glad I did not flinch.

Randy agreed to represent me, and we began a slow and deliberate process of strategizing how to best approach Cameron, getting my music in front of him in a credible way. Part of that strategy included composing a brand-new theme that we hoped would capture the spirit of the new film. That was a tall order, since very little information was available about *Avatar 2* in 2018.

"Listen," he said, "When you're pitching for a film score, don't try to impress anyone with fancy orchestrations or complex writing chops. All you want is for the director to hear their film in your music." That was Randy's key piece of advice as I set out to produce a compelling demo package. He suggested that I pull together eight or nine tracks that sounded great and reflected everything we could guess about the scope and tone of *Avatar 2*.

We knew the RDA were exiled back to earth at the end of the first film, and we assumed that part of the sequel would celebrate a flourishing of the Na'vi people and their culture. Then, as a few trade articles began popping up, we learned other important details about *Avatar 2* – some of the film would take place underwater, Jake and Neytiri would raise a family, and Colonel Miles Quaritch, *Avatar*'s first villain, would somehow return to Pandora.

That was a pretty thin thread to weave from, but I thought it was enough for me to make a bold stab. Several tracks from my original *Avatar* score seemed to work to our purpose. But nothing from the game conveyed the kind of resurgence, optimism, and native cultural celebration we assumed would open the new film. For that, I would need to create something fresh. And to match the sound quality of the *Avatar* video game tracks, that meant finding financial support for a live orchestral demo.

GAYLEN RUST

By this time, I had been leading the music division at HUGEsound Post Production for nearly two years (see Chapter 15). Still, the CEO at the top of our umbrella investment company, Gaylen Rust, had to approve any major expenditures outside of client projects. Since my pitch for *Avatar 2* was a total speculation, a long shot roll of the dice for a major film score, I needed Gaylen's approval for the budget. I made an impassioned pitch and he agreed to get behind me 100%. Gaylen was all in. He said, "whatever was required" to finance the recording sessions, go for it.

I pulled together a 53-piece orchestra and 24-voice choir for the new theme, which I titled, *Dawning of a New Day*. The tracks were recorded and edited at HUGEsound and sounded sensational. Choral conductor Jane Fjeldsted did wonders in bringing the singers' voices to a brilliant nasal pinch. The orchestra was sweeping and solid. Ethnic woodwinds hissed and snarled. Darren Bradford's work on the Penny Whistle was particularly tasty, dancing high above the broad orchestral themes, hanging emotional ornamentation all across the song. Mike Roskelley and I mixed everything at The Pod, though I did additional touch-up mixing afterward at HUGEsound.

Dawning of a New Day was a terrific opening track. Exploding out of the speakers with massive percussion transients and overblown Peruvean nose flutes, the music drifted into a thick alien atmosphere, setting up for the opening statement of the new theme. Violins rose cautiously out of the chaos, offering a stepwise, halting theme, ornamented by Penny Whistle and ethnic flutes. As the theme gained confidence and momentum, the strings were joined by French horns, throat singing, bright female voices, and deep African percussion. The anthemic celebration reached a joyous crescendo, then relaxed into a sweet and tender rendering of Horner's love theme from the original film. Listening to the final master, I tried to temper my enthusiasm, but I was ecstatic. Everyone involved had knocked it out of the park. This track was a home run.

Randy guardedly agreed, though he was jaded enough not to invest too much emotion into any given pitch. When we combined *Dawning of a New Day* with the other tracks I had curated and edited from the *Avatar* video game score, even Randy had to smile, admitting that this was a pretty compelling and comprehensive pitch.

Within a few days of compiling our pitch package, Randy was contacted directly by Jon Landau, Cameron's producer. Landau wanted to gather demos from a few top composers, so when Cameron was ready to think about music for *Avatar 2*, he would have some options to consider. He told Randy that he was only reaching out to a few of the most exclusive composer agents, and that he would accept no more than three or four submissions from each. We figured that probably meant Fortress, Gorfaine-Shwartz, and William Morris Endeavor.

That was some rarified air.

With so few submission slots available to Fortress, and a whole stable of experienced film composers at the agency, I worried that I might not make the cut. After all, Fortress only made money if one of their composers was selected. It seemed risky to give up one valuable submission slot to someone like me, with limited film-scoring experience.

But Randy responded by putting my pitch package at the top of the Fortress submission, along with a personal note to Landau. He referred to me as "a spiritual successor to James Horner, cut from the same cloth." I almost cried when I read that. Who could ask for a better endorsement? All I had ever wanted was for my *Avatar 2* music submission to be heard by Cameron. Maybe the odds were finally swinging in my favor.

Now came the waiting.

After several months of radio silence, Randy checked in again with Landau and was told nothing had happened with music yet.

More waiting.

After several more months, Randy reached out again and received the same response. None of the composer submissions had been listened to. It had been almost a year and I was getting impatient. What now? I decided to try a pincer move on social media. Somehow, I had to get Cameron's attention.

SOCIAL MEDIA

One of Randy's competitors, Richard Kraft, had just posted a challenge on a Facebook composer forum. Kraft invited composers in the forum to "be bold" and make "one bold, proactive, comfort zone-pushing action to help propel your career forward" before the week was over. Out of frustration with the glacial pace of my previous *Avatar 2* attempts, I took up the challenge.

Maybe a social media post would dislodge some unexpected connection. It was a Hail Mary, to be sure. But up they went, all eight tracks from my *Avatar 2* pitch, in a Facebook post and link. In the post, I added this introduction:

> All right Richard Kraft, you've inspired me. I'm taking my moonshot. To your recent "be bold" challenge, I am absolutely shooting for the moon. Not Earth's moon. But Polyphemus' moon. Otherwise known as Pandora.
>
> I've pulled out all the stops in a pitch to score *AVATAR 2*. Brand new music. Live orchestra. Choir. Ethnic instruments. Whale song.

Eight original music tracks. With an open letter to James Cameron at the bottom of the page. Taking it public. Meanwhile, my agent is working normal channels…[1]

Along with the music tracks, I posted an open letter to James Cameron on my website, linked in the Facebook post. Here is what I wrote in my open letter:

Dear Mr. Cameron,

I enthusiastically invite you to hear this original music I've put together for *Avatar 2* – the dawning of a new day for the Omaticaya, the exploration of Pandora's oceans, new conflicts, the return of old enemies – all performed by live orchestra, choir, ethnic instruments, solo voice… even a hint of whale song!

This open letter is a creative attempt to reach you, to invite your consideration, to catalyze your curiosity enough to listen to eight original music tracks, prepared especially for *Avatar 2*.

I'm not desperate. But I would like to get your attention.

James Horner mentored me. *Avatar* inspired me. I think life experience has prepared me.

I grew up in Oklahoma, hearing and re-hearing stories of the infamous Trail of Tears. It turned my heart to the plight of the Native Americans, their civilization upended, their lives broken.

As a child, I read and re-read *Chariots of the Gods*, which stirred a fascination for the indigenous civilizations of South and Central America, with an eye turned towards the stars.

From these formative influences, my immersion into Pandora's story came quickly, easily, and comprehensively as I began composing music for *Avatar*'s video game release in 2009.

I fell in love with that world. I loved the Omaticaya, and the way their warrior spirituality connects them to their ancestors and all living things. I loved the conflict against an aggressive, arrogant, military industrial complex. I loved how rival Na'vi tribes came together to triumph over their aggressors. I'm drawn to Jake Sully, a broken man given new life and purpose.

James Horner led me to understand his musical interpretation of that world, as I composed under his tutelage to create *Avatar*'s original video game score. James shared his ideas with me about rhythm, pace, harmonic structure, theme, and palette. Such a stunning gift!

These pieces of music encapsulate what I learned from Horner's guidance, while also including my own inspiration about Pandora's future.

Randy Gerston, my Hollywood agent, once described me as a spiritual successor to James Horner, cut from the same cloth (those are his words, not mine). I won't go that far. But I do recognize that blending Horner's mentoring influences with my own natural connection to *Avatar*'s story has, at the very least, created a uniquely relevant combination!

Mr. Cameron, if you somehow find your way to this page, I hope you will recognize in these tracks a musical voice that is both familiar and appropriately fresh.

If you hear inklings of your next film in this music, then we may have some interesting things to talk about. If not, no harm done.

Either way it's been my pleasure to put this music together with great love and admiration for the rich and evocative world you've created.

Thank you for the inspiration,

Chance Thomas

DREAM SIDEBAR

By now you may think I was completely obsessed with scoring this film. If so, you would be right. I was so obsessed, I literally dreamed one night that I was in a room with James Cameron. He was walking back and forth, not in an agitated way, but more like pacing around to clarify his thinking. I introduced myself and asked if he had ever listened to my music pitch for *Avatar 2*. In the dream he told me, "I listened to your music. I was blown away. The music really is a perfect fit for *Avatar*. But I can't hire you. The money people want a name composer, a big name."

In my dream, I wondered if a big name film composer would really add financial value to the production, aka, seats in the theater. The "money people" Cameron mentioned in the dream didn't think I could generate any kind of pull in the marketplace.

As the dream continued, I asked, "Do your money people understand that the video game business is about three times the size of the movie business?"

He stopped pacing and perked up. I got bolder, "125 million people are playing *Fortnite*, right now. More than 10 million people play *DOTA 2*, which I scored a few months ago. *Lord of the Rings Online* has been played over 23 million times, and I've scored that game for years. These are big numbers, meaningful numbers. Gamers will respond in droves to the news that I'm scoring *Avatar 2*. Tell that to your money people."

Cameron seemed intrigued, and impressed with my resolve and the hard data. But as dreams tend to do, this one drifted off without resolution. Just a dream.

But isn't it fascinating how the subconscious mind works on our obsessions while we sleep?

CRICKETT GOODSELL TYACKE

The Facebook post generated a tremendous groundswell of interest. And just as I had hoped, it unearthed a connection I never would have discovered otherwise. Crickett Goodsell Tyacke, an old friend from my high school days in Oklahoma, messaged me with the news that Cameron's wife, Suzy Amis, had once attended Heritage Hall, a private school in Oklahoma where Crickett's father David Goodsell was headmaster. Crickett had personally been friends with Suzy's brother Charlie Amis, and offered to reach out to Charlie and ask if we could send my music to Cameron up the family tree.

Charlie actually listened to the music tracks and read the letter. He responded positively to Crickett, but added that the family "never forwards anything like that to Jim." Cathy Crystal had actually warned me about this years ago, telling me that Cameron was an exceptionally private and independent spirit when it came to his business. She had told me, "He likes his ideas to be his own." And while there was great mutual respect between Cameron and his wife, Charlie made it clear that they kept a thick divide between their personal and professional lives.

I knew it was a last ditch effort. But I had to try.

POST SCRIPT

In my final conversation with Randy Gerston about the *Avatar 2* pitch, he confided that he wasn't sure if anyone in Cameron's camp ever listened to a single note of my music. It may have all been in vain. In fact, he learned that one of James Horner's former assistants, Simon Franglen, had been in Cameron's ear the whole time, and was probably going to get the gig. Franglen's hiring was confirmed a few months later in the press.

It was over.

My quest to score *Avatar 2* had taken so many unexpected twists and turns. Film music agents, movie editors, a writer for Billboard, a crystal shop in Malibu, even a private school in Oklahoma. I leaned hard into every one of them. But like an elusive life ring floating away on windswept waters, *Avatar 2* just kept drifting beyond my reach.

As I write this post script, I have recently returned from experiencing *Avatar 2: The Way of Water* in my local IMAX theater. I have to admit, Simon Franglen did a terrific job scoring the film. I was entertained and loved Franglen's many homages to Horner throughout the score. Yet, it was bittersweet. And even though I have now retired from composing, I could not stop myself from imagining how I might have scored many of the scenes differently.

As I exited the theater, nursing a little twinge of pain and regret, I thought of Ed Kitsell, a good Englishman I had known of particular grace and wisdom, who recently passed away. He once reminded me of this timeless quote attributed to Siddhartha Gautama Buddha, which seems apropos: "In the end, only three things matter: how much you loved, how gently you lived, and *how gracefully you let go of things not meant for you.*"

Avatar 2 was not meant for me, though I pursued it with all the dogged determination and ingenuity I could muster. I took my leap and rode hard, leaving no stone in my reach unturned. I loved the chase and found the pursuit exhilarating. I am very proud of the music and grateful for the dear people who supported me along the way. There is no useful purpose in retaining any bittersweet emotions about the experience.

Avatar 2 was not meant for me. Time for me to gracefully let go.

To listen to the full music pitch submission for Avatar 2, *as described in this chapter, please visit: HUGEsoundRecords.com/Memoir-18*

NOTE

1 Facebook. Thomas, Chance. Avatar pitch post; August 7, 2019; 2:14 pm. https://www.facebook.com/ChanceThomas.composer/posts/pfbid02sUt-MfGYfxrkAnqQAsodu5HKEw8ibaAy562ePB7wbeVUGBCx3MSU8A69f-G2UkW1Mel

CHAPTER 19

The Settlers

INTENSE PAIN, RADIATING FROM my wrists back up through my arms. I shake my hands down at my sides, reposition my elbows and forearms, trying different angles throughout the day, and push forward. There are still so many files to edit and export.

Fatigue. I am so tired. My eyes sting. My back aches. My ears are buzzing. I can barely keep going. But I still have over 200 files to get through before I can call it a night. I will not relent until I am done.

Oh crap. I started misnaming the files 42 exports ago. Now I have to go back and fix all of the errors. As if this wasn't overwhelming enough already.

Grinding. This feels like the musician's equivalent of digging graves with a spoon. Or maybe cutting an overgrown lawn with a hand sickle. Why am I doing this?

The Settlers: New Allies is the largest known procedural music score in history. This dynamic music score unfolds across 16,327 music files. The music is never the same twice and potentially never ends.

The score adapts on the fly to each player's individual style; it reacts to gameplay and delivers a thematic experience without being repetitive; it evolves in aesthetically delightful and meaningful ways. That is pretty much the holy grail of game music.

Technically and creatively, this wildly ambitious score was the magnum opus of my music scoring career.

But *The Settlers* also sucked all the life out of me. Months after delivering the last music file I was still an empty shell. No energy. No motivation. My mind was in a perpetual fog. I had days of borderline depression, other

DOI: 10.1201/9781003199311-20

times inexplicably punchiness, laughing at nothing at all. Is this what a nervous breakdown looks like?

Let us rewind the story and see how we got here.

BENEDICTE OUIMET

In 2009, I attended GameSoundCon in San Francisco, California. I arrived late to a particularly crowded session, and grabbed an open chair next to a young woman with tussled blonde hair and wide-frame glasses. The session was a yawner, so we struck up a quiet conversation to pass the time. Her name was Benedicte Ouimet, and she worked in the music department at Ubisoft in Montreal. She was funny, intelligent, loved to shop, and seemed ambitious. We exchanged business cards and went our separate ways.

You never know when a random business encounter may turn into a valued client. It is important to keep in touch. I would send Benedicte occasional updates, say hello when crossing paths at conferences, and congratulate her on successful scores she was involved with. I recruited her to serve on a music awards screening committee for G.A.N.G. I even invited her to contribute a sidebar to my textbook.[1]

Years went by. We periodically discussed the possibility of working together on something cool, but never found the right project. Then one late summer day in 2018, she called me out of the blue. With a surprising amount of sparkle in her voice she said, "You know all that interactive music stuff you talk about in your textbook? I have a new project that needs just that! I think it's perfect for you. Do you want to hear more?"

Yes, yes, absolutely yes!

She began describing an interactive music score that would marry the fingerstyle acoustic guitar sound of a Michael Hedges, Tommy Emmanuel, or Antoine Dufour with a symphony orchestra. This vision was the brainchild of Stefan Randelshofer, audio director at Ubisoft's newly acquired Blu Byte Studios in Germany. I was definitely intrigued.

DEMOS

With most opportunities in the video game industry, your relationships of trust and a strong track record will open the door for you. But that is only the beginning. Generally, you still have to prove yourself anew by pitching a custom demo for each gig. That is just the way the business rolls.

Still, Benedicte was asking for something I had never encountered before. For this demo, she said the Blu Byte audio director wanted to see

video footage of me working with fingerstyle guitarists in my area, to demonstrate that I had access to local resources and possessed the savvy to
work with them. That was definitely a first.

I will admit, fingerstyle guitar is a rare specialization. Although I had
worked with a number of brilliant studio guitarists such as Rich Dixon,
Michael Dowdle, and Tommy Hopkins, none of them could claim that
particular weapon in their arsenal. In fact, there was no one I knew, nor
anyone who *they* knew possessing such a skill in Utah.

What do you do when a client's need arises but your stable is empty?
Where can you turn for a need so highly specialized and rare as this?
I have found that diligent research is the great unequalizer. It can tilt an
otherwise impossible situation in your favor.

I began with my guitar playing friends, but went three and out. Google
came up empty too. Contractors in the area all drew a blank. So far my
research was going nowhere. But diligence does not blink, it just keeps
digging.

I located an acoustic guitar specialty store in downtown Salt Lake City,
Utah. I planned a visit and stopped by to talk with the store employees and
owner. After gushing over their collection of rare acoustic instruments,
and discussing our mutual admiration for great fingerstyle guitarists of
the day, I asked if they knew of anyone in Utah who played fingerstyle.
Unfortunately, they could not think of anyone.

I visited a second specialty store and went through the same scenario.
The store owner scratched his head for a minute, and then said, "I think
I know a guy. His business card might still be pinned up on our bulletin
board." Sure enough, he plucked a yellow card from the wall and handed
it to me. I cannot recall the guitarist's name, but I jotted down his number
and waved thank you to the owner as I headed out the door.

Research and persistence. I made the call and the guitarist was excited to
come over to HUGEsound and show me his chops. Once he had unpacked
his instrument, he started to play *These Moments* by Antoine Dufour,
which is a terrific song and a nice showcase for the style. He had obviously
worked hard on the song, but mastery was eluding him. I made a couple
of suggestions about dynamics and strum patterns, capturing video of us
working together. It was not great, but it was a start. Before he left, he recommended two other guitarists who were studying the same style. Both
were contacted and invited to visit with me at HUGEsound. One of them
turned out to be pretty good. We had a great time experimenting and shot
some additional video while working together.

I was now ready to gather my resources and put the demo package together. Besides video, Blu Byte also wanted to hear some relevant examples of my music scoring work. From my repertoire, I gathered six tracks of epic orchestral music and six tracks of acoustic guitar with orchestra. I added the video footage we had shot with the local guitarists, and uploaded everything to a DropBox folder, sending the link to Benedicte. After so many decades of submitting demos, I crossed my fingers and hoped for the best, but had no expectations either way. Within a couple of weeks, Benedicte called again with the good news. I had won the audition. How soon could I come to Düsseldorf, Germany?

GRAND DESIGNS

A few weeks later, I was on a flight to meet with audio director Stefan Randelshofer and his handpicked audio team. Benedicte was flying in from Canada to be there too. We were all coming together to brainstorm about the flavor, scope, and design of this new video game soundtrack.

Stefan's vision was startlingly ambitious. He wanted nothing less than an endlessly generative music score from live-recorded parts. He envisioned an ever-evolving and infinitely varied underscore that was immediately responsive to changes in gameplay. However, and this is the caveat that would place *The Settlers* apart from any previous procedural music score ever deployed, the generated score had to sound like real music, as if created with *linear artistic intent,* rather than by soulless computer AI.

No small task.

We spent the better part of three days continuing the discussion. Two key contributors from the audio team who joined us were audio programmer Arne Hertel and audio designer Chiara Haurand-Schlagkamp. I was so inspired and impressed by everyone's intelligence, creativity, ambition, and camaraderie. We were innovating, igniting real sparks of magic during those brainstorming sessions. I had the feeling we were on a path toward something truly spectacular.

As our summit in Düsseldorf drew to a close, we settled on six primary objectives for *The Settlers* soundtrack:

1. The game's music would sound natural, as if the generated parts of the score had been composed on purpose. The music accompanying each player's journey would sound organic, live, musical, and compelling.

2. Shifting game states would be reflected in the music score, foreshadowing upcoming events, highlighting key moments, and tightly following the player's actions.

3. The score would not loop mindlessly, avoiding the bane of bad game music, but remain fresh and evolving in content, color, and mood.

4. Potentially, the score could play forever without ever being quite the same.

5. The music would feature the guitar virtuosity of Antoine Dufour, Michael Hedges, Tommy Emmanuel, or another comparable fingerstyle guitarist. Contacting and contracting this guitarist, then bonding creatively and collaborating throughout the project, would be a top priority for me.

6. The score might also include percussion, some configuration of orchestra, and other elements, TBD.

I went home to ponder how I could possibly create a music design to achieve all of those ambitious objectives.

Drawing upon principles I distilled while authoring my textbook,[2] it became clear that I would need three primary branches in this music score. (1) An **Event-Driven** branch where the music would highlight key gameplay events or game state changes, such as achievement, discovery, combat, victory, defeat, training, menu selection, and the like. (2) A **Cinematic** branch where the music would underscore pre-rendered linear content, usually dramatic or narrative. (3) A **Procedural** branch for everything else throughout the game. This would include exploration, building, traveling, harvesting, conversations, anticipation, and aftermath of important events. The procedural branch would provide the synapses of the score, threading among and between all the other music files in the game, connecting everything into one dynamic and cohesive soundtrack.

Since the first two branches are well understood in game music design circles, I will touch on those later. Most of the true innovation took place in designing the procedural branch. The procedural part of the score required the most brainpower and manpower, generating the largest number of assets. So I will start there. Let us explore how the procedural music branch was conceived and developed.

PROCEDURAL MUSIC DESIGN

I began by asking the most fundamental question of all. What makes music... music?

One could answer melody, harmony, rhythm, texture, and color. But what really drives the mood and emotion in music? While all components in a composition make a contribution, I resolved that harmony supplies the primary vector for mood and emotion. Let me take a quick sidebar to explain my reasoning.

Research in neuroscience has revealed that musical harmony connects directly to human biology in predictable, even measurable ways. For example, imagine that you are feeling sad right now. If we measured key indicators in your body, we would see that your temperature is lower than normal, your skin conductivity has decreased, your blood pressure is slightly elevated, and your pulse has slowed. That is what a human body does when we feel sad.

But did you know that the same physiological conditions can be triggered by exposure to minor chord progressions? Using the same measuring equipment, we would find that your temperature is lower than normal, your skin conductivity has decreased, your blood pressure is slightly elevated, and your pulse has slowed. Exactly the same biological reaction as if you were actually sad.

That is not all. Major music harmonies produce respiratory changes and limbic system responses identical to genuine happiness. Dissonant harmonies increase your pulse rate and light up areas of the brain associated with fear. This is so universal and predictable that I teach young video game composers – *while the player is playing the game, a great music score is playing the player*. It is like having access to a custom array of switches, knobs, and sliders to seduce and manipulate the player's emotions. When you get the harmony right, it always works.[3]

Harmony

Yes, harmony would be the foundational building block of this procedural music design. Harmony would provide the mood and also provide *vector* within that mood. That is how I would ensure musicality and perceived purpose as the score unfolded across time.

Harmony for any mood is built from germanely evocative chords and chord patterns. The game state design called for four different moods – Neutral, Happy, Sad, and Tense. In order to build chord progressions to conjure each mood, I would need asset buckets filled with suitable chords for each mood.

But buckets of chords alone do not make meaningful harmony. How could I create musically suggestive harmonic structure from among these chords within each mood bucket? How could a bit-driven music system come up with expressive chord *phrases*?

This was the greatest wrestle I had during the music design phase of the project. As a young man, I had earned a living as a contract pianist (Chapter 1), often improvising for long stretches during each gig. Now, I spent weeks at the keyboard experimenting with chord progressions of all kinds, trying to reverse-engineer my improvisational *vector*. To wit, while improvising, what factors determine the choice of whichever chord I select "next"?

It was during those weeks at the keyboard that the realization struck me like lightning.

Somewhere in my brain I had developed a probability table that drove my decisions about which chord to select "next" during any given improvisation. If I was noodling around in a pensive mood on an Am7 chord, there was a high probability that my next chord would be a Dm7. There was a very low probability that I would move from Am7 to C# major add 9. I realized that whichever chord I was playing during any given moment in time, would generate an intuitive range of probabilities for a host of other "next" chords, in order to drive a mood forward and give the music relevant *vector*. That internal probability table was a surefire predictor for the musicality of my improvisation.

That was the lightbulb moment. All I had to do was synthesize a harmonic probability table for each mood in order to drive the procedural branch of the score. With that realization, the project suddenly jumped from theoretical to likely.

Immediately, I began to experiment with chords for various moods, finding my way along various paths. I would make notes about which chords would evolve the mood without breaking it, which chords tended to sound the most natural following other chords, and sketching out a large matrix of probabilities to govern the AI selection mechanic. In the distillation process, a simplicity emerged beyond the complexity, crystalizing into four probability tables for each required game state mood – Neutral, Happy, Sad, and Tense.

Here is how they would work. Whatever chord was currently playing for a given mood, the system AI would check with the probability table to determine which chord to play next.

For example, here is a probability table for the game's Happy mood. It tells the game engine, "Given the current chord in the table's left vertical column, what is the probability of selecting each possible chord from the horizontal row across the top 'next'?"

	E	G9	A6	A59	C1v	D1v	B	B7
E	80%	70%	40%	50%	60%	70%	10%	40%
G9	70%	60%	80%	80%	80%	70%	50%	50%
A6	70%	60%	40%	80%	60%	20%	70%	50%
A59	50%	60%	70%	70%	90%	20%	50%	30%
C1v	70%	40%	20%	60%	70%	90%	50%	20%
D1v	70%	30%	10%	40%	70%	70%	60%	70%
B	60%	80%	50%	60%	40%	60%	70%	90%
B7	90%	80%	50%	60%	60%	10%	70%	40%

This was such a breakthrough design element for this project! I was now confidant we would be able to build a natural-sounding procedural music system for *The Settlers* original score.

This was a great start. But now I had to figure out what kinds of *structures* I could use to *deploy* harmony throughout the score.

The audio team wanted the music built around acoustic guitars, so I could deploy harmony with both strummed and finger-picked chords on guitar. For additional variety, I could record the strums and finger picking across a range of varied patterns. And for diversity, I could spread the recordings out among different types of guitars – nylon string acoustic, steel string acoustic, and 12 string. Finally, for increased flexibility, I could record each pattern variation in blocks of different beat lengths – 4 beats, 8 beats, and 12 beats.

These were innovative ideas. Now I needed to distill them down to specific asset lists. Using the Happy mood harmonic table with its eight chords as an example, I would need:

- Strums on acoustic 12-string and six-string guitars for each chord, recorded in 4, 8, and 12 beat blocks (48 recorded files);

- Fingerpicking recorded on nylon string acoustic guitar with four rhythmic variations each in 4, 8, and 12 beat blocks (96 recorded files).

That is a total of $48 + 96 = 144$ recorded files on acoustic guitars to provide foundational harmony assets for the Happy mood.

The Neutral mood was even bigger, requiring 13 different chords, resulting in $78 + 156 = 234$ recorded files.

The Sad mood and Tense mood requirements were closer in size to the Happy mood, approximately 140 files each.

Thus, just to provide foundational harmony assets on guitar for all four mood packages, I would need to produce over 650 recorded files. Yes, that is a lot of time in the studio with my guitar players. But just think of the unprecedented variety, diversity, and flexibility provided by such a wealth of component assets!

Green Light

I presented this breakthrough to Ubisoft's audio team and they responded with measured enthusiasm. Using a probability table as an engine to drive the selection of assets solved our most difficult procedural problem. But the team expressed concern about the proliferation of assets. I did not want to tell them this was just the tip of the iceberg (you will understand what I mean in the following sections). I assured them that the number of files would not be problematic, as long as we developed an intuitive file structure and robust naming convention. I had already envisioned both in rudimentary stages.

During the same team discussion, we generated another terrific ancillary idea. What if we envisioned our proliferation of recorded files like musical Lego pieces? Not only could they be assembled in real time by the system AI following the probability tables, but audio team members could also use them like Legos *literally*, building prefabricated blocks of chord progressions for specific areas or functions in the game.

This opened up additional possibilities. For example, we could prefabricate the beginning of a level and then turn the balance over to procedural generation. Or we could custom design a framework, and insert degrees of variability within that framework.

To achieve these ends, audio programmer Arne Hertel suggested creating wildcards (X) for any place in the music system where we want the system AI to generate the "next" chord (including its duration and variant). Custom-designed sections would designate specific chord names, while wildcards (X) would be used for AI-generated chords using the probability tables.

Ultimately, everything that happens in the procedural part of the score begins and progresses through chord selection, whether assembled like Lego pieces in advance by custom design, or by wildcards (X) selected by the system AI through harmonic probability tables. Either way, chord selection lays the score's harmonic foundation.

We decided that chord phrases could also include silences too, simply by indicating the number of beats of silence.

Multiple chord phrases could also be stitched together to form a sequence. And multiple sequences could be stitched together to form a song. Since each component could be prefabricated or generated procedurally, this flexible structure allowed for unprecedented elasticity in the game score.

Please understand that the term "system AI," as used in this chapter does not mean, *music written by a computer*. The system AI only accesses and runs through harmonic probability tables that were painstakingly created by me, a human composer, to generate harmonic progressions based on my personal musical tastes. Put another way, the system AI simply reflects an encoding of what I would do if I were sitting behind each player, improvising music in response to actions in the game. From that perspective, even the most densely procedural parts of the music are still outcroppings of my own original scoring work.

Rhythm

Harmony needs a scaffolding to build on. That scaffolding is rhythm. For a stable and easily connectible scaffolding, we needed a constant tempo and meter. I settled on 104 bpm and 4/4 time. Variety came from the previously described block lengths of 4 beats, 8 beats, and 12 beats. I introduced beat subdivisions within each block for additional diversity – triplets, quarters, eights, and sixteenths – recording several variations of each beat subdivision for each block length.

To reiterate, the entire game system runs at 104 beats per minute. Every single beat is tracked within the game engine. This allows for accurate pinpointing and seamless stitching of each block of files as the score progresses.

Melody

Harmony and rhythm form a solid musical foundation together. But music requires melody to tell the story. Melody must match the underlying harmony and rhythm to create music instead of cacophony. Thus for each chord, I created melodies matching each block length and each rhythmic pattern. Since melody is more noticeable and memorable than any other musical component, I had to proliferate the number of melodic variations for every chord and phrase length, recording as many as 45 different melodic variations for each chord.

As an example, for the Neutral mood, we recorded a total of 585 melody fragments on the steel string acoustic guitar. This enormous pool of melodic fragments allowed for vast variation during the Neutral part of the score. Additional melody fragments were recorded for the Happy, Sad, and Tense moods in sufficient numbers.

The composing challenge was significant. Each melody fragment had to flow naturally between segments. Using the larger 12 beat blocks, I could establish bits and pieces of thematic content. But for the shorter eight beat and four beat blocks, I could only compose transitional bits of melody, parts seemingly snatched out of mid-sentence, easy to connect to – whether coming or going in either direction. I won't lie, figuring that out was an enormous endeavor of trial and error.

Color

Color comes from instrumentation and orchestration. Adding color to this branch of the score meant recording optional layers with different instruments. Imagine Lego pieces of specific colors matching specific layers of instrumentation and orchestration. These were now also available to add onto the score, whether by custom design or procedural generation.

Since the team's original specification called for a music score built around acoustic guitars, the harmonic and melodic guitar parts formed the foundational layers and color of the score. However, if the entire score were only guitars, it would quickly feel stale and monochromatic, in spite of notational variety. I added other arrangement layers to keep the score sounding fresh, varied, colorful, and evolving. These included live orchestra, sampled orchestra, and percussion. Notably, I also included a host of solo melodic instruments – violin, viola, cello, flute, alto flute, bass flute, bansuri, duduk, and bassoon. Additional melody fragments were recorded on each of these instruments to compliment the hundreds of guitar fragments already recorded for the score. Now I had a truly unprecedented assortment of colors, layers, and options to build with.

For the Neutral mood alone, I would need 2,559 total music files to scatter among the primary asset buckets of harmony, rhythm, melody, and color. Multiply that by the Happy, Sad, and Tense moods in the game and you are beginning to get a handle on the scale and scope of this project.

It was like having four mood-themed swimming pools filled with thousands of individual, musical Lego pieces.

I think that is a sufficient framework for envisioning the procedural branch of the music design.

EVENT-DRIVEN MUSIC DESIGN

In addition to the procedural music branch, the music design also needed an *Event-Driven* branch. The audio team referred to music in this branch as *Magic Moments*. There are many, many types of game events that trigger Magic Moments, but they roughly fall into four categories: (1) Activity, such as prep for battle, fighting, and training; (2) Discovery, such as finding a new ally or enemy, an important landmark, or building anticipation; (3) Objectives, such as completing a building, conquering a territory, or leveling-up; and (4) Outcomes, including victory, defeat, and aftermath of important events.

You can think of Magic Moments like traditional bits of game music – prefabricated stingers, loops, intros, and outros, which underscore key game events. In *The Settlers'* music system, each bit had to be swappable and interconnectible with other Magic Moments. For example, battle music could be built from any number of various swappable, interchangeable looping segments, stitched together as needed. Intros and outros were composed with variants fitting any number of loop segments. This allowed for extensive random or customized assembly.

Magic Moments also had to be intra-connectible within the procedural branch of the music score, taking the handoff from generative music and handing back to it seamlessly once the event duration had passed.

Magic Moments could be of any duration appropriate for their role in the game. A combat loop segment might be 56 beats long, an intro transition might be only 4 beats. Opening a new map might last 36 beats, while discovering a landmark could be 12 beats. Each asset bucket in this event-driven branch of the music score would therefore be filled with hundreds of large and small prefabricated, swappable, layerable, interconnectible files, ready to be called up when the appropriate event is triggered. All of these assets were further subdivided into harmony, rhythm, melody, and arrangement layers or stems.

Another way to think of the event-driven branch is like having four more swimming pools categorized for event types, each filled with hundreds of large and small musical Lego starter kits – prefabricated, swappable, layerable, and interconnectible.

CINEMATIC MUSIC DESIGN

The game design called for 40 short films, or linear cutscenes, which would be interspersed throughout the game. These were all individually scored according to their dramatic and/or narrative content and flow.

In addition, there were 32 points of interest in the game, which were similarly linear in nature, and required music score matched to the timing and flow of the pre-rendered camera movements.

Each cinematic element, whether cutscene or point of interest, had to connect seamlessly within the procedural or event-driven branches of the score. Thus, each cinematic file name was tagged with its beginning chord and ending chord. To insure a smooth connection, we developed a *Pathfinding* algorithm.

The Pathfinding algorithm could most easily be described as a look-ahead feature. Once the player triggered the last game state prior to the cinematic, the system calculated how many beats until the cinematic would likely play. Then, it calculated the fastest harmonic path from the current chord, through the probability tables, to the beginning chord of the cinematic. The resulting path drove the remaining chord selection so that the flow into each cinematic would sound natural and musically satisfying.

BUCKETS WITHIN BUCKETS

We will now zoom out and look at the big picture in another way. We have discussed three branches in our music design, yielding three categorical buckets of music assets: (1) a HUGE bucket of **Procedural** music assets, (2) a large bucket of **Event-Driven** music assets, and (3) a small bucket of cinematic music assets. Let us now consider the buckets *within* those buckets.

Inside the **Procedural** music bucket are four Mood buckets – Neutral, Happy, Sad, and Tense. Remember that each Mood has its own distinctive collection of harmonies, melodies, and matching arrangement components.

But additionally, inside each of the four Mood buckets are three Regional biome sub-buckets, one for each biome in the game. These Region sub-buckets contain melodies recorded on Region-specific melodic instruments. For the Forgotten Plains, the regional instruments are violin, viola, and cello. For the Veiled Islands, the regional instruments are flute, alto flute, and bass flute. For the Cursed Lands, the regional instruments are bansuri, duduk, and bassoon.

Inside the event-driven bucket, components are very similar, except there are no Mood buckets. Event-driven music may play in any Mood. Instead, there are event *type* buckets – Activity, Discovery, Objectives, and Outcomes. Still further are Regional biome sub-buckets for event-driven music in the Veiled Islands, Forgotten Plains, and Cursed Lands.

The cinematic bucket is very small, holding only the 72 linear music scores for the 40 Cutscenes and 32 Points of Interest in the game.

TOTAL ASSETS

All of the individual music files, which I composed, recorded, and produced to fill every bucket and sub-bucket, totaled 16,304 files. At the end of the project, I also assembled 23 additional tracks from the music design for a 55-minute original game soundtrack (OST). This brought the grand total of music assets to 16,327 music files.

ORGANIZATION

Keeping track of all these files would be impossible without a powerful organizing system in place. I started by designing a naming convention that would include hooks for every relevant descriptor. There is a lot of information that needs to be conveyed for each file. For example, which design branch does the file belong to – procedural, event-driven, or cinematic?

Procedural files were designated with the mood type (neu, hap, sad, ten). Then the regional biome. Next, the type of chord function, and so on. Which chord from the harmonic table is it? What technique was the chord played with? What pattern is being played? How many beats is this particular music block? And which variation is it?

I developed a naming convention that could convey all of that information with relative succinctness. For example, a file from the procedural music branch might look like this:

mus_neu_upl_cho_arp_A6_p03_12b_v5.mp3

This file identifies all of the following bits of information:

> (mus) – This is a music file.
> (neu) – The file belongs to the neutral mood package in the Procedural branch.
> (upl) – The file plays in the upland regional biome (Forgotten Plains).
> (cho) – This is a base layer guitar chord file.
> (arp/str) – This guitar chord is played with an arpeggio. NOTE: Arpeggios (arp) play in the guitar accompaniment when the camera is zoomed out to a bird's eye view, while strums (str) play in the guitar accompaniment when the camera is zoomed in to the player's first person view.
> (A6) – The chord is A6.

(p03) – This file contains a recording of the third arpeggio pattern.
(12b) – The file lasts for 12 beats.
(v5) – Among the variations available for the third arpeggio pattern, this is variant number five.
(mp3) – It is an mp3 file.

Event-driven files were designated with many of the same tags, with a few notable exceptions. Rather than using a chord function descriptor, these files included an event type identifier. Here's an example name of an event-driven file or Magic Moment:

mus_mag_sou_bat_lp_v1_E5_54b_mel.mp3
(mus) – This is a music file.
(mag) – The file belongs to the event-driven (Magic Moment) branch of the score.
(sou) – The file plays only in the southland regional biome (Cursed Lands).
(bat) – This file is for combat.
(lp) – This is a looping music file.
(v1) – This is variation number 1.
(E5) – The loop begins and ends on an E5 chord.
(54b) – The file lasts for 54 beats.
(mel) – This file contains recorded melodic variations on steel string guitar.
(mp3) – It is an mp3 file.

This naming convention provided the game engine with every relevant bit of information needed to grab the right file at the right time, keeping the score fresh, relevant, and evolving for each game state.

SAMPLE SCENARIOS

Even with a good understanding of all these design pieces, you might still wonder how it all comes together. How does this music system actually work? A simplified walk through of two sample game state scenarios should help.

Scenario one. The game starts for the first time and introduces a series of menus. After the menus the game transitions to an opening cutscene. At the end of the cutscene, gameplay opens with your ship approaching the coast of a Veiled Island. Once ashore, you instigate exploration of the beach and surrounding woods. The first settlement begins to take shape and construction culminates with a few key buildings. Meanwhile, an army commences growth and training. You send the army out on a recon mission, and they encounter an opposing army. Battle ensues and the enemy is victorious. The remaining troops retreat back to your camp to fortify the settlement. Let's explore how the music system would work in this first scenario.

The start of the game is considered a Magic Moment, calling for an Event-driven track. In this case, the main theme, "Return of The Settlers", was composed for this specific purpose. This three minute track loops while the player navigates through the menus. The track is arranged in twelve layers or stems, and as the player progresses deeper into the game, the system adds arrangement layers to the song. Since this is the player's first time in the game, the music system plays only the first layer, which is solo fingerstyle guitar.

Exiting the menus transitions to the first cutscene, which begins with a low drone in the same key as the main theme. A simple cross fade brings the music along. The cutscene score plays through, and ends on an F# major chord, which fades out as the screen fades to black.

As the screen next opens upon the game world, the camera is zoomed out, giving a bird's eye view of the beach. This is where the Procedural music system branch takes over. It picks the first chord in the neutral package, an E major chord, from the uplands regional biome (Veiled Islands). Since the camera is zoomed out, the system selects arpeggio technique for the chord accompaniment layer, and randomly selects one of the finger picking patterns in a randomly selected length (eight beats for this example), and plays one of its randomly selected variants. That particular layer 1 (L1) file would be designated as: mus_neu_upl_cho_arp_E_p01_8b_v2.mp3

Simultaneously, the system AI also selects any guitar melody variation file that matches the type, pattern, and length of the selected chord in the accompaniment layer. That particular layer 2 (L2) file would be designated as: mus_neu_upl_cho_mel_E_p01_8b_v6.mp3

Note that the file for the chord accompaniment layer (L1) and the selected file from the melody layer (L2) will play simultaneously.

The system AI then checks the probability table to determine which chord to play next. With the chord selected, perhaps an E7, the system recycles all of the steps just outlined. So eight beats after playing the first chord, at 104 bpm, the system plays the 'next' selected E7 chord, randomly choosing a length (4, 8, or 12 beats) in the accompaniment layer (L1), and randomly choosing one melody variant (L2) that matches the type, pattern, and length of the selected chord in the accompaniment layer. This process recycles, continuously creating a procedurally generated neutral mood in the underscore until the game state changes.

The game state changes with the completion of a key building. For example, the Keep. The Procedural music plays to the end of its current block, then immediately plays the Magic Moment music for finishing the Keep in the Veiled Islands. The Keep completion music lasts for eight beats, at which point the system AI transitions back to the Procedural music branch. This process recycles between the Procedural and Event-driven branches each time an additional key building is completed (Keep, Fort, Castle, Tower, Tower upgrades). Specific Magic Moment music is composed and produced for each key building's completion.

When the army leaves the settlement to recon the surrounding areas, the Neutral Procedural music continues. However, once the game detects that the army is in moderate proximity to an enemy army, the system AI switches to the Tense mood package. Now chords are selected from the Tense mood buckets and progressed according to the Tense probability table. Files are selected for each layer in the same systematic way that the Neutral mood music files were selected.

Once battle begins, the last Tense mood block finishes and the music system switches to the Event-driven branch. The system AI randomly selects a battle music group for the Veiled Islands and plays its intro block for four beats, followed immediately by its loop segment. Battle music can stitch diverse loop segments together as needed from associated groups, or it can loop any segment or combination of segments for as long as battle continues. In scenario one, your army loses. At the signal to retreat, the music system plays the defeated outro block.

Once the outro block concludes, the system switches back to the Procedural branch again. Since your army was defeated, it now pulls from the Sad mood package. Each chord accompaniment and melody is selected from the Sad mood as the army retreats to the settlement. Once the army has returned, and fortifications begin, the system AI switches back to the Neutral mood package, and continues.

Everything in this scenario happens at the very beginning of the game, so generally only the first two arrangement layers are played. This can be customized, like anything else in the system, by audio designers testing, tweaking, and seasoning the score to taste. But the general idea of the design was to grow the arrangements across time and locations as player progress more deeply and broadly in the game.

Let's look at another scenario happening much later in the game in the Cursed Lands.

Scenario two. By this time you have many settlements on many different islands. You have progressed through more than half of the game's missions. A new cutscene introduces your next mission, which is to traverse hostile territory in the Cursed Lands to the ruins of an ancient throne room and retrieve an important relic. You encounter enemy resistance along the way, fighting three battles, and successfully locate the throne room and relic. During the return trip, you discover deposits of gold and silver. You return to your base camp and deliver the relic to the castle, bringing the level to completion. Let us see how the music system would work in this second scenario.

The first cutscene opens with its accompanying linear score. As the scene fades to black, and the score fades to silence, the music system switches to the Procedural branch of the score and begins selecting chords from the Neutral package. This time, instead of only playing the first two layers, playback involves all available layers of the score – guitar chord accompaniment layer (L1), guitar melody layer (L2), percussion layer (L3), orchestra layer (L4), regional melodic instruments (L5). This is because we are more than half way through the game, and by now all arrangement layers are active. In the Cursed Lands, the regional melodic instruments (L5) are bansuri, duduk, and bassoon.

The army leaves the settlement in search of the ancient throne room and the Neutral music continues. As in scenario one, once the game detects your army in moderate proximity to an enemy, the system AI switches over to the Tense mood package, playing all five layers of the arrangement.

When the first battle begins, the last Tense mood block finishes and the system AI switches to the Event-driven branch. The system selects a battle music group from the Cursed Lands and plays its intro block for four beats, followed immediately by a loop segment. In this scenario, you win the battle. As the enemy retreats, the music system plays the victorious outro block.

Once the outro block concludes, the system AI switches back to the Procedural branch again. Since you won the battle, the Procedural branch plays from the Happy mood package. This mood keeps playing until another enemy group is detected, or for a designated duration determined by the audio designers. If the Happy mood plays until another enemy is detected, then the mood transitions to Tense and then combat music, with the process recycling as previously described.

The same cycle occurs for the third battle, transitioning to the Happy mood package after the victory once again.

The throne room is a Point of Interest, so when you find it, the Procedural system prepares to transition to the POI linear score by using the Pathfinding algorithm. It then plays the POI linear score, then transitions back to the Neutral mood package while the player searches for the relic.

When the relic is found, the Procedural branch hands off to the Event-driven branch to play the 'relic found' Magic Moment score. Then, the system AI transitions back to the Procedural music branch, again using the Happy mood package. This continues as the player returns toward base camp.

Along the way, the player stumbles upon gold, triggering the Magic Moment music for finding gold. As that music ends, we transition back to the Happy or Neutral procedural branch. That continues until the player discovers silver, triggering the specific Magic Moment music for finding silver. Keep in mind, all of these transitions happen seamlessly, on the correct beat as one block ends and another begins. And they play back all five arrangement layers, so the orchestration is consistent.

Once the player returns to base camp and delivers the relic, this triggers another Event-driven Magic Moment music stinger for completing the mission, with the music transitioning from Procedural to Event-driven accordingly.

As the level concludes, the event-driven branch plays the Magic Moment music for level completion and fades to black.

Is it starting to make sense yet?

LAYERS

One component of the system we should probably revisit in more granularity is the arrangement component of the system, which is organized into interactive layers. Arrangement components are included in the score to add color, interest, and variety. To wit, guitars (both accompaniment and melody), orchestra, percussion, and regional instruments. Let's examine this in more detail.

In the first Layer (L1), we find guitar accompaniment chords, both strums and arpeggios.

In the second Layer (L2), we find multiple variations of guitar melody fragments for each beat length and pattern.

The third Layer (L3) contains the orchestral parts, matching each chord and beat length.

The fourth Layer (L4) contains several variations of percussion patterns for each beat length.

The fifth Layer (L5) has regional instrument melody fragments that complement the guitar melody fragments.

As the game progresses, layers are added to the arrangement. As the player moves between different biomes, regional instruments are introduced, which bring color variation and regional flavor to the score.

Using layers or stems with Event-driven music is not new. It is a well-established method that has been used in game music for many years. What is innovative about this system is the way it allows the music to flow seamlessly between procedural music and Event-driven music, matching chords, melodic fragments, beat lengths, and arrangement layers to give an impression of a single, through-composed score for the entire game.

The system always knows what chord is playing, how many beats the current music segment lasts, and what accompanying files are authorized to play along with it. This allows the system to hand off from chord to chord, according to the probability tables, in musically pleasing ways throughout the game experience.

Coding and hard functionality of the system is provided by custom software developed by Ubisoft's Düsseldorf audio team. The game also utilizes two middleware programs: Wwise and Snowdrop.

COMPOSITION AND PRODUCTION

I have been typing for 19 pages and all I have managed to cover was the *design* of this music system! Obviously, that was the most innovative part of the experience. But it was not the only part. There are also stories to tell from the composition and production experiences.

With the music design in place, I began writing the score. Though I had reverse engineered the structure of music improvisation for the music design, it was quite another challenge to compose note strands that sounded interesting and even thematic at times, no matter when they were played, or what order they played in relative to other melodic fragments and variants. Each strand needed to connect seamlessly to and from all others.

I must have made dozens of quick mockups from these composed fragments so I could hear different possible pairings. Some fragments that sounded good alone failed to play nice with others. Those had to be rewritten. Others seemed to work well when connecting to one cross section of harmonies, but worked poorly when connecting with others. Those too had to be reworked.

This testing process eventually distilled melody fragments that possessed universal utility. These I put into my working version of the game, listening to judge if they functioned as intended. It was like magic hearing it all come together!

I worked through the score mood by mood. I began with the Neutral mood. It was by far the largest, since it would underscore the bulk of the game. Next, I developed melody fragments for the Happy mood. This is where I allowed more fingerstyle artistry to come through in the guitar parts. The Sad mood package followed, and finally I composed melodies for the Tension package.

It was while testing the game, and considering the broad scope of the regional biomes, that I realized guitar alone would not adequately support the game world. This was the point in development where I suggested adding regional variants for the arrangement layers. I suggested three different but related instruments for each biome. When proposing this to the team, they responded with caution. Everyone could see how the regional flavoring would improve the game experience. But adding all of these regional instruments would bloat the asset count exponentially. It would also drain the budget, as I now had to pay a significantly expanded group of soloists.

I mocked up some examples using digitally sampled instruments as a demonstration. The added color instantly drew distinctions between the biomes, and relieved the ear fatigue from hearing only guitar. It would inflate everyone's workload, but the results were too dramatic to ignore. We made the decision at that point to add a regional layer to the system.

Composing music for the Magic Moments and cutscenes was much easier. In fact, it seemed like child's play compared to writing music for the procedural parts of the score. Event-driven music needed intros, loops, outros, layers, and stems. Cutscenes needed nothing more than linear scoring to picture. This was stuff I had done for 25 years. Easy-peasy.

ANTOINE DUFOUR

Antoine Dufour was a complete unknown to me when I started this project, having never heard of him nor his ground-breaking work before. During my first music meeting in Düsseldorf, Stefan Randelshofer explained that his vision for *The Settlers* included a music score wrapped tightly around the fingerstyle artistry of a Michael Hedges, Tommy Emmanuel, or Antoine Dufour. Part of my job would be to contract one of these musicians to work with us on this score. Stefan had a particular affinity toward Antoine's playing, so I figured I would pursue him first.

I googled Antoine Dufour and discovered a young, pensive, Canadian guitarist with fiery chops and radiant creativity. I was so impressed by his talent and instrument mastery. I thought that collaborating with Antoine had the potential to open up a completely unanticipated and thrilling new vein of creativity in my writing. That is, if he was willing to work with me. Inviting his collaboration might be a hurdle, since Antoine had never before worked on a music score nor collaborated with another composer.

Approaching a valuable collaborator requires at least as much tact, respect, preparation, and graciousness as approaching a potential client. So I poured over Antoine's YouTube videos, I read about him in the press, and studied his website. First contact needed to be well-informed and respectful. He deserved nothing less.

We ended up having a great chat. Antoine appreciated my genuine respect for his talents and decent knowledge of his skillset and achievements. He was reciprocally impressed with my own track record and professionalism. We shared a good sense of humor, an animated enthusiasm for music, and a deep connection about our families. I felt we had built a good foundation so far. This was a solid start.

It was now time to paint a vivid and compelling picture of the game and its ambitious music score.

When I described our aspirations for *The Settlers* soundtrack – a procedural music score of such massive scale and live-recorded quality that had never been done before, he was instantly intrigued. Although he was uninitiated to the world of interactive music design and adaptive playback, I described a high-fidelity music score unfolding in real-time across infinite variations, never ending and never playing the same twice. I revealed the basic construct of the harmonic probability tables I had designed, the multilayered approach to orchestration, and the many melodic variations we would record to feed the system. He listened intently and accepted my invitation to collaboration with eagerness. If he had fully understood what was coming, he might have turned tail and run away in the other direction.

The truth is, none of us, including me, had the smallest clue what we were getting ourselves into. *The Settlers* music score would require hundreds of hours of specifically focused recording sessions in order to capture thousands of live-performed melodic fragments and supporting chords. I had composed each fragment to hand off seamlessly to every other fragment, creating unbroken, natural-sounding, spooling melodies in real time. Every fragment had to be perfect in terms of timing, expressiveness, and intonation. Recording these fragments was tedious, gritty, gut-wrenching work.

This degree of extended hyper-focus laid a heavy toll on everyone who participated in producing the score. But it hit Antoine especially hard. During one prolonged slog through the Neutral package, he nearly reached a breaking point. With Antoine's permission, here are a few edited excerpts from a particularly desperate email he sent to me at the end of an especially difficult day:

> "Chance – I just need to tell you how I feel, cause it's not good. I find this stuff overly hard on my mental. If I had any pride before, I have absolutely no trace of it now. I lost my mind a few times yesterday and went in all phases of discouragement and frustration.
>
> It's like the torture of the Chinese drop... I mean, I can take that for maybe 2–3 hours a day, but after that, I lose my mind and think I should kill myself. So here I am, about a third of the way

climbing Everest, realizing I'm naked and I will die if I turn back or if I continue. I also am losing my voice cause I've been shouting so loud yesterday.

I would take jail for three months over doing this, I'm not even kidding.

Don't worry, I won't kill myself, but if I burn out, the job won't get done either. I'm sorry, it's the real first time I hit a wall like this."

I quickly sent a supportive and encouraging email, and called Antoine first thing the next morning. I told him to take as much time off as he needed, and reassured him that the tracks he had already sent me were terrific. And they *did* sound terrific. The tone of his guitar, the artistry of his playing, and the fidelity of the recordings he had capturing at his home studio were outstanding.

Even so, most of his tracks required further editing on my end, tweaking them to fit the rigorous specifications of this music system. Post editing was always anticipated, as Antoine's contract required two takes of each fragment.

From Antoine's recordings of each melody fragment, I would edit together a single game asset. For example, I would pull from both of his takes, beginning with a note from take one, editing into a note from take two, and so on. Antoine's tuning was nearly flawless, and his timing was excellent. It pains me to say this (literally, refer back to the opening paragraphs in this chapter), but excellent timing still was not quite good enough for the final assets. The timing had to be perfect. In spite of Antoine's incredible effort, most of his tracks still needed note-nudging to make each phrase snap with vigor. I also edited the dynamics, punching a note out here, pulling another note back there, so that each fragment delivered the right lilt for its particular segment of the melody.

The interactive flexibility that this fine-tuning delivered was truly unprecedented and everything sounded spectacular. But it was mind-numbing, painful work to get there.

MAIN THEME

I should tone down that last statement. It wasn't all drudgery. There was joy along the way too. For example, Antoine and I both felt invigorated, challenged, and fulfilled in our collaboration on the main theme, *Return of the Settlers*.

I had composed this theme early in the project and arranged it using digital samples. It was a simple, catchy theme, easy to hum and accessorized with fun and flamboyant guitar ornamentation. Being primarily a keyboard player and percussionist, not a great guitarist, I feared there would be some unplayable parts in my arrangement. But since I had worked with exceptional guitarists for decades, including the peerless Rich Dixon, I had a good feel for what the instrument was capable of. Still, I felt nervous when the time came to send Antoine my mp3 mock-up, MIDI file, and written descriptive notes.

Why are composers often anxious when exposing their work to others for the first time? Have you ever felt that way? Maybe it is just an inherent part of the artistic personality. Remember the story about James Horner with all of his disclaimers, when he was getting ready to play the new *Avatar* cue for me (Chapter 9)?

As it turned out, I need not have worried so much. Antoine dug the track, and quickly went to work learning the parts. As expected, some of my keyboard guitar parts needed reworking to find their way under Antoine's fingers. So we had daily meetings, working through one section at a time. Antoine would play his transcription of the part, and then we would talk about what was working and what could be cooler. He would suggest ideas and I would react. I would sing ideas to him, and he would react. In this way, we worked through the entire theme until we had an arrangement that faithfully captured the essence and most of the details from my original arrangement, upgraded with the fireworks of Antoine's guitar virtuosity and creativity.

At the end of our collaboration, I had a fabulous recording of Antoine performing the main theme in real time sounding better than I ever dreamed. I had hundreds of gorgeous, interchangeable melodic fragments for *The Settlers'* procedural music system. Fortunately, neither Antoine nor I fell completely off the deep end, though we were both taxed to our respective limits by the grind.

Yes, everything worked out in the end. Our collaboration was a triumph, made all the sweeter because of the joy we shared during moments along the path, and the seamless way the final tracks all worked together.

STUDIO MUSICIANS

Antoine Dufour was just one of several studio musicians whose hard work and artistry contributed to the making of this soundtrack. I will highlight a few others for you.

Jeannine Goeckeritz

Flutist Jeannine Goeckeritz practically moved into my studio for this score. There were weeks and weeks of recording sessions, spread across many months. At one point, she had recorded 154 pages of bass flute music alone. After the first few long sessions, the pain in Jeannine's shoulders and neck were becoming unbearable. But Jeannine has the determination of a pit bull, so instead of withdrawing from the project, she fashioned an innovative metal stand that could support the weight of her bass flute while she sat and played the parts. It was genius. The new stand saved critical wear and tear on her shoulders and looked savvy in the studio too. Jeannine was always delightful, somehow keeping a smile on her face, a lilt in her voice, and spikes in her hair for endless hours of recording studio tedium. She played all of the bass flute, alto flute, and nearly all C-flute parts for this score – literally hundreds and hundreds of music files, more than any other instrument except the guitar. At the very end of production, Jeannine did have one small scheduling conflict, so Daron Bradford came in and played the final few flute parts for the cinematics.

I want to commend Jeannine on another aspect of her involvement with the project as well. When it became clear that I had wildly underestimated the time required to record so many melody fragments for the procedural part of the score, Jeannine was the first musician who suggested reducing her hourly rate in return for the endlessly expanding hours of recording time we were racking up. Most other local studio musicians followed suit, which saved me from financial losses on this project.

Nicole Pinnell

Nicole Pinnell has long been a favorite studio musician in the Intermountain West. Her virtuosity on the cello, sparkling personality, can-do attitude, and colossal range of techniques, always lead to the most productive and delightfully enchanting sessions.

Her first recording sessions for *The Settlers* were scheduled at the beginning of the 2020 COVID-19 pandemic, and she was serious about protecting our health. When Nicole arrived at the studio, she was prepared with masks, gloves, sanitizer, and antiseptic wipes. I did my part by sanitizing the studio and wearing my own mask too. I will admit it was an adjustment, acclimating to masks while trying to be creative. But we soon found our groove and worked very hard to get the endless pages of cello parts just right.

I typically keep a cheerful disposition and encouraging demeanor while running recording sessions. But I can be a ferociously exacting producer. Some studio musicians say I am the most demanding music producer they have ever worked with. Here is how I see it. My clients are entrusting me to deliver the most exquisite soundtrack possible. That is why I push and pull for perfection in recording sessions. And when I say perfection, I am not talking about music that is soulless, bland, or uninspiring. I am talking about beautiful intonation, snappy timing, precise pitch, fluid phrasing, and expressive dynamics. Most experienced session musicians will give you two or three of those in a typical performance. But it takes extra work and concentration to achieve all five in a single, extraordinary take. Nicole consistently put in that extra effort. That is why the results of our recording sessions together have always been exceptional.

Aaron Ashton and Becca Moench

Aaron Ashton and Becca Moench split the violin work between them. Aaron is well known among fans of my *Riders of Rohan* soundtrack for his outstanding fiddle work in that score. His artistry on *Theme for Rohan* is especially magical. Aaron recorded all of the procedural violin parts for *The Settlers*, while Becca recorded violin parts for the main theme, Magic Moments, and cinematics. I think Aaron got burned out while recording this project, though he delivered solid tracks for his part of the score. He recorded the first few hundred phrases at my studio, then moved to Idaho to work on his dad's ranch for several months. He recorded the remainder of the procedural violin parts there, by himself in a small room at the ranch. The tracks turned out good enough, but I missed the quality control and interaction of our in-person sessions. When I was ready to record violin parts for the main theme, recorded at HUGEsound Records studio, Aaron declined. That is when I called on Becca to step in.

Becca first crossed my radar while recording the *Mines of Moria* score. We had just finished tracking the strings for *Ages of the Golden Wood*, and sent the musicians on break. I went up to the control room to hear the final pass. Becca asked if she could come in and listen too, seeming truly enthralled by the song. She was incredibly gracious and complimentary in her comments, and that has always stayed with me. Becca usually played second chair in the first violin section during my orchestral recording sessions in Utah, but I had never hired her as a soloist.

She was marvelous to work with, super eager to get things just right, and always ready for another take if needed. Some musicians will play a line just the way they play it, and do not respond well to requested changes. Becca was just the opposite, nimble and chameleon-like, she took suggestions to heart and delivered the part. Having access to so many deeply talented studio musicians on this project was like an embarrassment of riches.

Many others gifted musicians participated in recording sessions. Leslie Richards and Emily Barrett Brown recorded the viola parts. Catherine Umstead recorded the violin solo in *Return of the Settlers*. Brady Bills recorded most of the rhythm and accompaniment guitar parts. I got in on the action too, recording some of the guitar parts myself.

Nashville Scoring Orchestra

Over the years of my career, I have recorded music scores in Seattle, Washington; Los Angeles, California; Prague, Czech Republic; and Fresno, California. However, most of my music scores have been recorded in Salt Lake City, Utah.

For *The Settlers*, my initial plan was to record in Salt Lake City as well, but then the COVID-19 pandemic engulfed us. Many of Utah's local municipalities were requiring masks and enforced distances for all indoor venues. We were early in the pandemic and reliable information was hard to come by. I thought I should comply with the government's directives. The only local studio large enough to accommodate the orchestra size I wanted was still too small to comply with the indoor distance requirements. That is when I reached out to Alan Umstead of Nashville Music Scoring to inquire about recording with his group.

Nashville had no such distance regulations. Nevertheless, I wanted to be cautious and protect the musicians from this virus that seemed harmless for some and deadly for others. Alan assured me that the venue at Ocean Way Recording was spacious enough to spread the musicians out. He added that everyone wore masks at their recording sessions. Alan and I worked out the details and I agreed to record the orchestra with his group.

But something always comes up. Wait for it…

Just a few days before my scheduled sessions in Nashville, Alan called with some alarming news. A heavy thunderstorm had engulfed Nashville, and lightning had struck Ocean Way Recording. I cannot recall all the gear that got fried, but Ocean Way was no longer an option for recording my score. Alan suggested The Sound Kitchen, another Nashville area studio, for our upcoming sessions. He said it was not quite as spacious as Ocean Way, and the room's acoustics would color the recordings differently, but he said the musicians would still have enough room to spread out safely.

What choice did I have? We recorded the orchestra at The Sound Kitchen, strings first and then brass. The musicians were terrific, playing the charts with energy, accuracy, and style. I even took a rare turn at the podium, conducting the strings for the main theme, *Return of the Settlers*. All of the tracks sounded awesome. As a bonus, my old friend Jason Hayes showed up to snap pictures and shoot some video footage. Alan treated us to authentic Tennessee barbecue for lunch after the first day. As you might imagine, it was delicious!

EDITING

Editing was necessary for every studio musician I tracked, and for all the live orchestral tracks. Editing this score was an obscenely bloated, massive job, considering the final delivery package was 16,327 music files. Much of this I handled personally. But the load would have crushed me without additional expert help. I outsourced chunks of the editing work to three other editors – Bobby James, Russell Scarborough, and Luis Morales.

Each melody fragment had been recorded at least twice, sometimes more. For each fragment, the editor would listen to the various takes and select the best one. That is, the performance that delivered the most fluid phrasing, beautiful intonation, snappy timing, precise pitch, and expressive dynamics. Then, the editor would massage individual notes, adjusting their timing, replacing them with the same note from another take, or even running a tuning process on any part of the phrase that momentarily slipped out of tune. The editor could pump steroids into the dynamics as well, giving additional emphasis to notes that should be brought out more, dipping the volume where a note should be ghosted, and so on. Editing is an incredibly meticulous process.

Editing is that phase of production where our quest for perfection zooms down to its most granular level. All aspects of recording receive a degree of microscopic attention during editing that is unavailable in any other phase of production. While editing, there is far less time pressure than during a recording session or mixing session. Also, the digital audio micro-tools available to editors are incredibly powerful.

I personally love editing. It is during editing that my highest ambitions for an emotional line, nasty groove, or turn-of-phrase can be surgically refined. I sought for additional outsource editors who held a similar view.

A word about outsourcing. In spite of your most strenuous screening efforts, other people's standards may not be the same as yours. But part of the music producer's job is to make those standards crystal clear, and to do so as quickly as possible to all outsourced technical and creative talent. There should be no doubt in their minds about what you expect finished work to sound like. Never be shy about sending files back for revision, with clear instructions about what needs improvement. A good contractor will quickly catch on to your specifications and make the necessary adjustments going forward. If there are those who do not make that adjustment, and continually send you work that you deem incomplete, do not hesitate to let them go. This business is overcrowded and highly competitive. There are always ten other people ready to step up and work for you. Just as there are hundreds of other people ready to step in and work for your client, taking your place if you fail to deliver.

MIXING

With so many individual music files to mix, we had to reinvent the mixing process. I say we, but what I really mean is that Mike Roskelley had to reinvent the mixing process. With thousands of files to mix, it would have taken months to accomplish our mix using traditional methods. It became necessary, even crucial to design a new pipeline that could mix thousands of files with exponential efficiency, without sacrificing quality.

Necessity moved Mike to an unexpected innovation. He created a matrix that fed all similar instrument files through a processing sequence designed for that instrument. For example, he would randomly select a handful of melody guitar fragments from the Neutral package, and mix them traditionally against the other parts of the score. Then he would capture just that sliver of the mix process that applied to the Neutral guitar – including any EQ, reflections, reverb, echo, and dynamics – and route it into a sequence, setting up a batch process that could run every raw file through that pipeline. He did this for melody guitar, accompaniment guitar, violin, viola, cello, bass flute, alto flute, C-flute, bansuri, duduk, bassoon, percussion, and strings, from all four mood packages – Neutral, Happy, Sad, and Tension. Then he spot-checked results to make sure the expected consistency had promulgated across each batch.

I went through and listened to each individual file personally, insuring a 100% inspection. I had to know that all files sounded uniform enough to work seamlessly in the music system. After the individual inspection,

I plugged different groups of files into my system to make sure the layers sounded like a properly mixed piece of music as they stacked up and played together, without overdriving the level. It was incessant, grueling labor around the clock.

We also had to mix the Magic Moment tracks. These received a more traditional mixing approach, treating each interchangeable, layerable segment as a typical piece of music built from stems.

Finally, months later, we mixed the cinematic scores. These fit into the mixing template used for the Magic Moments.

By this point, we had developed such rapport and such an unconscious communication language that I did not even need to be at his studio for the lion's share of the mixes. Once we got the basic sound set up for the project, I returned to my own studio to review the mixed tracks as they came in over the Internet – procedural music tracks, event-driven music tracks, and cinematic score tracks.

Mike's work was superb, and our rapport had never been better. The performances were riveting and the editing had fine-tuned the tracks to perfection. The final music assembly sounded fantastic. Oh, that everyone in the creative arts could experience the matchless gift of such peerless collaborators in their artistic endeavors!

SOUL CRUSHING NEWS

The game's original release date was Fall 2020. As September and October came and went under radio silence, I began to worry. Then on November 5, 2020, the audio team invited me into a transatlantic video conference with some soul crushing news. Ubisoft had canceled the game. I could not believe it. We had built a truly revolutionary music score, like nothing ever before in the history of game audio. It was working brilliantly in the game, just as designed. But it was all for naught. The game was being canceled, and all our work was heading to the trash bin.

Or so I thought.

A few months later in early 2021, Blu Byte's audio director told me that a group at the studio had proposed a new game design for *The Settlers,* which was subsequently approved. A new version of the game was being restarted. The audio team had saved the music and music system from the original game to try and wedge into the new game. That seemed a bit dodgy to me, but at least the music was not being thrown away. Maybe the team would find a way to make it work. I offered to come out to Düsseldorf and assist with the transplant. But there was no budget. In fact, I learned that the audio team was instructed to minimize resources for any music-related work on the new game.

As 2021 was drawing to a close, Ubisoft sent me a new batch of cinematic cutscenes to score. I completed my work in February of 2022, in anticipation of the new game's scheduled release in March 2022. But just two weeks before the March release date, the game was postponed again. Indefinitely. I was so discouraged. It was around this time that I decided to retire from composing. Stefan Randelshofer also left Ubisoft for other pursuits.

I kept in touch with the new audio team, but every contact was disheartening for me. The newest version of the game was dumping many of the music assets. Some of the most sublime features of the system were being dumbed down or ripped out completely. I again offered to come out to Düsseldorf and lend my expertise and manpower to make the best of whatever was left of the music system, but again I was rebuffed.

As 2023 dawned, I learned that a substantially reworked version of the game was finally going to be released. The target date was now February 17, 2023. After the previous stops and starts, I was unsure whether to believe it or not. But when Ubisoft called and asked me to record a Twitch session with their PR team three days before the game's scheduled release, I figured it was finally going to happen.

Sadly, when I saw footage from the reworked game, the music system seemed a mere shell of what we had originally built. Even some of the simple features were broken, such as music for small battles, which now played Tension exploration music instead of combat music. This was very disappointing to me, a diminished conclusion to a gloriously conceived and meticulously produced ambition.

SAVING GRACE

There is one saving grace. Ubisoft contracted me to put together an original video game soundtrack (OST) from the game score assets, and it sounds fantastic. It also accurately portrays the results of the original game music design.

In producing the OST, I methodically followed the music specs from the original game design. The music follows the probability tables, building tracks from thousands of individual musical Lego pieces. Additional layers and variants are introduced as music segments repeat and evolve. Interwoven between many of the gameplay music tracks are cinematic cutscene scores from the final game.

I loved assembling this soundtrack, and the result is a terrific sounding album that successfully hits all of the targets we set for ourselves way back at that first Düsseldorf meeting in 2018:

1. The music sounds natural, as if it had been composed on purpose. The music sounds organic, live, musical, and compelling.

2. Shifting game states are reflected in many of these tracks, foreshadowing upcoming events, highlighting key moments, and tightly following changing game states.

3. The music does not loop mindlessly, avoiding the bane of bad game music, but remains fresh and evolving in content, color, and mood.

4. We achieved the goals of endless variety in the original game with a potential never-ending score, which is showcased to a degree in the hour-long OST.

5. The soundtrack album spotlights the guitar virtuosity of Antoine Dufour, and his brilliance really shines through.

6. The score includes some very cool hand percussion tracks, live orchestra, and other small acoustic ensemble instruments.

With the OST assembled, I sent all of the music tracks to the Bit Farm for mastering. Again, if tracks do not come back to you as expected, never hesitate to ask for reasonable revisions. Great professionals want their clients to be thrilled with the results of their work. That was the case here. We had several rounds of revisions, but ultimately gathered a collection of music files that sizzle together and sound great on any playback system.

Early response to the soundtrack album has been overwhelmingly enthusiastic.

SUMMARY

In spite of everything, I could not imagine a more ambitious way to conclude my music scoring career. One of my fellow composers said that *The Settlers* music score was a magnum opus for me, a pièce de resistance, the crowning achievement of a long and highly decorated professional career. Certainly, the elegance and complexity of this music design far surpass anything I had ever done before, not to mention the scale and scope of the undertaking. The sheer number of music assets alone dwarf any other score I am aware of.

I am also immensely proud of the work others contributed to this score. The original game team built a miraculous musical experience, fulfilling the music design completely. The score adapted on the fly to each player's individual style; it reacted to gameplay and delivers a thematic experience without being repetitive; it evolved in aesthetically delightful and meaningful ways, never the same twice and potentially never ending.

That was pretty much the holy grail of game music.

Every studio musician, engineer, and editor brought their A-game to this production, showing tremendous grit and determination in grinding through the interminable recording sessions and endless hours of editing and mixing. Antoine Dufour deserves particular applause for his artistry and dedication. The whole experience evidenced a triumph of the human creative spirit.

Most importantly, the music sounds terrific. Curling up with the soundtrack album now, listening to the crisply recorded and smoothly flowing music – with Antoine's fiery guitar playing, the Nashville Scoring Orchestra's rousing performances, and every soloist shining their color beautifully and seamlessly – I feel a tremendous sense of joy and satisfaction.

The Settlers was the final score of my composing career. It is a substantial enough achievement for me to walk away with a feeling of going out on top. On top of my own game, on top of my own creative envelope.

I was never blessed with generation-defining talent. But I always had just enough talent coupled with an outrageous work ethic. Both came to full fruition with *The Settlers*.

Riding off into the sunset, I can look back and live with that.

To watch video and listen to music from The Settlers: New Allies, *as described in this chapter, please visit: HUGEsoundRecords.com/Memoir-19*

NOTES

1 Chance Thomas, *Composing Music for Games: The Art, Technology and Business of Video Game Scoring*, pp. 102–103; Boca Raton: CRC Press, 2016.
2 Chance Thomas, *Composing Music for Games: The Art, Technology and Business of Video Game Scoring*, Chapters 4–5; Boca Raton: CRC Press, 2016.
3 Chance Thomas, *Composing Music for Games: The Art, Technology and Business of Video Game Scoring*, pp. 33–34, 36; Boca Raton: CRC Press, 2016.

CHAPTER 20

Church Music

THIS COULD ALMOST QUALIFY as a separate career, all by itself.
Parallel to the music I composed for video games runs a second body of work comprised of more than 80 credits, stretching from the early 1990s to the early 2020s. You will not find them listed on IMDB. Rather, this was music I composed and produced for media projects of the Church of Jesus Christ of Latter-day Saints. These media projects run the gamut from documentary films, to television commercials, stage musicals, YouTube videos, and much more.

This was not traditional worship music. Stylistically, it was all over the map. Sometimes that was literal – Pacific Island music, Caribbean reggae, European Renaissance, Motown, Middle Eastern, rustic American folk, New Orleans jazz, bluegrass, and many other styles I was asked to compose in. Researching these cultures and their musical idioms led to dramatic increases in the breadth and depth of my music scoring vocabulary. What composer would not welcome that?

At other times, I was asked to compose in a contemporary orchestral film scoring style. Think James Horner, Jerry Goldsmith, John Williams, James Newton-Howard. Studying the music of these masterful film composers became a joyful exercise for me, though it could also be intimidating. Nevertheless, through experimentation and abundant trial and error, I began to acquire competency in orchestral writing. These blossoming orchestral writing and arranging chops also found their way into my video game music. In fact, those skills led directly to the composing job I won at Sierra (Chapter 2).

DOI: 10.1201/9781003199311-21

Perhaps instead of describing church music as a parallel career path, I should label it an interlaced career path. Certainly, any story of my music scoring career would be incomplete without it. Let us see how it began.

In the early 1990s, I was growing a fledgling composing business, byChance Productions, working primarily in the advertising industry. One local agency I was trying to make inroads with was Fotheringham and Associates. I would send demos quarterly and check in by phone monthly. A year went by and then another, but I kept showing up. Eventually, one of the senior partners, Dave Newbold, offered me a small project. "I have five public service announcements from the Church of Jesus Christ of Latter-day Saints that need music," he said. "These are radio spots, and the budget is really small. Normally, I would just use needle drop, but you've been so persistent, I thought I would offer them to you."

Yes, yes, absolutely yes!

These five public service announcements (PSAs) were clever, funny, and heartwarming. The script writing was terrific, and the voice actors were top notch. I did not want to cheapen the presentation with bad music. This was very early in my career, and I did not have much scoring experience yet. I decided to try leveraging my improvisational piano skills to create five solo piano scores, timed to perfection against the dialog. Nuances and pratfalls abounded, and you could almost understand each story just by listening to the music. When I turned in the scores, Newbold was impressed with the attention to detail, the craftsmanship, and the individuality carved out for each spot. He called it a home run.

During a follow-up call, I asked Newbold if he frequently produced PSAs for the church. He said not frequently, only the occasional spillover project when the church's in-house audio/visual (A/V) department was overwhelmed. I did not know that the church had an in-house A/V department. He mentioned that a producers' group for the church met every Tuesday morning, and that sometimes they invited potential vendors to come and make presentations. Continuing the conversation I asked, "If I wanted to submit my name to present, who would I contact for an invitation?" He responded, "Call Lyle Shamo, he's the head of Audio Visual Production for the church." He gave me Shamo's number and wished me well.

Happy clients can be a fertile resource for finding new prospects.

Within 60 seconds I was on the phone, making the call. Shamo's assistant greeted me pleasantly, and after some amiable small talk, I asked her about the producers' meeting. "Yes," she said, "They meet each Tuesday morning at 9:00 am."

Let us pause to consider this situation. What would you do with that information? Would you give the assistant your phone number and ask her to have her boss call you back? Would you thank her and try calling again later? Maybe you would think, "Dave referred me to Lyle Shamo. This girl is just the assistant. There's nothing more she can do."

All of those possibilities ran through my mind. And then a new idea illuminated me. What if I asked the assistant directly about making a presentation. What could it hurt?

I ventured, "You've been very gracious. May I share something with you? I'm a music composer. I recently scored five new public service announcements for the church. Dave Newbold at Fotheringham and Associates hired me, and he was really happy with how the music turned out. He suggested I call your boss."

She was still listening, so I continued, "I had a terrific experience scoring those PSA's for the church. I would love to introduce my work to the producers group at an upcoming meeting. Could you assist me with that?"

Her voice sparkled with enthusiasm, "Well, you're in luck. We have an opening in two weeks, and I personally handle all the scheduling. What was your name again?"

Assistants often have more power than their titles imply. Sometimes they can open important doors for you. Tuck that lesson away for safe keeping.

PRODUCERS' GROUP

The day for my presentation arrived. I located the conference room, and walked in just as the meeting was starting. There must have been 25–30 producers in that room, and they all turned to watch as I awkwardly looked for an open seat. After the group handled their administrative business, I was invited to come forward and introduce myself. I walked to the front of the room carrying a portable cassette player with speakers dangling from either side (aka, ghetto blaster), along with a handout I had printed at Alpha Graphics. Keep in mind, this was barely 1992. I did not own a laptop. There was no PowerPoint, no thumb drive to plug seamlessly into their system. No tech to speak of.

I said hello, and asked one of the producers to pass around copies of my handout to everyone. I described my work in advertising and played a local jingle and a few commercials for them. Next, I talked about scoring the recent church campaign for Dave Newbold, and played one of those radio spots. It would have been prudent to end my presentation there, followed by a brief invitation to try my scoring services. But instead, I thought it would be a good idea to close my presentation by singing an original song with a spiritual message. Since this was a group of producers who worked for a church, I figured it might resonate with them.

It was an ill-advised decision. The song was called *The Keeper of the Temple*, and it was little more than pseudo-philosophical tripe clothed with vague religious connotations. I had written it very recently, and was too infatuated with my own creation to realize it was drivel. Nevertheless, I stood in front of those 25–30 media professionals and sang a very mediocre, four-minute song for them. My voice cracked, I shuffled nervously during the long instrumental breaks, and while the music was fading out at the end, I even bowed and said "thank you," although no one was clapping.

Where is the nearest hole I can crawl into?

I thanked them for having me, reminding them of the recent work I had done for the church PSA campaign, and asked them to please hold on to my contact information. Perhaps they could give me a try sometime? I returned to my chair and began packing up my things as the meeting concluded. Everyone scattered quickly, but before I could slip away, one of the producers came over and introduced himself. "Hi, I'm Quinn Orr," he said with a broad smile, "Do you have a few minutes to come and visit in my office?"

Quinn struck me instantly as a man with no pretenses. He wore brown loafers that looked lived in and comfortable. His white shirt was partially untucked, drooping over a belt holding baggy trousers snug against a slight paunch. His thick black hair was parted on the right side, with a few feisty spikes poking up here and there. If Quinn was wearing a tie that day, it was loose at the neck, with wide diagonal stripes, likely brown and white with gold at the edges. It may have had a small stain on it.

We walked back to his office, and spent no more than ten minutes talking about music and media. He gave me his business card, and said I was welcome to check in with him from time to time.

Allow me editorialize for a moment. This man gave me the courtesy of his personal attention after my unexceptional presentation. No one else did that, and I do not blame them. But Quinn Orr walked over to me, looked me in the eye, smiled at me, shook my hand, and invited me to spend ten minutes with him, talking about my work and his work in a general way. I am not sure if he had any intention of ever hiring me, but taking a few minutes with me was classy and kind. It helped me feel better about myself after such an amateur performance.

Best of all, Quinn told me I could call and check in with him from time to time.

Of course, me being me, I was not about to let any moss grow under that invitation. We will circle back to Quinn at the end of the chapter, as he would become my most loyal client and dear friend.

Quinn was not the only person I ended up working with from that producers' group. As the years went by, I had the opportunity to compose music for Gary Cook, Grant Baird, Curt Dahl, Jerry Craven, Ron Muns, Gary Esterholt, John Garbett, John Bigler, Michael Dunn, and others. We will not meet all of them in this book, but I will introduce you to the first few before we return to Quinn at the conclusion of the chapter.

GARY COOK

Summon a mental picture of any movie director or producer you can imagine. None of them look anything like Gary Cook. A sweet man with a razor-sharp mind, Gary was short and rounded, and completely bald except for a small patch of stubborn hair clinging behind each ear. He always wore a heavily starched, long-sleeve white shirt and polished black shoes. His complexion was both reddish and pale, which sounds like a contradiction, but somehow describes him exactly right.

Gary was not physically striking. He could probably disappear in a group of three. But once the man opened his mouth and began speaking about film, all eyes and ears quickly fastened on him. Everyone was riveted by his insights. He was like the old EF Hutton commercial: when Gary Cook spoke, everyone listened.

I am not sure where Gary picked up his expertise about filmmaking, but he had incisive perceptions about dramatic flow, character development, script accessibility, and a true north concerning historical accuracy and principled relevance in whatever media he was overseeing. If Gary had not been such a sweet and easy conversationalist when discussing anything but film, you might label him a savant.

In late 1992, Gary was directing a film for the church called *On the Way Home*. It portrayed the dramatic story of a family coming apart at the seams, who manage to recover and thrive through good friends and gospel influences. A gifted local composer, Sam Cardon, who would later become a good friend and mentor, was doing the film score. But Gary needed another composer to score the trailer. He had heard some of the work I did for Quinn, and offered me a shot. Gary was the first church producer besides Quinn to take a chance on me, and I have always been grateful.

He carried disproportionate influence within the producers' group, and once I had completed a successful score for him, my reputation for doing good work began to spread rapidly.

GRANT BAIRD

On the other end of the spectrum was Grant Baird. Grant actually looked like a movie director *meme*, with his expensive leather jacket, salon-styled blonde hair, big colorful glasses, brand new jeans, and tan-colored cashmere boots. He was Hollywood style all the way, and he pulled it off effortlessly. The first day I met Grant, he was sporting a blonde mustache like a fashion accessory against a perfectly tanned face. It was like meeting a Utah doppelganger of George Hamilton.

Grant had been directing a highly successful campaign of filmed PSAs for the church called the *Home Front* series. These spots were always well-written, heartwarming, and usually ended with some clever plot twist encouraging people to spend more time with their families. But media was changing and the *Home Front* series was starting to wind down. Grant was directing one of the last *Home Front* spots in the series, and wanted fresh blood for the music score. Michael Dunn was his producer.

Years ago, Michael Dunn and Grant Baird had worked at the same agency as Dave Newbold. Remember, Newbold was the person who connected me with the church producers' group in the first place. Many long months after my presentation, Newbold recommended my work personally to Michael, who also passed the recommendation on to Grant. Incredible how much goodwill can come from a single, delighted client.

Michael and Grant made arrangements to meet with me. At our meeting, they described the story behind the new spot, the setting, the emotional arc, the cinematography, and how they hoped the audience would feel. It was a sweet story centered on a father and son who love fishing together. I cannot recall what the plot twist was, but I do remember being enthusiastic about everything they explained. We felt a good connection during the meeting, and they agreed to hire me. Grant made it very clear that he wanted a lush orchestral sound for this score, blended with something sweet and slightly humorous. He cited James Horner's work as an example. I told them I knew just what to do.

Actually, I had no idea what to do, except to take the SMPTE-striped video back to my studio and start imagining music in the style we spoke about. At the very least, I could do that. That is how all of my best scores came to life anyway. I would imagine myself in the story, drawing upon past experiences to help me feel similar emotions. You might call it a method actor approach to composing. Gems of inspiration always arrived whenever I immersed myself in that way.

The inspiration did come. It came for a solo clarinet line, slightly whimsical, but mostly sweet and tender. The clarinet took the lead throughout the score, joined by a lush string section with warm, slow-moving chords in the trombones and French horns. This was my first gig composing and orchestrating for a large, live orchestral ensemble. It took many rewrites to get it close-to-right.

One problem I wrestled with was this. The score sounded great by itself, but when I laid it up against the dialog, the clarinet kept competing in the same sonic space as the narrator, getting in the way. Mixing engineer Michael Chadbourne, who had tracked the orchestra and was now mixing the spot, just grinned. "Rookie!" he quipped. And then he suggested that I should use the clarinet more delicately, more sparsely under dialog, commenting on the emotional narrative, rather than carrying the role of a lead vocal. This was an important lesson to learn, a lesson which impacted how I would approach scoring for the balance of my career.

CURT DAHL

If Grant Baird represented the past of church media, Curt Dahl represented the future. While Grant's *Home Front* campaigns left people with a smile on their face and a lump in their throat, Curt wanted church media that would lift people out of their seats toward concrete action. The Church of Jesus Christ of Latter-day Saints has always been an evangelizing organization. You may know that, especially if you have encountered its missionaries – young men going two-by-two, wearing white shirts, ties, and name tags, often riding bikes together. Or pairs of young women walking door to door, wearing modest dresses and name tags. Because of this missionary orientation, Curt wanted to produce content that would attract people in a much more direct way.

This new era of church media would retain the heartwarming legacy of its predecessors, while also incorporating a compelling call to action. At the end of each new spot, a friendly narrator would invite people to dial a toll-free number to receive a free *Holy Bible* or *Book of Mormon: Another Testament of Jesus Christ*. The book would arrive within just a few days, hand-delivered by missionaries from the church.

Curt wrote and directed all of these spots. His running mate, John Bigler, produced them. They made a terrific team, producing dozens of direct response campaigns for the church over many years. The content was rich and diverse, ever changing and continually expanding to reach across geography, cultures, and styles. Scoring these campaigns pushed me to continually develop new composing and arranging chops, just to keep up. I learned to write for many new instruments – blues harmonica, bass flute, steel drums, soprano sax, ukulele, and others. So many flavors to explore in composing music for this evolving menagerie of media. Of course, Curt sometimes requested a traditional film scoring approach too, so my orchestral writing skills continued growing.

This new breed of church media began producing dramatic results. Thousands of people called requesting free scriptures. Local missionaries were dispatched for each delivery, sometimes leading to meaningful discussions. Discussions with missionaries raised the potential of changing lives for the better – marriages being strengthened, addictions being overcome, self-reliance improving, and deeper spiritual connections being forged. Many people joining the church as a result. During one year, Curt once told me that the church's statistical department traced 16 convert baptisms *every day* to this new media. I told myself that maybe the music had played a role in that process.

Generally, when I delivered a new batch of music for these campaigns, I felt good about the artistry, production quality, and fit. Curt always seemed pleased and satisfied with my work too. However, the next gig was never a given. I always expressed appreciation, but one day Pamela suggested I could reward Curt with more than just a thank you. She suggested including a batch of home-made chocolate turtle cookies with each delivery.

Imagine these culinary works of art with me for just a moment. Each chocolate turtle cookie was the size of a rolled-up fist, slightly flattened. Five pecan halves protruded prominently from all sides, representing a head and four legs. The flavor was decadent chocolate upon chocolate, blended with other mysterious and delicious savors known only to the chef. They looked awesome and tasted heavenly. Pamela's cookies were a huge hit. Curt began telling me that he liked my music, but loved the cookies. Maybe that was the real reason he continued hiring me. Whatever it took to keep my clients happy and coming back for more!

Pamela's cookies actually helped me take an important step forward in how I viewed the client–composer relationship. Up to that point, I thought the extent of my job was to provide clients with excellent service, while being polite and professional. In that way, I was really no different than a retail sales clerk or fast-food counter help. Now I was beginning to realize that I could take the relationship further. And in the best cases, my clients could also become my friends.

With that in mind, I invited Curt to come over and take my new car for a drive. I had just bought a bright red, Mitsubishi 3000 GT VR-4 Twin Turbo. It was everything a great sports car ought to be. Curt hopped in and began steering the car timidly down the road. I thought he was being overly conservative. I goaded him about his manhood, encouraging him to really open it up. Boy did he! When the twin turbos kicked in, the thrust nearly shoved us into the back seats. His face flashed bright red with fear and delight, and he blurted out, "Chance, this is too much fun!"

I resolved to make a more active effort to develop friendships with all of my clients.

JERRY CRAVEN

Cultivating friendship opportunities with clients began in earnest with Curt Dahl, but may have reached an apex with Jerry Craven. Jerry had joined the producers' group at the same time that Quinn Orr did. The two of them were buddies, brothers in arms, finding their way in a media business within the unique constraints and resources of a large worldwide church. After Quinn and Gary Cook began hiring me, Jerry jumped on the bandwagon too. He first contracted me to score an instructional film for Brigham Young University. Then he asked me to score a handful of commercials for Deseret Industries and LDS Family Services. Jerry was fun to work with and I enjoyed his sense of humor.

By the mid-1990s I had moved to central California, not far from Yosemite National Park. One year, Jerry and his family wanted to spend their vacation in Yosemite, but hotel costs in the park were high. Our home was just 16 miles south of the entrance, so Jerry asked if his family could stay with us. We said yes, and I offered to show Jerry some of my favorite places inside the Park – gems that had been introduced to me by another good friend in the business, sound designer and fellow composer Tim Larkin.

If you visit Yosemite's Bridal Veil Falls in the spring or early summer, you will see massive sheets of water plummeting hundreds of feet, feeding a roaring overflow, rapids, and streams that empty into the Merced River. But Jerry came to visit in late August, with only a whisp of runoff remaining, hanging a sheer veil of mist high above the granite. There were no rapids, no river running free. Only boulders with sliver-thin crevices to grip while pulling ourselves up, and small rocks to scamper over, splashed with sunshine and dry moss. The cool mist tickled our faces as we reached journey's end – a gorgeous hidden pool, fed by dozens of web-like mini-falls, sweating from the rock face just under the cliff. Standing at the top, Jerry lit up like a Christmas tree, delighted by such an unexpected and stunning gift of nature, unveiled just for us.

Bridal Veil was only the beginning. Afterward, we took Glacier Point road to the trailheads of Taft Point and Sentinel Dome. From a common starting point, each trail stretches out for a mile in opposing directions. We hiked to Taft Point first, sitting on the precipice of a 3,500-foot sheer cliff, dropping away from its northern edge to Yosemite Valley far below. After soaking in the views, we retraced our steps and journeyed on toward Sentinel Dome, the sweet smell of Spruce filling our senses. Sentinel Dome offers a spectacular 360-degree view of the entire western park – Yosemite Valley, El Capitan, Yosemite Falls, Cloud's Rest, and Half Dome. It is the view of views, impossible to share without catalyzing some level of bonding. Jerry and his family loved their trip, and it was an important step in moving our business relationship deeper into the friend zone.

Shortly after the Yosemite trip, Jerry left his employment with the church producers' group, and we never worked together again. But we have remained friends, keeping in touch in all the intervening years, happily cheering each other on from the sidelines.

QUINN ORR

As promised, I now return to the story of Quinn Orr. Quinn gave me his business card and invited me to check in from time to time. I waited two weeks, then anxiously took him up on the offer.

Quinn picked up the ringing phone in his office. A nervous voice on the other end stammered, "Hi, uh, Quinn? This is Chance Thomas, um, the composer? We met a couple of weeks ago. You gave me your card and, uh, asked me to check in with you occasionally. Is this a bad time?"

Sheesh. I would have hung up on myself.

But Quinn was patient, magnanimous, and maybe even a little bit curious. He took my call, and opened a dialog about a short documentary segment he was producing for an upcoming broadcast. The segment was two or three minutes long, featuring interviews with several men and women giving their opinions about the futility of materialism. He wondered if I would be interested in scoring this short piece of media.

Yes, yes, absolutely yes!

I can still remember one of the best lines from that segment, word for word. Spoken by a well-tailored woman, probably in her late 50s, was this timeless gem: "I spend money I don't have, buying things I don't need, to impress people I don't like … who never come over anyway."

I scored the segment with sustained chords on a chorused electric guitar, fading in from silence. Deep reverbs gave the chords an ethereal wash, keeping the score far in the background. The colors were interesting, adding a serviceable underpinning for the dialog to stand against. Quinn was pleased, and thanked me for the music. Best of all, he invited me to check in with him again in the future.

Emmy Award

Quinn and I began working together periodically, taking on projects of increasing profile and creativity. In 1995, we made a short music video together, a public service announcement encouraging viewers to "rise above the blues." Visually, this PSA opened with a sea of blue balloons hugging the ground, while a single yellow balloon wrestled to find its way through the thick layers. At length, the yellow balloon squeezes free and floats unencumbered into the sunny skies above. A text overlay at the end simply states: *Rise Above the Blues*.

Musically, I followed the yellow balloon around with piano and clarinet, Mickey-Mousing its movements in a Carl Stallings style, playing against a dark bed of low strings. It all turned out adorably, winning an Emmy Award for Best Regional Film PSA from the Rocky Mountain region. The statuette still stands proudly on a shelf inside my studio office.

Quinn's projects spanned a broad gamut of subjects and style. After our Emmy-winning success with *Rise Above the Blues*, Quinn was tasked with filming a heart-rending story of the Martin handcart company, caught in heavy blizzards across the highlands of Wyoming, lurching to a stop on the snowbound banks of the icy Sweetwater River. The story is both tragic and heroic, climaxing as three 18-year-old boys pick up each wearied member of the handcart company and carry them across the icy river, one by one. "The strain was so terrible and the exposure so great, that in later years all the boys died from the effects of it."[1]

While working on his script, Quinn had been listening to my score for *Quest for Glory V: Dragon Fire*, specifically a track called, *The Rite of Freedom*. He asked if I could bring some of that flavor to bear in scoring his Sweetwater River film. I took the pulse, the harp, and the big French Horn ideas from *The Rite of Freedom*, then wrapped them around urgent, tug-at-your-heart harmonies and rhythms in the string section, topped with a soaring flute. The result was a poignant music score that accompanies the tragic unfolding and tender end of the story, underscoring its emotional narrative.

Creativity and Flow

Other projects came and went as Quinn continued flexing his artistic muscles across a wide range of media, bringing me along for the creative ride. One highlight was composing music for a worldwide branding effort, designed to unify all church media under a uniform visual and musical logo. The original idea was a 13-second animation featuring the name of the church, accompanied by a climactic orchestral buildup. Think along the lines of the iconic 20th Century Fox logo, but with an inspirational bent. Quinn and I felt that the music I composed and orchestrated hit the target and matched the animations perfectly.

But the coolest part of the experience was having my music performed by the Orchestra at Temple Square under the baton of Tabernacle Choir director Mack Wilberg. Mack is one of my musical heroes, perhaps the finest choral and orchestral arranger on planet Earth, not to mention a world-class conductor. With Mack conducting, the orchestra performed magnificently, beginning tenderly and growing to a powerful crescendo. The music was recorded in the old Tabernacle with its endless rows of wooden benches, plastered ceiling, and never-ending natural reverb. When the timpani, trumpets, gran casa, and low brass hit the climax with their tremendous energy, I thought the ceiling would split open and rain plaster down upon the hall.

Unfortunately, the church's PR team kept tinkering with the logo, cutting the length shorter and shorter, editing the music down to match. Except, the music *did not* match. The edited music was truncated, without proper dynamics, meaningful development, or harmonic language. Imagine cropping most of the 20th Century Fox logo and playing just the last three notes. Ultimately, the musical component was discarded and only the short animation remained. That was a disappointing end to a promising project, but the process was still memorable. Sometimes composers have to find their satisfactions where they can.

Onward we marched, continuing to produce a variety of inspiring content for the church. Short films, interviews, documentary segments, commercials, PSAs – it seemed like Quinn could do it all. He wrote scripts, cast actors, directed, produced, contracted, managed, and promoted. I was right there with him, composing original music scores and sometimes even trying my hand at acting in his productions.

One of my favorite experiences with Quinn was composing music for an uplifting promotion of FamilySearch.org, the popular Internet portal used to trace family roots and compile genealogies. For this piece, Quinn interviewed a dozen people regarding their experiences searching for information about their ancestors. I was deeply touched by the stories they all shared. I had always imagined digging through genealogy records as a tedious undertaking. But the people in these interviews had been enlivened by it. The joy they exuded really impacted me.

I wanted to capture that feeling and amplify it in the music. I used ukulele and steel string acoustic guitar to lay down a bouncy rhythm, while a catchy melody danced across the top, played on nylon string classical guitar. A lush string section provided support, while light percussion reinforced the lively vibe. There are some tender moments along the way too, but most of the score highlights this infectious feeling of enthusiasm. That is what I hoped to convey, rallying a response of enthusiasm for the quest.

Capstone Project

As of this writing, there are 17 million members of the Church of Jesus Christ of Latter-day Saints scattered across every populated continent. Members worldwide sustain church president Russell M. Nelson as a living prophet, seer, revelator, and a special witness of Jesus Christ.

During the spring of 2018, President Nelson traveled to Jerusalem to film his testimony about Jesus. Standing on the Mount of Olives, passing through the Garden of Gethsemane, and at other historic sites in the ancient holy land, the prophet bore his witness of the sublime life and ministry of the Savior.

Quinn received the assignment to film and edit the prophet's testimony, and to deliver it for public release. By this point, Quinn and I had built a genuine friendship and deep relationship of trust after working on so many projects together. Still, it was an extra special thrill when he called and asked if I would like to score this one.

Quinn came to my studio, bringing along the final edit. We watched the film together, discussing ideas for music placement, melody, and tone. It struck me that the prophet's speaking voice ought to be the melody of this production. In other words, nothing in the music should compete with his voice, such as a solo violin, a clarinet, a brass section, or a singer. I suggested that perhaps a subtle counter-melody to the prophet's voice, playing in the string choir, might be a favorable approach. Quinn liked that idea and instructed me to proceed with the score.

I had a couple of false starts before I found my footing. The first approach felt too vapid and meandering. There was no substance, no discernable feeling. If I could not conjure emotion in the score, what was the point of having music anyway? That version had to go in the trash. The next approach called too much attention to itself. This time the music overshadowed the prophet's message. I was reminded that the key word in underscore is *under* – under the prophet's voice, not over it, against it, or before it. That version also went in the trash.

While working on the third version, I heard a gentle knock at the studio door. When I pulled it open, I was stunned to see President Nelson's wife, Wendy Nelson, standing there. When she heard I was scoring her husband's witness of Jesus, she asked if it would be OK to drop by and check on me. After shaking off the shock, I welcomed her into the room.

She asked me how I was approaching the music. I told her that I was treating her husband's voice as the melody, building the rest of the music around his narrative in support of the message. She smiled and nodded, her face and body language gently relaxing, as if her work here was done. I imagined she might want to listen to some of the score in-progress, perhaps even offer a suggestion or critique. But she never said anything else about the music. Instead, she shared a personal experience that was sacred to her.

Wendy said that when the previous president of the church, Thomas S. Monson, was on his deathbed, she and her husband were called to the hospital. As President Monson passed away, she received an unmistakable divine impression, like a still small voice penetrating her mind and heart, which told her tenderly:

"Russell is my prophet now."

That is a profound statement. For a believer like me, it was riveting. She continued sharing other cherished spiritual impressions, confirming her faith in God and ratifying her husband's call to serve as a special witness of Christ. I thanked her, and expressed how deeply her visit had inspired me. I suspected that some vestige of Wendy Nelson's faith would now find its way into the music I was composing, intertwined with the testimony of her husband.

A beautiful image of Jerusalem hung in the background as we spoke, paused on the big screen behind us. It seemed an appropriate backdrop for our conversation, stopped at the very spot I had been scoring.

Isn't it interesting how many remarkable people and special experiences music scoring can bring into our lives? Some may have little to do with music itself. But they all enrich us in unexpected and fulfilling ways. It is part of the profession I never anticipated, but have come to love and deeply appreciate.

At length, I finished composing the music and pivoted into production. The final score was performed by a large orchestra, comprised of top-notch studio professionals and talented musicians from the Utah Symphony and Orchestra at Temple Square. Jenn Sprague contracted the orchestra with Aaron Ashton as concert master. Michael James Greene engineered and mixed the recording. I conducted and produced the sessions. Everyone did a stellar job and I felt honored and deeply satisfied sending the master recording over to Quinn.

This was the culmination of decades of trust Quinn had placed in me, drawing out the very best from me in the service of a cause we both loved, and a work we believed could make a positive difference for individuals and families across the world. For 30 years, I had composed music for church media, more than 80 productions in all. Creating music for a prophet's witness of Jesus in the holy land was the capstone experience of it all, a pinnacle achievement for a believer like me.

To watch video and listen to music composed by Chance Thomas for the Church of Jesus Christ of Latter-day Saints, as described in this chapter, please visit: HUGEsoundRecords.com/Memoir-20

NOTE

1 Gordon B. Hinckley, "Tried in All Things"; Quoted in documentary film, published by the Church of Jesus Christ of Latter-day Saints, copyright 1999.

CHAPTER 21

Securing the Future

Making money has always been an integral part of my music career paradigm. I was never among those who claimed they did not care about money. One experience in particular is illustrative.

I was asked to join an afternoon panel at a regional Comic Con, which featured four composers. In answering an audience question about art versus commerce, the other three composers stated that money was not a motivating factor in their work:

"It's not about the money, man. It's about the art, the purity of expression, being true to yourself."

"I never think about the money. I just think about the music."

"If you're in it for the money, you might as well hang it up now." And so the dialogue went.

But I disagreed. I posited that music scoring was a business. Although the business delivers a highly artistic service, it was nevertheless a business. Only with sufficient money would a composer be empowered to devote full-time efforts to composing.

Full-time devotion leads to higher-quality work, because the more time a person devotes to a particular pursuit, the more proficient they become at it. Additionally, a robust cash flow provides money to upgrade capital assets, engage in professional education, and employ outside experts who can make artistically elevating contributions to the composer's work. All of these positive actions flow from a prosperous business, allowing the composer to deliver music scores of increasingly enhanced artistry and excellence.[1]

DOI: 10.1201/9781003199311-22

That was where I gravitated. I always wanted to treat composing as a viable business that delivered an artistic service.

Every composer who cultivates their craft and business long enough will eventually strike a decent payday. When that happens, some may party away their money, or spend it all on the latest gear. Granted, we should all celebrate occasionally. And periodic gear investments are an important enhancement to your arsenal. But I encourage composers to reserve a portion of any big payday for investing in appreciable assets. We live in a capitalist economy, which means those with appreciable assets win. I am talking about real estate, stocks, precious metals, copyrights, and brands.

Beginning 25 years ago, I began investing a portion of my music earnings in real estate and stocks. Those investments have grown to a point where I am comfortably retired today. That is not because I am a unicorn or extraordinary outlier. The strategy can work for anyone.

My composing business has always been the engine that fed our other investments. After my wife and I brought children into our family, she stopped working outside the home. My composing profession had to be robust enough to support the family, keep the business liquid, and generate extra cash to invest. I hate the image of the starving artist. I would love to debunk that idea forever, giving young composers tools and training to find financial success, as well as artistic satisfaction in their careers.

With that in mind, here are ten financial practices that have proven beneficial for me and for my family. Perhaps some version of these will work wonders for you too:

FIND CREATIVE WAYS TO SAVE MONEY

Right after college, my wife and I worked as entertainers on cruise ships, all expenses paid. For two and a half years, we saved nearly every penny we earned while seeing the world for free. I also wrote lots of music. By the time we returned to land, we had enough money saved to make a down payment on a home and buy some basic studio equipment.

BUY THE WORST HOME IN THE BEST NEIGHBORHOOD

Our first home was a run-down duplex in an otherwise upscale neighborhood. We remodeled the tenant side first and rented it out, bringing in enough money to pay the mortgage each month. Between music scoring gigs, we fixed up the landlord side next, doing as much labor as we could ourselves. When the market heated up, we sold the duplex for a big profit. Subsequent real estate purchases have followed a similar pattern.

INVEST EXTRA CASH INSTEAD OF BLOWING IT

We took our duplex profits and invested in stocks, bonds, and mutual funds. We spread the investments around – large cap stock fund, small cap stock fund, government bond fund, and a handful of individual stocks. I set up every investment to perpetually reinvest the dividends, eventually creating an exponential growth curve. Additional investments have been made when extra cash was available from my music scoring business and when opportunities seemed timely.

BUILD YOUR BUSINESS TO OWN ASSETS

I started HUGEsound in 1998. I trademarked the name and bought high-quality equipment. Whenever possible, I negotiated for copyright ownership in my music scoring projects. I slowly built up a library of music assets which I owned. Years later, I sold the business, including the name, equipment, and music library for a substantial sum. Most of the cash proceeds were invested in real estate.

REACH FOR MORE LUCRATIVE SCORING GIGS

Wherever you are today, don't be afraid to stretch for the next financial wrung on the music scoring ladder. If you are doing indie films, start submitting for TV shows. If you are doing mobile games, start submitting for console games. There is great money to be made in music scoring, but you have to hunt upward for it. And you have to pitch hard and smart to get it. The right relationships can open those doors for you.

GET SOME TRACKS INTO COMMERCIAL MUSIC LIBRARIES

I do not have tons of music in libraries. But I have enough placements to generate a nice revenue stream of passive income every quarter. Over the past 25 years, what started as pizza money has grown into travel-the-world money.

AVOID ALL AVOIDABLE DEBT

Pay off your credit cards in full every month. Save for things you want, rather than buying them on credit. Exceptions would include essential gear to start your business, a home, and maybe your first car. Otherwise, try to survive with what you have, without ever going into debt. Also, pay off your mortgage as early as possible. Making double payments is a good strategy whenever you can. Debt will drown you. Avoid it like the plague.

GIVE TO GREAT CAUSES

There is karma in charitable contributions. I think we all know that intuitively. Not only does charitable giving make the world a better place, but somehow it comes back to you and then some. Give judiciously of your money and your talents to great causes you believe in. Even starting with a tiny amount can create a marvelous habit over time.

INVEST IN A STABLE LIFE PARTNER

Incredible balance, synergy, and love can come from having a stable life partner. It will certainly impact your finances. I met Pamela in 1980, and we are still going strong today. She is smart, talented, reliable, frugal, fun-loving, stubborn, healthy, and incredibly supportive. Her primary job in our partnership was full-time mother and home-school teacher, but her wise and frugal influence on our financial condition has been stabilizing and empowering.

HAVE SOME FUN ALONG THE WAY

Be thrifty, but not miserly. Everyone needs to have some fun and enjoy the journey. Our family loves to travel. We love roller coaster parks, tropical beaches, old European cities, national parks, NBA games, and great restaurants, usually with a coupon. You can build great memories without necessarily spending a ton of cash. That leaves you extra dollars for investing in the future without loathing life in the present.

RETIREMENT

There is a lot more financial stuff we could talk about – PROs, speaking fees, advertising revenues, stock options, capital gains, tax strategies, and the like. But I think this is a good start.

I began composing music when I was 12 years old. It was my first love, and it blossomed into a wonderful career. For decades, I worked incredibly hard to create a body of work that I am proud of artistically. Along the way, I also tried to be smart about money.

At the end of February 2022, I retired from composing. As I told many friends and colleagues at the time, after completing the massive score for *The Settlers: New Allies*, I simply had nothing left to say as a composer. For decades, I had dipped my little creativity cup into an internal wellspring of inspiration, and it always came back full. Now, there is nothing left inside but a parched, splintery void. As a creator of music, I am all poured out.

As they say in competitive sports, I left everything on the court.

Looking back, I experienced more than I ever deserved. I met and worked with the most magnificent people you could ever imagine – individuals of such remarkable creativity, talent, and imagination as to forever exalt my view of the human race. What a run.

I extend to each reader my optimism for the very best of success in your life pursuits, both personal and professional. Planet Earth offers so much richness, variety, challenge, love, delight, struggle, and laughter.

May you pursue your loftiest ambitions with vigor and purpose!

May you achieve much of what you dream!

And as reliably as possible, may you ever live in joy and harmony with those within your many circles of influence.

With love and enthusiasm,

Chance Thomas

NOTE

1 Chance Thomas, *Composing Music for Games: The Art, Technology and Business of Video Game Scoring*, p. 245; Boca Raton: CRC Press, 2016.

Acknowledgments

No one was more supportive throughout this endeavor than my loving wife, Pamela Thomas. Above all others, I would like to acknowledge and express endless love and gratitude for her invaluable encouragement.

This work would not have been possible without the belief and patience of my publishing editor, Sean Connelly. I am likewise indebted to Danielle Zarfati, Uma Maheswari and Jennifer Stair, whose able assistance guided me through the final details leading up to publication.

Many smart and generous peers gave time and expertise in reviewing early drafts and sharing beneficial suggestions and feedback with me. Their universal encouragement endowed me with the confidence I needed to pursue this undertaking. Among them were:

Gonzalo Varella, Steve Blumenthal, Stefan Angelov, Nathalie Bonin, Karina Pardus, Sasha Stevanoska, Russell Nollen, Rachel Robison, Jared Le Doux, Andrew Bong, Craig Dodge, Argyro Christodoulides, Laura Stevens, Amanda Lavin, Helen Lynch, Arhynn Descy, Kimberly Hou, Leo Voin, Jordan Davis, Bonnie Corral, Jess Henderson, Annina Melissa, Daisy Coole, Ryn Jorgensen, Jamie Striegel, Jesse Zuretti, Marie-Anne Fischer, Claire Batchelor Morris, Byron Beasley, Elaine Gallant, and Julie Elven.

I express overflowing gratitude, love, and appreciation to each and every one.

Special shout out to graphic designer Scott Sharp, whose tireless work, attention to detail, and artist's eye gave the book its eye-catching and informative cover. Likewise, to everyone at Routledge Press, Taylor & Francis, and CRC Press working in editorial, production, layout, and print, you have my thanks for handling this project with professionalism and expertise.

Finally, I acknowledge our beloved Creator for the glorious gift of human life. Mine has been filled with wonder, sparkle, people I adore, and experiences I cherish. I will be forever grateful.

Outrodiction

ALL CONTENTS OF THIS book are pulled from the weathered and fossilizing, gray matter hard drive nestled between my ears. As of this writing, I am 61 years old and not nearly as sharp as I once was. Which may not be saying much.

Some events in this book occurred a long time ago. In a comprehensive attempt to ensure accuracy, I have reviewed email archives, old journal entries, contracts, social media posts, and daily planners for fact checking. And while I cannot promise that every date, every word of every quote, and every minor detail is 100% punctilious, I can assure you that all of the key points and substance are right.

To the best of my recollection.

Everything written herein is my own personal work, and reflects the personal interpretation of my own experiences and viewpoints, and not necessarily those of my publisher.

Please visit the book's companion website for videos, music samples, photos, and other bonus content accompanying each chapter:

www.HUGEsoundRecords.com/Memoir

Index

Author

This is not your grandfather's video game music.

Chance Thomas has been a trailblazer in the video game industry since the 1990s, pushing the bleeding edge of music soundscapes from 8-bit chiptunes into gorgeous symphonic orchestral scores, and from endlessly repeating loops into adaptive and massively generative musicscapes.

Chance has composed original video game music for some of the most valuable entertainment properties in the world, including **Avatar, Marvel, The Lord of the Rings, Dungeons & Dragons, King Kong, Warhammer, DOTA 2, Might & Magic,** and many more. Additionally, his music has underscored critical acclaim and blockbuster success in film and television, including an Oscar™, an Emmy™, and billions of dollars in sales worldwide.

In 1998, he launched HUGEsound to provide world-class music and sound for video games. With dozens of successful titles, HUGEsound grew until its acquisition by a large investment firm for exponential expansion. The new HUGEsound Post Production became a state-of-the-art playground for creative artists, well on its way to national distinction. In 2018, a massive Ponzi scheme was uncovered at the investment firm and HUGEsound was lost to the courts.

With help from family, friends, and peers, Chance bounced back with HUGEsound Records and composed the magnum opus of his career, *The Settlers: New Allies.* This was the largest known procedural music score in history, unfolding across 16,327 music files. The music adapts to each player's individual style, reacts to game play, and delivers a thematic experience without being repetitive.

Chance previously authored the landmark textbook, *Composing Music for Games: The Art, Technology and Business of Video Game Scoring.*

Discover books and music by Chance Thomas at: HUGEsoundRecords.com